Archaeology
of the
Central
Mississippi
Valley

Dan F. Morse
Phyllis A. Morse

New World Archaeological Record

Archaeology of the
Central Mississippi Valley

NEW WORLD ARCHAEOLOGICAL RECORD

Under the Editorship of

James Bennett Griffin

Museum of Anthropology
University of Michigan
Ann Arbor, Michigan

In preparation:

**Michael J. Moratto, with contributions by David A. Frederickson,
Christopher Raven, and Claude N. Warren,** California Archaeology
Robert E. Bell (Ed.), Prehistory of Oklahoma

Published:

James L. Phillips and James A. Brown (Eds.), Archaic Hunters
and Gatherers in the American Midwest
Dan F. Morse and Phyllis A. Morse, Archaeology of the Central
Mississippi Valley
Lawrence E. Aten, Indians of the Upper Texas Coast
Ronald J. Mason, Great Lakes Archaeology
Dean R. Snow, The Archaeology of New England
Jerald T. Milanich and Charles H. Fairbanks, Florida Archaeology
George C. Frison, Prehistoric Hunters of the High Plains

Archaeology of the
Central Mississippi Valley

DAN F. MORSE
PHYLLIS A. MORSE
Arkansas Archeological Survey
State University, Arkansas

ACADEMIC PRESS, INC.
Harcourt Brace Jovanovich, Publishers
San Diego   New York   Berkeley   Boston
London   Sydney   Tokyo   Toronto

Most Southeastern Indians conceived of their world as a circular flat island suspended by four cords attached to the Upper World. The turtle was an important bridge between this world and the Under World. The bone pendant pictured on the cover and on the chapter opening pages was found at the Hazel site in Northeast Arkansas and dates to approximately A.D. 1500.

ACADEMIC PRESS, INC.
1250 Sixth Avenue, San Diego, California 92101

United Kingdom Edition published by
ACADEMIC PRESS, INC. (LONDON) LTD.
24/28 Oval Road, London NW1 7DX

Library of Congress Cataloging in Publication Data

Morse, Dan F.
    Archaeology of the central Mississippi Valley.

    (New world archaeological record)
    Bibliography: p.
    Includes index.
    1. Indians of North America--Mississippi River
Valley--Antiquities. 2. Indians of North America--
Mississippi River Valley--History. 3. Mississippian
culture. 4. Mississippi River Valley--Antiquities.
5. Mississippi River Valley--History. I. Morse,
Phyllis A. II. Title. III. Series.
E78.M75M67 1982   977'.01   82-22734
ISBN 0-12-508180-4
ISBN 0-12-508181-2(paperback)

PRINTED IN THE UNITED STATES OF AMERICA

87 88 89   9 8 7 6 5 4 3 2 1

This book is dedicated to
DAN AND ANN MORSE
for their Golden Wedding Anniversary

Contents

1

The River

2

The Archaeology

3

Paleo-Indian Beginnings (9500–8500 B.C.)

4

Dalton Efflorescence (8500—7500 B.C.)

5

The Hypsithermal Archaic Disruption (7000—3000 B.C.)

6

Archaic Expansion (3000—500 B.C.)

7

Woodland Beginnings (500 B.C.—0)

8

The Hopewellian Period (0—A.D. 400)

9

Woodland Conflict (A.D. 400–700)

10

Mississippian Frontier (A.D. 700–1000)

11

Mississippian Consolidation (A.D. 1000–1350)

12

Mississippian Nucleation (A.D. 1350–1650)

13

Epilogue: Historic Archaeology

Preface

In the Central Mississippi Valley, the De Soto expedition of 1539–1543 encountered "the best villages seen up to that time, better stockaded and fortified, and the people were of finer quality . . . [Bourne 1904: 140]." This was the climax of a prehistoric cultural evolution that had begun 11,000 years earlier with sophisticated Paleo-Indian hunters, fishers, and wild plant gatherers. The process continued into the Historic period until the inevitable wave of the Euro-American frontier changed the region beginning in the seventeenth century. This book describes an archaeological reconstruction of the preceding 11,000 years of an extraordinarily rich environment centered within the largest river system north of the Amazon.

The scope of the book is all of the lowlands of the Mississippi Valley from just north of the Ohio River to the mouth of the Arkansas River, from Cape Girardeau to Arkansas Post. Organization is by period, from Paleo-Indian through the Archaic, Woodland, and Mississippian into the Historic. The treatment is comprehensive but not redundant. Artifacts and sites were carefully selected to exemplify the increasing complexity of a wide range of cultural behavior through time. Illustrated artifacts, with very few exceptions, are in institutional rather than private collections. This was intentional so as not to enhance the commercial value of investor-owned artifacts.

Archaeology of the Central Mississippi Valley is oriented toward the specialist as well as the nonarchaeologist. Phillips's (1970) book includes the latest available widely distributed summary of the Central Mississippi Valley, although it is essentially about the Yazoo Basin located to the southeast. Phillips's summary is both brief and incomplete. More detailed treatment of the Central Valley consists of scientific papers in local journals or series and many unpublished reports available only to specialists working in this region. Avocational archaeologists living in or near the Central Valley have not even had access to many of these works. Public libraries have also lacked a comprehensive summary of the archaeology of this region. The lay view of archaeology is largely biased toward treasure seeking and sensationalism and there is a significant communication gap between tax-supported research and taxpayer knowledge of that research.

Archaeology is a set of techniques developed to recover the data of past human events remaining in and on the ground. Because of this, the hardier lithic and ceramic artifacts are necessarily emphasized. Scientific archaeology is the exercise of logic and the objective control of these data so they may be properly interpreted. Thus, experimentation in artifact replication and use is also emphasized. Anthropological archaeology is a set of techniques developed to incorporate these data into other sets of human behavioral data. Whenever possible, the book attempts to humanize the archaeological interpretations by reference to settlement system, social organization, religion, economy, and politics.

The major emphasis in this volume will be on understanding the nature of change through time in the Central Mississippi Valley. Environment and climate change through time are thought to have influenced human behavior. In particular, the dry hypsithermal period of about 7000–3000 B.C. and the difference between an older braided stream surface and the younger meander belt system are examined from this standpoint.

Radiocarbon dates have been corrected wherever possible (Damon *et al.* 1974). Pottery types used are defined in Phillips (1970:21–238). Since even the very identification of a potsherd type changes with time, all that we can be certain of in this volume is that its interpretations will change. Statements are definite and controversy is minimized to allow easier reading, but not to suppress the uncertainty of it all. After all, debate is the basis of scientific progress and there is still much to debate about in Central Mississippi Valley archaeology.

REFERENCES

Bourne, Edward G. (Editor)
  1904 *Narratives of the career of Hernando De Soto.* New York: Trailmakers Series.
Damon, P. E., C. W. Ferguson, A. Long, and E. I. Wallick
  1974 Dendrochronologic calibration of the radiocarbon time scale. *American Antiquity* **39**:350–366.
Phillips, Philip
  1970 Archaeological survey in the Lower Yazoo Basin, Mississippi, 1949–1955. *Papers of the Peabody Museum, Harvard University* **60**.

Acknowledgments

First and foremost, gratitude must be extended to Philip Phillips, James A. Ford, and James B. Griffin for their classic *Archaeological Survey in the Lower Mississippi Alluvial Valley, 1940–1947.* We are indebted not only to the enormous amount of work accomplished by these three gentlemen but also to their professionalism and scientific honesty. Philip Phillips in addition contributed another important milestone, *Archaeological Survey in the Lower Yazoo Basin, Mississippi, 1949–1955,* which refined in considerable detail the ceramic classification used in the Central Valley and summarized the known phases. Another very important document is Stephen Williams's 1954 doctoral dissertation, Archeological Study of the Mississippian Culture in Southeast Missouri.

Three individuals deserve a very special thanks from us. Mary Ann Richardson typed the entire manuscript through all drafts and corrections. She also advised us on some of the figures and handled much of the administrative detail. Timothy A. Jones drew all of the illustrations for this book with the exception of the base maps themselves. Marvin D. Jeter helped us enormously by editing chapters as they were written. He not only helped us with the use of the English language but made several comments of archaeological importance as well.

The Arkansas Archeological Survey merits our thanks. Charles R. McGimsey III is the director and Hester A. Davis is the state archaeologist. Without their support the book could not have been written.

Gratitude is expressed to W. Frederick Limp, Assistant Director, and Pamela Ashford, Photographer, Arkansas Archeological Survey, for ensuring that we were supplied with requested Arkansas Archeological Survey photographs; to Hubert B. Stroud, Associate Professor in Geography, Arkansas State University, for drawing our primary base map and one of the other two maps; to Richard A. Marshall, Mississippi State University, for conducting us on an archaeological tour of southeast Missouri; and to Roger T. Saucier, U.S. Army Corps of Engineers, for commenting on our representation of his important work in the Quaternary geology of the Central Valley.

Many papers and books by numerous investigators helped us understand the specifics of Central Valley archaeology. Acknowledgment is generally made with references to particular publications, but not all are referenced because many papers are not readily available in normal university libraries or because the papers were not published. Wherever possible, the investigators themselves are named in the text in conjunction with their contributions. At least that has been our intent and we apologize here and now to anyone whose name was inadvertently omitted.

Institutions and corporations directly helpful to us include: Arkansas Archeological Survey; Arkansas Archeological Society; Arkansas State University Museum; University of Arkansas Museum; Thomas Gilcrease Institute of American History and Art; Peabody Museum, Harvard University; Office of State Archaeologist, University of Kentucky; Memphis Pink Palace Museum; University of Michigan Museum of Anthropology; University of Missouri American Archaeology; Missouri Archaeological Society; Department of Anthropology, National Museum of Natural History (Smithsonian Institution); Tennessee Historical Commission.

Individuals directly helpful to us include Leonard W. Blake, Jeffrey P. Brain, Ronald C. Brister, Sam Brookes, Ken Carstens, Carl H. Chapman, R. Berle Clay, Mary E. Coles, John Connaway, John Corbet, Don Crabtree, Kenny Davis, Paul and Hazel Delcourt, S. D. Dickinson, Robert C. Dunnell, David Dye, J. Allen Eichenberger, Tom Emerson, David R. Evans, Charles Figley, Doyle J. Gertjejansen, James B. Griffin, John E. Guilday, Marion Haynes, E. Thomas Hemmings, Michael P. Hoffman, John House, Richard W. Jefferies, John Kelly, Jim King, Frances King, George Lankford, R. Barry Lewis, Jim McCarty, Lloyd H. McCracken, Mary McGimsey, Dan M. McPike, Robert C. Mainfort, Jr., Walter L. Manger, Larry Medford, Jim Michie, George Milner, Michael Million, Daniel A. Morse, John F. Morse, Robert J. Morse, Jack D. Nance, Anna Parks, Gregory Perino, Howard Pierce, David Pratt, Cynthia R. Price, James E. Price, Frank Reynolds, Gordon Rice, Steve Rogers, Michael Sierzchula, Frank Sloan, Bruce D. Smith, Samuel D. Smith, Charles Snell, Fritz Snell, Caryl Steele, Neal L. Trubowitz, Iris Weaver, and Stephen Williams.

Most of the artifacts illustrated belong to the Arkansas Archeological Survey and are in storage at the Arkansas State University station in Jonesboro, Arkansas. Several of the illustrated artifacts belonging to the Arkansas Archeological Survey were donated by avocational archaeologists and landowners. Nine artifacts used as models for illustration are in the private collections of Jerry Johnson (Figure 12.4i), Buddy Miller (Figure 12.4b,m), G. D. Morse,

M.D. (Figures 5.3j; 6.2h; 12.2f), Ralph Olson (Figure 12.4g), Gordon Rice (Figure 6.3g), and Iris Weaver (Figure 3.7j). Individuals providing photographs were Leonard Blake (Figure 10.3), Frances Hampson (Figure 2.2a), Jim Michie (Figure 4.4), Gregory Perino (Figures 11.3 and 11.4), and Frank Reynolds (Figure 3.2).

Four of the illustrated artifacts are in the Henry Clay Hampson II Memorial Museum of Archaeology: Figure 3.8, Figure 12.4d, and Figure 12.6b. Six illustrated artifacts are in the collections of the Arkansas State University Museum: Figure 3.7a (Catalog number 70), Figure 3.7k (17190), Figure 5.3d (17448), Figure 6.2c (9573), Figure 6.3e (16205), and Figure 10.4e (16718). Nine specimens in the University of Arkansas collections are illustrated: Figure 3.6b (AAS Neg. 804561, UAM Cat. 74-5-30), Figure 11.5f (33-43C), Figure 13.3a (AAS Neg. 744020; UAM Cat. 66-30-177), Figure 13.4a (32-101-13A), Figure 13.4c (32-101-5A), Figure 13.4d (32-101-38A), Figure 13.4e (32-101-44A), Figure 13.4f (32-101-35B), and Figure 13.4h (32-101-12C). Figure 2.2 is also courtesy of the University of Arkansas Museum (Neg. No. 000415).

The Department of Anthropology, National Museum of Natural History, Smithsonian Institution provided photographs used as the basis for all or portions of five figures: Figure 6.5 (Neg. 80-15923, Cat. 62975), Figure 10.4c (Neg. 80-15920, Cat. 31137), Figure 12.2g (Neg. 80-15924, Cat. 114486), Figure 12.4f (Neg. 80-15917, Cat. 31135), and Figure 13.3j (Neg. 80-15926, Cat. 369475). Artifacts in the collections of the Thomas Gilcrease Institute of American History and Art are illustrated as Figures 4.5a, 11.4a–e, and 12.6a, c, f–h. Vessels illustrated as Figure 12.6d–e are in the Alabama Museum of Natural History Collections. The Memphis Pink Palace Museum provided the illustrations for Figure 3.4 (1936.10.1), Figure 3.5a (1940.7), and Figure 3.5b (1979.116.1). The Tennessee Department of Conservation Division of Parks and Recreation provided Figure 8.2 and the Tennessee Department of Conservation, Tennessee Historical Commission provided Figure 13.7. The Mississippi Department of Archives and History Archaeological Survey provided most of Figure 2.1. The insert in Figure 2.1 and Figure 2.3 were due to the efforts of the University of Michigan Museum of Anthropology, Central Mississippi Valley Archaeological Survey, and to Harvard University and to the Peabody Museum Lower Mississippi Survey.

C. B. Moore illustrations published in 1910 by The Academy of Natural Sciences of Philadelphia were used as the basis for several figures as follows: Figure 6.7a (Moore Figures 73,74), Figure 9.8a (Moore Figure 64), Figure 9.8b (Moore Plate XXVIII), Figure 9.8c (Moore Figures 71,72), Figure 9.8d (Moore Figure 67), Figure 12.4a (Moore Plate X), and Figure 12.4n (Moore Figure 11). The American Museum of Natural History, New York, illustrations utilized as the basis for figures are as follows: Figure 8.3 (Ford 1963:Figures 3, 12), Figure 8.4a (Ford 1963:Figure 37), Figure 8.4b (Ford 1963:Figure 9), Figure 8.4d (Ford 1963:Figure 10b), Figure 8.4e–f (Ford 1963:Figure 11),

Figure 8.4g (Ford 1963: Figure 21a), Figure 8.5 (Ford 1963:Figures 15a, 15b, 33a, 32a, 25b, 31b, 31d, 31e), Figure 13.4b (Ford 1961:Figure 14n), and Figure 13.4g (Ford 1961:Figure 16p). The *Arkansas Archeologist* provided the basis for the illustrations in Figure 13.4a, b–f, h (Hoffman 1977) and in Figures 11.5a and 10.6b (McGimsey 1964:Figure 3). The *Missouri Archeologist* provided the basis for the illustrations in Figure 11.5e (Hamilton, Hamilton, and Chapman 1974:Figure 101), Figure 10.4a (Evans 1977:Figures 44, 45), and Figure 10.9b, c, e (R. Williams 1974:Figures 13, 20, 221). Figure 11.5d was based on an illustration in the *Bureau of American Ethnology Bulletin* **37** (Fowke 1910: Plate 16) and Figure 11.9h is drawn after an illustration in the Twelfth Annual Report (Thomas 1894:Figure 108). Figures 11.5b and c were adapted from Phillips and Brown 1978, courtesy of the Peabody Museum Press. The University of Missouri Press published the illustration used as a basis for Figure 11.8f (Chapman 1980:Figure 5-44B). Figure 11.9 is based primarily on illustrations published by Academic Press (Price 1978:Figures 8.4, 8.10, 8.8). The Arkansas Archeological Survey has previously published portions of the Zebree site features in Figure 10.9 (Morse 1975:Figures 7 and 12; Morse 1980:Figure 21-5), Figure 9.3a, c (Million and Morse 1980:Figures 16-2a,b), the illustration of Parkin in Figure 12.7a (P. Morse 1981:Figure 5), and the basis for Figures 12.4d and 12.6b (Morse 1973:cover, Figure 42).

Artifacts and specimens in the collections of the Arkansas Archeological Survey and stored, except where noted, at the Arkansas State University station which were used for illustrations are identified by the following catalog numbers for appropriate figures: 3.6 (82-332), 3.7b (70-164), 3.7c (82-330), 3.7d (79-653, Pine Bluff station), 3.7e (79-859), 3.7f (82-331), 3.7g (68-70), 3.7h (82-329), 3.7i (72-230), 3.7l (69-153), 3.7m (71-555), 3.8 (77-535), 4.2a (74-107-390), 4.2b (74-107-307), 4.2c (74-107-102), 4.2d (74-107-74), 4.2e (74-107-116), 4.2f (74-107-36), 4.2g (78-345), 4.2h (74-107-68), 4.2i (74-107-487), 4.2j (74-107-235), 4.2l (74-107-194), 4.2m (70-917), 4.2n (74-107-49), 4.2o (70-687), 4.2p (70-355-3099), 4.2q (82-334), 4.2r (74-107-377), 4.2s (71-386), 4.2t (70-355-347), 4.2u (74-107-91), 4.2v (74-107-441), 4.2w (69-137), 4.2x (74-107-233), 4.5b (74-107-294), 4.5c (74-107-133), 5.2a (70-329), 5.2b (71-319), 5.2c (68-364-207), 5.2d (69-645), 5.2e (70-478), 5.2f (68-323), 5.2g (69-139), 5.2h (70-475), 5.2i (72-320), 5.2j (73-40), 5.2k (70-320), 5.2l (71-486), 5.2m (68-780), 5.3a (71-529), 5.3b (82-333), 5.3c (73-17), 5.3e (73-40), 5.3f (68-395), 5.3g (70-319), 5.3h (69-645), 5.3i (70-477), 5.3k (71-563), 5.3l (70-335), 5.3m (70-329), 5.3n (67-717), 6.2a (69-144), 6.2b (69-324), 6.2d (69-144-12), 6.2e (81-315), 6.2f (68-364-181), 6.2g (68-364-10), 6.3b (68-364-172), 6.3d (79-367), 6.3f (79-367), 6.3h (71-16), 6.3i (73-603), 6.3j (74-790), 6.3k (74-776), 6.4a (75-674), 6.4b (68-364), 6.4c (70-315), 6.4d (76-1254), 6.6 (67-144-94), 6.7b (71-423-111), 6.7c (68-364), 7.2a (81-315), 7.3 (81-315), 7.4 (81-315), 7.5a (81-315), 7.5b (81-315-121), 7.6 (81-315-177), 7.7 (81-315), 7.8a–j (81-315), 7.8k–l (81-315-15), 7.8m (81-315), 7.8n

(81-315-67), 7.8o (81-315-60), 7.9a (81-315), 7.9b (81-315-44), 8.4c (70-720-189), 8.6a–b (71-340), 8.6c (68-140-21), 8.6d (71-340), 8.6e (79-891), 8.6f–g (71-489-38), 8.6h (68-140-6), 8.7a (70-923-92), 8.7b (68-140-57), 8.7c (70-923-3c), 8.7d (70-923-4), 8.7e (68-140-7), 8.7f (70-923-126), 8.7g (68-140-80), 8.8 (70-923-141), 9.3b (76-1247-746), 9.3d (69-656-1519), 9.3e (68-400-6), 9.4a (69-656-523), 9.4b (69-656-920), 9.4c (67-144-178), 9.4d (67-144-72), 9.4e–f (67-144), 9.4g (67-144-276), 9.4h (67-144-132), 9.4i (69-656-1474), 9.4j (69-656-1524), 9.4k (69-656-2314), 9.6a–d (82-312), 9.6e (70-720-283), 9.7a (67-159-F5), 9.7b (67-144-37), 9.7c (67-144-129), 10.4b (69-711-71), 10.4d (69-528), 10.6a (74-120), 10.6c (69-656-1597), 10.6d (68-263), 10.6e (72-588), 10.7a (69-656-2029), 10.7b (69-656-475), 10.7c (69-656-2154), 10.7e (75-671-3715), 10.7f (68-399-29), 10.7g (76-1247-209), 10.7h (75-671-4130), 10.7i (75-671-6219), 10.7j (76-1247-328), 10.8a (69-656-77), 10.8b (69-656-66), 10.8c–d (69-656-118), 10.8e–g (69-656-211), 10.8h (69-656-867), 10.8i (69-656-349), 10.8j (69-656-1557), 10.8k (69-656-1682), 10.81 (69-656-1108), 10.8m (75-671-6007), 10.8n (68-400-245), 10.8o (69-656-659), 10.8p (68-363-58), 10.8q (69-656-2038), 10.8r (69-656-2176), 10.8s (69-656-358), 10.8t (69-656-1240), 11.2a–c (69-711-83), 11.2d–e (67-144-130), 11.2f (69-711-83), 11.2g (82-310), 11.2h (82-328), 11.2i (72-215), 11.2j (67-171-4), 11.2k (67-144-93), 11.21 (81-315-230), 11.4f (69-705-21, 69-705-19), 11.6f (71-589), 11.7a (70-718-51), 11.7b (77-1065-5), 11.7c (68-140-61), 11.8a (69-656-464), 11.8b (69-656-1502), 11.8c (69-711-138), 11.8d (69-711-26), 11.8e (76-1247-657), 12.2a (73-426), 12.2b–d (74-120), 12.2e (74-919), 12.2h (71-498), 12.2i (73-367), 12.3a (68-140-10), 12.3b (76-1247-326), 12.3c (72-658), 12.3d (76-1239), 12.3e (72-305), 12.3f (75-671-726), 12.3g (71-567-14), 12.4c (69-711-80), 12.4e (82-326), 12.4h (69-711-95), 12.4j (79-1040-177), 12.4k (79-1040-196), 12.41 (73-370), 12.4o (69-711-82), 12.5a (73-50), 12.5b (68-436), 13.3c–e (80-376), 13.3f–g (71-392), 13.3h (82-327), 13.3i (80-376), 13.5 (78-1149-214), 13.5b (78-1149-211), 13.5c–d (78-1149-213), 13.5e (78-1149-292), 13.5f (78-1149-245), 13.5g (78-1149-246), 13.5h (78-1149-296), 13.5i (78-1149-236), 13.5j (78-1149-323), 13.5k (78-301), 13.51 (69-656-1284), 13.5m (78-1149-295), and 13.5n (78-1149-240).

Arkansas Archeological Survey negative numbers pertain to the following figures: 2.2a (713546), 2.3a (814995), 2.3b (814992), 2.4a (753947), 2.4b (735201), 2.5 (682483), 2.6a (702701), 2.6b (763788), 3.2 (822627), 3.6a (692588), 3.6b (804561), 4.2a (752490), 4.2b (752477), 4.2c (752488), 4.2d (752488), 4.2e (752479), 4.2f (752488), 4.2h (752500), 4.2i (752494), 4.2j (752494, 752495), 4.2l (752492), 4.2n (752490), 4.2r (752490), 4.2u (752492), 4.2v (752497), 4.2x (752496), 4.3 (712131-712150), 4.5b (752480), 4.5c (752483), 4.8a (703018), 4.8b (702657), 4.10a (742666), 4.10b (742703), 4.10c (742402), 4.10d (742492), 6.2i (723477), 6.3c (712055), 6.8a (682794), 6.8b (682498), 9.5 (813110), 10.5a (743818), 10.5b

(743819), 11.4f (713556), 11.5f (671087), 11.6a–b (712880), 11.6c–d (712874), 11.6e (744002), 11.6f (713848), 12.6a (695599), 12.6c (695545), 12.6d (723020), 12.6e (723028), 12.6f (723027), 12.6g (694792), 12.6h (695230), 12.7b (813117), 12.8 (794229), 13.3a (744020), 13.3c–d (822631), 13.3e (822633), 13.3f–g (822630), 13.3h–i (822629), 13.6 (724664), 13.8a (752284), 13.8b (785806), 13.8c (752339), and 13.8d (785820).

Archaeology of the
Central Mississippi Valley

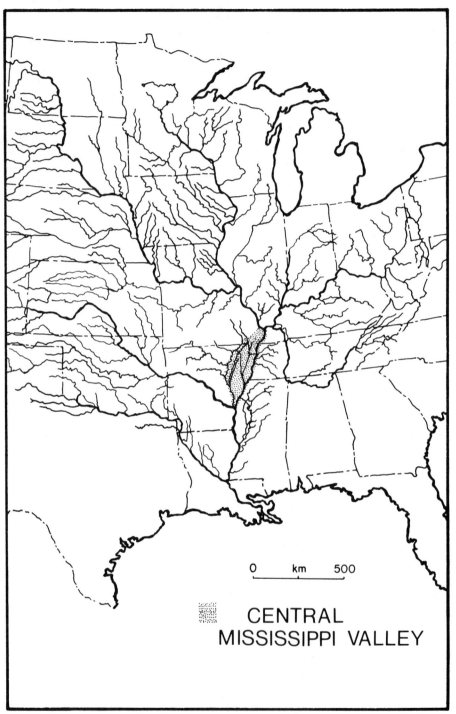

FIGURE 1.1. Location of the study unit in reference to the Mississippi River drainage of the eastern United States.

1

The River

Everywhere you look, the Mississippi River is evident. It created the topography. Even many of its modern tributaries flow in its relict channels. No one can live here and not be aware of the river; it influences everyone's life. It was also the most important environmental influence on human behavior in the past.

The Mississippi River is 4100 km (2560 miles) long and drains 3.25 million km² (1.25 million square miles) (Figure 1.1). It joins the Ohio River at Cairo, Illinois, halfway between New Orleans and Minneapolis–St. Paul. This location marks the northern limit of the lowland alluvial valley of the Mississippi. Almost 800 km (500 miles) downriver from the Ohio is the Arkansas River, third only to the Ohio and Missouri in volume flow. The area between the Ohio and Arkansas rivers is the *Central Mississippi Valley* of this book.

The central lowlands vary between 80 and 160 km (50 and 100 miles) in maximum width. Elevation above sea level immediately adjacent to the Mississippi River ranges from about 90 m at the north to 45 m at the south. Nearly 40,000 km², at least 15,000 contiguous square miles, are classifiable as the Central Mississippi Valley (Figure 1.2). Adding the valleys of tributaries flowing from the bordering uplands would increase this even more.

The territory between the Ohio and Arkansas rivers seems to have been inhabited from an initial Paleo-Indian occupation until the recent past. However, there has been relatively little archaeological work toward the northern and southern extremes or along the eastern and western fringes. This artificial gap in knowledge may emphasize or misrepresent what appears to be a natural border of a cultural area through time. As in most cultural areas, there were population shifts through time complicated by sociopolitical evolution and environmental changes, the most notable of which were changes in the nature and location of the Mississippi and proto-Mississippi rivers.

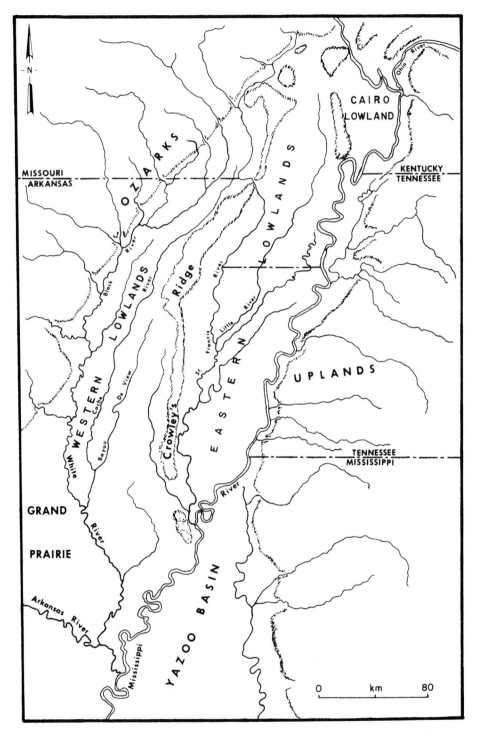

FIGURE 1.2. Major subdivisions of the Central Mississippi Valley and bordering regions.

GROSS DIVISIONS

The Central Lowlands lie mainly to the west of the Mississippi River. The major lowland subdivisions are located either west or east of an erosional remnant upland named Crowley's Ridge, after the early nineteenth-century pioneer Benjamin Crowley. Appropriately, they are known as the Eastern Lowlands and the Western Lowlands (Figure 1.2).

The two principal modern drainage systems in addition to the Mississippi are the White and St. Francis rivers. They are associated primarily with the Western Lowlands and Eastern Lowlands, respectively. Each drainage consists of a complex of watersheds. Watersheds and complexes of watersheds undoubtedly formed important cultural subregions in the prehistoric past, just as they do in the historic present.

The St. Francis River was named after Marquette's favorite saint. It flows out of the Ozark Highlands near the northern extreme of the region, bisects Crowley's Ridge, and forms the western boundary of Arkansas and Missouri in the "Missouri Bootheel." It then flows southward, draining all of the Eastern Lowlands and most of Crowley's Ridge, to near Helena, where it joins the Mississippi River. Major tributaries are the Castor River, both Right Hand and Left Hand chutes of Little River, Big Bay Ditch, Tyronza River, L'Anguille River, and a confusing series of bayous, ditches, and sloughs. Almost all of the drainage in the Eastern Lowlands flows southward and westward into the St. Francis River. The modern Mississippi River's natural levee system effectively blocks eastward drainage.

The White River flows out of the Ozarks near the center of the western border of the region, where it is joined by the Black River. Its principal drainage is the Western Lowlands and the Ozarks from just north of the Arkansas–Missouri state border. Major tributaries of the White River are the Black River, Current River, Eleven Point River, Strawberry River, Little Red River, La Grue Bayou, Village Creek, Bayou De View, and Cache River. Drainage is basically eastward and southward out of the Ozarks into the White River, which joins the Mississippi River immediately north of the mouth of the Arkansas River. The White River, based on volume of flow, is larger than the St. Francis River.

A narrow strip of lowlands is found east of the Mississippi River. It is little investigated archaeologically but is believed to be closely related to remains west of the river. The Hatchie, Obion, and Forked Deer rivers are major tributaries.

There are two basic kinds of soils and landforms within the Central Lowlands (Figure 1.3). Most of the region is characterized by older deposits, which are called the braided stream surface, named for the character of the river at the time of deposition. This surface is the favorite for rice cultivation because a water-retaining clay "hardpan" can be artificially created with the use of heavy machinery. Within this landform there are interruptions by alluvial floodplains and alluvial fans created by later meandering streams.

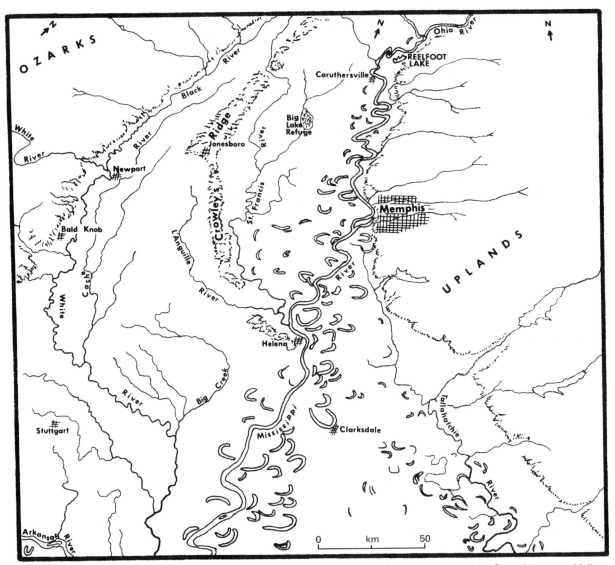

FIGURE 1.3.   Location of the major meander belt surfaces within the Central Mississippi Valley. [Adapted from John H. Corbet, *Physical Geography Manual* (Dubuque, Iowa: Kendall-Hunt Publishing Co., 1974).]

The Mississippi River flows within a meander belt. Actually, there has been a sequence of meander belts since the cessation of the braided stream nature of the Mississippi River (Saucier 1974, 1981). The loamy natural levees of the meander belt have traditionally been the favorite soil area for cotton and the premium land to own within the valley. An unfavorable interruption for modern farmers is the clayey backswamp, an area of poor drainage along the outer margins of levees.

These two regional divisions reflect contemporary historical significance. They also have relevance to an understanding of the prehistoric behavior of human beings. In particular, the Woodland and Mississippian periods may be understandable only in terms of the relationship of phases to this general regional topography.

Most of the major streams flow out of an upland into the lowlands. They provide access to upland resources, especially lithic. They also provide alluvial floodplains for hunting, gathering, fishing, and farming. Relict channels exist often as ponded lakes. The territorial importance of a drainage system to a people is exemplified by the De Soto expedition's reference to the "River of Casqui," the Casqui being a tribe in northeast Arkansas who inhabited sites along the St. Francis and Tyronza rivers.

GEOLOGICAL HISTORY

In this section we emphasize not only the sequence of major environmental changes but also the origins of modern landforms and particularly the accessibility of lithic resources. There has been little modern geological investigation within this region. A notable exception is the work of Roger Saucier, of the U.S. Army Corps of Engineers, whose work is restricted to the Quaternary period. Considerable work has also been accomplished by Walter Manger, of the University of Arkansas Department of Geology, and his students and colleagues. Actually, almost the whole of observable geological time is present within and adjacent to the region. A simplified version of the depositional history is shown in Figure 1.4.

Upland Formations

The Precambrian is represented in nine counties in the Ste. François Mountains of southeast Missouri (Branson 1944). Elevation above sea level ranges between 330 and 390 m. Porphyries and granites are the rocks mostly represented. Basalt, both in the classic and in a generic sense (including granite and rhyolite), is present in volcanic cones, which only rarely occur. Banded iron deposits also are present and include specular hematite. Basalt was particularly important for the manufacture of heavy cutting tools; hematite was prized for red paint. Hematite or other natural iron deposits occur as seams in much of the Ozarks, but basalt appears to be restricted to the Ste. François Mountains.

Heavy erosion of Precambrian rocks was followed by the superimposition of deposits, indicating a long period of inundation by the sea. Disconformities between deposits indicate a continuous cycle of inundation and exposure for

ERA	PERIOD			
CENOZOIC ERA	QUATERNARY PERIOD	POST-GLACIAL (HOLOCENE) 11,000 B.P.	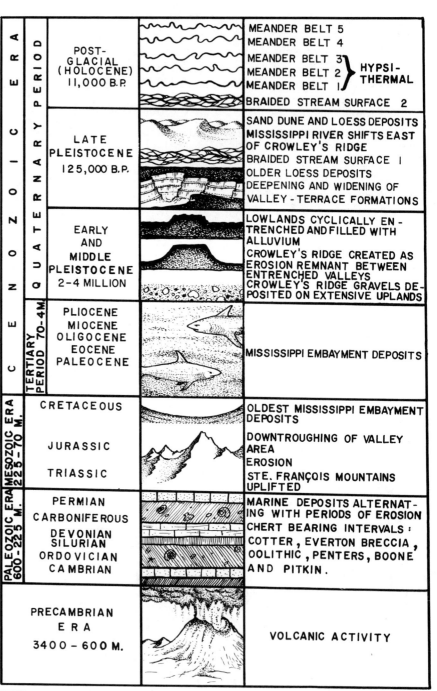	MEANDER BELT 5 MEANDER BELT 4 MEANDER BELT 3 MEANDER BELT 2 } HYPSI-THERMAL MEANDER BELT 1 BRAIDED STREAM SURFACE 2
		LATE PLEISTOCENE 125,000 B.P.		SAND DUNE AND LOESS DEPOSITS MISSISSIPPI RIVER SHIFTS EAST OF CROWLEY'S RIDGE BRAIDED STREAM SURFACE 1 OLDER LOESS DEPOSITS DEEPENING AND WIDENING OF VALLEY - TERRACE FORMATIONS
		EARLY AND MIDDLE PLEISTOCENE 2-4 MILLION		LOWLANDS CYCLICALLY ENTRENCHED AND FILLED WITH ALLUVIUM CROWLEY'S RIDGE CREATED AS EROSION REMNANT BETWEEN ENTRENCHED VALLEYS CROWLEY'S RIDGE GRAVELS DEPOSITED ON EXTENSIVE UPLANDS
	TERTIARY PERIOD 70-4M.	PLIOCENE MIOCENE OLIGOCENE EOCENE PALEOCENE		MISSISSIPPI EMBAYMENT DEPOSITS
MESOZOIC ERA 225-70 M.		CRETACEOUS		OLDEST MISSISSIPPI EMBAYMENT DEPOSITS
		JURASSIC		DOWNTROUGHING OF VALLEY AREA EROSION STE. FRANÇOIS MOUNTAINS UPLIFTED
		TRIASSIC		
PALEOZOIC ERA 600-225 M.		PERMIAN CARBONIFEROUS DEVONIAN SILURIAN ORDOVICIAN CAMBRIAN		MARINE DEPOSITS ALTERNATING WITH PERIODS OF EROSION CHERT BEARING INTERVALS: COTTER, EVERTON BRECCIA, OOLITHIC, PENTERS, BOONE AND PITKIN.
PRECAMBRIAN ERA 3400 - 600 M.				VOLCANIC ACTIVITY

FIGURE 1.4. Geological chart of the Central Mississippi Valley. The Pleistocene dates in the chart are current maximum beginning dates (B.P., before present, or years ago; M, million years ago).

erosion. Sandstones, dolomites, and limestones that include fossils are characteristic Paleozoic deposits immediately adjacent to the Precambrian outcropping in the ancient Ste. François Mountains. These rocks extend southward along the Ozark Escarpment, which borders the western edge of the valley. Sandstones from these deposits were useful as abraders and for use in earth ovens.

Cherts are available along the Ozark Highlands escarpment, particularly along eroded outcrops within the Ozark valleys, from the Ordovician through the Mississippian formations. These cherts are available both in eroded cobble form as parts of gravel deposits near outcroppings and as blocks from within the outcrops themselves. Walter Manger has been attempting to unravel these complex series of cherts, which were potentially useful to and are known to have been used by the aboriginal populations of Arkansas. This study is currently only a preliminary investigation, and most of the results are in draft archaeological reports and theses.

The Ozark Escarpment itself usually varies only about 30–60 m above the adjacent Western Lowlands. More extreme elevations are only observed back from the immediate border of the lowlands. The Paleozoic deposits form a downtrough or depression, which is the geological bedrock substrata of the Central Mississippi Valley. This downtrough was filled with Cretaceous, Tertiary, and Quaternary deposits and is known geologically as the Mississippi Embayment, an extension of the Gulf Coastal Plain.

The uplands east of the Mississippi River vary between 75 and 90 m above sea level near the lowlands and rise to between 120 and 210 m adjacent to the Tennessee River. The surface is gently rolling, and deposits consist of sands, silts, clays, and gravels. Western Tennessee is also part of the Mississippi Embayment.

The Pleistocene

The Early and Middle Pleistocene witnessed the washing away of most of the embayment deposits, leaving Crowley's Ridge as an erosional remnant within the Central Mississippi Valley. There are a variety of lithic sources on Crowley's Ridge. Cherts, as well as agates and quartzites, occur in large amounts in gravel beds of prominent streams, such as Big Creek and Crow Creek. The debris from lithic workshops are found on the banks of streams near where these gravel beds existed. Orthoquartzite outcrops on the west side of the ridge north of Jonesboro. Poorly cemented sandstone, locally known as "ironstone" because of an iron oxide cement, was used for abrasion. Petrified wood is present but does not constitute a very high grade of stone and was only rarely used for knapping purposes.

Approximately 75,000 to 80,000 years ago the final period of glacial advances, the Wisconsin, began. Subsequent deepening and widening of the valley resulted primarily from a significant change in river regime. At least two "loess" or windblown silt episodes have been recognized from deposits on

Crowley's Ridge and in western Tennessee that have been dated to the late Wisconsin. Another significant eolian phenomenon is a 1025 km^2 (396 square miles) of sand dunes in the Western Lowlands, tentatively correlated with the first third of the latest major loess episode, the Peoria Loess of 20,000–10,000 B.C. During or at the end of the later portion of this period of time, small, scattered, windblown silty deposits were formed on both of the lowlands. During this period silts were picked up by winds in both lowlands and deposited widely. At this time the Mississippi River abandoned the Western Lowlands, wherein it was flowing, and joined with the Ohio River to form a larger stream system in the Eastern Lowlands. At about the end of the Pleistocene, human beings first entered the Mississippi Valley, quite possibly one of the richest environments in the New World.

Late Pleistocene and Early Holocene

The commonly recognized boundary between the Pleistocene and the Holocene (postglacial) periods is 11,000 B.P. or 9000 B.C. (Butzer 1977). Postglacial warming conditions in the Central Mississippi Valley seem to have occurred earlier, perhaps by 12,500 B.P. or 10,500 B.C. (Delcourt *et al.* 1980). Spruce along with fir and larch gave way to a mixed oak deciduous forest, reflecting a shift from a cool–temperate to a warm–temperate climate.

Relict braided stream channels, possibly ponded, made up much of the Western Lowlands. A large meandering stream occupied the Cache Basin and apparently was a combined Cache–Black–St. Francis system. Braided stream sandbars had already been transformed into large areas of sand dunes.

In the Eastern Lowlands, adjacent to Crowley's Ridge, was a relict braided stream surface bordered on the east by a prominent escarpment. Immediately east flowed a terminal Pleistocene braided stream, which promptly shifted even more eastward with the advent of the early Holocene. Mastodon, tapir, and giant ground sloth bones have been found deposited on top of a sandbar that existed during the active terminal Pleistocene braided stream. The sandbar was beneath the clay of a ponded inactive channel that existed after stream abandonment.

The Hypsithermal Period

By around 9000 B.P. or 7000 B.C. the mixed oak deciduous forest was firmly established. Ponded relict braided stream sections provided the forest edge that is important for animal life. The Mississippi River system had begun converting from a braided into a meandering stream (called Meander Belt 1) farther south and probably in the southern extreme of the Central Valley. Modern drainage patterns were beginning to take shape in both lowlands.

Around 7000 B.C. the Hypsithermal period began in the Central Valley (King and Allen 1977). During this period conditions became significantly drier, forest cover declined, and grasses increased. The driest conditions extended from around 6700 to 4500 B.C., but dry environments continued until about 3000 B.C., when forests began to make a significant comeback. Roger Saucier's study of sequential meanders of the Current River indicates that a decrease in volume flow was taking place during this interval. The mean annual discharge of the Mississippi River also appears to have declined during this period (Saucier 1974:20). By 5500 B.C. the second Mississippi River meander belt had formed as far north as Memphis. By 4000 B.C. the Mississippi River was flowing in Meander Belt 3 continuously from Cairo. It is at this time that the Mississippi and Ohio rivers joined at Cairo, as they still do today. Meander Belt 3 is mapped northward from the modern meander belt along the east side of Crowley's Ridge to Parkin, then follows a course to Osceola, where it merges once again with the modern Meander Belt 5 system. The shift of Meander Belt 3 to Meander Belt 4 took place about 2800 B.C., near the end of the Hypsithermal period. Meander Belt 4 essentially occupied the same location as the earlier Meander Belt 3 but shifted south from Osceola to near Memphis.

After the Hypsithermal

Wetter conditions with more widespread forests characterized the region after about 3000 B.C. Around 800 B.C. Mississippi Meander Belt 5 came into existence and has continued until today. Climatic variations during the post-Hypsithermal period sufficient to influence cultural behavior are an expectation, but virtually no relevant data have been collected.

Subsequent to the shift from braided to meandering stream flow in the Eastern Lowlands, a series of abortive attempts by the Mississippi River to change its course westward occurred (Saucier 1970). Most were of very short duration and not too significant. One, however, indirectly created the so-called sunk lands, erroneously attributed by local folklore to the New Madrid earthquake of 1811–1812. The new stream was composed of about 4% of the Mississippi River volume. It originated near Hayti, Missouri, perhaps about A.D. 800 and flowed to the southern edge of Big Lake, which it created by damming the older braided channels with its natural levee. At this point, Little River was diverted slightly, and there are two "chutes" of Little River to Marked Tree flowing parallel to each other to this very day. At Marked Tree relict braided channels were also dammed by natural levee construction, and Lake St. Francis came into being. The new stream flowed southward within the older Mississippi River meander belt near Parkin and exited back into the Mississippi River once again near Helena.

THE RECONSTRUCTED RIVER HABITAT

Modern drainage consists of a series of ditches that drain portions of the lowlands for the cultivation of rice, soybeans, cotton, wheat, milo, and alfalfa, and land leveling is apparent everywhere. Irrigation agriculture, particularly for growing rice and soybeans, is popular. Even catfish farming is practiced. Few forests and little indigenous wildlife remain. Driving through an area of monotonous lowland topography, high temperatures, high humidity, and predominant mosquitoes, one may ask why anyone would want to live in this area. Yet, the Central Valley is seemingly one of the richer archaeological zones in the United States, if not the richest, and it is apparent that people lived here in relatively large numbers for thousands of years.

Climate and Weather

The Central Mississippi Valley is low in elevation above sea level and surrounded by higher land masses. It is located between about 37° and 34° north latitude and longitudes 89° and 91.5° west, oriented in a north-northeast to south-southwest direction. The influence of peripheral uplands, Crowley's Ridge, and the surface waters upon climate and weather is not well known. Nor is there really a long period of weather data available for this region. Modern influences on weather include urban centers such as Memphis, where concrete, vehicle exhaust, and industrialization are significant factors. Large-scale land clearance and irrigation rice cultivation have also changed local weather patterns.

The mean annual temperature for the region is around 15°C (60°F). In January the mean monthly temperature is about 4°C (40°F), and in July it is about 27°C (80°F). The average daily range in January is around −2–10°C (28–50°F), and in July it is about 20–34°C (68–94°F). Occasionally, temperatures will drop below −18°C (0°F) in January and soar to above 40°C (105°F) in July.

Natural atmospheric fronts or storm tracks influence precipitation in the region by drawing moisture from the Gulf of Mexico. There is a winter and early spring maximum of precipitation that coincides with the period of least evaporation and allows for maximum ground water recharge and storage. Most of the precipitation is rain; snow does not contribute significantly to the mean annual figure of approximately 125 cm (50 in.). Rainfall is normally fairly evenly distributed throughout the year. Humidity is relatively high; the mean daily noon and midnight figures are about 60–80%, respectively.

Winter is short and only moderately cold, and summer is long and hot. Frostfree days number in excess of 200, extending from the end of March through the end of October. The generally cloudless summer months allow considerable sunshine, approximately 65% the maximum amount possible, which is significant in an agricultural region. However, severe drought is possible when too much sunshine is associated with little rain, low humidity, and high temperatures. Drought is a severe problem in the valley, particularly for agriculture.

Spring storms, often spawning tornadoes, are characteristic. Wind velocity, particularly in the spring, is often high and originates in the west and southwest. Floods occur in the early spring and often again in the early summer as a result of snow melt in northern latitudes drained by the Mississippi River and its tributaries. If there is little snow, river and ground water levels drop significantly. Severe flooding will result from large northern snowfalls. Before the construction of modern restrictive river levees and the large-scale clearance of the lowlands, the severity of floods was eased by natural back-swamps and vegetation transpiration.

Landforms and Hydrology

Crowley's Ridge ranges between 40 and 75 m higher than the surrounding lowlands. The ridge is central to and parallel with the Central Valley. It varies between .80 and 24 km wide, and there are two important gaps, permitting the St. Francis and L'Anguille rivers, north and south, respectively, to flow from the west to the east. The slopes are not very steep. The surface is gently rolling to steeply dissected, the latter of which is partially due to earlier farming practices. Springs exist in profusion, and numerous valleys are present on both sides. Two long valleys are present within the ridge: Big Creek near Jonesboro and Big Crow Creek near Forrest City. Many of the local valleys are relatively wide, considering the narrowness of the ridge. Attempts to locate deeply buried or stratified deposits within the valleys have proved negative to date. No attempt has been made to investigate the possibility for stratigraphy in colluvial ''apron'' wash lateral to the ridge or in alluvial fans.

The larger tributary valleys of the Ozark Highlands are wider, and alluvial fan development is more obvious there than in the valleys of Crowley's Ridge. Farther west in the Ozarks, greater elevation is characteristic, and rock shelters are numerous. These uplands were important in providing immediate access to contrasting biological resources and climate. Each 90 m in elevation is approximately equal to a northern latitude displacement of 160 km (100 miles). The possibility of alternative exploitative systems is greatly enhanced within a region as favorably located as the Central Mississippi Valley.

Drainages in the lowlands are essentially parallel with the valley, and streams tend to flow in a southerly direction completely through the region. East-west movement in the valley is very difficult. As the De Soto expedition discovered, it is much easier to follow a stream than to cross one after another.

Essential lowland divisions are the older braided stream surface, the younger braided stream surface, the older meander belts and the younger or modern meander belt. Modern and older streams have carved and deposited paths through these basic surfaces, and wind activity has modified considerable portions of the older surfaces.

A braided stream regime is an alternative to a meandering one. Two factors favored braided stream development in the Central Valley. First, there was an abrupt change in gradient from the more northern uplands. Second, glacial meltwater provided much of the flow and coarse sediment. Changes in sea level may have influenced stream gradient as well. This flow concentrated into a seasonal pattern. Deposition of elongated sandbanks diverted flow laterally, which in turn deposited more sandbanks destined to become islands as stream beds deepened. Equilibrium is approached when the system of sandbanks and channels is sufficiently wide enough to accommodate flow. In the case of significantly increased flow or buildup of the drainage system bed in elevation, diversion to an entirely new location can result. Thus relict channels are silty to clayey, and interfluvial areas are sandy. Clayey soils also result from more modern drainages involving meandering streams once the Mississippi River shifted to the east of Crowley's Ridge.

Braided surfaces are divisible into distinct levels dating to sequential periods. Within the Western Lowlands, the older and higher level is located to the east and the younger to the west. These gently rolling surfaces differ in elevation on the order of 3–6 m.

Sikeston's Ridge and a narrow section of land immediately east of Crowley's Ridge are remnants of the oldest braided stream terrace in the Eastern Lowlands. The youngest braided stream terrace is separated by a distinct ridge or escarpment ranging in height up to 4.5 m (15 ft.) and parallel with Crowley's Ridge. Big Bay Ditch flows along much of this escarpment. The border of these two subterraces is essentially the channel now occupied by Right Hand Chute of Little River to Marked Tree and the St. Francis River south of Marked Tree.

The oldest meander belt is represented only in the southern portion of the Eastern Lowlands. A river meanders to achieve an equilibrium between discharge and sediment load. By a process of erosion along one side with subsequent deposition on the opposite side, a snakelike pattern develops within a single stream channel. Meander loops tend to be cut off, become lakes, and then evolve into swamps. Meandering erodes out a valley within which the river flows. Bars are built within the stream and become islands. Floods cause natural levees on the banks of the river because of an abrupt decrease in current allowing the deposition of coarser sediments. Farther back, increasingly finer sedimentation occurs, creating a marshy floodplain that slopes back from the levees. Low knolls also are formed here, but in general the floodplain is flat. Levee construction often blocks smaller tributaries, causing them to flow parallel with the river until they are finally forced to join it, resulting in backswamps, shallow lakes, and complicated lateral stream patterns. Together all these features constitute a meander belt.

Stress existed in the past and still exists today in the region. Volcanic activity in the Precambrian was followed by obvious earth movements resulting in the Ste. François Mountains and the Central Valley depression. Folding is evident through the Cretaceous. The New Madrid earthquake of 1811–1812 scared local Indians and settlers and was felt hundreds of kilometers away (Penick 1976). Ignoring the large body of local folklore, most of it invalid, we can, nevertheless, attribute some landforms to this earthquake.

This early nineteenth-century earthquake did not significantly disturb archaeological deposits, with a few exceptions. Cracks filled with clean subsurface sand indicate that the edges of sloughs slumped, with the resulting cracks being instantly filled with clean fluvial sand from beneath. "Sand blows" often exist over these areas in the Eastern Lowlands and are conspicuous by not containing pre-1811 artifacts on their surface. That cracking usually follows the line of least resistance is evidence of insignificant topographic deformation. Alluvial soils roll with an earth tremor and usually crack only when sections of soil slump into lower elevations as landslides. Reelfoot Lake in Tennessee is thought to have been caused by such a landslide damming the reservoir. The sunk lands of Arkansas and Missouri did not sink during the earthquake but did experience several years of abnormal flooding due to blocked drainage channels. They originated as the result of alluvial drowning, mostly caused by older channels being dammed by the construction of natural levees by later river systems. Although no solid evidence of earlier earthquakes has been recorded to date, tremors may have frightened local inhabitants and disrupted normal behavior patterns.

Sand dunes make up a significant topographic subdivision, mostly associated with the latest braided stream surface in the Western Lowlands and an area near Cairo (Saucier 1978). Dunes concentrate in areas up to 75 km² and range individually as high as 9 m and in area as much as 10 ha (25 acres). Other windblown hillocks are present over much of the Western Lowlands and Eastern Lowlands associated with braided stream surfaces, but these are much lower and less extensive in area. All, however, provide well-drained locations for encampment.

Another strange phenomenon in the region, also restricted to the western edge of the Western Lowlands, is the "prairie bump." These rounded mounds range in size from around 8 to 30 m in diameter and 30 cm to 1 m high. The two main speculations of their origin are biological (plant or animal) and geological (eolian). They are not of human origin, although often artifacts left by human occupation can be found on their surface.

The Grand Prairie area bordering the southern portion of the Central Valley is a series of relict backswamp and meander belt deposits of the Arkansas River. It is characterized by numerous prairie bumps. It is distinct from the Western Lowlands because of the wide expanse of alluvial features.

Soils

Soils are important for a number of reasons. They are the basis for plant growth and animal habitat and for horticulture. No less importantly, they provide the very foundation for habitation.

In the Central Mississippi Valley, an upper ground temperature of 20°C (68°F) is attained by the final 2 weeks of April. This is above the minimum growth temperatures for hot-season crops and is sufficient for seedlings. Corn in particular requires relatively high day and night temperatures. The optimum air temperature for plant growth such as corn is around 31–37°C (88–99°F). This range is achieved during much of the summer.

Crop productivity of soils without drainage or fertilizer ranges from impossible swampy situations to the preferable fine sandy loams on natural levees. Coarse sandy soils are normally productive but are vulnerable to nutrient leaching and to drought conditions. Most soils are naturally acid.

Natural levees and sand dunes provide topographic relief for the inhabitants of these lowlands. There are well-drained sandy and silt loam soils on these higher elevations. Clays suitable for pottery manufacture are always located nearby in slackwater situations. Logs buried in the ground for structural support generally last for 20–30 years.

Vegetation

Probably the best description of the vegetation of this region is the southeast Missouri inventory of plants in Steyermark's *Flora of Missouri* (1963). Probably 2000 or more species of plants, several hundred of which were edible, existed in this region. Major biotic communities are listed in Table 1.1. In an active meander belt environment, nutrients are constantly added to alluvial soils and to water habitats from swamps. The fluctuating water levels and relatively large amount of surface water present create ideal browse undergrowth along forest edges.

Within this region, midwestern and northern species overlap in distribution with southern species. Examples of southern plants whose ranges extend up the valley are water hickory, cane, bald cypress, pecan, cherry bark oak, and overcup oak. From the north and midwest extend several species of hickories as well as pin oak and dogwood. Spanish moss is characteristic only south of the Arkansas River. Bald cypress and cane extend today only about as far north as the Ohio River but probably extended as far north as St. Louis in the recent past.

The importance of plants for sustaining animal life cannot be overemphasized. For instance, oaks provide critical food, in the form of acorns, for white-tailed deer and even ducks. Foods important to humans include persimmon, greenbrier, pokeweed, wild potato, wild rice, Indian turnip, cattail, amaranth, dock, lamb's-quarters, Jerusalem artichoke, wild onion, spring beauty, and a variety of other fruits, nuts, and berries.

TABLE 1.1
Major Biotic Communities in the Central Mississippi Valley

Upland	Lowland	Wetland
Beech–tulip	Cottonwood–willow–sycamore	Limnetic (open water)
Oak–pine	Sweetgum–elm–hackberry	Littoral
Oak–hickory	Whiteoak–"sweetgum"	Cypress–tupelo
		Cypress–hardwood
	Fields and second growth	

Fauna

The Central Valley is one of the richest areas known for hunting and fishing in the eastern United States. The primary land mammal throughout this region was the white-tailed deer. Raccoon ranked second, followed by cottontail and swamp rabbit and the fox squirrel. Bear was rarely hunted. Buffalo and elk apparently did not exist in the Central Valley in prehistoric times, although they are described in the contemporary literature of the Historic period.

Approximately 400,000 mallards winter in northeast Arkansas alone, so it is no surprise that ducks comprised the primary bird eaten, with numerous species represented. Geese were next in importance, followed by turkey and the now-extinct passenger pigeon. Turkeys are upland birds and are not prominent in most prehistoric animal bone inventories.

Fish were extremely important, particularly since many achieve very large sizes, such as the flathead catfish, alligator gar, drum, and buffalo. In addition, fish constitute a concentrated protein source. Turtles and frogs abounded, especially the large meaty snapping turtle and one of the largest bullfrog varieties found anywhere. Smaller but still large common fish were largemouth bass, walleye or sauger, channel catfish, bowfin, gar, and suckers. Numerous smaller fish were also available. Shellfish do not appear to have been an important primary food but certainly were collected and probably eaten.

REFERENCES

Branson, E. B.
   1944   The geology of Missouri. *University of Missouri Studies* 19:3.
Butzer, Karl W.
   1977   Geomorphology of the Lower Illinois Valley as a spatial–temporal context for the Koster Archaic site. *Illinois State Museum Reports of Investigations* **34**.
Delcourt, Paul, Hazel Delcourt, Ronald Brister, and Laurence Lackey
   1980   Quaternary vegetation history of the Mississippi Embayment. *Quaternary Research* **13**:111–132.
King, J. E., and W. H. Allen, Jr.
   1977   A Holocene vegetation record from the Mississippi River Valley, southeastern Missouri. *Quaternary Research* **8**:307–323.
Penick, James Jr.
   1976   *The New Madrid earthquakes of 1811–1812.* Columbia: University of Missouri Press.
Saucier, Roger
   1970   Origin of the St. Francis sunk lands, Arkansas and Missouri. *Geological Society of America Bulletin* **81**:2847–2854.
   1974   Quaternary geology of the Lower Mississippi Valley. *Arkansas Archeological Survey Research Series* **6**.
   1978   Sand dunes and related eolian features of the Lower Mississippi Alluvial Valley. *Geoscience and Man* **19**:23–40.
   1981   Current thinking on riverine processes and geologic history as related to human settlements in the Southeast. *Geoscience and Man* **22**:7–18.
Steyermark, Julian
   1963   *Flora of Missouri.* Ames: Iowa State University Press.

2

The Archaeology

Speaking of vandals, no state has suffered more at the hands of reckless, careless mound diggers than Arkansas, and especially the "pottery belt" of that state. The fine clay vessels found in considerable numbers are highly prized by wealthy collectors. Four or five adventurers, trappers and men who have a superficial education and no regard for science, floated down the Mississippi on house boats and carried on explorations in the past. A number of large collections have been made, and perhaps twelve or fifteen thousand pieces of pottery are now in museums, in the hands of collectors and otherwise scattered throughout the country as a result of their labors. No notes, drawings or photographs accompany the specimens. No reports have been published. One simply sees the long rows of "pots" on the shelves and a general label, "From mounds in Arkansas," accompanying the exhibit [Moorehead 1904:114–115].

HISTORY OF ARCHAEOLOGICAL INVESTIGATIONS

The first archaeologists undoubtedly were Indians who speculated about the origin of stone debris concentrated at locations in a stoneless environment. The De Soto expedition accounts provide the first ethnological observations of the aboriginal cultures of the Central Mississippi Valley. The narratives describe flourishing, highly organized societies with large populations, presided over by powerful chiefs. There then was a gap of over 130 years until Louis Jolliet and Jacques Marquette came down the Mississippi from New France in 1673. They described only two villages in the entire Central Mississippi Valley area. After this, occasional records such as those of fur traders and French and Spanish officials at Arkansas Post refer to the shifting Indian groups in the area. Fewer than 2000 Europeans lived between New Madrid, Missouri, and the Arkansas River before the Louisiana Purchase of 1803.

In the nineteenth century the area was explored and described by various travelers and naturalists. Such persons as Henry Schoolcraft, Thomas Nuttall, and even Sir Charles Lyell, the author of *Principles of Geology,* visited the wilderness of the Central Valley and published their observations. Their major interests were botanical and geological, but they often noted the presence of mounds. For instance, Thomas Nuttall in 1819 observed low mounds near New Madrid, Missouri, which "as usual, abound with fragments of earthern ware [1821:46]."

After the Central Valley became a part of the United States, a comprehensive plan to map the entire Louisiana Purchase using the basic township, range, and section grid began at a point in Arkansas. These early maps often show such features as "Indian Mound" or "Abandoned Delaware Village." The study of archaeological resources began in the mid-nineteenth century. For instance, an Antiquarian and Natural History Society was formed in Little Rock in 1837, 1 year after Arkansas became a state. This society kept a cabinet of specimens, including clay pots and novaculite items from the Hot Springs area. These specimens were placed on display at the old state capitol and have since been lost.

A gap exists in the literature from the 1840s until the 1870s. Then an intensive period of archaeological activity took place. Much of the recorded observations were preceded by commercial exploitation of large mound sites, centering around Charleston, Missouri. Pots became a cash crop for the local farmers. In response to this activity, the St. Louis Academy of Science conducted fieldwork from 1876 to 1878 in southeast Missouri (Potter and Evers 1880). William Potter and Edward Evers published professionally surveyed maps of five sites using a scale that included such valuable details as house mounds, which have since been destroyed by cultivation. The maps also clearly showed large flat-topped temple mounds with their heights and surrounding ditches. They included accurate drawings of 147 complete pottery vessels, again including scales. The goal was clear presentation of data as a foundation for future research rather than as support for various theories of origin or interpretation of symbolic meanings. Evers studied over 4000 specimens of pottery from southeast Missouri before choosing the various specimens to be illustrated. The high standards of this brief work were seldom achieved during the next 100 years.

In the year 1877–1878, Dr. Frank James was practicing medicine in Osceola, Arkansas (Baird 1977). Joseph Henry of the Smithsonian Institution contracted with James to open mounds in the area and send specimens to Washington. Pipes, hoes, and "vases" were sent to the Smithsonian and were regarded as having "exceptional interest." Unfortunately, the exact site provenience of this collection was not noted by James in his diary or in the extant Smithsonian correspondence. James also supplied specimens to European museums, including one in Vienna, Austria (Baird 1977:53). These are the first documented collections from the Mississippi County, Arkansas, area.

One of the first recorded uses of the probe or feeling rod for discovering the presence of complete pots was by a Captain C. W. Riggs, who spent several years in the 1880s digging sites along the Mississippi, St. Francis, Ohio, and Missouri rivers (Brose 1980). Riggs worked from a houseboat that included a library and equipment for developing photographs. The Riggs collection of 3000 pottery specimens was exhibited at the World's Columbian Exposition in Chicago in 1892 and later was sold at Wanamaker's Department Store. Riggs kept the site provenience of his collection, but his catalog was lost. Specimens from this collection are now at institutions such as the Cleveland Museum of Natural History, Field Museum of Natural History, Chicago, and the Buffalo Museum of Science. All his notes and photographs are still missing.

"Captain" Wilfrid Hall was another person who spent many years accumulating and redistributing artifacts from the Central Valley during the late nineteenth century (Griffin 1981). Hall sent barrels of pottery and stone tools to his patrons to the north, particularly the Putnam Museum in Davenport, Iowa, and the Cabinet Association of Jacksonville, Illinois. These artifacts were shipped without suitable packing and often arrived in poor condition. Provenience was not of much importance to Hall, and a considerable number of artifacts from Arkansas and Tennessee cannot be assigned to any particular site. Hall was sent both money and barrels of useful objects such as coffee, sugar, and the *Sunday School Times* as payment. The Davenport collection served as a major data base for W. H. Holmes's *Aboriginal Pottery of the Eastern United States* (1903), in which he first defined a Middle Mississippi Valley group.

The first well-documented archaeological excavations in northeast Arkansas were conducted by the Peabody Museum of Harvard University in 1879 (Putnam 1881:12). Edwin Curtis spent the winter along the St. Francis River making collections from the Rose Mound, Fortune Mound, Stanley Mounds (Parkin), and the Halcomb Mound. Although these excavations were never published in detail, Curtis left a brief diary, and the materials recovered, including over 900 pots, are still available for study at Harvard. Curtis observed that it was difficult to reach the area and that he had to bring his own camp equipage and "corpse of laborers" with him. He saw mounds full of pottery in deep woods that had never had a shovel in them.

By far the most comprehensive and fully reported research during this period of early exploration was that of the Bureau of Ethnology Division of Mound Exploration (Smith 1981). An earmarked appropriation of 5000 dollars began this project, which lasted from 1881 until 1890 (Thomas 1894). A small group of assistants aided Thomas in mapping over 2000 mounds and collecting over 40,000 specimens in 23 states. The overall research plan involved sampling typical mounds and mound groups over as wide an area as possible rather than concentrating on one region. The leveling of mounds by the encroachments of agriculture and destruction through commercial sale of archaeological relics were already seen as dangers to the data base.

Field workers were ordered to collect specimens without bias to be used by future students. The accuracy of detail demanded by Thomas included complete measurement of mound groups using diagrams, recording of strata and the relics within them in field books, field cataloging of specimens by provenience, and the subsequent recataloging by the bureau and the Smithsonian. Fieldwork was done throughout the year, working in the South during the winter.

The most important question the bureau asked was that of the origin of mounds. Many writers believed that an extinct race built the observed prehistoric monuments and that the American Indian was incapable of such achievements. The Thomas survey, using the contents of the mounds themselves as evidence rather than romantic speculation, concluded that the Indians and mound builders were one and the same people. Evidence to the contrary was discussed and often shown to be fraudulent.

A considerable amount of the Bureau of Ethnology survey time was spent in the Central Mississippi Valley. The survey provided detailed maps and tables of measurements for such large mound groups as the Rich Woods, Beckwith's Fort, and Powers Fort sites in southeast Missouri and the Webb group, Miller Mounds, and Taylors Shanty group in northeast Arkansas. Large-scale excavations were undertaken at many of these sites. The emphasis of the survey was on the Missouri–Arkansas lowlands area, with only two sites briefly mentioned in West Tennessee and one each described in Kentucky and Illinois. Artifacts from these excavations were used as a basis for other studies such as surveys of prehistoric pottery and shell art of the American Indian. Thomas attempted a typology of all the mounds surveyed in eastern North America, naming eight primary archaeological districts. His Arkansas District included much of the Central Mississippi Valley plus the rest of Arkansas and northern Louisiana (Thomas 1894:586).

As the one hundredth anniversary of this survey approached, the Smithsonian Institution and the Lower Mississippi Survey of Harvard's Peabody Museum sponsored a restudy of the Mound Exploration Division at the Smithsonian in 1980. All surviving photographs, notes, correspondence, and collections were made available for study to archaeologists working in the regions covered by the original survey. After 100 years, the collections made were still intact for study.

Gerard Fowke conducted excavations in Missouri in 1906 and 1907 financed by the St. Louis Division of the Archaeological Institute of America (Fowke 1910). He visited southeast Missouri, hoping to excavate several sites that would produce complete pottery specimens. He interviewed collectors and landowners in four counties and became convinced that all the good sites had been found and dug out 20–30 years earlier by prospectors with probes. He found two untouched sites, but the landowners forbade any excavation.

Fowke reported the discovery of the Malden or Wulfing plates, an isolated find of eight embossed copper plates featuring humans wearing hawk regalia. Fowke also wrote an artifact handbook for the Missouri Historical Society as their first *Bulletin*. This handbook featured only stone tools.

An ambitious archaeological survey was supported by Louis Houck while he was writing his three-volume *History of Missouri* (1908). He sent Lewis Bean and D. L. Hoffman "accurately and definitely [to] locate every mound and settlement" [p. 41] of the mound builders of Missouri. These energetic individuals recorded over 28,000 mounds, which are all mapped and listed by county and then section, township, and range in footnotes in one chapter of Houck's book. Houck saw that the center of the Mississippi Valley was an area of distinct prehistoric activity, with southeast Missouri being a subarea or center. He noted that a concentration of mounds was present in a band 9.7–16.1 km (6–10 miles) wide on alluvial flatlands not far from the Ozarks, particularly along creeks feeding into the St. Francis River. He also observed that these sites were always on extensive bodies of good soil. It was later discovered that many of the "mounds" located were natural sand dunes. The site locations were a good basis for the beginnings of a comprehensive state site file, as even the sand dunes are the most likely spots for prehistoric habitation. This kind of information was not available for the other states in the Central Valley.

Clarence Bloomfield Moore of Philadelphia (Figure 2.1) is one of the most noteworthy contributors to Southeast archaeology. Moore, a wealthy gentleman, was a Harvard graduate who spent his winters directing the excavation of sites from the shell heaps of the Florida coast to large mound sites on inland rivers. He did the archaeological work from his stern-wheel steamboat, the *Gopher*, 30 m (100 ft.) long and 6 m (20 ft.) wide. It carried a captain, a pilot, an engineer, a crew of five men, six men to dig, and special guests such as an anatomist. Moore's steamboat captain explored the territory in advance, locating promising sites and getting landowner permission to excavate.

Moore spent four field seasons between 1908 and 1916 in the Central Valley area, first on the Lower Arkansas, Yazoo, and Sunflower rivers, then on the St. Francis, next on the Mississippi River itself, and finally on the Mississippi above Memphis and into the Ohio and Green rivers in Kentucky. Moore's main publication emphasis was on pottery. For instance, at Pecan Point in Mississippi County, Arkansas (Moore 1911:447–474), he recovered 349 burials, which included 535 pottery vessels.

It has become almost traditional to deplore the work of Moore, because of his emphasis on recovery of fine specimens from burials. However, this kind of acquisition is an evolutionary first step in the archaeological history of any region. Moore was unusual in that he immediately published his excavation results, with superb illustrations in the *Proceedings* of the Academy of Natural Sciences of Philadelphia. He also took field notes, cataloged all his material, and donated it to scientific institutions. He had animal bones identified by

FIGURE 2.1.   C. B. Moore's boat, the *Gopher*. [Courtesy of John Connaway and Sam Brookes, Mississippi Department of Archives and History Archaeological Survey.] Inset: C. B. Moore in 1873 when he graduated from Harvard College. [Courtesy of James B. Griffin.]

zoologists, sent off skulls to be measured, noted particulars such as burial positions and the occasional inclusion of European artifacts, and had copper analyzed to see whether it was native. Moore's publications and Thomas's Bureau of American Ethnology Mound Survey became the basic archaeological literature for the Central Valley and must still be frequently referred to today.

There was little archaeological literature published from the World War I period all through the 1920s. One exception was Calvin Brown's *Archeology of Mississippi*, published in 1926 by the Mississippi Geological Survey. Brown was on the staff of the Geological Survey and the University of Mississippi, and the book was the result of many years of fieldwork. One chapter discussed archaeological sites by region, and other chapters detail various artifact classes such as axes and celts, pipes, pottery, and post-Columbian material. Over 300 excellent photographs accompanied the report, furnishing data for newer interpretations such as the presence of fluted points. An extensive 30-page description of pottery from the Walls site near Memphis was the basis for the definition of the Walls phase by later researchers.

One of the leading amateur archaeologists in the Central Valley was Dr. James K. Hampson of Nodena Plantation near Wilson, Arkansas (Morse 1973). Dr. Hampson was a physician who conducted excavations at the Upper and Middle Nodena sites from 1932 to 1941 (Figure 2.2a). Hampson never finished a monograph on his excavations, but he was always most generous in showing interested people his specimens and helping professional archaeologists with information about the area. He permitted the University of Arkansas Museum and the Alabama Museum of Natural History to excavate at Nodena in 1932 (Morse 1973). Dr. Hampson mapped all burials and houses found, making a master map of these features and filling out a card on each burial excavated. He was particularly interested in paleopathology, saving all burials with evidence of disease or trauma. The specimens from over 1200 graves and 65 houses were preserved at a private museum in the old plantation store building. These were donated to the state at Hampson's death and are now on display in the Henry Clay Hampson II Memorial Museum of Archaeology at Wilson, Arkansas.

Samuel C. Dellinger was the lone representative of institutional archaeology in Arkansas for almost 30 years (Figure 2.2b). He was curator of the University of Arkansas Museum from 1925 to 1960 (Hoffman 1981), as well as chairman of the Zoology Department. Although he was not an anthropologist, his main endeavor was to accumulate archaeological collections from Arkansas for the museum. He resented that large eastern museums had fine displays of Arkansas materials and felt that these specimens were collected by expeditions similar to those that pillaged the more backward countries. Dellinger spent considerable energy discouraging both nonprofessional and professional archaeologists from working in Arkansas, including trying to stave off Philip Phillips, James Ford, and James Griffin from "skimming the cream" during their monumental survey in the 1940s (Phillips, Ford, and Griffin 1951:40).

Dellinger's most positive contributions to Arkansas archaeology were made in the 1930s. He received a $20,000 grant from the Carnegie Foundation to establish a state archaeological survey. With these funds, enormous for the Depression era, he excavated in over 100 rock shelters of the Arkansas Ozarks, in large Mississippian sites of northeast Arkansas such as Nodena and in sites in the Central Arkansas River Valley. Several articles based on Carnegie-financed data were published (Dellinger and Dickinson 1940), but he never produced a major monograph. Works Progress Administration (WPA) money financed a second series of major excavations, most of which were in southwest Arkansas. More than 8000 pottery vessels are now in the University of Arkansas collections as a result of Dellinger's efforts.

In 1930 the University of Kentucky Department of Anthropology received money from the National Research Council to purchase a truck for fieldwork.

(a)

(b)

FIGURE 2.2. Two early Arkansas investigators. (a) Dr. James K. Hampson in his museum in 1942. [Courtesy of Mrs. Frances Hampson.] (b) Samuel Dellinger in late 1930s or early 1940s. [Courtesy of the University of Arkansas Museum.]

Additional funds from the Smithsonian helped underwrite major field excavations. From this began the University of Kentucky *Reports in Archaeology and Anthropology,* the majority of which were published in the 1930s. W. D. Funkhouser and Colonel William S. Webb of the University of Kentucky published their *Archaeological Survey of Kentucky* in 1932. They visited each county, mapped and photographed sites, and published a site map for each county. They divided the state into eight major physiographic regions and included the Central Valley in their Muskhogean area, where the Mississippi, Ohio, Tennessee, and Cumberland rivers joined. They saw this region as a center of prehistoric trade and travel, with affinities to the South. The only site report for the Central Valley area published in this series was that for the McLeod Bluff site in Hickman County, Kentucky, where all the burials uncovered had been previously disturbed.

The "Ancient Buried City" near Wickliffe, Kentucky, was excavated and developed as a tourist attraction in the 1930s by Colonel and Mrs. Fain King. Five mounds, including one containing only infant burials, were roofed over. The site is still operated as a tourist attraction. Collections from other sites were placed on display along with objects from the "Buried City" itself.

The University of Missouri began sponsoring archaeological research in the 1930s when J. Brewton Berry joined their Sociology Department (Berry 1975). His initial enthusiasm for archaeology came from a meeting with Jesse Wrench of the History Department, and these two individuals began surveying sites in the university area. When large-scale federal relief programs were begun by President Roosevelt in 1933, Wrench and Berry drew up plans for a statewide archaeological survey program, and the Civil Works Administration sponsored it for a trial period. An archaeological investigator was appointed for each county and assigned to report locations of mound and village sites and owners of large relic collections. Thousands of forms were turned in. One such county investigator was Carl Chapman, now known as the dean of Missouri archaeology.

After this initial enthusiasm, a small group met at Columbia and formed the Missouri Archaeological Society in December 1934. The goals of the society were to locate every prehistoric site in the state, preserve remains for parks and study, arouse public interest in archaeology and publish a bulletin dealing with Missouri Indians and their remains. The first issue of the *Missouri Archaeologist* was published in 1935, and it has continued to publish articles and memoirs on Missouri archaeology.

In 1937 Wrench, Berry, and Chapman conducted an archaeological survey of the proposed Lake Wapapello area, where the St. Francis River was to be dammed in Wayne County. Over 500 sites were located, and 14 were tested. This was about the only reservoir salvage conducted in the Central Mississippi Valley and was small compared with the large Tennessee Valley Authority dam salvage projects of the 1930s.

One other WPA project was carried out on the northern fringe of the Central Valley in New Madrid County, Missouri. The Academy of Science of

St. Louis sponsored excavations by Robert M. Adams and Winslow Walker at the Matthews site in 1941–1942. This site had been mapped in 1878 by William Potter, and houses shown on his old map were found and excavated. Data on the typical floor plans of Mississippian houses were recovered. This was one of the first site reports published in the Central Valley.

World War II serves as a useful transition zone for a history of regional archaeology. At that time there was little fieldwork because of lack of manpower and fewer scientific publications because of restrictions on paper. Fieldwork done in the 1930s waited for the return of archaeologists for analysis and final reports. Many of these collections are still waiting, as it has always been far easier to get funds for excavations than for the subsequent unglamorous analyses. The beginning of modern archaeology in the valley took place during this time period. Philip Phillips of Harvard University, James B. Griffin of the University of Michigan, and James A. Ford, then of Louisiana State University, began their archaeological survey of the Lower Mississippi River Valley in 1940 and waited to finish in 1947 (Phillips, Ford, and Griffin 1951).

The major goal of this survey was to investigate the northern two-thirds of the Lower Mississippi River Valley, an area where nothing was known about pre-Mississippian societies and little was published about Mississippian itself (Figure 2.3a). Their initial research focused on gathering data to explain the origin and development of Mississippian societies. From their first day in the field, the relationship between Baytown (Hopewellian) and Mississippian became their major survey problem (1951:40). Accompanied by a very small staff, they gathered surface collections from 385 sites, analyzed the ceramics from these sites (Figure 2.3b), and placed small test excavations in 11 sites selected from this analysis. They used new Mississippi River Commission maps to plot sites. Samples of over 10,000 sherds were collected from some sites. A card was made out for each site, and maps were made of the larger mound group sites. They developed a pottery typology that is still the basis for that used today. The pottery collections were seriated and sites dated relative to one another. The various old channels of the Mississippi River were correlated with sites to set up a chronology of occupation. Types of sites were defined, and a temporal ordering of these site types was made. A lengthy discussion of both the De Soto expedition route and early French accounts of Indian groups tied these in to archaeological data. Final conclusions of this monumental work were that a single center for origin of Mississippian culture did not exist in the survey area and that multiple origins were present.

Chucalissa, a large Mississippian site south of Memphis, was discovered by Civilian Conservation Corps (CCC) workers while they were building a camp in the 1930s. Brief excavations were undertaken under the direction of University of Tennessee archaeologists in 1940 (Nash 1972). Plans for excavation and development as a park were postponed until the 1950s, when an archaeologist was provided to supervise volunteers from the Memphis Archaeological and Geological Society and laborers from the Shelby County Penal

(a)   (b)

FIGURE 2.3.   The Phillips—Ford—Griffin survey. (a) Crossing the St. Francis River on Dillon's Ferry with James A. Ford on board. (b) James B. Griffin examining potsherds at the Vernon Paul site, Cross County, Arkansas, on April 1, 1940. [Courtesy of University of Michigan Museum of Anthropology and Central Mississippi Valley Archaeological Survey.]

Farm to clear the site, excavate burials and features, and reconstruct thatch houses and the temple mound. The site was donated to Memphis State University in 1962 and is now a museum and archaeological laboratory. Regular archaeological field schools conducted at the site have made this one of the most intensively sampled large prehistoric sites in the valley.

A formal Central Mississippi Valley Archaeological Survey was begun by the University of Michigan in 1949 (Griffin and Spaulding 1952). Griffin and Spaulding defined their research area as stretching along the Mississippi floodplain from the mouth of the Illinois River to southeast Missouri, where the Lower Valley survey had stopped. Their major goal was to gather data to set up a complete cultural sequence. Support for this survey came from the Viking Fund. To augment the data on Mississippian societies, both Late Archaic and Middle Woodland period sites were discovered and excavated. In connection with this survey Stephen Williams produced the first detailed synthesis of archaeology in southeast Missouri (1954). Enough data were gathered by Williams to set up a sequence of regional phases by area, including four distinct Mississippian phases. Williams's cultural sequence interpretations are the basis for those still used in southeast Missouri today.

Growth in the archaeological knowledge of southeast Missouri was fostered by the creation of a Department of Anthropology at the University of

Missouri in the 1950s. The Department and Division of American Archaeology provided funds for field research. In the 1960s land leveling of fields for irrigation became standard agricultural practice for southeast Missouri and northeast Arkansas. This process was destroying many large obvious archaeological sites, and funds for land-leveling salvage archaeology were obtained from the National Park Service. Local informants notified university personnel of planned leveling in southeast Missouri, and test pits were placed in selected sites before destruction. As the site was leveled, features were mapped in by the archaeologist, and artifacts were collected.

Several theses were based on this work, including J. Raymond Williams's (1974) study of Baytown phases and Hopgood's (1969) study of Baytown pottery. Klippel (1969) excavated the Hearnes site in the Cairo Lowland. Lewis (1974, 1982) used data gathered during the land-leveling study to study Mississippian settlement locations, ecological adaptation, and exploitative strategies. The site of Beckwith's Fort, or Towosahgy, was acquired by the Missouri State Park Board in 1966, and various students have conducted research at the site (Cottier and Southard 1977).

Federal funds were provided for highway salvage archaeology, including preliminary surveys and excavation in the right of way of sites threatened by highway construction. Along Interstate Route 55 (Marshall 1965) in Missouri, 30 sites were found, and 7 were then excavated by personnel from the University of Missouri.

Cooperation with and encouragement of avocational archaeologists by University of Missouri personnel also furthered research. Most notable are the publication of the Campbell site excavations of Leo Anderson (Chapman and Anderson 1955) and the Lawhorn site report of John Moselage (1962), both of which are detailed site reports. In fact, the Lawhorn monograph is the first complete descriptive report published on any site in northeast Arkansas. After the Lilbourn site was chosen for the location of a technical school, the University conducted a considerable amount of fieldwork at the site (Chapman and Evans 1977). The sampling of a large Middle Mississippian town, including cemetery areas, fortifications, residential clusters, and a plaza was accomplished. Chapman is currently summarizing Missouri archaeology in a series of volumes (1975, 1980).

The Thomas Gilcrease Institute of American History and Art of Tulsa, Oklahoma, sponsored several excavations in northeast Arkansas in the late 1950s (Perino 1966, 1967). After the institute had purchased a large collection of Arkansas artifacts, it planned excavations to augment these data for better interpretation. The Banks site in Crittenden County produced at least 385 burials and seven house patterns. The Cherry Valley Mound excavation uncovered a previously unknown Mississippian phase. One of the first mentions of the important Dalton period occupation of Arkansas was noted in this report.

Hopewellian burial mounds at the Helena Crossing site were excavated by James A. Ford, then of the American Museum of Natural History, in 1960 (Ford 1963). Ford revisited the site while conducting an excavation at the Quapaw Menard site and found that three of the five mounds mapped by Phillips, Ford, and Griffin in 1940 were already destroyed by highway construction. Emergency funding by the museum enabled Ford to dig the remaining mounds and publish a report (1963) on the previously unknown Middle Woodland occupation in Arkansas.

Michigan's Central Mississippi Valley Survey was reactivated when the National Science Foundation funded the Powers phase project in southeast Missouri in the late 1960s (Price and Griffin 1979). As a student, Price had discovered two burned village sites that were occupied for only a short period of time and had not been seriously damaged by collectors. Complete excavation of both the Turner and Snodgrass sites and surface collections and test excavations at other sites in the phase have produced vast amounts of data on both intrasite patterning and on Mississippian settlement systems. Bruce Smith, another University of Michigan graduate student, studied the exploitation of animal populations in the Powers phase through analysis of faunal remains (1975) and later (1978) described in detail the assemblage present at a Powers phase farmstead. The Powers phase headquarters in southeast Missouri later became a research station of the University of Missouri and is presently connected with the Center for Archaeological Research at Southwest Missouri State University.

Beginning in 1948 the University of Arkansas also grew as an archaeological research center (Davis 1969). Activity intensified in the late 1950s. In 1960 university personnel helped form the Arkansas Archaeological Society, which grew to over 300 members the first year. The society published a *Bulletin* and began to sponsor summer digs to train members in field techniques. Several of these digs were at sites in northeast Arkansas, such as Parkin. Charles McGimsey III, who in 1960 became museum director, has been the editor of the *Bulletin* from the beginning.

After various efforts had been made to initiate a state archaeological program funded by the Arkansas legislature, the Arkansas Archaeological Survey was both created and funded in 1967 and a state antiquities act was passed (McGimsey 1972). The Survey was founded as a separate state agency. The administrative staff was located at Fayetteville and originally consisted of a director, state archaeologist, editor, photographer, draftsman, registrar, graduate assistant, and a few clerks and typist–technicians. Funds were also provided to place archaeologists at eight state institutions of higher learning, along with their own typist–technicians, vehicles, and field and lab equipment. The cooperating institutions provided office and lab space. The primary job of the Survey archaeologist was to conduct research in a particular area and to undertake both problem-oriented and emergency-salvage excavations.

Knowledge about Arkansas prehistory has grown enormously since the founding of the Survey. Preliminary local sequences were defined by the Survey archaeologists during their first year (e.g., D. Morse 1969). In northeast Arkansas major accomplishments have included research on Dalton culture (Goodyear 1974), Mississippian societies such as those at the Nodena (D. Morse 1973), Parkin (P. Morse 1981), and Zebree sites (Morse and Morse 1980), surveys of regions such as the Cache River (Schiffer and House 1975), and historic archaeology at Davidsonville (Stewart-Abernathy 1980). A summary of what was accomplished in the first 13 years of the Survey, *Arkansas Archeology in Review*, has been published (Trubowitz and Jeter 1982).

In 1974 the Moss–Bennett bill or Archaeological Conservation Act was passed by Congress. This legislation required all federal agencies to mitigate the impact upon archaeological resources in any project in which federal funds would be used and expanded the former highway and reservoir salvage aspects of archaeology. Out of this has grown a multitude of private firms doing archaeology, as well as an increase in personnel stationed at universities to assess properly archaeological resources. Agencies such as the U.S. Army Corps of Engineers, Soil Conservation Service, and Forest Service began adding archaeologists to their staffs as well as contracting out archaeological work. The contract branch of the Arkansas Archaeological Survey grew and has become formalized, with up to 100 people in the field at one time and a core staff of professional archaeologists stationed in Fayetteville. In northeast Arkansas, surveys of areas from small sewage plants to the entire St. Francis basin have been done using federal funds. The impact of generous funding upon archaeological research is currently causing considerable change in the whole profession.

FACTORS AFFECTING SCIENTIFIC ARCHAEOLOGY IN THE CENTRAL VALLEY

There is no local or regional permanent multidisciplinary research group in the Central Valley. Such investigative or cooperative teams exist only during the duration of a project and usually are most cemented during the excavation phase. Most nonartifactual analyses have to be accomplished outside the region, often quite distant from the excavation focus. Most artifactual analyses are accomplished by the nucleus of the team, usually stationed in the valley or nearby. Oddly, the recent "contract period" of archaeological work has tended to fragment this situation further rather than to help provide the atmosphere for large-scale cooperation. Although both the Arkansas Archeological Survey and the Southeast Missouri Field Station of the Southwest Missouri State University Center for Archaeological Research are primarily dedicated to research and both are headed by a resident archaeologist, neither is large enough in personnel or varied enough in expertise to conduct multidisciplinary investigation, except in an expedient way. However, the presence of these two organizations has to be considered a significant plus for area research.

Cooperation and communication among colleagues interested in the same region is a difficult goal, complicated by employment at different institutions and state boundaries. In the Central Valley, attempts have been made since about 1967 to create such a group. First called the Mid South Archaeological Conference, this informal organization temporarily changed into the Central Lowland Archaeological Seminar and Society (CLASS) in 1975. One meeting was held at the Zebree site during excavations there in 1975. Open communication between long-range investigators working in the Central Valley has been on a relatively effective level.

Environmental and cultural resource protection laws passed in recent years have created a group of short-range investigators, often referred to as contract archaeologists. The total money spent on these projects is greater than the previous cumulative total in the Central Valley. Normally, when a project is contracted to resident university-based organizations, the work and results are on a high level (e.g., Schiffer and House 1975). But when the project is contracted to nonresident private firms, the archaeological results are sometimes minimal and occasionally not even useful for interpretation. Confidence in the data base—artifact description and site location and nature as reported by some private firms—is not very high. Such individuals are not familiar with local resources and do not have a long-range commitment to the regional archaeology.

Avocational archaeologists, those whose hobbies involve some aspect of archaeology, are prominent in the Central Valley. Most belong to a formal state society of avocational archaeologists and some have been quite helpful, such as James Hampson of Nodena, Arkansas (Figure 2.2a; S. Williams 1957). Many have reported sites to the appropriate state survey or helped out in many ways during emergency salvage, and some have even published important papers.

There are probably fewer actual scientific hobbyists in the Central Valley than elsewhere simply because the region is so rich archaeologically. This situation promotes treasure seeking rather than scientific investigation. Several thousand individuals surface collect from sites in the Central Valley. Many artifacts are sold, and the commercial value of Indian artifacts has soared in the last few years. Several hundred actually dig for Indian treasure in the form of pots and other items (Figure 2.4). Some individuals have amassed quite sizable collections, sometimes available to the public as private museums. In some cases sites are leased, and the diggers pay the lessor a daily fee to dig.

Digging for treasure accomplishes several things adverse to scientific archaeology. First, no record beyond a possible site location exists of the discovery; in some cases even county and state provenience is lost or deliberately disguised. Second, most landowners think all archaeology is treasure seeking since that is what they usually see. Sites have been closed to such investiga-

(a)

(b)

FIGURE 2.4. Typical treasure seeking at archaeological sites in the Central Mississippi Valley. (a) Treasure seeker using a probe. (b) Burial pit with probe holes evident. [Courtesy of the Arkansas Archeological Survey.]

tion—which is good in theory—but many treasure seekers ignore this as an inconvenience. Third, broken grave pottery distributed over the surface with kitchen ceramics significantly changes the artifact counts when one is doing a controlled surface collection. Fourth, strata destruction occurs, and living floors are significantly altered.

RECOVERY TECHNIQUES

Certainly the most basic portion of an archaeological investigation is good control of the sampling process. In particular, knowledge of the limitations conditioning interpretation is crucial. Control must be good enough for another investigator to be able to duplicate the process or be able to judge its effectiveness. Unfortunately, few reports state specifically how samples were collected.

Surface Collections

Approximately 90% of the land surface of the Central Valley is farmed. This affords a unique opportunity to examine the upper 20 cm or so of a vast region for archaeological debris. This also means that every discovered site has been destroyed at least in its upper layers, and often totally, in the sense of displaced or disturbed artifact context. But this very destruction allows the investigator to observe patterns of human debris easily.

The most common collecting methodology has been the *grab sample* technique. On smaller sites everything observed is collected. On more intensively occupied sites the techniques range from filling a certain-sized sack to consciously selecting certain kinds of artifacts, such as all rim sherds, all observed decorated sherds, all identified lithic tools, and samples of lithic raw material variation, including fire-cracked rock. Surface collecting is usually accomplished by having personnel walk in closely spaced parallel transects within identified areas. A less intensive technique that involves less time is to walk wider-spaced transects with lateral viewing up to approximately where the other person is looking, or to walk in a zig-zag pattern. This latter variation allows for fewer actual transects across the field and closer observation of concentrated areas of debris, such as plowed-up house floors.

Controlled collections on sites vary from investigator to investigator and through time. One technique is to specify a specific restricted area for total collection. For instance, every third cultivation row in a field may be selected. Sometimes in sparse sites every artifact is plotted. After a controlled sample has been collected, selected artifacts are collected from other parts of the site. These are usually recognized lithic tools, rim sherds, and decorated sherds.

The ideal method of collecting a surface sample is by dividing the site into equal-size squares, then selecting squares or circles by the use of a table of random numbers for intensive sampling. There are many drawbacks to the technique. Primarily, it is time-consuming since in the Central Valley numerous sites contain enormous quantities of artifacts.

Farming practices, lay persons, and commercial treasure seeking have biased surface collections to an unknown extent. Environmental factors include rain and wind erosion. Experience has demonstrated that the best time to collect or to discover sites is in early spring when visibility is best; the worst time is midsummer, when crops are flourishing.

Definition of Site

The definition of *site* has become a crucial decision. Earlier, sites were large contiguous or nearly contiguous scatters of artifacts "worth collecting." The problems of vehicular support, number of bags, time to process, and space to store collections helped dictate this kind of definition. The fewer sites, the fewer problems there were. In particular, the problems of archaeology during the initial periods of survey did not depend upon a specific definition of site since attention was upon artifact association and seriation for temporal control. This was a consciously and specifically stated part of the methodology. Later, the definition of site became a loose, unconsciously unstated variable difficult to objectify. More recently, the demands of archaeology have focused attention on variations in settlement types. Historic archaeology has also developed considerably. Hence, any evidence of human interaction with the environment is significant. Now, a "site" is any geographical location where there is either documentary or physical evidence of such interaction. An early reference to a mound now washed into the Mississippi River is ample evidence to complete a site form. The finding of a single artifact such as a stone ax is also ample evidence. However, most investigators prefer to restrict the single-artifact site definition in view of the vast amount of paperwork generated and the disturbing possibility that a small flat chip of stone can move a considerable distance, particularly if aided by a muddy tractor tire.

Sites are discovered by three major techniques: intensive areal survey, an intuitive feeling that a site should be located there, and leads gotten from documents or from people. Informants include farmers who accidentally discover a site or avocational archaeologists who look for sites as a hobby, or sometimes as a business. The latter are least apt to report a newly discovered site. Until recently, most surveys were conducted by intuition or through informants. As a result, most recorded sites before the mid-1970s were relatively large, almost exclusively prehistoric, and produced enough artifacts to make fairly definite statements concerning temporal placement.

Intensive areal surveys are usually of locations such as a proposed sewer plant or pipeline and are archaeological clearances done under contract. These developed during the 1970s but become tightly controlled surveys only in the late 1970s and early 1980s. Another type of intensive survey consists of observation within a certain distance of a known site to discover other sites and environmental resources. A total of 128 prehistoric sites were discovered in a very intensive 1-km radius survey around a Late Mississippian site (P. Morse 1981).

A third kind of intensive survey is the transect. A sampling corridor .40 km wide extending from the Mississippi River to the Ozarks was established in 1976 to discover the full range of sites present, to see whether there were patterns that could be related to environmental variation, and to begin to form a basis for an estimation of the number of sites potentially discoverable in the Central Valley (Morse and Morse 1980:17–26). Student volunteers were used during the March spring vacations—the optimum time to look for sites in this region. The first 3-day period of fieldwork covered 24 km (15 miles) and generated almost 2 years of lab work and paperwork. One of the problems involved in doing Central Valley archaeology is that fieldwork is possible year round except for perhaps 2 weeks or so in January. Unlike the situation in northern climates, there is no weather-enforced period of lab work and report writing.

As of January 1971 approximately 2700 sites were recorded in the Central Valley. In the decade that followed this number increased to around 8000. In 1971 this total was over 80% of the sites recorded in the entire Central and Lower valleys; if anything, the percentage has increased. Probably only around 2% of these sites have been investigated beyond a simple surface collection. The total recorded to date probably represents less than a 1% sample of those actually present. Based on the minimal definition of *site* there are approximately 1 million surface sites in the Central Valley.

Subsurface Data

Various techniques are used in subsurface exploration of a site. A soil probe produces a hollow core sample that barely reaches below the cultivation zone. This is used throughout the Central Valley to check for undisturbed midden. In some cases a solid probe or rod is used to locate a refuse deposit or burial under varying circumstances. Shovel tests are accomplished in a systematic fashion during an areal survey to check for buried shallow deposits, to locate sites in a freshly cultivated field where artifacts and midden can be masked by dust, and to determine whether a site has undisturbed deposits. Deeply buried sites (e.g., Koster in Illinois) have not been discovered in the Central Valley, but they almost certainly exist.

Deliberate subsurface exploration in the Central Valley has been limited traditionally to test pits. One very major exception is the excavation of the Snodgrass site in southeast Missouri (Price and Griffin 1979). This was a single component, shallow Mississippian village consisting of over 90 structures. No other excavation in the Central Valley even approaches the magnitude and effectiveness of this one. The data potential in even larger sites with midden deposits ranging up to 3 m deep is staggering. Many of the sites dating to the late prehistoric and the protohistoric periods are extremely sensitive to stratigraphic control, a control that promises generational temporal control. However, the cost of excavation and retention of a research group means that it is not possible for local support to finance such projects. The Snodgrass site was excavated by the University of Michigan over a 7-year period with significant National Science Foundation sponsorship.

Even test pitting is not an extensively used tool of recovery in the valley. Probably fewer than 100 sites have been tested by the excavation of one to half a dozen test squares. Most of these are located in southeast Missouri. Test pitting is usually initiated to learn what a site can provide. However, many investigators in the Central Valley have viewed the test pit as sufficient data from a site, but in all fairness this situation often is dictated by the shoestring budgets typical of this region or by the destruction of the site itself.

Single test pits, usually 2 m or so in extent, are the most common examples of a test pitting program (Figure 2.5). A linear grouping of test squares constitutes a more intensive test. A more major excavation is rare (Chapman and

FIGURE 2.5.   Test pit at an Archaic site in Craighead County, Arkansas. [Courtesy of the Arkansas Archeological Survey.]

Evans 1977; Ford 1963; Goodyear 1974; Price and Griffin 1979; Smith 1978). Fewer than 20 major tests and excavations have ever been conducted in the valley, so there has actually been relatively little research-oriented major excavation, in comparison with the potential. As more of the archaeological richness of the Central Valley is destroyed, research attention might increasingly focus upon state-acquired large sites as semipermanent field schools.

Salvage probably accounts for approximately 100 sites investigated to a greater extent than surface pickup. Salvage normally involves sites in immediate danger of agricultural destruction. Most often, the site is already being leveled when the archaeologist is notified, and 1 day (Figure 2.6a) to perhaps a few weeks of unplanned recovery is the result. Sometimes, the landowner will set aside the site area for longer periods of time, but this situation is very rare and basically impractical for the archaeologist and the landowner. Another type of salvage, planned rather than unplanned, is the "mitigation" of a site known to be slated for destruction at a future date by a governmental agency.

Methodology

Recovery technology has been questioned recently within the Central Valley. The more constant employment of lithic, ceramic, and environmental specialists from the start of an investigation involving a major excavation has demonstrated just how weak our data base might be. The use of one-quarter in. (.62 cm) and one-half in. (1.25 cm) mesh screens in particular has been reexamined from the standpoint of biased data being recovered.

At the Zebree site, screen-mesh-size experiments were conducted as part of the archaeological project to discover quickly what sizes to use in the excavations and to gain control over the material recovered. The one-eighth in. (.31 cm) mesh size was discovered to be best for representative recovery, particularly of faunal remains. The one-quarter in. (.62 cm) size was most efficient in terms of excavation and processing time. Sampling control was made possible by the regular collection of flotation samples and examination of the heavy element caught by one-sixteenth in. (.16 cm) screen. Some screening using one-sixteenth in. mesh control is now dictated by the discovery that most chert debitage, including the chips most characteristic of arrowhead production, can be recovered almost only with that size screen. Another discovery—that different pottery types break down into varying minimum sizes of sherds—can be controlled only by the investigator describing the recovery techniques used.

The Zebree excavation is also interesting from the standpoint of comparing varying excavation techniques used in the Central Valley (Figure 2.6b). The site was test pitted in 1968, extensively tested mainly with block excavations in 1969, substantially excavated in 1975 with a variety of current and innovative techniques including the employment of random squares and backhoe trenches, and finally in 1976 salvaged with the help of a bulldozer and other equipment as the site was being ditched away. The whole complex of ap-

(a)

(b)

FIGURE 2.6. Site destruction in Arkansas. (a) Archaeological salvage at an Arkansas Woodland site being land leveled with dirt buggies. (b) Drainage ditch excavation that destroyed the Zebree site, Mississippi County, Arkansas. [Courtesy of the Arkansas Archeological Survey and Cohen Construction Company.]

proaches helped our interpretation immensely, but any one of them used exclusively would have provided only a small part of the total site picture.

DATA INTERPRETATION AND INCORPORATION

Scientific control is crucial to sound archaeological interpretation. In archaeology the sampling is so minimal and the investigators characterized by such diverse backgrounds in recovery expertise that there is a real credibility problem. This problem has intensified during the latest period of archaeological investigation.

Data Description

Once artifacts are hidden within lists of categories, it is almost impossible to tell what is really represented—unless there is an adequate description. There has been a conscious effort toward more uniform terminology in the Central Valley, which is in step with the process of sophistication in world archaeology. The attempt to restrict terminology to a descriptive name indicating a set of defined physical attributes has not been wholly successful. Functional names persist, but most are justified by specific attribute descriptions.

In step with sophistication in terminology has been experimentation and microscopic examination as tests of interpreted function. The Dalton point is now viewed as a knife, and the beveled edges no longer are a mystery. In fact, understanding the Dalton point through experimentation and prediction became an integral part of the understanding of Dalton culture as research emphases shifted around the late 1960s from artifact types to patterns of human behavior. By the 1970s attention also expanded from examination of grave furniture to kitchen ceramics. This expansion was supplemented by experimentation in ceramic container manufacture and use. Just as an understanding of lithic categories is not complete until the technology is mastered, control of ceramic technology is absolutely necessary for interpreting the significance of ceramic types. This is most important when attempting interpretations of changes in paste over time. Closer observation of sherd cross sections with the use of a microscope, pioneered in the Midwest by James Porter (1964), has revealed a ceramic sophistication not earlier attributed to the aborigines of the Central Valley. Observation of vessels themselves has resulted in evidence of use, particularly in reference to ladle damage on lips. Investigation of vessel capacity can even furnish data for social organization and economic studies.

The lowlands of the Central Valley provide a practically unique opportunity to study all lithic debris. With the exception of ice-rafted pebbles, all lithics must be explained as a result of human endeavor. No lithics can be simply discarded as "natural." If they are in the collection, they are classified as artifacts. Even "manuports" had to be transported here and must be accounted for.

Virtually everything collected at a site is regarded as an artifact, including bone and shell debris, debitage, and the more traditional artifacts. This method is simply the easiest approach. At Zebree the processing lab was adjacent to the site for quick cataloging and immediate feedback to the field. The lab was divided into specific artifact category labs such as ceramic, faunal, and botanical. Everything was cataloged for final computer printout, and artifacts were identified with numbers so that identifications could be checked later. The only real problem, still not solved, was the time involved in examination of the heavy fraction of flotation samples. The basic overriding concern should always be that the data base be organized, clearly identified, and properly curated for future reference.

Temporal Control

The two major techniques of dating events in the Central Valley are seriation and stratigraphy. In the latter, superimposition of strata and the recognition of intrusion are important concepts. At the Dalton period Brand site, windblown silt was superimposed over water-laid clay. At many Mississippian period sites, soils were brought into the site and distributed over previous land surfaces. Some of these sites will prove to have extremely sensitive stratigraphy. The recognition of intrusions is particularly important in the Central Valley due to the clearing of forests from sites with tree-root intrusions and the prevalence of treasure seeking with a probe and shovel.

Seriation as a concept was developed to a great extent by James Ford in the Lower Mississippi Valley (1952). Sequences of styles or motifs are particularly important, especially if they may be viewed as horizon types. Projectile point and ceramic types are most used in seriation. The type–variety classification is used traditionally for ceramics.

Not nearly enough radiocarbon dating has been done in the Central Valley. This is the cheapest, most proven, and most objective dating technique of wide application available. Only 125 radiocarbon dates are published for the Central Valley; 59% of these are from sites in southeast Missouri and 38% from northeast Arkansas. Approximately one-third of the dates are not considered accurate in terms of anticipated results.

Archeomagnetic dating has shown promise but as yet is not a significant independent dating technique. Dendrochronology also shows promise but to date has been applicable only for historic sites. Geochronological association has not yet been used to its full potential.

Environmental Control

The Central Valley is a region of drastic recent environmental change. Ongoing land leveling and drainage for intensive commercial agriculture is changing the area even more drastically. In much of the lowland area there are virtually no forests. Even cultivation zones are becoming sandier as wind blows away silt during the early spring disking. The largest and most modern agricultural equipment is being used. Irrigation has become increasingly important as cotton has declined and rice has increased in production.

Environmental reconstruction is dependent upon the early nineteenth-century General Land Office records (maps and field notes), soil maps, U.S. Geological Survey (USGS) topographic quadrangle sheets, and older journals of travel in the preceding century. Some pollen control has been exercised on earlier time periods but is far from complete.

Habitat investigation is still in a preliminary stage in the Central Valley. This is largely dependent upon soil maps and most useful for later time periods when agriculture is important. Bruce Smith's approach (1975), for instance, indicates that beneficial cooperative investigations are possible in the near future.

Ethnographic Parallelism

Simply by using certain terms—such as *hoe, ax, house, band*—we are extrapolating from our knowledge of anthropology, which tends to be done in a rather informal manner in the Central Valley. The rigor of controlled terminology is not attained here, but this is pretty much characteristic of almost everywhere archaeology is done.

ARCHAEOLOGICAL SEQUENCE

In the Central Mississippi Valley the archaeological sequence is made up of periods and cultural phases. This book is organized along these lines, and each chapter describes a period of time from oldest to the latest. Here we wish to present a very brief description of the sequence as an introduction to the more detailed chapters that follow (Figures 2.7, 2.8).

Paleo-Indian Period

The oldest period is that of fluted points. Approximate dating based on the dates of locations outside the valley are 9500 to 8500 B.C.—about the end of the Pleistocene and the beginning of the Holocene. The Central Valley is rich in fluted point discoveries, but as yet no intact deposits are known. Primary association is along both sides of a major meandering stream in the Western Lowlands and west of the braided Mississippi stream system in the Eastern Lowlands (see Figure 3.1). These were hunters, fishers, and gatherers of wild foods. There is no evidence of megafauna exploitation.

Dalton Period

In striking contrast with other preceramic periods, Dalton remains have been extensively investigated. Radiocarbon dates outside the Central Valley

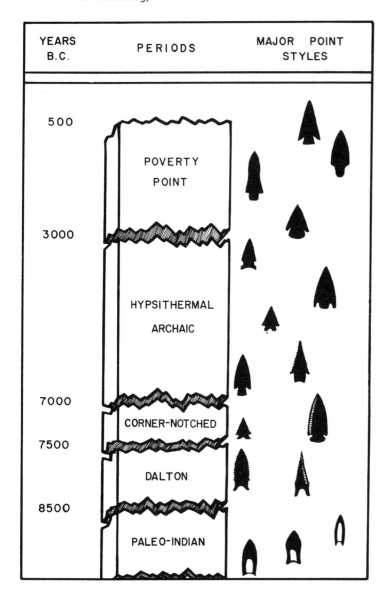

YEARS B.C.	PERIODS	MAJOR POINT STYLES
500	POVERTY POINT	
3000	HYPSITHERMAL ARCHAIC	
7000	CORNER-NOTCHED	
7500	DALTON	
8500	PALEO-INDIAN	

FIGURE 2.7. The preceramic archaeological sequence in the Central Mississippi Valley.

indicate that the period extends from just after 8500 to almost 7500 B.C. Continuity from the Paleo-Indian period is evident in tool types, whereas affinity with later Archaic expressions is seen in other tools and inferred behavior. Territories were oriented within watersheds (see Figure 4.1). Recognized sites have been interpreted as villages, hunting camps, and cemeteries. Behavior was sophisticated, and most of the lowlands were occupied to some extent. Dalton artifacts are plentiful in the Central Valley compared with most other regions in the eastern United States.

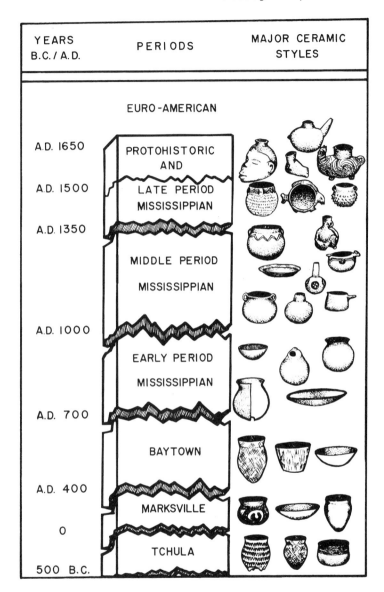

FIGURE 2.8. The ceramic archaeological sequence in the Central Mississippi Valley.

Early Corner-Notched Horizon

This period dates between about 7500 and 7000 B.C. It is characterized by corner-notched points and side-notched points, including San Patrice.

Hypsithermal Archaic Period

Between about 7000 and 3000 B.C. the Central Mississippi Valley experienced a climatic trend toward dryness and grasslands. People responded to this change and moved their primary habitation sites to upland regions such as the Ozark Escarpment (see Figure 5.1). It was not a hiatus but a settlement shift. Lowland artifacts datable to this period (and the 500 years or so immediately preceding it) are rare. The Hypsithermal is thought to have become less severe about 4500 B.C., and a major point style believed to date after 4000 B.C. is much more prominent in lowland assemblages than are earlier styles. Point horizon styles allow this long period to be subdivided into 500- and 1000-year units.

Poverty Point Period

Lowland activity significantly increased, and recognizable artifacts that can be dated to the period 3000–500 B.C. are very common. Most probably tribal social organization (in contrast to the earlier band social organization) had emerged by 3000 B.C. If so, this was a reflection of increased population and smaller territories. It allowed much greater variation in sociopolitical complexity. A variety of village and extraction camp sites have been recognized. Most notable of the recovered artifacts are those produced by the "lapidary industry." These include well-made beads and atlatl weights ("bannerstones") made of exotic stone. All of the valley except for the easternmost portion was intensively occupied. Major areas of villages are spaced far enough apart to indicate that the population still was relatively low (see Figure 6.1). Horticulture developed during the Poverty Point period in the eastern United States.

Tchula Period

About 500 B.C. ceramics appeared suddenly in the Central Valley (Figure 2.8). Horticulture and outside exotic trade may have increased in intensity, but otherwise there was very strong local continuity. This continuity has made it virtually impossible to identify sites based only on small surface samples. All of the Central Valley was available for occupation for the first time. Population still seems to have been relatively low. Differences in ceramic paste between the northeast and the central portions of the Central Valley are evident (see Figure 7.1).

Marksville Period

From 0–A.D. 400 full participation in the eastern United States Hopewellian tradition is evident. The most exotic sites, mostly early Marksville, are located in the meander belt. The population was still dispersed in autonomous communities, but a significant increase in numbers is evident in late Marksville times (see Figure 8.1).

Baytown Period

During the period A.D. 400–700 the ceramic difference climaxed between meander-belt- and braided-stream-surface populations. The sand-tempered Barnes tradition and grog-tempered Baytown tradition differences are also evident in settlement systems and probably politics and economy. In the southern portion of the Central Valley, Baytown changed into Coles Creek rather than into Mississippian. Baytown period sites are common (see Figure 9.1).

Early Period Mississippian

By around A.D. 700 politically complex chiefdoms were developing in various portions of the eastern United States. The most spectacular development was occurring within the American Bottom east of St. Louis, where the important Cahokia site is located. Earliest expressions in the Central Valley are evident in the Cairo Lowlands. By A.D. 800–900 a significant portion of the northern half of the Central Valley was controlled by Mississippian chiefdoms (see Figure 10.1). This was a period of tremendous ideological, social, political, economic, and technological change. Intensive agriculture formed the economic base to support relatively large populations in dispersed villages and farmsteads.

Middle Period Mississippian

By A.D. 1000 the whole Central Valley evidently was controlled by numerous Mississippian chiefdoms (see Figure 11.1). By A.D. 1200 a characteristic chiefdom was made up of a fortified ceremonial center and fortified villages and household "farmsteads" scattered within its region to exploit effectively the prime arable land and still protect its population. Mississippian sites exist virtually everywhere, and conflict appears to have been an increasing problem.

Late Period Mississippian and the Protohistoric Period

At approximately A.D. 1350 a significant settlement shift took place (see Figure 12.1). Formerly independent chiefdoms consolidated. The population abandoned much of the braided surface and primarily shifted onto the meander belt. Mostly only fortified villages existed in much of the Central Valley. These villages were located within large concentrations of prime agricultural land. By the Protohistoric period (A.D. 1500) most of the Central Valley was controlled by six major chiefdoms. One in particular seems to have been expanding at the expense of the others. Both historical records of the De Soto expedition and archaeological data agree here. A single "Quapaw" tribe emerged around A.D. 1680, when French explorations penetrated the region, as the culmination of a political consolidation evolution that by then had been adversely affected by contact with European powers.

Euro-American Period

The eighteenth and early nineteenth centuries date the role of the Central Valley in Indian displacement west of the Mississippi River and the increasing intensity of the settlement of Euro-American pioneers on the American frontier. Shortly after the beginning of the nineteenth century, towns and farmsteads—recognized by considerable debris incorporating English tableware and other artifacts—abound.

REFERENCES

Baird, W. David (editor)
  1977 *Doctor Frank L. James in Arkansas, 1877–1878*. Memphis: Memphis State University Press.
Berry, J. Brewton
  1975 Looking backward. *Missouri Archaeological Society Newsletter* **296**:1–8.
Brose, David
  1980 How Capt. Riggs hunts for mound builders relics: An historical investigation of some influences on C. B. Moore. *Southeastern Archaeological Conference Bulletin* **22**:145–152.
Brown, Calvin S.
  1926 *Archaeology of Mississippi*. University, Miss.: Mississippi Geological Survey.
Chapman, Carl
  1975 *The archaeology of Missouri* (Vol. 1). Columbia, Mo.: University of Missouri Press.
  1980 *The archaeology of Missouri* (Vol. 2). Columbia, Mo.: University of Missouri Press.
Chapman, Carl, and Leo O. Anderson
  1955 The Campbell site. *Missouri Archaeologist* **17**:1–140.
Chapman, Carl, and David R. Evans
  1977 Investigations at the Lilbourn site, 1970–1971. *Missouri Archaeologist* **38**:70–104.
Cottier, John, and Michael Southard
  1977 An introduction to the archaeology of Towosahgy State Archaeological Site. *Missouri Archaeologist* **38**:230–271.
Davis, Hester
  1969 A brief history of archeological work in Arkansas up to 1967. *Arkansas Archeologist* **10**:2–8.
Dellinger, S. C., and S. D. Dickinson
  1940 Possible antecedents of the Middle Mississippian ceramic complex in northeastern Arkansas. *American Antiquity* **6**:132–147.
Ford, James A.
  1952 Measurements of some prehistoric design developments in the Southeastern states. *American Museum of Natural History Anthropological Papers* **44** (Part 3): 313–384.
  1963 Hopewell culture burial mounds near Helena, Arkansas. *American Museum of Natural History Anthropological Papers* **50**.

Fowke, Gerard
  1910   Antiquities of central and southeastern Missouri. *Bureau of American Ethnology Bulletin* **37**.
Funkhouser, W. D., and W. S. Webb
  1932   Archaeological survey of Kentucky. *University of Kentucky Reports in Archaeology and Anthropology* **2**.
Goodyear, Albert
  1974   The Brand site: A techno-functional study of a Dalton site in northeast Arkansas. *Arkansas Archeological Survey Research Series* **7**.
Griffin, James B.
  1981   The acquisition of a little-known pottery haul from the Lower Mississippi Valley. *Geoscience and Man* **22**:51–55.
Griffin, James B., and Albert C. Spaulding
  1952   The Central Mississippi Valley archaeological survey, Season 1950: A preliminary report. In *Prehistoric pottery of eastern United States,* edited by J. B. Griffin. Ann Arbor, Mich.: University of Michigan Museum of Anthropology.
Hoffman, Michael
  1981   The father of us all: S. C. Dellinger and the beginning of Arkansas archaeology and anthropology. Paper presented at 38th Southeastern Archaeological Conference, Asheville.
Holmes, William H.
  1903   Aboriginal pottery of the eastern United States. *Bureau of American Ethnology 20th Annual Report.*
Hopgood, James F.
  1969   *Continuity and change in the Baytown pottery tradition of the Cairo Lowland, Southeast Missouri.* Unpublished M.A. thesis, Department of Anthropology, University of Missouri.
Houck, Louis
  1908   *A history of Missouri.* Chicago: R. R. Donnelley.
Klippel, Walter
  1969   The Hearnes site. *Missouri Archaeologist* **31**.
Lewis, R. Barry
  1974   Mississippian exploitative strategies: A southeast Missouri example. *Missouri Archaeological Society Research Series* **11**.
  1982   Two Mississippian hamlets: Cairo Lowland, Missouri. *Illinois Archaeological Survey Special Publication* **2**.
McGimsey, Charles R., III
  1972   *Public archeology.* New York: Academic Press.
Marshall, Richard A.
  1965   An archaeological investigation of Interstate Route 55 through New Madrid and Pemiscot counties, Missouri, 1964. *University of Missouri Highway Archaeology Report.*
Moore, Clarence B.
  1910   Antiquities of the St. Francis, White and Black rivers, Arkansas. *Journal of the Academy of Natural Sciences of Philadelphia* **14**:255–364.
  1911   Some aboriginal sites on Mississippi River. *Journal of the Academy of Natural Sciences of Philadelphia* **14**:367–478.
Moorehead, Warren K.
  1904   Commercial vs scientific collecting: A plea for "art for art's sake." *Ohio Archaeological and Historical Publications* **13**:112–117.

Morse, Dan F.
   1969   Introducing northeastern Arkansas prehistory. *Arkansas Archeologist* **10**:12–28.
Morse, Dan F. (editor)
   1973   Nodena. *Arkansas Archeological Survey Research Series* **4**.
Morse, Dan F., and Phyllis A. Morse (editors)
   1980   *Zebree archeological project.* Report submitted to U.S. Army Corps of Engineers by Arkansas Archeological Survey.
Morse, Phyllis A.
   1981   Parkin: the 1978–1979 archeological investigation of a Cross County, Arkansas, site. *Arkansas Archeological Survey Research Series* **13**.
Moselage, John
   1962   The Lawhorn site. *Missouri Archaeologist* **24**:1–104.
Nash, Charles H.
   1972   Chucalissa: excavations and burials through 1963. *Memphis State University Anthropological Research Center Occasional Papers* **6**.
Nuttall, Thomas
   1821   *A journal of travels into the Arkansa Territory.* Philadelphia: Palmer (Readex Microprint).
Perino, Gregory
   1966   The Banks village site. *Missouri Archaeological Society Memoir* **4**.
   1967   The Cherry Valley mounds and Banks Mound 3. *Central States Archaeological Society Memoir* **1**.
Phillips, Philip, James Ford, and James B. Griffin
   1951   Archaeological survey in the Lower Mississippi Alluvial Valley, 1940–1947. *Papers of the Peabody Museum, Harvard University* **25**.
Porter, James W.
   1964   Thin section descriptions of some shell tempered prehistoric ceramics from the American Bottoms. *Southern Illinois University Museum Lithic Laboratory Research Report* **7**.
Potter, William, and Edward Evers
   1880   Archaeological remains in southeastern Missouri. *St. Louis Academy of Science Contributions to the Archaeology of Missouri.*
Price, James, and James B. Griffin
   1979   The Snodgrass site of the Powers phase of southeast Missouri. *University of Michigan Museum of Anthropology Anthropological Papers* **66**.
Putnam, Frederick Ward
   1881   Report of the curator. *Fourteenth Annual Report of the Peabody Museum of American Archaeology and Ethnology.*
Schiffer, Michael B., and John H. House
   1975   The Cache River archeological project: An experiment in contract archeology. *Arkansas Archeological Survey Research Series* **8**.
Smith, Bruce D.
   1975   Middle Mississippi exploitation of animal populations. *University of Michigan Museum of Anthropology Anthropological Papers* **57**.
   1978   *Prehistoric patterns of human behavior.* New York: Academic Press.
   1981   The division of mound exploration of the Bureau of (American) Ethnology and the birth of American Archaeology. *Southeastern Archaeological Conference Bulletin* **24**:51–54.
Stewart-Abernathy, Leslie C.
   1980   The seat of justice: 1815–30. *Arkansas Archeological Survey Research Report* **21**.
Thomas, Cyrus
   1894   Report on the mound explorations of the Bureau of Ethnology. *Bureau of American Ethnology 12th Annual Report.*
Trubowitz, Neal, and Marvin Jeter
   1982   Arkansas archeology in review. *Arkansas Archeological Survey Research Series* **15**.

Williams, J. Raymond
  1974   The Baytown phases in the Cairo Lowland of southeast Missouri. *Missouri Archaeologist* **36.**
Williams, Stephen
  1954   *An archeological study of the Mississippian culture in southeast Missouri.* Ph.D. dissertation, Yale University. Ann Arbor, Mich: University Microfilms.
  1957   James Kelly Hampson. *American Antiquity* **22:**398–400.

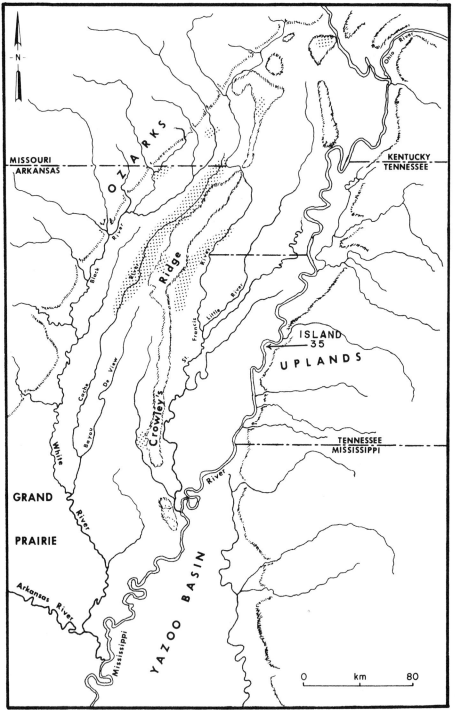

FIGURE 3.1. Major regions of fluted point discoveries in the Central Valley. Much of the surface area east of Crowley's Ridge was not available for permanent occupation.

3

Paleo-Indian Beginnings (9500–8500 B.C.)

In 1965 Stephen Williams and James Stoltman hypothesized that in the Southeast "during the Paleo-Indian Era fluted-point makers roved the countryside in pursuit of big game, primarily the mastodon [p. 677]." They thought there was a correlation between the distribution of fluted points and known mastodon discoveries. However, although there was a high incidence of mastodon in the Lower Mississippi Valley, there were few recorded fluted points. But they attributed the lack of fluted points to "rapid recent alluviation that has covered most of the surfaces available for occupation by Paleo-Indians [1965: 677]."

Later, Roger Saucier (1968) demonstrated that a considerable portion of the modern land surface area was exposed during the Paleo-Indian period. This reinterpretation of the geological time depth was reinforced by the discovery of fluted points, which are dated elsewhere to the end of the Pleistocene, in the Central Valley (Figure 3.1). This chapter will begin with a survey of Pleistocene fauna in deference to the Williams–Stoltman hypothesis, then describe fluted points, a considerable number of which have been recorded, and other possible Paleo-Indian points found here.

PLEISTOCENE FAUNA IN THE CENTRAL VALLEY

Pleistocene fauna have been discovered for 170 years in the Central Valley (Figure 3.2). Bones were collected in New Madrid Country, Missouri, about 1812 and 1820 (Mehl 1962:93). Jefferies Wyman described Pleistocene finds from the Memphis area in 1850 and 1851. Prior to 1889 R. E. Call was informed of mastodon bone found near Helena, Arkansas.

FIGURE 3.2. Frank Reynolds with mastodon bones he unearthed in 1936 near Marmaduke, Arkansas. [Courtesy of Frank Reynolds, Paragould, Arkansas.]

The major regional clusters of discoveries are apparent from Figure 3.3. On a sandbar near *Friars Point*, Mississippi, a number of fossils have been recovered. Farther south in Bolivar County, Mississippi, sandbars have produced Pleistocene fauna as well. Those near Friars Point form part of a secondary deposit and probably originated from Crowley's Ridge to the northwest, near *Helena*, where fossils have been reported occurring in a blue-black carbonaceous clay beneath a loess mantle. At and in the vicinity of *Forrest City* numerous fossils were recovered from several locations, mostly exposed by Crow Creek. Within and in the vicinity of *Memphis* there is another concentration of fossils. An impressive cluster occurs along and near a drainage ditch system known as *Bay* of the St. Francis River east of Crowley's Ridge in Arkansas. Only a few discoveries have been made in the Western Lowlands of Arkansas. In West Tennessee the discoveries are also scattered. There is an apparent cluster at or near the mouth of the *Hatchie River*, including Richardson's Landing. A whale identified as Eocene (*Basilosaurus*) was found in the center of this cluster, and its discovery emphasizes that not all extinct mammals are restricted to the Pleistocene in this region. Another Eocene whale bone was found near Forrest City. Little is known about west Kentucky and

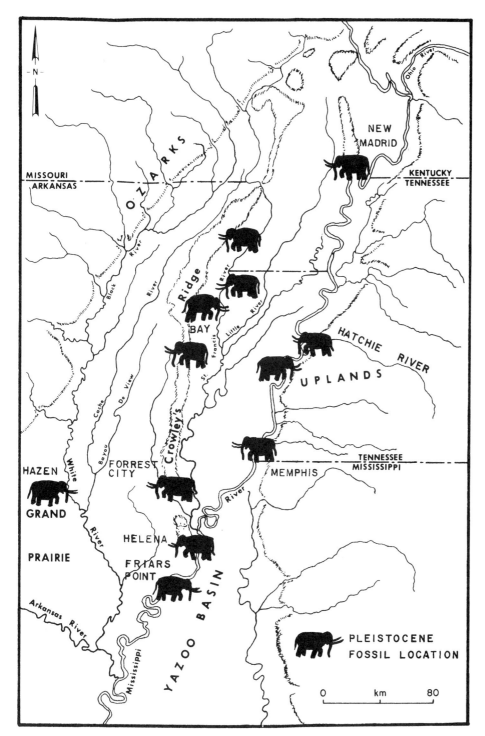

FIGURE 3.3.   Some major Pleistocene megafauna discovery sites in the Central Mississippi Valley.

southeast Missouri except for two discoveries made near the beginning of the nineteenth century near *New Madrid*, Missouri.

The Pleistocene is mainly symbolized by repeated glaciation and the appearance of essentially modern mammals, particularly the true elephant, horse, and bison. Despite local folklore to the contrary, this region was never covered by a glacier. However, typical Pleistocene animals were characteristic, and the various species found here, described in the following subsections, will be added to significantly in the future as more bones are found. This catalog of species found in the Central Valley is based on files kept by the Arkansas Archeological Survey in Jonesboro and the Memphis Pink Palace Museum in Memphis.

Mammut americanum (Mastodon)

Mastodons comprise the most characteristic Pleistocene animals in the Southeast. Since they are so large, bones and teeth (Figure 3.4) as well as tusks are usually easily recognized and reported when found. A total of 28 mastodon locations are known for the Central Mississippi Valley; 19 of these are located in Arkansas.

The Island 35 mastodon (actually, two animals) is probably the most famous, since the bone was allegedly associated with two artifacts (Williams 1957). It was found in a sandbar deposit, most probably derived from the Hatchie River locality. Mastodon bone was found in 1982 on a sand and gravel bar upriver from Island 35. It had been recently redeposited on the bar. The discovery site was adjacent to the Chickasaw Bluffs which is composed of loess on top of an organic clay strata at this point. The clay contained wood and spruce cones and probably originally contained the mastodon bone.

Mastodon has been found below the loess (Helena and western Tennessee), in the lower portion of the loess (northwest Tennessee), and associated with Braided Stream Terrace 2 (Bay). These discoveries indicate that the known mastodon finds may have been contemporaneous with much of the later portion of the Wisconsin stage, becoming extinct at the end of the Pleistocene, and it is important to realize that the earliest human occupation was only at the very end of this period.

A mastodon from the campus of Southwestern College in Memphis was dated to 21,000 B.C. (Corgan 1975:84), and one at Nonconnah Creek, Tennessee, near Memphis was radiocarbon dated to about 15,000 B.C. (Delcourt *et al.* 1980). This period of time was during the first of the Woodfordian substage, when the last loess episode was in existence. This substage was a period of full glacial conditions with forests of spruce to the east of the Mississippi Valley in western Tennessee, and of jack pine and spruce extending west of the valley across Missouri. The loess hills east of the Mississippi Valley provided a less extreme environment and fertile soil that allowed mixed deciduous forest to persist in local pockets through the full glacial period. Climatic

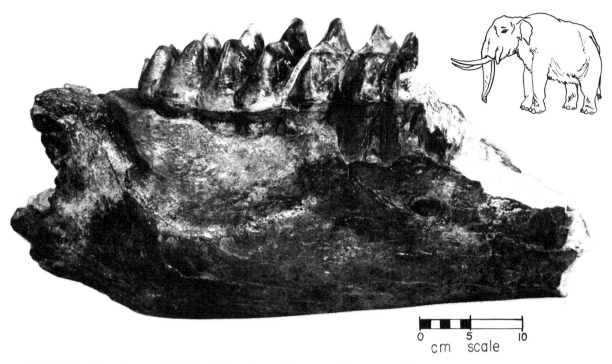

FIGURE 3.4. Mastodon mandible from Obion County, Tennessee. [Photograph of bone courtesy of the Memphis Pink Palace Museum.]

warming after 15,000 B.C. resulted in rapid expansion of hardwood forests at the expense of boreal coniferous forest (Delcourt *et al.* 1980).

The mastodon was a woodland animal, feeding on coarse vegetable food. "Analysis of undigested plant remains found in the ribcages of some specimens has revealed twigs and cones of conifers, leaves, coarse grasses, swamp plants, and mosses [Kurtén and Anderson 1980:344–345]." As the deciduous forests increased to the detriment of the pine and spruce forests in the lowlands after around 15,000 B.C., the mastodon must have experienced some difficulty finding winter food. In particular, increasingly swampy conditions would have proved troublesome for such a large animal. It is quite possible that the mastodon left the area or became extinct before the appearance of human beings, after about 9500 B.C.

The only known evidence of the direct association of man and mastodon has been found recently at Kimmswick, Missouri, north of the Central Valley (Graham *et al.* 1981). Two fluted points, several hundred chert flakes, and a few unifacial tools were found in pond deposits with mastodon and other bone. Kimmswick is interpreted by Russell Graham as a kill and processing site for both mastodon and other animals. Several species adapted to deciduous woodland and grass areas were found, indicating that the mastodon could exist in a habitat containing deciduous trees.

Mammuthus (Mammoths)

Remains identified as *Mammuthus primigenius* (probably actually *M. jeffersonii*; see Kurtén and Anderson 1980:348–354) were collected from the Friars Point locality and sandbars to the south. Another was reported from deep under the Ohio River bed near Cairo, Illinois (Hay 1923:140–141). A mammoth (*M. jeffersonii*) tooth was found 5 km downstream from New Madrid, Missouri, and is identified as *Parelephas columbi* in Mehl (1962:50). A mammoth found near Hazen in Prairie County, Arkansas, has not been identified more specifically; it was buried at a depth of 6.8 m. The mammoths found in the Central Valley may predate the mastodons, but the stratigraphic relationship is obscure. The mammoth was a prairie animal, and the last major prairie conditions during the Pleistocene in the Central Valley were terminated at the initiation of the Woodfordian substage about 21,000 B.C. (Delcourt *et al.* 1980:125).

Bison (Buffalo)

Several remnants of *Bison* sp. (Figure 3.5a) are known from the Memphis area and Friars Point. A probable *Bison bison antiquus* skull was found just south of Memphis (personal communication, Donald C. Allen, Memphis). Reports from other areas are complicated by the known presence of *Bison bison* (*bison* or *athabascae*) in the nineteenth century and the general size and tooth similarity to domesticated *Bovidae*. Buffalo are considered to be basically a prairie animal, and the extinct species are believed to have coexisted with mammoth rather than with mastodon.

Symbos cavifrons (Musk-ox)

The posterior portion of a musk-ox skull is recorded from Cape Girardeau County, Missouri (Mehl 1962:63). A skull was found near New Madrid in 1812 (Mehl 1962:93). Other remains have been identified in the Friars Point collection. The musk-ox is thought to have become extinct by the Woodfordian substage (Parmalee and Oesch 1972:46).

Megalonyx sp. (Ground Sloth)

Megalonyx is known from Friars Point and south. The Forrest City area has produced a tibia and a humerus, found in Little Crow Creek, which are probably *jeffersonii* (personal communication, E. Thomas Hemmings, Arkansas Archeological Survey; see Figure 3.6b). Another bone from Crow Creek

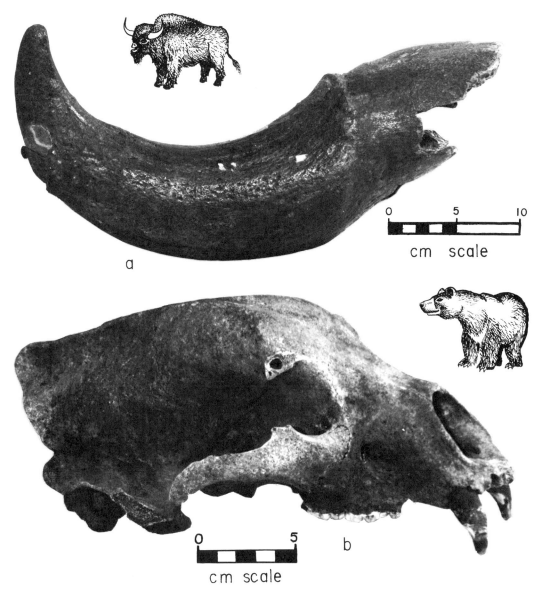

FIGURE 3.5. Extinct animals from Richardson's Landing, Tipton County, Tennessee. (a) Bison horn core. (b) Bear skull. [Photographs of bones courtesy of the Memphis Pink Palace Museum.]

was once identified as *Megalonyx*, but that identification is now being questioned. A "toe-bone" identified as *Megalonyx jeffersonii* was described in 1850 (Corgan 1975:84; Hay 1923:280) as having been found near Memphis. It was associated with mastodon, giant beaver, and beaver. A caudal vertebrae found with a mastodon and a tapir near Bay may be from *Megalonyx* (person-

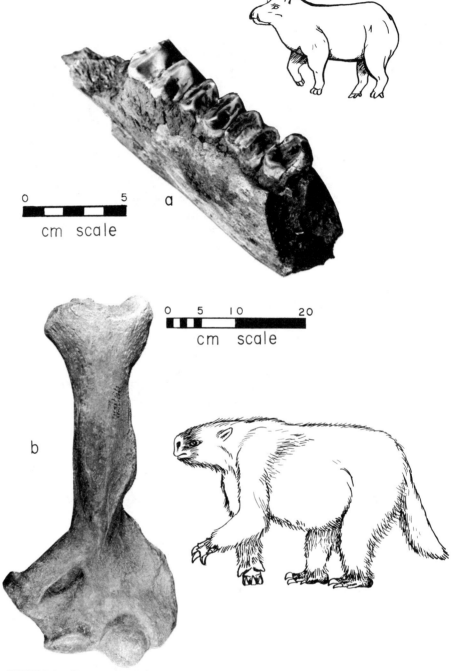

0   5

cm scale

0   5   10   20

cm scale

a

b

FIGURE 3.6. Extinct animals found in Arkansas. (a) Tapir mandible from Bay ditch location, Poinsett County. (b) Ground sloth longbone from Crow Creek location, St. Francis County. [Photographs of bones courtesy of the Arkansas Archeological Survey.]

al communication, John Guilday, Carnegie Museum of Natural History). These sloths were primarily forest animals that could have coexisted with mastodon (Kurtén and Anderson 1980:138).

Tapirus sp. (Tapir)

The left mandible of a large *Tapirus* was found in association with mastodon and a possible sloth bone in the Bay drainage (Figure 3.6a). It may be *T. veroensis* or *T. excelus* (personal communication, Claude W. Hibbard, University of Michigan). The tapir is comfortable in a forested parkland where it is relatively warm and wet.

Equus sp. (Horse)

Friars Point and sandbars to the south have produced some Pleistocene horse remains. A left humerus was found on another sandbar, near Memphis (Corgan 1975:84). Horses may date relatively earlier in the Wisconsin in this region.

Tayassuidae (Pigs and Peccaries)

Pig bones occur at Friars Point (personal communication, John Connaway, Mississippi Department of Archives and History). They are either modern pig or the Pleistocene peccary (*Platygonus* sp.). However, peccaries are associated with upland cave deposits rather than with bog deposits, and they are not expected in the lowlands of the Central Valley (Parmalee and Oesch 1972:41).

Cervus canadensis (Elk)

In Dyer County, Tennessee, remains of an elk, *Cervus* cf. *c. canadensis*, were found (Corgan 1975:66). Elk did not exist in the Central Valley during the prehistoric portion of the Holocene, or at least that portion of it represented by faunal collections. An occasional elk tooth ornament or astralagus die is found in Mississippian sites, reflecting trade, perhaps from central Illinois or some other suitable habitat. In the nineteenth century, elk and buffalo were hunted in this region, but there are no elk in the Central Valley today.

Odocoileus sp. (Deer)

Deer, possibly *O. virginianus*, the white-tailed deer, is known from Friars Point and points south. It should be more common based on deposits in Missouri and Alabama. Since it is so common in prehistoric deposits, the bone hardly creates much excitement when discovered.

Ursus sp. (Bear)

A right mandible was found below Friars Point in Bolivar County, Mississippi (personal communication, Jack M. Kaye, Mississippi State University). A skull was found at Richardson's Landing (Figure 3.5b). Both are probably *U. americanus*, black bear. It is not known how common the black bear was in the lowlands. Archaeological deposits do not contain much bear, but this might reflect hunting practices as much as occurrence. Bear probably denned in the Ozarks.

Canis dirus (Dire Wolf)

A left humerus is from Friars Point. Dire wolf was a predator and undoubtedly fed upon many of the smaller mammals. More bone should be present in local deposits.

Castoridae (Beaver)

Both *Castor canadensis* and *Casteroides ohioensis* are recorded from near Memphis (Corgan 1975:84). The latter is the giant beaver, as large as a bear. There are at least two *Casteroides* known from Memphis (personal communication, Ronald C. Brister, Memphis Pink Palace Museum). There is one known from Little Crow Creek, near Forrest City, Arkansas (Arkansas State University Museum files), which may be from the same deposit that has produced ground sloth. *Castor* has also been found at Friars Point. Ponds and forests are indicated as part of the habitat.

Other

Turtle bone has been found on Mississippi River sandbars and in association with mastodon, tapir, and possibly sloth in the Bay drainage. This animal should be more commonly represented. Also expected are bones of the raccoon (*Procyon lotor*), a very common part of Indian diet after the Pleistocene and a known Pleistocene inhabitant of other regions. Similarly, rabbit and squirrel occur in a Pleistocene context elsewhere. An investigation at Crankshaft Cave in Missouri has provided an indication of the number of mammals present during the Pleistocene (Parmalee, Oesch, and Guilday 1969). Very few birds have been identified, and fish have not been described at all in this general region. Both constituted an important part of the prehistoric diet in the Holocene.

FLUTED POINTS

More than 120 fluted points are on record for the Central Valley. The majority of these are from northeast Arkansas. Eight have been found in northeast Arkansas since 1967 by personnel of the Arkansas Archeological Survey. According to local relic dealers, many more have been found and sold before they could be recorded in any manner. It is abundantly clear that the fluted point period is well represented in the Central Valley area. However, nowhere in the Central Valley is there a localized concentration that definitely could be considered a fluted point site comparable to sites such as Lindenmeier.

There are two major concentrations of points known in northeast Arkansas (Figure 3.1). One exists along the east side of Crowley's Ridge, west of the Bay drainage and on an escarpment marking the border between the two braided stream terraces in the Eastern Lowlands. This escarpment is very prominent and almost certainly was dry the year round, in contrast to the lower elevations found to the east. Very few points have been reported from east of this concentration, indicating the possibility of occasional occupation of the braided stream system that existed there. One point allegedly found on the spoil bank of a prominent ditch also indicates the possibility of buried components in the terrace.

The second major concentration is west of and parallel to Crowley's Ridge. The Cache River is bordered by prominent escarpments and flows within a floodplain approximately 1.6 km (1 mile) wide near Jonesboro. Fluted points are found on both escarpments. It is possible that buried sites may exist within the floodplain.

Two points are recorded from on top of Crowley's Ridge itself. The Arkansas Archeological Survey collected another point on the lower slope of the ridge where deposits have built up from a ridge stream changing gradient, and quite possibly there are buried sites beneath the ridge's apron or where streams emerge from the ridge. The same phenomenon may be true of the Ozark Highlands escarpment as well, particularly where Ozark streams emerge from the highlands to the lowlands, depositing recent sediments. Immediately south of a prominent alluvial fan on the Black River, five points allegedly were found at a single site. Significant portions of the land surface that existed during the Paleo-Indian period are masked beneath more recent deposits. A point was recently discovered protruding from a ditch side almost a meter beneath the surface in Woodruff County, Arkansas. The apparent settlement system involving two linear patterns of points along both sides of Crowley's Ridge, indicating possibly two bands of people, may arise in part from the geological history of this region.

Considerable variation exists within the category of fluted points from the Central Mississippi Valley. Most seem to fall into a "Clovis-like" or a "Folsom-like" classification. These have been named the Crowley's Ridge point and the Sedgwick point, respectively. These are also the names used for the two recognized fluted point phases in the Central Valley. All points are surface collected, and no associated artifacts have been recognized.

Crowley's Ridge Point

The point is essentially oval in outline with lateral grinding and fluting scars extending to near the center, where the point is widest (Figure 3.7a–c).

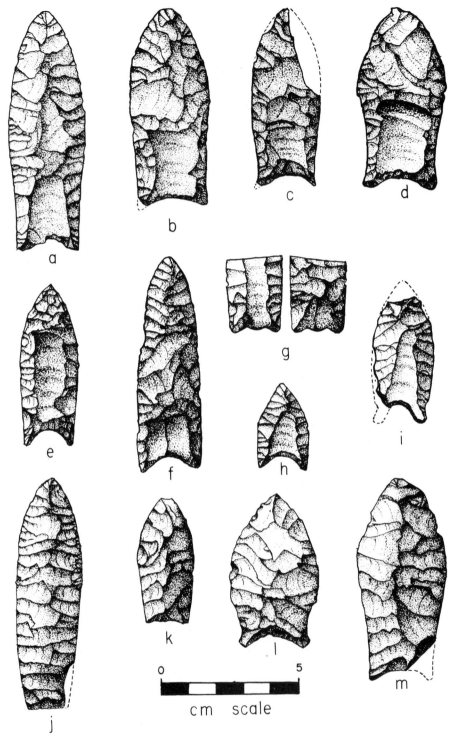

FIGURE 3.7. Fluted and possible early unfluted points found in the Central Valley. (a)–(c) Crowley's Ridge points. (d) Possible variant of Crowley's Ridge point. (e)–(h) Sedgwick points. (i) Probably reworked Sedgwick point. (j)–(k) Agate Basin–like points. (l)–(m) Coldwater points. [(a), (k) Courtesy of Arkansas State University Museum; (b)–(i), (l)–(m) courtesy of Arkansas Archeological Survey; (j) courtesy of Iris Weaver.]

The pointed half seems to have been shortened by resharpening on most specimens. The basal half exhibits a gentler curve and is recurved slightly, but it is usually not eared significantly, if at all. The basal concavity tends to be shallow. Most often only a single fluting scar is visible; sometimes lateral remnants of preparation flutes are apparent. Both faces above the hinged fluting scars exhibit preform knapping patterns. The base tends to be mostly retouched on the face of the initial flute, probably due to preparation of a platform for fluting the opposite face.

These points are fairly typical of fluted points found throughout the eastern United States, but they tend to be shorter than those found in the Great Plains. However, fluting lengths and extent of lateral grinding seem to be similar in eastern and Plains points, and the shortening relationship in fluted points is in that portion of the point above the fluting scars. The tip end is stubby, with relatively steep lateral retouch, as if it were resharpened. This feature suggests that penetration may not have been a primary consideration, but the thickness of the point decreases at the tip, benefiting penetration as a knife or as a thrusting spear, and there are a few impact fractures on tips. In addition, the slight shoulder and flutes of a point would have accommodated the haft so that there was not an impenetrable obstacle where the haft terminated. The Central Valley surface finds may have been at the sites of camps, where points were discarded as worn out or no longer functional for various reasons. The fauna hunted here may have been the white-tailed deer rather than elephants or bison, and deep penetration might not have been as critical in hunting deer as in hunting elephants.

In summary, the Crowley's Ridge point is fairly typical of Clovis-like points found elsewhere in North America except perhaps for the apparent consistent foreshortening of the distal half. These points are part of a strong horizon style that is well dated elsewhere. They provide adequate evidence of the existence of human beings in the Central Mississippi Valley during at least the latter half of the tenth millennium B.C.

Sedgwick Point

Smaller, more triangular fluted points also occur in large numbers (Figure 3.7e–h). Unfinished points exhibit a central basal nipple (Figure 3.7g). Sedgwick points also exhibit a foreshortened distal end. The Sedgwick point appears to have been made as a long, narrow triangular point that afterward undergoes resharpening. The resharpening concentrates on the most distal portion, indicating that penetration was a primary consideration. Most Sedgwick points tend to be shorter than typical Folsom points. Many exist in local collections, and they usually are not recognized as fluted points.

Other Possible Fluted Points

The range of variation within the two major categories is not known; therefore, other types may or may not exist. For example, one possible variation of the Crowley's Ridge type is vaguely similar to points from South America, particularly Fell's Cave (Figure 3.7d). Another possible variation may simply be a reworked Sedgwick point (Figure 3.7i).

Often, reference is made to a "fluted Dalton" or "Graham Cave Fluted" point. As far as we know, these are Dalton points with generous basal thinning scars. On occasion these scars will have removed the central ridge on both faces. They appear to be part of the preform preparation leading to a Dalton point rather than a final fluting process. All of these points exhibit relatively short hafting areas as defined by lateral grinding in contrast to the relatively long hafting area on typical fluted points.

OTHER POSSIBLY EARLY LANCEOLATE POINTS

Dalton points are discussed in considerable detail in Chapter 4, where it is obvious that the great deal of variation observable upon unmodified Dalton points can accommodate many suspected Paleo-Indian lanceolate outlines. As with fluted points, there are no well-controlled site contexts in the Central Valley that allow us to identify specific cultural complexes manufacturing and using most named styles of lanceolate points. We are dependent upon a technique of identifying horizon styles that appear to be characteristic of the southeastern United States and that are firmly established in context outside of the valley. In the case of fluted points, we are on fairly firm ground. But with nonfluted lanceolate forms, the assumptions become very shaky indeed.

Agate Basin

Frison warns us that "there are later manifestations that resemble Agate Basin at least in projectile point form [1978:32]." The "Nebo Hill complex," located in north-central Missouri, is an example. Since the reconstructed Nebo Hill assemblage includes grooved axes and other characteristic Late Archaic artifacts besides points somewhat similar to Agate Basin, the current view is that Nebo Hill is Late Archaic in age. This interpretation is reinforced by radiocarbon dating (Brown and Ziegler 1981).

A few points referable to the Agate Basin type have been recorded in the Central Valley (Figure 3.7j, k). They are not nearly as common here as they are farther north, particularly north of St. Louis in Illinois, which may be part of a continuous distribution into the Plains region. The possible Agate Basin examples found in the Central Valley appear to be made of local chert. That they do not represent points traded into this region or brought here by traveling hunters is also indicated by a different basal treatment for local forms. Bases do not tend to be rounded; they are very definitely straight and steeply retouched or slightly concave. Otherwise, they are very similar to the points described from the type site although they do cluster in the lower size range for the type.

Coldwater

Rather than continuing to identify possible rarely occurring types recognized outside the Central Mississippi Valley, we would prefer to retain Brown's (1926) type name, Coldwater, but to restrict it to nonfluted lanceolate examples (McGahey 1981; Figure 3.7l, m). Coldwater points may represent an early stage in the development of the Dalton point, but they are quite different in the sense of an absence of lateral beveling. Often they exhibit very short areas of lateral grinding. It is noted in Chapter 4 that possible Coldwater points are included in a very tight Dalton context. Here we are selecting specimens from surface collections without being able to cross-check with an assemblage context.

A point that is almost identical to the Alabama Quad type exists. However, our current interpretation is that most probably this is a variant of Dalton. The same is true for a specimen similar to the Alabama Beaver Lake type. This too very possibly is a variation of the Dalton point type. The ears are very prominent, and the point was not utilized much beyond an initial stage of manufacture.

MAN AND MASTODON

The Central Valley is rich in Pleistocene fauna and in early artifacts, particularly fluted points. These are contemporaneous at the end of the Pleistocene. Much of the faunal assemblage continued beyond the Pleistocene and included the white-tailed deer, raccoon, rabbit, squirrel, and undoubtedly many other small mammals as well as a variety of fish and birds. Before the appearance of humans in the Central Valley there was a change from cool–temperate to warm–temperate conditions and a demise in spruce and jack pine together with an increase in oak and other deciduous trees. Mastodon may date into the Paleo-Indian period, but much or all of the extinct Pleistocene fauna remains discovered to date seem to have predated this period.

The emphasis in the literature has traditionally been on megafauna, particularly the mastodon, as the primary food of eastern Paleo-Indian hunters. The Williams–Stoltman hypothesis reflects this traditional view. This is in part due to the emphasis on kill sites in the Plains that involve now extinct megafauna. The megafaunal association, particularly with *Bison bison antiquus* and *Mammuthus*, was important in the history of American archaeology since it demonstrated the existence of "Ice Age Man." There is no evidence, however, to support the view that the mastodon was the primary protein focus of Paleo-Indian hunters.

Mastodon finds have been made along both sides of Crowley's Ridge. Most of the discoveries in the Eastern Lowlands are along a stream system that borders an escarpment noted for producing many of the known fluted points recorded east of Crowley's Ridge. The Hyneman mastodon is the only find over which we have excavation control (Morse 1970: Figs. 2, 3). The bone was deposited upon a braided stream sandbar by a sluggish, clay-laden stream. The chance of associated artifacts in a situation such as this is minimal; even most of the bone was not present. Most probably portions of the decaying corpses of a mastodon, a tapir, and possibly a sloth were washed together into this locality.

Mastodon localities in the Central Valley to date, with one exception—Island 35—have not produced evidence of human association. There were two artifacts, found beneath an ilium, at the Island 35 locality, but both artifacts, unfortunately, are badly fragmented and almost impossible to pinpoint culturally or temporally (Williams 1957). The point fragment (Figure 3.8a) appears

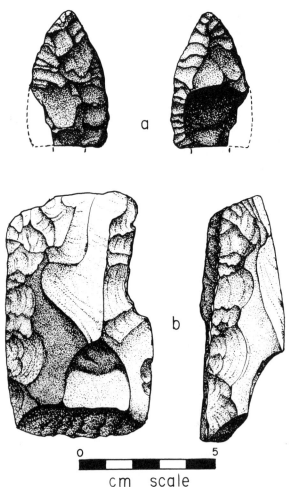

a

b

0   5

cm scale

FIGURE 3.8. Two artifacts found associated with the Island 35 mastodon remains. (a) Side-notched point fragment. (b) Biface or chopper. [Courtesy of the Henry Clay Hampson II Memorial Museum of Archeology.]

to have been originally stemmed or side-notched. It exhibits much of its pre-form flaking pattern in a manner reminiscent of Hickory Ridge Side-Notched. The rectangular chopper or scraper (Figure 3.8b) is not diagnostic of any particular period. The artifact assemblage probably postdates 4000 B.C.

Sandbars, of course, are redepositional phenomena typical of a meandering stream. Just upstream from Island 35, the main channel of the river flowed adjacent to the bluffs and apparently redeposited sand at the head of the island over a reported 30-ha (75-acre) area. A course change caused the sandbar to be washed away after about 1880, and by 1900 the gravel was being exposed. At Nonconnah Creek (Delcourt *et al.* 1980) loess overlay clay deposits (one of which included a mastodon) as well as sand and gravel deposits. The Island 35 bone and artifacts are best viewed as a secondary deposit, and their coincidental association relates to only the final phase of deposition, not the primary one.

There are no other known associations of artifacts with Pleistocene megafauna in the Central Valley. At the Kimmswick locality south of St. Louis, fluted points in physical association with a bone deposit including mastodon recently have been found by the Illinois State Museum. The association is a stratigraphic one, not conclusive evidence of the killing and butchering of mastodons. Bones of other species, including the white-tailed deer, were also found near the points. There seems to be little question of the contemporaneity of fluted-point makers with Pleistocene megafauna at Kimmswick. What can be questioned is the assumption by some archaeologists that fluted-point makers in the eastern United States depended primarily upon mastodon meat. The environment was exceptionally rich, conducive to a variety of animal life including practically all of the fauna that continued to exist after the end of the Pleistocene.

CULTURAL RECONSTRUCTION

Archaeologists often interpret their finds by reference to contemporary societies. For hunters and gatherers, the societies used range from the Australian aborigine and South African Bushman to the Eskimo. Anthropomorphizing artifacts and sites is both necessary and important, so important that some archaeologists even collect their comparisons first hand (Binford 1978). Breathing life into stones is a very imperfect art at our level of understanding in the Central Valley, but archaeologists have a responsibility to at least try.

Most probably the fluted-point makers lived in bands rather than in tribes (Service 1962). The *band* is a loosely defined group of people who recognize kinship with one another to the extent that they are exogamous. Marriage must be to someone belonging to a different band. The band performs ceremonies together but does not necessarily associate together as a group year round. The nuclear family, made up of husband, wife, children, and probably an older grandparent or two, is the normal year-round group. Often, and possibly almost year round, the extended family, composed of the core of the nuclear families of brothers, constitutes the group working together. Families belonging to the same band come together seasonally, particularly if group hunting or gathering is necessary. A hunting party of five males out of the band should be potentially available for maximum efficiency.

Males need to be familiar with the territory in which they hunt, singly or as a coordinated group, in order to be able to predict the behavior of the animals being hunted in that particular region. Males tend to stay with the band of their birth. To be effective in gathering, females can accommodate to different but similar territories since their resource base is stationary and more predictable on a wider basis. Females tend to leave their band at marriage.

Exogamy brings females from other bands into the local band, forming and reinforcing kinship ties between adjacent bands and allowing equitable gift exchange or trade between bands. Exogamy also allows for the potential movement of families from one band to another should resources become scarce in an area. If resources shift, people must be moved. The male is usually the decision maker, the protector, and the wandering hunter and trader. The female is the gatherer, the homemaker, the mother. Females gather wild food in groups as well, although their range from the base camp may not be as great as the males'. Children learn their future adult roles by play. Earlier, they are cared for by other children and adults. Grandparents are revered for their knowledge of past events in a world that does not greatly change from generation to generation. They also may be more stationary and tend to stay more than do others at the base camp and care for children who are too young to accompany work groups. The Central Valley seems to have been a rich region for food. Probably very little time (relative to today) was spent on the food quest.

The distribution of fluted points in the Central Valley suggests that there are two concentrations of humans, one along each side of Crowley's Ridge. Two bands are possibly indicated. At least one additional band is expected to be located near the Ozark Highlands. Population was low. The environment was not particularly stable. Movement along major waterways through time is expected, as adjustments to the environment were made from time to time. Extreme nomadism is not expected since infants and older adults, some possibly infirm, were necessary to the groups' continued success and existence and simply could not travel long distances in short time periods. In addition, Paleo-Indian groups existed throughout the more favorable environments of the eastern United States, and long trips would necessarily have involved encroachment upon the territories of bands without close kinship ties. Once the Central Valley was occupied by people, population would have increased to fill the niche. One band would soon become two, then more bands, since intermarriage was the key to continued existence and economic well-being. It is possible that the Paleo-Indian bands within the Central Valley were part of a larger regional band network.

REFERENCES

Binford, Lewis R.
  1978 *Nunamiut ethnoarchaeology*. New York: Academic Press.
Brown, Calvin S.
  1926 *Archeology of Mississippi*. University, Miss.: Mississippi Geological Survey.
Brown, Kenneth, and Robert Ziegler
  1981 Nebo Hill settlement patterns in Northwestern Missouri. *Missouri Archaeologist* **42**:41–55.
Corgan, James X.
  1975 Vertebrate fossils of Tennessee. *Tennessee Department of Conservation Division of Geology Bulletin* **77**.
Delcourt, Paul, Hazel Delcourt, Ronald Brister, and Laurence Lackey
  1980 Quaternary vegetation history of the Mississippi embayment. *Quaternary Research* **13**:111–132.
Frison, George C.
  1978 *Prehistoric hunters of the High Plains*. New York: Academic Press.
Graham, Russell, C. Vance Haynes, Donald Johnson, and Marvin Kay
  1981 Kimmswick: A Clovis–mastodon association in eastern Missouri. *Science* **213**: 1115–1117.
Hay, Oliver, P.
  1923 The Pleistocene of the United States and its vertebrate animals from the states east of the Mississippi River. *Carnegie Institute of Washington Publication* **322**.
Kurtén, Björn, and Elaine Anderson
  1980 *Pleistocene mammals of North America*. New York: Columbia University Press.
McGahey, Samuel O.
  1981 The Coldwater and related late Paleo Indian projectile points. *Mississippi Archaeology* **16**:39–52.
Mehl, M. G.
  1962 Missouri's Ice Age animals. *Missouri Division of Geological and Water Resources Educational Series* **1**.
Morse, Dan F.
  1970 Preliminary notes on recent mastodon and tapir finds in northeastern Arkansas. *Arkansas Archeologist* **11**:45–49.
Parmalee, Paul W., and Ronald D. Oesch
  1972 Pleistocene and recent faunas from the Brynjulfson caves, Missouri. *Illinois State Museum Reports of Investigations* **25**.
Parmalee, Paul W., Ronald D. Oesch, and John E. Guilday
  1969 Pleistocene and recent vertebrate faunas from Crankshaft Cave, Missouri. *Illinois State Museum Reports of Investigations* **14**.
Saucier, Roger
  1968 A new chronology for braided stream surface formation in the Lower Mississippi Valley. *Southeastern Geology* **9**:65–76.
Service, Elman R.
  1962 *Primitive social organization*. New York: Random House.
Williams, Stephen
  1957 The Island 35 mastodon. *American Antiquity* **22**:359–372.
Williams, Stephen, and James B. Stoltman
  1965 An outline of southeastern United States prehistory with particular emphasis on the Paleo-Indian era. In *The Quaternary of the United States*, edited by Henry Wright, Jr., and David G. Frey, pp. 669–683. Princeton, N.J.: Princeton University Press.

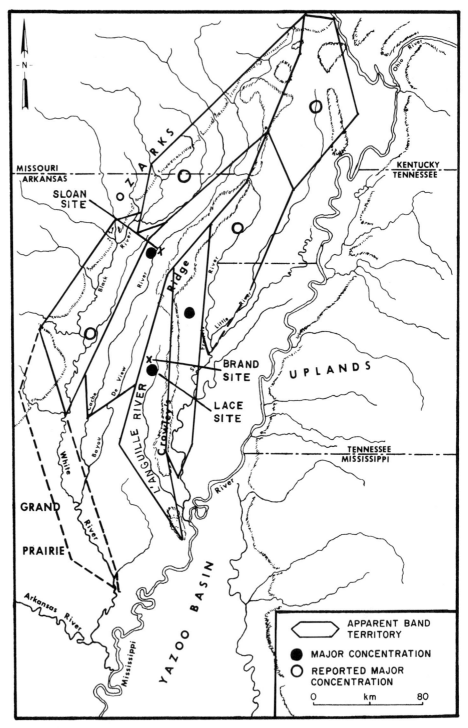

FIGURE 4.1. Interpretive model of Dalton period site clustering in the Central Valley.

4

Dalton Efflorescence (8500–7500 B.C.)

By 8500 B.C. fluting had ceased in the Americas as a horizon style. Radiocarbon dates in Alabama and Missouri bracket the Dalton period (Figure 4.1) to somewhere between 8500 and 7000 B.C. No direct dating has been achieved in the Central Mississippi Valley, but conservative dating dictates a period from about 8500 to 7500 B.C. Goodyear (1982) dates Dalton even more tightly, 8500–7900 B.C. Only Dalton points occur in context in Dalton sites, indicating a temporal distinction from other early points.

There is little doubt that Dalton represents a base out of which the Archaic developed in the southeastern United States. Diet focused on the white-tailed deer, with smaller animals, fish, and birds being included as well (Price and Krakker 1975:32). It was once thought that much of the reconstructed behavior did not emerge until the Late Archaic, or even later. This behavior includes cemeteries, the true woodworking adz, artifact caches, exotic artifacts, vegetable-grinding implements, permanent settlement, widespread trade, and other traits not usually attributed to preceramic or nonhorticultural peoples.

Dalton points have been found throughout the Central Valley (Morse 1976; Brain 1970). The Dalton period expression in much of the Central Valley is called the L'Anguille phase, after the L'Anguille River, which flows near the type site, Lace (Morse 1973). The Bloomfield Ridge phase was named in southeast Missouri (S. Williams 1954:35).

THE DALTON TOOL KIT

Extensive surface collections from almost 1000 sites with Dalton components contain much of the total variability within Dalton lithics. Two sites have been extensively excavated, one completely, and have provided contextual control and much technological information. There has been some experimentation on technology of point manufacture, and a start has been made on an understanding of nonlithic industries based on probable functions of lithic tools.

The Dalton Point

Like the earlier fluted points, the Dalton point is basically lanceolate in outline with a concave base. Differences include: (*a*) a more proximal location of the widest measurement, (*b*) a shortened basal portion as indicated by the maximum extent of lateral grinding and basal thinning scars, (*c*) a basal concavity that extends almost as far as the whole base, and (*d*) resharpening attributes that straighten the lateral edges and often constrict them to a width less than that of the base. Although Dalton preforms look very similar to Clovis preforms in outline (Figure 4.2a–b), the point was manufactured by pressure flaking, which usually completely masked the earlier preform pattern.

The typical Dalton point, when first formed from the preform, exhibits convex lateral edges that are serrated (Figure 4.2c). As the point was resharpened, the edges straightened out (Figure 4.2d). Typically, points were retouched unifacially, resulting in beveled edges (Figure 4.2e). The striking platform utilized for retouch was the worn, now nonserrated edge. Resharpening in this manner minimized the loss of the point's width. Serrations were chipped directly into the worn edge. Wear from use of the point was on the serrations.

The typical Dalton point is both a serrated knife and a saw. It has proved useful in butchering experiments on the white-tailed deer and is efficient for sawing bone. Probably relatively short handles or foreshafts were attached. Most points are beveled, showing they were resharpened by a right-handed knapper with the point held toward the knapper. The rare opposite-beveled Dalton point apparently was made by a left-handed knapper. After several resharpening stages, the thickness of the point's central ridge does not allow further serration. In addition, the working edge is very steep, perhaps too steep to be useful for cutting. The point may be discarded or, more rarely, recycled. A typical recycling stage involved the burination of the tip (Figure 4.2f); sometimes up to six burin flakes were removed. The resultant chisel edge was efficient for grooving bone preparatory to splitting the bone into awl and needle preforms. End scrapers were manufactured from other worn-out or broken points (Figure 4.2g). Often the point was removed from its haft and chipped into a drill or awl shape (Figure 4.2h). No obvious drill wear has been observed on such specimens, and the implement had to be hand held. These may have functioned as awls or gimlets, perhaps in leather or wood.

Jim Spears experimented on the replication of a Dalton point and subsequent resharpening of the point to exhaustion (Goodyear 1974:27–30). Although Spears retouched the point bifacially rather than unifacially, the experi-

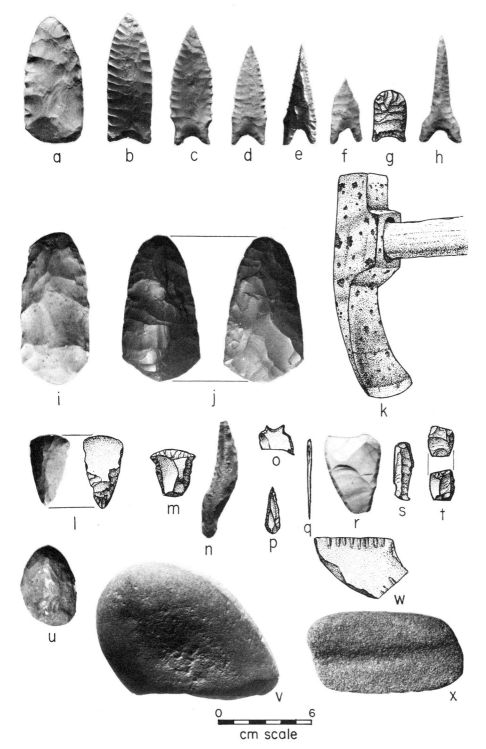

FIGURE 4.2. Typical Dalton artifacts. (a)–(b) Point preforms. (c) Unresharpened point. (d)–(e) Resharpened points. (f) Burin. (g) End scraper. (h) Awl. (i) Adz preform. (j) Adz. (k) Nineteenth-century English hand adz for comparison. (l) End scraper. (m) End scraper with "graver spurs." (n) Backed uniface. (o) Graver. (p) Microlith. (q) Bone needle found at Graham Cave in Missouri. (r) Retouched scraper. (s) Unretouched blade. (t) *Pièce esquillé.* (u) Discoid hammer. (v) Edge-abraded cobble. (w) Notched abrader. (x) Grooved abrader. [Courtesy of the Arkansas Archeological Survey.]

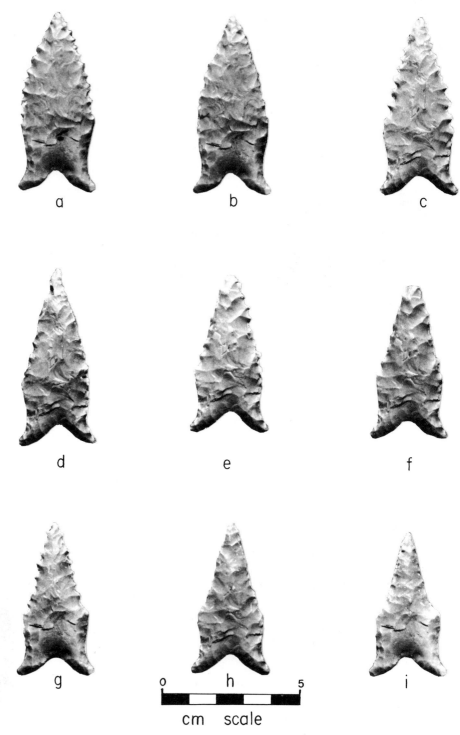

FIGURE 4.3. Dalton point manufactured and resharpened by Jim Spears. (a) Newly made point. (b), (d), (f), (h) Point serrations worn away on antler. (c), (e), (g) Resharpened point. (i) Exhausted point after unsuccessful attempt at final resharpening. [Goodyear 1974: Fig. 12.]

mentation demonstrated that several rejuvenation stages are potential on a given point (Figure 4.3). James Michie (1973) conducted experiments on the butchering of a white-tailed deer. Replicated Dalton points of local South Carolina material were hafted on relatively narrow hardwood foreshafts suitable for attachment in a spear for thrusting and minimizing the potential hazards of penetration due to shaft blockage at the skin surface. The serrated points proved to be efficient tools (Figure 4.4a–b). Skinning, entrail removal, and sectioning were all performed successfully with Dalton points.

The "Dalton point" has emerged as a complex concept. Rather than several formal types of points with discrete temporal and spatial dimensions, there is a single typical point with several shape categories reflecting manufacturing, resharpening, and recycling stages. Preform vagaries could account for other variations. Most of the significantly larger Dalton period points are similar to the typical point but normally are in a pristine (unresharpened and unbeveled) shape and not serrated. An exception is the very large point (up to 325 mm) that is essentially triangular in shape (Figure 4.5a,c). This largest point style, the Sloan point, includes specimens that do not appear to be ground for hafting and that may be better interpreted as fulfilling a sociological rather than a strict technological function. More traditional Dalton point shapes were also manufactured (Figure 4.5b). Analogous extralarge points occur in the Solutrean in France (Smith 1966: figs. 43, 72) and in a Clovis site in Idaho (Butler 1963; Butler and Fitzwater 1965).

The Dalton Adz

A triangular and relatively heavy biface has been identified as an adz for several reasons (Morse and Goodyear 1973; Figure 4.2j). Its "poll" is ground both laterally and lightly over both faces. The wide working transverse edge is gougelike. Polished facets on the convex surface of the distal end on some adzes exhibit straight striations oriented either parallel with or diagonal to the long axis of the biface. None of the over 100 adzes observed appear to have been thermally treated. All these features suggest a heavy-duty tool hafted in a substantial handle and used in the unidirectional scraping of a straight to concave surface. Size suggests a short handle. A contemporary analogy is the hand adz (Figure 4.2k).

Like points, adz preforms were manufactured from carefully selected chert cobbles. Often the poll area exhibits cortex, sometimes on both faces. Point and adz preforms occurred in caches at the Sloan site. Many of these preforms, however, seem too small to have been manufactured into useful tools, and it is probable that these represent symbolic preforms and were not meant to be processed any further. Other preforms are in surface collections, without good Dalton context, and presumably most were aborted due to difficult knapping developments. No experiments in the manufacture or use of nonpoint Dalton artifacts have been attempted.

(a)

(b)

FIGURE 4.4.   Butchering experiment with Dalton points by James Michie. (a) Removing the hide. (b) Initial cut to remove intestines. [Courtesy of James Michie.]

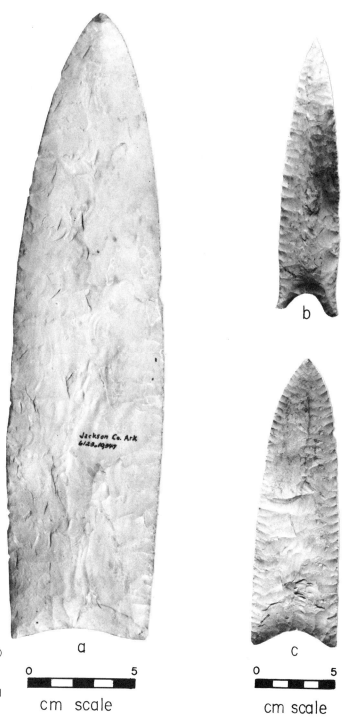

FIGURE 4.5. Large Dalton points. (a) Sloan
point from Jackson County, Arkansas; length:
298 mm. (b)–(c) Points from Sloan site,
Arkansas; length: 190 mm and 182 mm. [(a)
Courtesy of The Thomas Gilcrease Institute of
American History and Art, Tulsa, Oklahoma;
(b)–(c) courtesy of the Arkansas Archeological
Survey.]

a

0   5

cm scale

b

c

0   5

cm scale

The pristine adz is pointed at its working edge (Figure 4.2i–j). This point apparently allows penetration of the material being adzed. Striation patterns found on such adzes are parallel with the long axis of the biface. As the working edge rounds off with wear and resharpening, the corners become more prominent, and apparently one is chosen for initial penetration of the working edge. Striations found on rounded bit adzes are oriented diagonally to the long axis of the biface. In all observed cases, these striations are straight, parallel with one another, and oriented toward the corner of the working edge.

Almost certainly, the adz was used to manufacture wood utensils such as bowls for preparing and containing food. They probably also functioned to manufacture dugout canoes. Possibly, adzes were used to shape or smooth out ax marks in house timbers, for carvings, and for grave markers. The adz was a universal and useful tool throughout history. How far into prehistory it extends is unknown, but it must date to a period earlier than Dalton. The adz and other tool types are generally ignored by archaeologists who emphasize temporally diagnostic point styles and assume a cultural pattern that does not include nonlithic artifacts.

Unifaces

A variety of categories of unifaces exist, many of which are not well understood. *End scrapers* are the most easily recognized and perhaps the most common retouched unifaces (Figure 4.2l). Most probably they were hafted in a socket shaft. Some seem to have been made with "graver spurs" (Figure 4.2m), but the spurs may well be due to the desire to retain a standard working-edge width while accommodating the scraper to a given shaft. Working edges seem to fall into two categories. The first is characterized by a relatively acute angle and polish. The second exhibits a relatively steep angle and crushing or "Quina retouch." Presumably, one related to the working of skins, whereas the other was used on woods and/or bone surfaces.

A second, rarer retouched uniface class is backed, has a steep working edge lateral to the tool and opposite the backed edge, and has a basal portion suitable for hafting in a socket shaft (Figure 4.2n). Like many of the end scrapers, the bulb of percussion was removed by thinning. Other variations exist, including a chisel-shaped uniface, a point, and a large side scraper.

Steeply retouched microliths belong in the Dalton assemblage (Figure 4.2p). Gravers also exist (Figure 4.2o), presumably used to incise the eyes in bone needles such as the one found at Graham Cave (Klippel 1971:45; Figure 4.2q). Some flakes were steeply retouched (Figure 4.2r), whereas others, particularly blades, were not modified for use (Figure 4.2s). Many are naturally backed with cortex. True blades were detached from disk cores.

Other Chipped-Stone Dalton Tools

The bipolar reduction technique was practiced in Dalton times to produce blocky flakes and cores (Figure 4.2t) often known as *pièces esquillés*. These are thought to have been employed as wedges in splitting bone lengthwise after the bone had been grooved with a burin. The bone preforms then could be manufactured into awls, needles, and perhaps points. Recent studies, however, indicate that most are core nuclei and were struck to produce flake tools (Hayden 1980).

A variety of choppers, scrapers, and knives were made on broken and worn-out tools (Goodyear 1974). Cores, both pebble and disk types, were also utilized or modified as tools. One distinctive tool, a small discoid hammer (Figure 4.2u), is made on a thick biface with a battered and lightly ground edge.

Cobble Tools

Cobbles of quartzite, chert, and dense sandstone were utilized and modified in various ways, although modification was minimal. Choppers were manufactured by the removal of a few flakes from one end either unifacially or bifacially. These probably were used in butchering, dicing vegetable food, and other heavy percussion tasks. At the Brand site, polish was observed for as much as 20 mm up the working edge.

Pitted anvils occur as well. These presumably constituted the anvils necessary for a bipolar technique. Pitted hammers also occur in these deposits. A very distinctive Dalton period cobble tool is the edge-abraded cobble (Figure 4.2v). Most probably this is a vegetable processing tool. Why these tools have not been documented elsewhere except for Panama and the North American Plateau is strange since, like adzes, these tools should not be unique to Arkansas in the eastern United States.

Abraders

Some cobbles with depressions exhibit a symmetrical, cylindrical hole with polished sandstone grains. The depressions average about 25 mm in diameter and 7.5 mm deep. These may have functioned somehow in the process involving the preparation of antler or bone since their context is apparently butchering activities.

A distinctive abrader is flat with lateral notching (Figure 4.2w). The notches fit the lateral edges of Dalton points perfectly. Thinner abraders fit the basal portion of points. They also might have been used on needle tips.

Another distinctive abrader is oval with a long central groove (Figure 4.2x). It could accommodate biface edges, particularly the adz, and even perhaps antler knapping hammers and punches. This type of abrader evidently fragmented easily during manufacture and use since several odd-shaped abraders can be identified as midsections or ends of the centrally grooved abrader.

A bewildering array of flat-surfaced and grooved abraders exist in Dalton contexts. One of the most neglected technological investigations in American archaeology has been abrasion. Particle size, hardness, angularity, size uniformity, spacing, and the strength of bonding are all unstudied important variables in the selection of an abrading tool. Until these attributes are investigated, there appears to be little reason for extensive speculation concerning the materials being abraded.

SETTLEMENTS

Almost 1000 sites with Dalton components have been recorded in the Central Valley. Most of these exist in Arkansas, more particularly in the lowlands north of Memphis. Each watershed seems to contain a spatial concentration, with site densities falling off to the south and north. This feature is most apparent in the case of the L'Anguille River, located between the Cache River and Crowley's Ridge. One site has been tested (Redfield and Moselage 1970) and one site extensively excavated (Goodyear 1974) within this drainage. Perhaps the next best control is over the Cache River region itself. One site has been completely excavated in this drainage (Morse 1975). In Missouri two multiple-component sites have been tested in the Little Black River drainage (Price and Krakker 1975).

Considerable discussion of Dalton settlement patterns has been published, based upon archaeological investigations in Northeast Arkansas. Two major contrasting territorial models have been proposed, one by Michael Schiffer (1975a,b; also see Price and Krakker 1975) and another by Dan Morse (1971, 1973, 1975, 1977). Both use ethnological data about how hunter–gatherer societies schedule their yearly round to exploit most efficiently the diverse resources in the environment to reach separate conclusions about the archaeological data.

Schiffer maintained that a band using a single river basin as a territorial unit would not have direct access to critical resources and that band territories should crosscut several drainages to best exploit a series of contrasting microhabitats. He also concluded that there were no permanent base camps present at the center of a band's territory, but that these were simply areas which were reoccupied frequently. Schiffer maintained that hunting–butchering camps would be archaeologically invisible, with hunters not discarding enough material to be recognizable later. Schiffer's criticism stimulated Morse to better define and refine his original model, which is presented here in more detail (Figure 4.1).

In Figure 4.1 a model of the possible settlement pattern suggested by Morse is presented. There has been less survey work that concentrated upon the Dalton period in the southern and northern extents of the Central Valley. The dark dots in the figure indicate known concentrations; the undarkened circles are placed in areas thought to approximate reported but unverified concentrations. The linear patterns of distorted hexagons encompass known areas of Dalton sites with a basic assumption of watershed association.

Figure 4.6 is an attempt to relate different types of sites to one another within a single watershed. The central interpretation is that each watershed represents a single band's territory and that the major concentrations of sites represent an area of base settlements, one of which is possibly inhabited year

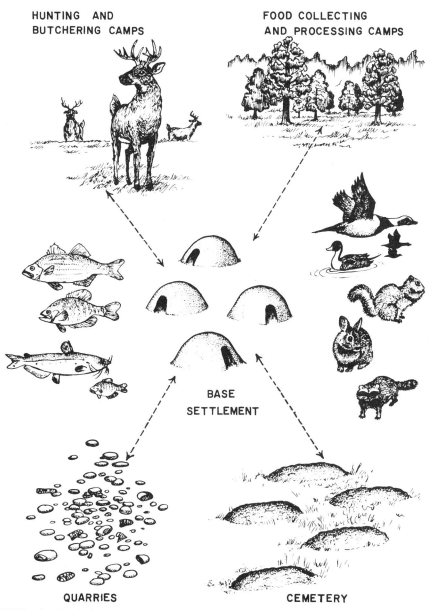

FIGURE 4.6.   Symbolic model interpreting relationships of sites found within a single watershed region. The "base settlement" is repesented in Figure 4.1 by solid dots or circles.

round by the whole group. Each territory is approximately of equal size and encompasses a portion of upland as well as a variety of lowland microenvironments. These presumably would be patrilocal exogamous bands tied together by marriage. Trade and intervisitation would blur any perceptible differences between these groups. Watershed or stream travel is easier than cross-country excursions. In addition, each watershed encompasses most of the plant and animal life available in all watersheds. The Ozark Highlands is richest in resource variation, particularly in lithics. Ozark cherts are very abundant in the Dalton sites of the lowlands; in fact, they are so abundant that if this resource is indeed scarce, there was considerable waste. It appears that social mechanisms strong enough to transport lithic resources in quantity throughout the lowlands were involved. Abundance of this nature did not exist again until the late prehistoric period, when the Mississippian chieftain sociopolitical system caused large amounts of exotic lithics to be distributed throughout the lowlands.

Three sites are good examples of what we mean by the different site types in Figure 4.6. Sites for the gathering and processing of wild plant food have not been recognized.

The *Lace site* (Redfield and Moselage 1970) is an example of a possible base settlement. It is prominent and central to a major distribution of contemporaneous sites. Midden may have been characteristic. All known classes of Dalton period artifacts are represented, indicating that a whole society was present and that it occupied the site over significantly long periods of time. The whole society may not have numbered much more than about 25 people. Perhaps as many as five small houses were present to accommodate nuclear families. There were other base settlement type sites nearby, but Lace is the largest and most prolific that has been mapped to date.

The *Brand site* (Goodyear 1974) is an example of a possible hunting camp. Artifact classes deposited here are restricted primarily to hunting and butchering and to the manufacture of bone artifacts. Only males seem to have been present, and significantly limited time periods at the site are indicated. A work force of perhaps five males may have occupied the campsite for from a few days to a week or 2.

The *Sloan site* (Morse 1975) is an example of a possible Dalton cemetery. Up to two dozen or more graves seem to have been present, reinforcing the concept of a band occupying a base settlement. Artifacts present are typically Dalton but in significantly different percentages than at living sites.

The Lace Site

Lace is the site that induced James A. Ford to initiate a survey of Dalton sites in the Central Valley during 1961–1962. It was called "the most important and impressive Dalton site examined [Redfield 1971:42]." This statement is still valid. Unfortunately, Lace, like all its known neighboring Dalton sites, was leveled for rice cultivation in 1980.

Lace was first cleared shortly before 1950 when "basketfuls" of points were picked up by children. In two visits to the site in the late 1950s, Gregory Perino and two other people collected 70 Dalton points and a number of end scrapers (Perino 1967:12). In 1961–1962 the Ford–Redfield survey team collected 101 Dalton points, 74 Dalton adzes, 110 or more preforms, and a large number of end scrapers and other unifaces (Redfield and Moselage 1970). During the 1960s and 1970s the site was a favorite target for collectors, many of whom were from out of state. During the last 10 years or more of the site's existence, the upper part of the cultivation zone was each year scraped away by a land plane to fill a low swampy area, and consequently any visit to the site was rewarding. The only collections known to exist, however, are those from the Ford–Redfield survey and the Arkansas Archeological Survey.

The total site mapped measured about 3 ha. However, the main portion of the site, wherein almost 90% of the artifacts occurred, measured less than .5 ha in maximum extent. This area was elevated about 1 m above the rest of the prominent knoll on which is located the remainder of the mapped site. In addition, the soil was dark, and most probably midden dating to the Dalton period existed here intact prior to clearing and cultivation. The prominent knoll is bordered by relict braided stream channels that were probably sloughs and lakes at the time of Dalton occupation. One relict channel leads to the L'Anguille River, located about 3.2 km (2 miles) distant. This river existed during the Dalton period, and its name has been used to designate the L'Anguille phase, which includes all known Dalton period sites in northeast Arkansas and most of southeast Missouri. The Lace site existed in the center of the cluster of known Dalton sites arranged along and near the L'Anguille River. Its prominence and immediate access to other site locations together with abundant evidence of all known Dalton artifacts suggest that this was a favorite base settlement for a Dalton band occupying this specific drainage throughout the Dalton period. This interpretation is reinforced by the probable presence of a midden deposit, an indication of occupation in permanent structures over a long period of time.

Despite this site's obvious importance, only two tests were made here. In 1961–1962 two avocational archaeologists under the distant supervision of James Ford spent a weekend at the site excavating three 1.5- × 3.0- m (5- × 10-ft.) test pits to a depth of 1–1.5 m. The reported results of that test were confusing in light of contemporary geological interpretations, so the Arkansas Archeological Survey excavated three small test pits in 1970 while the nearby Brand site was undergoing excavation to help clarify the apparent contradictions.

One test pit was placed near the center of the apparent midden area, which measured about 30 × 9 m in extent. Dalton artifacts were recovered at depths of 40–75 cm below the surface. A similar situation was reported by the Ford–Redfield test. However, their interpretation was that these artifacts were included within an active river levee. Our observations were that the deepest artifacts were introduced downward by mixture. In addition to being disked, the site had been chisel plowed. This plowing had mixed the windblown silt deposits with the weathered upper portion of the water-laid clays. Dalton artifacts probably originally were deposited on the surface of the weathered clay and within the base of the silt. Tree and burrowing animal disturbance displaced Dalton artifacts to even deeper depths. This interpretation of stratigraphic mixture is based on the clear stratigraphy observed at the Brand site.

Intact deposits probably had existed prior to the chisel plowing, and midden probably had existed as well. The difficulty in interpreting Dalton midden arises from the presence of the later sparse ceramic occupations at the site.

The Brand Site

Brand was partially excavated under Dan Morse's direction in 1970, and the report of excavations was accepted as an M.A. thesis in anthropology at the University of Arkansas (Goodyear 1974). These excavations were never completed, and the site was later destroyed.

The choice of Brand as our initial Dalton period excavation was not entirely due to chance, but chance certainly played an important part. Two local avocational archaeologists (Charles and Fritz Snell) showed us the site and donated all their finds because they felt the site was important. It was added to the list of approximately 250 known Dalton period sites and was still included when the list had been pared to the final five sites being considered for excavation. Brand was first on the list, whereas the other four were backup sites in case the reasons for excavation were not satisfied at Brand.

The process of elimination took a year because the basis for elimination—the reasons upon which to judge whether the excavation would be successful—had to be clearly formulated. The primary goal was to establish the Dalton lithic assemblage. We wanted to know what kinds of tools besides points were being used by Dalton people. We wanted to be able to reconstruct some of the main categories of Dalton behavior as they related to lithic technology and to the function of tools.

The base settlement and hunting camp dichotomy model was utilized to predict what classes of artifacts were expected at the Brand site. That Brand had been newly cleared and had produced only a few Dalton artifacts was important. Compared with other sites, Brand had the highest potential for stratigraphy, undisturbed deposits, a restricted assemblage, and less interference from other components.

An initial test at Brand indicated the possibility of intact stratified deposits. By feeling the profile with fingertips, the archaeologists could discern a difference between a lower clayey stratum and an upper silty stratum (Figure 4.7).

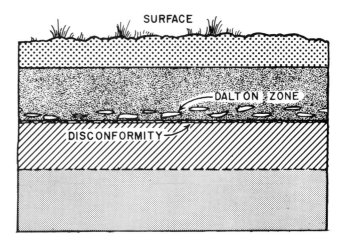

SURFACE

DALTON ZONE

DISCONFORMITY

 MODERN DISK ZONE

 WIND-DEPOSITED SILT

WEATHERED CLAY

 UNWEATHERED CLAY

FIGURE 4.7.   Summary profile of the Brand site.

There was a very slight difference in color, but the line of contact was confusing to sight because the upper portion of the clay stratum had undergone extensive weathering. This line was sharply demarcated by touching, a technique learned from Earl Swanson of Idaho, a blind archaeologist who had studied extensively with Zeuner, the noted European glacial geologist. The test square adjoining the initial test was excavated so that the weathered surface could be exposed. Dalton artifacts lay flat upon this surface, an indication of minimal disturbance since disturbed artifacts tend to be displaced vertically in burrows and root cavities. Dalton artifacts found away from this disconformity were so displaced.

The Brand site was on a knoll measuring around .8 m high and 1500 m² (about .25 acre). It was very typical of the class of sites interpreted as Dalton hunting camps. The Dalton component was the major occupation at the site. Besides Dalton remains, there was evidence of Archaic camps, a Late Archaic house site, a Baytown house site, and a Mississippian camp.

The braided-stream-surface clay formed a natural knoll. This clay was deposited approximately 30,000–50,000 years ago. The uppermost portion of the clay stratum then weathered over a considerable time period. Possibly incorporated into this weathered zone were windblown sediments occurring as part of a major episode of loess deposition that took place around 17,000–22,000 years ago. The surface of the weathered clay and/or loess probably was the ground surface at the time of initial Dalton occupation. This surface is a disconformity upon which Dalton artifacts were recovered (Figure 4.8a, b).

A stratum of windblown silt was deposited upon this knoll. Deposition probably continued through the Hypsithermal, up to as late as 6000 years ago. Dalton artifacts are associated in original context only with the base of this stratum. Above was a level mostly free of artifacts. The upper portion of the silty stratum contained post-Hypsithermal artifacts in a general disturbed condition. The disturbances for the most part seemed to be human, that is, due to the digging activities of the latest occupants at the site. Storage pits, house foundations, and other disturbances are expected in such sites. In addition the upper portion of the site was darker in color, probably because of a higher organic content due to midden formation.

The actual knoll is larger than the cap of wind-deposited silt. Beneath the cap were living floors dating to the Dalton period. These were recognizable artifact clusters (Figure 4.9). Five were excavated, and there may have been more in the area not excavated or tested by us. Each investigated floor was about the same size (range of 8–16 m²; average of 11.7 m²). Each contained about the same number of tools (range of 74–89; average of 83). Furthermore, the tools were classified into the same classes. The cumulative curves of each floor were essentially identical.

The floors are distinct from one another in space. Since each reflects the same activity, this is a rather unexpected situation. Butchering cooperation would imply spatial sharing, not discrete territories, unless it were a sort of assembly line, which is certainly not indicated by the evidence. The floors (or at least four of them) are either contemporaneous or sequential in time. If sequential, there should have been some spatial overlap. If contemporaneous, each floor is the site of a single male butchering his share of meat and making appropriate tools. The hunt may have been cooperative, but the butchering may have been private. Each floor is oval and oriented slightly north of an east–west direction. A gambing device for hanging deer and/or a drying rack to reduce meat weight are appropriate inferences. The worker's back could be to the sun all day, or the meat strips could be hung most efficiently for drying in the sun.

Despite the large number of tools, there is a class restriction. Only very limited activities took place at Brand. Woodworking and point manufacture seem to be absent. A short period of time as well as a limited part of the society participating are indicated. The butchering activities are removal of skin, the cutting of joints, crushing and chopping of bone and joints, and the resharpening of knives (points). Bone artifact manufacture is indicated by sawing of bones (serrated Dalton points), grooving of bone, scraping of bone, and fine

(a)

(b)

FIGURE 4.8. Excavations at the Brand site. (a) Two adjacent units being excavated; the Dalton floor is being exposed on the right, and the weathered clay is being removed on the left. (b) After completion of the two zones being excavated in a. [Courtesy of the Arkansas Archeological Survey.]

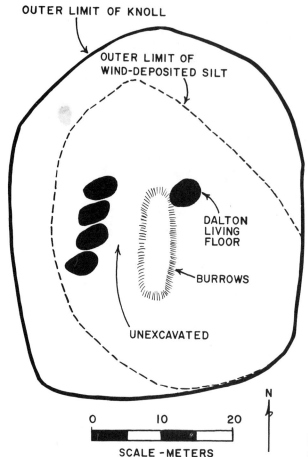

OUTER LIMIT OF KNOLL

OUTER LIMIT OF
WIND-DEPOSITED SILT

DALTON
LIVING
FLOOR

BURROWS

UNEXCAVATED

0   10   20

N

SCALE - METERS

FIGURE 4.9. Schematic sketch of the primary features discovered at the Brand site.

incising of bone (gravers) or the making of eyed needles. Preliminary skin work is indicated by the presence of end scrapers and perforators.

According to Frison's (1978:301–328) discussion of butchering, there were several important steps necessary to render the meat edible. The animal had to be gutted within an hour after death on a warm fall day to prevent maggot damage. The animal had to be properly cooled to prevent meat souring. Emptying the stomach cavity immediately after death solved the first problem. Hanging and field dressing fairly quickly after the kill solved the second problem. The kills must have occurred fairly near the campsite where tools were cached and possibly where racks were already constructed. Hanging also helped prevent dirt from hindering cutting operations. To prevent fly problems and to reduce weight, meat was stripped and hung to dry.

Butchering included a number of tasks, involving the use of choppers, hammerstones, and knives. A deer was best butchered by a single knowledgeable person. As predicted by Frison (1978:318), there is high point attrition at Brand. A total of 116 point fragments and 46 complete points were recovered from the living floors.

The Brand site may be interpreted as indicating the following behavior. The site was chosen as a butchering camp based on past success and/or upon a prediction of where the kills would take place. Stone butchering tools were cached there. Some deer may have been herded and driven into water for easier killing with or without the use of dogs. Clubbing, spearing, or drowning from canoes would have been effective. The dead deer may have been gutted before removal to the camp.

Game racks probably were constructed if they did not already exist, and field dressing commenced. It is possible that deer carcasses were cooled in the center of the site and that preliminary butchering took place here before they were moved to racks for field dressing. It is also possible that this was the sleeping area of the camp.

Each living floor may have been the site of a single male first butchering a deer carcass, then hanging up strips of meat to dry, and finally making bone tools while the meat dried. Without the benefit of bone debris to help make an interpretation, we cannot speculate much beyond this and still retain an acceptable degree of credibility.

The Sloan Site

We completely excavated the Sloan site in the spring of 1974. Frank Sloan, an avocational archaeologist with an interest in Dalton archaeology and the son of the owner of the site, insisted that we test it because he thought it was important, based on a tenant's selling some excellent-quality points found there. Once the excavation was in progress and the immensity of the find obvious, he continued to be highly supportive.

Caches of early artifacts are rarely found. Often the discoveries occur in soils not conducive to the preservation of skeletons. The discoverers often are not trained to observe archaeological context. In addition, we tend to divide human behavior into two mutually exclusive categories: nomadic hunters and settled agriculturalists. The latter usually are uniquely characterized by settlements, cemeteries, and trade. Graves with exotic burial furniture are not a normal part of the interpretation of hunting behavior.

However, skeletons do occur with some early caches. Most notable is the Anzick site in southwestern Montana (Lahren and Bonnichsen 1974). Two skeletons and over 100 stone and bone artifacts including fluted points were recovered.

The southern Idaho Simon site Clovis cache did not include a skeleton (Butler 1963), but the circumstances of that find clearly indicated a grave was probably involved. The soil predates the Clovis period, so the cache had to have been buried. The artifacts found there were complete and unused for the most part, and debitage was rare. Two Clovis points measure 18.5 cm in length—huge by fluted point standards.

The Sloan site (Morse 1975) is in the summit of a low sand dune, one of several strung out along the edge of the Cache River floodplain in the Western Lowlands of the northern Mississippi River delta. During the spring of 1974, a square area 14 × 14 m and 50 cm deep, which completely encompassed the site, was excavated. A total of 448 Dalton-culture artifacts were recovered from an area measuring 11 × 12 m.

The sand dune itself probably dated to between 20,000 and 16,000 B.C. (Saucier 1978:28), and the artifacts are intrusive into the dune. The Dalton artifacts were in clusters, with a few exceptions, and the total collection included little manufacturing debris and very few worn and broken specimens. There was no recognizable midden deposit. Non-Dalton artifacts were few in number, concentrated in the cultivation zone, and easily correlated with occupations subsequent to the Dalton one. Apparently only a minor portion of the Dalton assemblage had been disturbed by cultivation.

The Dalton artifacts were clustered into groups that seem to be components of 2-m-long patterns suggesting burial furniture associated with extended burials (Figure 4.10a). Orientation was northeast–southwest, parallel to the dune's long axis. Within these linear patterns were groups of artifacts in very close association as though buried in containers. Some of these groups were somewhat scattered when found; others, particularly two preform caches, were in actual physical contact (Figure 4.10b). Four Dalton points appeared to have been rolled into a bundle as hafted tools. These were recovered as two pairs of points with their tips in opposite directions spaced as if the short foreshafts or handles of one pair extended to the tips of the opposite pair. Artifact clusters at the site were not vertically stratified but were horizontally discrete, implying that the clusters are specific, perhaps marked, deposits, whether graves or not. These characteristics strongly suggest that these 448 artifacts were intentionally deposited in a deliberate pattern over a relatively short time period by a single society.

Proof that the Sloan site was a cemetery will depend upon the identification of 214 small, badly eroded fragments of bone recovered from the artifact clusters. Four are almost certainly human (personal communication, Jerry Rose, University of Arkansas). If skeletons were ever present, they would have disintegrated during the long time period involved between burial and excavation in this acid sand matrix. In addition to the bone fragments, a total of 602 soil samples were collected, including 415 recovered at .5–1-m intervals across the base of the main excavation. These soil samples can be tested for calcium and phosphorus, two elements that should have leached into the sand as the bone disintegrated. Carol Spears, under the direction of Leslie Hielman (University of Arkansas, Department of Agronomy), conducted several soil tests on a selected series of samples. The results of tests on acid-digested soil samples

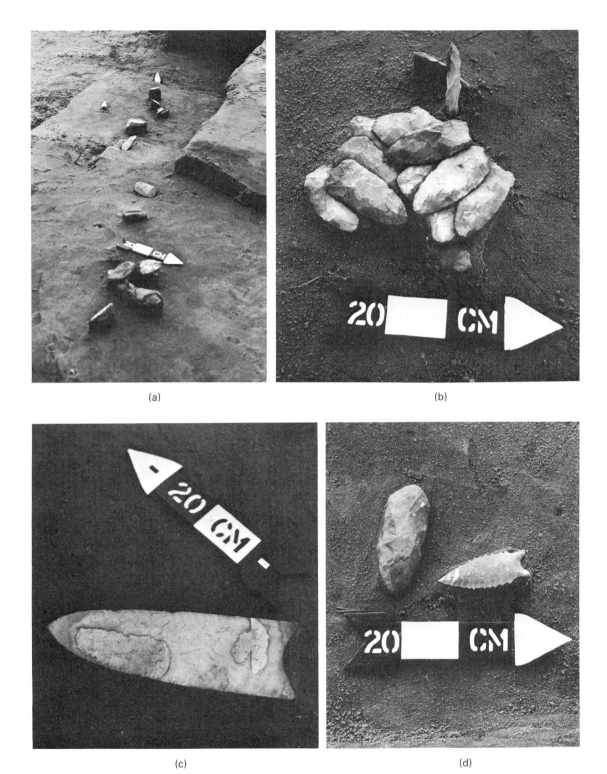

FIGURE 4.10. Excavations at the Sloan site. (a) Linear pattern in a group of artifacts. (b) Preform cache indicating a general lack of postdepositional displacement. (c) Large point *in situ*. (d) Point and adz *in situ*. [Courtesy of the Arkansas Archeological Survey.]

for phosphorus were inconclusive, but the results for calcium were in support of a cemetery hypothesis (Table 4.1).

The 448 Dalton-culture artifacts recognized to date are categorized in Table 4.2. Obvious differences between the Sloan assemblage and collections from other Dalton sites are the large number of points (144) in relation to other tools and the rare occurrence of debitage and cores, usually overwhelmingly prevalent at living sites. Sandstone abraders are more numerous than usual, and other cobble tools much rarer than normal. End scrapers, adzes, preforms, and backed unifaces are significantly prominent, whereas other unifaces are rarer than expected, based on the work at the Lace and Brand sites. The true blade is entirely absent, although it usually is a fairly common artifact at living sites. Since this is a completely excavated site, these differences cannot be due to sample vagaries. The nearest base settlement is about 1 km distant.

The presence at the Sloan site of so many unbeveled denticulate points that are not resharpened is unique. The Sloan site points are complete with very few exceptions and range up to almost 19 cm in length. At Brand most points were broken or obviously worn out as functional knives, and none were longer than 6.8 cm. Many Sloan site points measured over this figure. The largest Sloan point is 5.9 cm wide at its base, around 2 cm wider than most of the other larger points (Figure 4.10c). The base is not ground significantly more than the entire length of the lateral edges, in contrast to the usual treatment for hafting purposes. This point is also fragile. It is difficult to view this particular point strictly as a technological tool; rather, it seems to be symbolic or sociological. Other large points possibly should be viewed within a sociological rather than a technological context. Some of the points found at Sloan appear to be made from cherts from as far away as St. Louis, over 320 km distant.

TABLE 4.1
Percentage of Calcium in Types of Loci, Sloan Site, Arkansas

Sample locus	Predicted value	Test results (parts per million)
Late Archaic grave	High	1500
Around bone fragment in suspected grave	High	1200
Beneath suspected grave	High	1000
Separate area of sand dune	Low	700
Separate sand dune	Low	600
Beneath large point in suspected grave	(?)	500
In cemetery but not beneath suspected grave	Low	500
Just outside cemetery area	Low	500

TABLE 4.2
Preliminary Analysis of Dalton Artifacts Found at Sloan Site,
Arkansas

Artifact category	Number
Bifacial tools	
Beveled and denticulate Dalton points	62
Unbeveled and denticulate Dalton points	34
Recycled denticulate Dalton points	14
Unbeveled and nondenticulate Dalton points	34
Probable point preforms	89
Probable adz preforms	12
Adzes	30
Other biface	8
Unifacial tools	
End scrapers	36
Backed scrapers–knives	10
Gravers	5
Retouched flakes	22
Utilized flakes	6
Cobble tools	
Sandstone abraders	55
Chert discoid hammers	3
Edge-abraded cobble	1
End-battered cobbles	2
Unmodified cobbles	2
Debitage and cores	
Flakes of bifacial retouch	16
Plunging bladelike flake	1
Incompletely prepared pebble core	1
Exhausted pebble cores	4
Bipolar core	1
Total artifacts	448

Recycled points functioned as awls, scrapers, and as burins. Burins probably were used to groove bone before splitting the bone into splinters for artifact manufacture. Bone and antler artifacts are very prominent in the Old World Upper Paleolithic, and there are indications that this is true of the New World Paleo-Indian as well. Triangular and oval bifaces found at the Sloan site are thought to be preforms or blanks for points and, in the case of thicker preforms, for adzes. Many of the biface preforms seem to be too short actually to be made into points similar to those found at the site. The discovery of preform caches at the Sloan site is the earliest documented incidence of this trait in the eastern United States (Figure 4.10b). During the period of 1500–500 B.C., caches of artifacts—in particular, chert preforms—are characteristic in the Midwest (Morse and Morse 1964). They are best known in Hopewellian sites dating to 0–A.D. 400.

It has been said that "the adz in the Dalton tool kit seems to be a frequent and expendable tool [Morse and Goodyear 1973]." The Sloan site remains certainly support this assertion. Some of the adzes appear to be in mint condition (Figure 4.10d), whereas others seem to have been resharpened with a rounded bit. None are broken, exhausted, or recycled, in contrast to the normal situation at other Dalton sites. The Dalton adz probably was hafted similarly to the cooper's adz, with a short handle. The Sloan site adzes allowed us to hypothesize the manufacturing and resharpening stages involved.

Of the end scrapers, 32 have a contracting base suitable for hafting in a socketed handle. All seem to have relatively steep-angled working edges, possibly indicating that they were made specifically for use on hard surfaces. Three have possible graver spurs. All of the backed unifaces have a steeply retouched concave working edge, are "backed" on the opposite edge, and have contracting bases, presumably for placement into a socketed haft. The working edges are somewhat similar to those on Edgefield scrapers (Michie 1968) and Albany scrapers (Webb, Shiner, and Roberts 1971:30–33). The finely nippled gravers made on flakes indicate that a bone incising function is represented in the tool kits.

Bone and antler work may also be indicated by the large number of sandstone abraders recovered. Abraders furthermore could have functioned to prepare biface edges for knapping with soft hammers or to grind edges of points and the edges and proximal faces of adzes preparatory to hafting so the edges would not cut the haft bindings. One type of abrader is centrally grooved and is coarse (a U.S. sandpaper designation would be about 35). The Sloan site data indicate that the "archetype" tended to fragment during manufacture and use and suggested a method of classifying these fragments within meaningful subcategories of a single type. Otherwise, the definition of a large number of types to account for shape variation and the presence of a complete or partial groove might have been necessary.

A major tool find is the edge-abraded cobble. There still is doubt as to the basic function of such tools, whether as a blade-knapping hammer or as a food processing mano (Butler 1966:95; Crabtree and Swanson 1968:50–57; McGimsey 1956:155–156). The lack of true blades at the Sloan site supports a food-grinding function, as suggested by McGimsey and Butler.

Based on site size alone, 35 burials can be easily accommodated. Using a .5- × 2-m outline over apparent clusters results in a maximum of 36 grave lots. Of these, 15 involve very few artifacts and for the most part are located on the periphery of the main concentration. This leaves a lower maximum of about 21. This figure can be reduced further by enlarging grave dimensions and combining linear clusters and by reorientation of some of the possible graves. The most conservative estimate would be no less than 12 graves. We estimate that between 12 and 25 graves were involved or between half and all of the total expected band population using the cemetery facilities.

This interpretation would make this the earliest recognized cemetery in the

New World. Indicated are stable territories and a rich ceremonial life in the Dalton period. The Sloan site discovery suggests a need for a reassessment of current concepts concerning the societal and intellectual structure of Paleo-Indian and Early Archaic groups.

We have little direct evidence to estimate Dalton population size. Most estimates of archaeological populations are based on contemporary hunters and gatherers (Hassan 1979). These, however, are populations that existed in crowded, marginal, often hostile environments, in contrast to the Dalton period in the Central Valley.

The sociological makeup of band-organized hunters is simple and allows population flow to accommodate changes in the availability of food resources. The regional unit consists of a network of local family bands. The important technological factor is the cooperative group consisting of at least 5 adult males for hunting and a slightly larger number of females for gathering wild foods. This dictates a normal size of 20–50. Regional network populations usually range around 500–1000, .01 to less than 1 person per square kilometer. It would be difficult to estimate the Dalton period population at more than about 300 in the Central Valley. This figure is based on the reconstructed existence of approximately eight bands of 20–50 individuals for each band (Figure 4.1). The reconstructed network may simply be too restricted since it is not extended outside of the Central Valley.

REFERENCES

Brain, Jeffrey P.
  1970 Early Archaic in the Lower Mississippi Alluvial Valley. *American Antiquity* **35**:104–105.
Butler, B. Robert
  1963 An early man site at Big Camas Prairie, south-central Idaho. *Tebiwa* 6:22–33.
  1966 *A guide to understanding Idaho archeology.* Pocatello, Idaho: Idaho State University Museum.
Butler, B. Robert, and R. J. Fitzwater
  1965 A further note on the Clovis site at Big Camas Prairie, south-central Idaho. *Tebiwa* 8:38–39.
Crabtree, Don, and Earl H. Swanson, Jr.
  1968 Edge-ground cobbles and blade-making in the Northwest. *Tebiwa* 11:50–58.
Frison, George C.
  1978 *Prehistoric hunters of the High Plains.* New York: Academic Press.
Goodyear, Albert C.
  1974 The Brand site: A techno-functional study of a Dalton site in northeast Arkansas. *Arkansas Archeological Survey Research Series* 7.
  1982 The chronological position of the Dalton horizon in the Southeastern United States. *American Antiquity* 47:382–395.
Hassan, Fekri
  1979 Demography and archaeology. *Annual Review of Anthropology* 8:137–160.

Hayden, Brian
1981   Confusion in the bipolar world: Bashed pebbles and splintered pieces. *Lithic Technology* 9:2–7.
Klippel, Walter E.
1971   Graham Cave revisited. *Missouri Archaeological Society Memoir* 9.
Lahren, Larry, and Robson Bonnichsen
1974   Bone foreshafts from a Clovis burial in southwestern Montana. *Science* 186:147–150.
McGimsey, C. R., III
1956   Cerro Mangote: A preceramic site in Panama. *American Antiquity* 22:151–161.
Michie, Jim
1968   The Edgefield scraper. *Chesopiean* 6:30–31.
1973   A functional interpretation of the Dalton projectile point in South Carolina. *South Carolina Antiquities* 5(2):24–36.
Morse, Dan F.
1971   Recent indications of Dalton settlement pattern in Northeast Arkansas. *Southeastern Archaeological Conference Bulletin* 13:5–10.
1973   Dalton culture in northeast Arkansas. *Florida Anthropologist* 25:28–38.
1975a Reply to Schiffer. In The Cache River archeological project: An experiment in contract archeology, assembled by Michael Schiffer and John House. *Arkansas Archeological Survey Research Series* 8:113–119.
1975b Paleo-Indian in the land of opportunity: Preliminary report on the excavations at the Sloan site (3GE94). In Cache River archeological project, assembled by Michael Schiffer and John House. *Arkansas Archeological Survey Research Series* 8:135–143.
1976   An analysis of the Dalton complex in the Central Mississippi Valley. In *Habitats humains anterieurs à L'Holocene en America*, edited by James B. Griffin, pp. 136–166. *Colloque 17, Union Internationale des Sciences Prehistoriques et Protohistoriques*. Nice.
1977   Dalton settlement systems: Reply to Schiffer (2). *Plains Anthropologist* 22:149–158.
Morse, Dan F., and Albert Goodyear
1973   The significance of the Dalton adze in northeast Arkansas. *Plains Anthropologist* 18:316–322.
Morse, Dan F., and Phyllis A. Morse
1964   1962 Excavations at the Morse site: A Red Ocher cemetery in the Illinois Valley. *Wisconsin Archeologist* 45:79–98.
Perino, Gregory
1967   The Cherry Valley mounds and Banks Mound 3. *Central States Archaeological Societies Memoir* 1.
Price, James E., and James J. Krakker
1975   Dalton occupation of the Ozark border. *University of Missouri Museum Brief* 20.
Redfield, Alden
1971   *Dalton project notes, volume one.* Museum of Anthropology, University of Missouri.
Redfield, Alden, and John H. Moselage
1970   The Lace place: A Dalton project site in the Western Lowland in eastern Arkansas. *Arkansas Archeologist* 11:21–44.
Saucier, Roger
1978   Sand dunes and related eolian features of the Lower Mississippi River Alluvial Valley. *Geoscience and Man* 19:23–40.
Schiffer, Michael
1975a Some further comments on the Dalton settlement pattern hypothesis. In *The Cache River archeological project: An experiment in contract archeology*, assembled by Michael Schiffer and John House. *Arkansas Archeological Survey Research Series* 8:103–112.
1975b An alternative to Morse's Dalton settlement pattern hypotheses. *Plains Anthropologist* 20:253–266.

Smith, Philip E. L.
  1966   Le Solutréen en France. *Publications de L'Institut de Préhistoire de L'Université de Bordeaux, Mémoire* **5.**
Webb, Clarence H., Joel L. Shiner, and E. Wayne Roberts
  1971   The John Pearce site (16CD56): A San Patrice site in Caddo Parish, Louisiana. *Bulletin of the Texas Archeological Society* **42**:1–49.
Williams, Stephen
  1954   An archeological study of the Mississippian culture in southeast Missouri. Ph.D. Dissertation, Yale University Department of Anthropology. University Microfilms, Ann Arbor.

5

The Hypsithermal Archaic Disruption (7000–3000 B.C.)

The term *Archaic* was first used in the 1930s to encompass preceramic complexes within the McKern or Midwestern Taxonomic System. In time it became differentiated from *Paleo-Indian* and was divided into three subunits: Early, Middle, and Late. It has been increasingly difficult to define these divisions in the Central Valley, since one merges into another very subtly. Our solution is to recognize the Hypsithermal as a significant climatic period and to hypothesize that people responded to these changes in their physical environment with corresponding culture changes. The Hypsithermal Archaic essentially equates with what is usually classified as "Middle Archaic."

Any recognizable Archaic before the Hypsithermal may be classified as "Early Archaic." Those portions not discussed in Chapter 4, which describes the Dalton period, will be covered in this chapter as a prelude to the Hypsithermal Archaic. In some regions, this "Early Archaic" is still called Paleo-Indian, but we wish to restrict *that* period to when fluted points were made. Our "Late Archaic" occurs after the Hypsithermal (see Chapter 6). It is a time period in the Lower Mississippi Valley that includes or equates with the Poverty Point period.

THE HYPSITHERMAL PERIOD

The Hypsithermal was a warm and dry climatic interval dating from about 7000 to 3000 B.C. in the present-day United States. It was a time of maximal warmth and dryness, with corresponding changes in plant and animal species. The incidence of summer drought increased, and this drought stress is evidenced by the types of pollen collected in cores and in the kinds of animal bone present at archaeological sites. Forest types both migrated and decreased in size during this period. Species dependent upon forest products, particularly upon acorns, also migrated, and their food base was decreased. Obvious evidence of this period has been recognized for a long time in the southwestern United States and in the Plains, where it is called the Altithermal. It is only recently that comparable data were collected in the Southeast.

Good evidence of this dry period has been found in the Morehouse Lowland area of southeast Missouri (King 1981; Figure 5.1). A 2.3-m-deep peat core taken from the Old Field swamp in Stoddard County contained well-preserved pollen deposits that showed changing percentages of plant species through time. Radiocarbon dates of 6800–2800 B.C. on the peat from various depths established a more exact chronology of these changes. Such changes are customarily diagrammed as relative frequencies of major genera charted by depth and percentage.

The base of the Old Field core showed a mixture of bottomland forests with a high percentage of oaks, grass, and open-water swamp. By 6700 B.C.

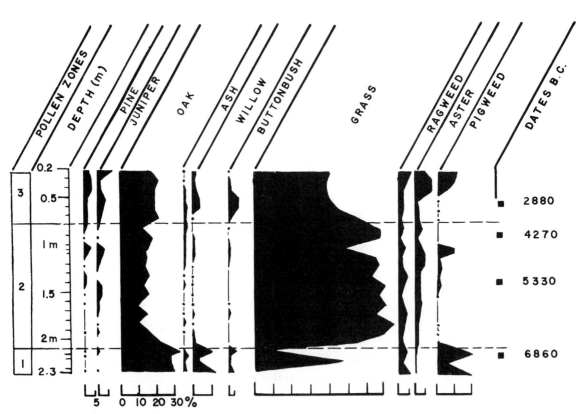

FIGURE 5.1.   Pollen-diagram based on work at Old Field, Stoddard County, Missouri. Each sample was made up of 400 grains. • = less than 1%. [After King 1981: fig. 11.]

open-swamp species declined, and herb and grass species increased. These latter species probably represent canebrakes. Some mixed oak forest was still present, but its habitat space and population was greatly reduced. Grasses and other nonarboreal pollen began to dominate the pollen profile. At 5000 B.C. up to 85% of the species were grassland inhabitants, and both the open-water and bottomland-woodland habitats were minimal in size. This percentage of grass-species pollen is even higher than that recorded for modern prairie communities; complete dominance by grass is evident. Some ponded water was still present but in very small amounts. The remnants of the upland forest communities showed changes to pine and juniper, which are drought resistant.

After about 4500 B.C. the time of extreme hot and dry climate ended. Grasses declined to under 50%, and the percentage of swamp species began to rise. Relatively dry conditions lasted until 3000 B.C., however. After that date, swamp size increased and arboreal pollen from bottomland forests also increased. Of particular note is an increase in species of oaks.

Geological observations also show evidence of the Hypsithermal. Roger Saucier has observed three distinct meander belt systems of the Current River dating after 8000 B.C. These belt segments are much smaller in size, with narrower belt widths and tighter meanders, than both previous and subsequent river belts. There obviously was a significantly smaller annual discharge of water carried by the river during this period in the southeast Missouri and northeast Arkansas area.

The Mississippi River itself probably began changing from a braided to a meandering stream near Memphis at about the beginning of the Hypsithermal. A slow decline in mean annual discharge is then seen for Meander Belt 1 (Saucier 1974), and Meander Belts 1 and 2 flowed together for part of their existence. Meander Belt 3 began about 4500–4000 B.C., when the extreme hot and dry climate ended. It terminated at about the same time as the Hypsithermal climatic interval, when Meander Belt 4 formed rather abruptly (Saucier 1974:20). Mean annual discharge of the Mississippi may have been only 40–60% of the present discharge during the Hypsithermal (Saucier 1981:12).

None of these changes occurred overnight. Recent research has tried to emphasize gradualism rather than abrupt transitions in both climate and related vegetational progressions (Wright 1976:594). However, the effects of climate on the potential food supply cannot be overstated. People can exist in seemingly harsh and unproductive environments, but their food preferences, extraction techniques, and population numbers must change with changing ecological conditions.

TEMPORAL CONTROL OF POINT HORIZON STYLES

There is a conflict in contemporary archaeological interpretation in the eastern United States that has not yet reached audible proportions. This complex disagreement involves questions of stratigraphy, recovery techniques, and philosophical orientation and is not likely to be settled here. Stated simply, the argument is essentially whether relatively brief horizon styles in point configuration do exist. Those who dig in rock shelters generally deny it. Many of those who excavate open sites support it.

In rock shelters, discernible strata exist and can be excavated as separate units. In particular, climatological data are readily available since a column sample can be obtained in a clear portion of the deposit that represents a great deal of time during which significant changes have occurred. However, drawbacks are numerous. Most of all, rock shelters restrict a population to almost exactly the location of all previous occupations. Thus, chances for mixture are maximized; there are no true sterile layers in rock shelters. In addition, samples tend to be minimal in rock shelters and are not always located in the best stratigraphic situations. Small samples simply increase the problematic nature of temporal interpretations.

Rock-shelter enthusiasts interpret different point styles as coexisting for long periods of time, sometimes even with little change in relative percentages. This picture of point succession derived from rock shelters has contributed to the confused impression of the Archaic. Little control is exercised over the non–rock shelter behavior of populations. Many reports exhibit a reluctance by rational investigators to pinpoint dates.

In some open sites where the depositional environment is sensitive to a succession of occupations through time, a quite different picture emerges. Work in East Tennessee, by Jeff Chapman (1977) in particular, has most recently demonstrated the succession of distinct point styles through time. Much earlier, however, this was clearly reported in a classic publication by Coe (1964): "When an occupation zone can be found that represents a relatively short period of time the usual hodgepodge of projectile point types are not found—only variations of one specific theme [p. 9]."

Each time period recovered in such open sites essentially is represented by a single point model. It has been demonstrated further by Chapman that relatively broad regional styles are involved. How broad a region those styles fit is not known since there are limitations to specific styles. However, independent dating of widely separate but similar point types indicates the possibility of pan-southeastern and pan-mid-western point families or clusters in many instances. This theory is very exciting because if it is true, it subjects our data to fairly tight temporal control against which to measure culture changes.

There are also drawbacks with open site stratigraphy. Biological mixture is more possible. Tree roots, burrowing animals, earthworms, and weathering distort open site stratigraphy. Some sites are very deep and impossible to excavate without enormous amounts of money. Another criticism is that active levee occupation may be specialized and seasonal and that only certain kinds of tools are used, resulting, the argument stresses, in a distorted picture of limited point variation through time. But rock shelters are also often specialized seasonal sites and are not characteristic of any one period of human occupation in the eastern United States. However, this fact does not negate the argument that specialized extraction sites could limit point variability.

Open-site enthusiasts may be operating with biased data, but Chapman's discoveries of separate horizons containing single point styles are impressive. In addition fluted points comprise another very broad horizon style. For the most part, assemblages for which there is tight control contain a single basic point style. The less control over time, the more variety there is in the points recovered.

Applying the concept of point horizon styles to the Central Valley is difficult. Extrapolation of data from neighboring regions is necessary because there are no known excavated samples within the valley dating to the Hypsithermal. When surface grab samples are used, the reliability of identifying specific point clusters is low. Furthermore, one must rely on whether specific styles are absent, present, abundant, or rare—an unsophisticated statistical statement in contemporary archaeology. But if we do not proceed, no one can attempt to disprove our conclusions.

We wish to test the hypothesis that the valley inhabitants shifted permanent site locations to the Ozark uplands and used the lowlands as a hinterland during the Hypsithermal. To test this, we should expect to find examples of all major point styles dated to this period in the area. Pre-Hypsithermal points should be relatively abundant. Styles expected during the 7000–4500 B.C. period should be only rarely represented in the lowlands but abundant on the Ozark Escarpment. Where found in the lowlands, they should concentrate along major streams, where water and wooded terrain are expected to have survived. From 4500 B.C. to 3000 B.C., points should be more prevalent than they were earlier in the lowlands but not yet as abundant as post-Hypsithermal examples.

We wish to emphasize that a complete hiatus is not being hypothesized. However, the potential subsistence variety in the lowlands decreased due to the development of grasslands. In addition, water and shade became rare in an environment in which a sunny day can be a curse. Dry soils also would have contributed to a hotter, more miserable environment. Exploitation of the lowlands became minimized and specialized, not terminated. There even must have been brief periods when particular portions of the lowlands were favorable for intensive exploitation. Certainly east–west travel was easier at this time than at any other time during prehistoric human occupation.

Although the work being done on open-site point style succession is for areas east of the Central Valley, that basic scheme has to be adopted as an outline for the valley. Many specific varieties expected in the Central Valley are based on rock shelter finds to the west, and these are the varieties that occur most often in the valley.

Early Corner-Notched Horizon (7500–7000 B.C.)

Classic Dalton points ceased being made some time between 8000 and 7500 B.C. An apparently transitional form exhibits bulbous basal ears and a corresponding deepening of the lateral haft area (Figure 5.2a). The appearance suggests a side- or corner-notched point rather than a lanceolate one. Lateral beveling on many is on the right side, similar to classic Dalton forms. This feature indicates that the tip of the point was held proximally by a right-handed knapper during resharpening. On others, the beveling is on the left side, a characteristic of points dating to a later time period. It is actually impossible to distinguish specific points made by left-handed knappers from those dating to a later time period, but the incidence of left lateral beveling increased significantly after the Dalton period. These points occur over a wide geographical area. Particularly noticeable is an eastern distribution well within the braided surface regions and relative prevalence in the deposits of Ozark rock shelters. Another Dalton point variety (Figure 5.2b) is similar in size and workmanship to a later type known as San Patrice (Figure 5.2c). The similarity of all of these early point types to one another is striking. The change from Dalton to the next period was not necessarily sudden.

Soon after about 7500 B.C. a variety of corner-notched points were being made throughout much of the southeastern United States. Some of these are technically side-notched but are treated as variations of a corner-notched mode. Some have been mislabeled, classified as "Big Sandy" in the literature. Coe's (1964) "Hardaway Dalton" might fit temporally here as well. In the Central Valley the basic similarity is to the San Patrice complex in Louisiana (Figure 5.2c) and to the "Kirk Cluster" (Chapman 1977) in Tennessee (Figure 5.2d–f).

The excavation of the John Pearce site in northwest Louisiana by Clarence Webb and his associates (1971) demonstrated the presence of a tight assemblage of seemingly similar corner-notched points. These are named San Patrice points (Figure 5.2c). In addition, an early type of assemblage of uniface tools was associated. These included gravers, end scrapers, and tools made on prismatic blades.

Many of the points in the San Patrice complex are almost (or are technically) side-notched. There are two named varieties — Hope and St. Johns — but most grade around a common theme. In fact, the observed tightness is greater than for the eastern Kirk cluster. A striking similarity is in size; both early Kirk cluster and San Patrice points tend to be small. There are exceptions, but the small size of most tends to mask their occurrence at multiple-component sites. Smallness arises from small chert stock in part, especially in San Patrice, and to considerable resharpening in general. These points were bifacially retouched, with very small final forms resulting. Many are serrated.

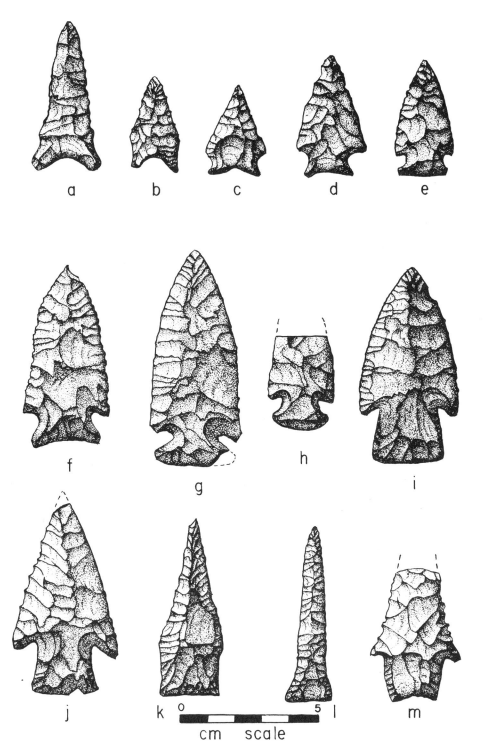

FIGURE 5.2. Points characteristic of the Early Corner-Notched and stemmed horizons in the Central Valley. (a) Dalton variety with bulbous ears and shortened hafting areas. (b) Dalton variety showing tendency toward San Patrice. (c) San Patrice variety. (d)–(f) Corner-notched points. (g) St. Charles. (h) Transitional corner-notched and stemmed point. (i)–(l) Hardin points. (m) Stemmed point. [Courtesy of the Arkansas Archeological Survey.]

Side-notching seems to be in free variation with this early corner-notched tradition. The side-notched Albany scraper is associated with the San Patrice complex, for instance. How this might relate to the Cache point, a possibly early side-notched variety currently dated to a much later time period, is not known. Bettye Broyles has reported a tentative point type in West Virginia (Kessel) similar to Cache that is dated to about 8000 B.C. (Perino 1971:14). Mason and Irwin (1960) also report an early occurrence of a side-notched point fragment in Wisconsin.

Corner-notched points are less abundant than Dalton points but are widely represented in the Central Valley. The literature does not reflect how prevalent they are in the Ozarks, but they seem to be fairly common and larger than those in the eastern and southern complexes. Based on this evidence, it would seem that occupation of the lowlands had lessened even before the onset of the Hypsithermal. This possibility does not seem to be a very promising development for the central hypothesis. However, the average radiocarbon date for eastern Tennessee's Kirk corner-notched cluster is 7270 B.C., and Saucier dates the onset of Meander Belt 1 at 7250 B.C. The onset of the Hypsithermal is usually set at "around" 7000 B.C. We need a better understanding of the immediate environmental effect of the very beginnings of the Hypsithermal on the lowlands of the Central Valley. There are abundant remains dating between 8500 and 7500 B.C. Between 7500 and 7000 B.C. recognizable archaeological debris is significantly less abundant. There is not an exact association dating with the onset of the Hypsithermal, but the timing is close enough so that the hypothesis has not yet been invalidated.

The St. Charles point (Figure 5.2g) is a relatively large corner-notched point found throughout the Midwest, with examples occurring in the Southeast and East. It is found very rarely in the Central Valley. Some of these points may have been manufactured with penetration as a primary function, but most have been resharpened laterally with a steep bevel. As on Hardin and Thebes points, the bevel is exactly opposite that found on most classic Dalton points.

The Thebes corner-notched point is normally thick and steeply beveled from lateral resharpening. This type is also mainly a midwestern phenomenon with rare southeastern counterparts. Its main distinctions are a relatively large size, a squared notch, and a thick, elongated base. The primary function seems to have been as a knife or scraper. Larger corner-notched points tend to be located in higher stratigraphic levels. St. Charles and Thebes points probably date relatively late, near the end of the Early Corner-Notched period and the beginning of the Hardin point period.

The Hardin and Early Stemmed Period (7000–6000 B.C.)

Perhaps the most impressive feature of the Hardin period is the influx of Plains-like styles at the very time the midwestern prairies are expanding. Radiocarbon dates indicate a date for the Cody complex in the Plains of about 7000–6000 B.C. (Frison 1978). The Hardin complex in the Midwest is very similar and is thought to be contemporaneous with Cody. Hardin points (Figure 5.2i–l) occur sparingly in the Central Mississippi Valley and are dated very generally to 7000–6000 B.C.

Hardin points are widespread in western portions of the eastern United States and differ from Scottsbluff and Eden types in being resharpened, usually as beveled knives rather than as unbeveled thrusting spears. Frison emphasizes that in the Plains Paleo-Indian period, points were developed that were long and narrow and with sharp tips (1978:33ff.). The point had to allow the foreshaft to enter the large mammals being hunted in order to be efficient. Frison questions the use of hafted Paleo-Indian points in the Plains as primary butchering tools (1978:318). The resultant edge dulling and haft stress would have meant an inefficient penetrating implement. Resharpening on Plains Paleo-Indian points was done so as to retip a spear broken by impact with bone, rather than to put a fresh edge upon a knife. Agate Basin and Hell Gap points, based on the extent of lateral grinding, had long shanks. The stemmed Cody complex points allowed a shorter shank with a corresponding longer blade. This would mean greater efficiency in the sense that a hafted point would be expected to be useful for a longer period of time. In addition, long points have a better chance of being lethal in case the foreshaft stops the penetration. Hardin points are like this development in one sense: They are longer than most earlier eastern points. Interestingly, some corner-notched varieties (e.g., St. Charles and Thebes) are also larger and beveled laterally.

The Hardin point, in contrast to Scottsbluff and Eden, was resharpened laterally and often has barbs that extend the cutting edge even further toward the base. Often Hardins are beveled laterally (but opposite the direction in Dalton points) as a result of resharpening. A use–life sequence of Hardins from wide, unbeveled points through a beveled increasingly narrowing series of points to a drill-shaped implement can be constructed that is very similar to that of Dalton points (Figure 5.2i–l). The indication is that Hardins are not so important in terms of penetration, and it may not be mere coincidence that bison were not characteristic fauna where Hardins are recovered. Hardin points are fairly rare in the Central Valley and have a distribution similar to that of Dalton points. None have been found in excavated Dalton levels or assemblages.

There is considerable variation within the Hardin type. Shank length varies tremendously, and even the shape of the shank often is different. Some points exhibit attributes of both corner-notched and stemmed forms (Figure 5.2h), which together with the emphasis on left-hand beveling suggests temporal proximity to early corner-notched forms.

Plains influence is evident in the Central Valley and contrasts with the distinctive eastern tradition of bifurcated stemmed points that was most characteristic in the East from around 7000 to 6000 B.C. The typical eastern bifurcate point has not been found in the Central Mississippi Valley. Besides Hardin points, several other identified point styles have been found that exhibit aspects of Hardin attributes.

These stemmed points probably date from the latter part of this period. They are abundant in the Ozarks but are fairly rare in the valley lowlands (Figure 5.2m). One probable example is the Searcy point. Searcy is similar to Kirk stemmed, which is radiocarbon dated to about 6000 B.C. in Tennessee. It is also possible that the stemmed Johnson and Hidden Valley points date to around this general time period as well.

The Rice Period (6000–5000 B.C.?)

During the period 6000–5000 B.C. the Stanly tradition existed to the east. Stanly developed directly out of the bifurcated tradition as a notched-base stemmed point. The closest analogy west of the Mississippi is Rice Lobed and related point types (Figure 5.3a). These points are smaller than the earlier stemmed varieties. They exist across the Ozarks but not in the Plains. If related to Stanly, Rice points extend this eastern tradition far to the west. Good examples do not exist in the valley lowlands to our knowledge, but very rare occurrences of notched-based points indicate that the period is represented.

Artifact styles found in good context outside the Central Valley suggest that there was a very minimum of human activity between 6000 and 4000 B.C. The tradition of making perforated stone atlatl weights, called "bannerstones," began in this period (Chapman 1977:90–92). The earliest known forms are crescent-shaped, with the perforation occurring through the short axis of the artifact. A very few similar weights have been found in the Central Valley, but they are exceedingly rare compared with other forms (Figure 5.3b). Rarer yet is the tubular form dated to the succeeding period.

Full-grooved axes may not have appeared until after about 4000 B.C. Grooved axes are very rare within the Central Valley. Ground faceted hematite "rubstones" occur rarely (Figure 5.3c) and are dated elsewhere at least as early as around 6000 B.C. Oval hafted knifescraper forms occur throughout the Hypsithermal outside the valley and are relatively rare within the valley proper (Figure 5.3d). Often they exhibit beveled and resharpened lateral edges and a short, unretouched basal region.

The Basal-Notched Horizon (5000–4000 B.C.)

Eastward in the Southeast this horizon was the period of Morrow Mountain points. Westward, varieties of basal-notched points such as Eva and Calf Creek were characteristic. Both Eva and Morrow Mountain points were reported at the Eva site, where the Eva level was dated to 5000–4000 B.C. (Lewis

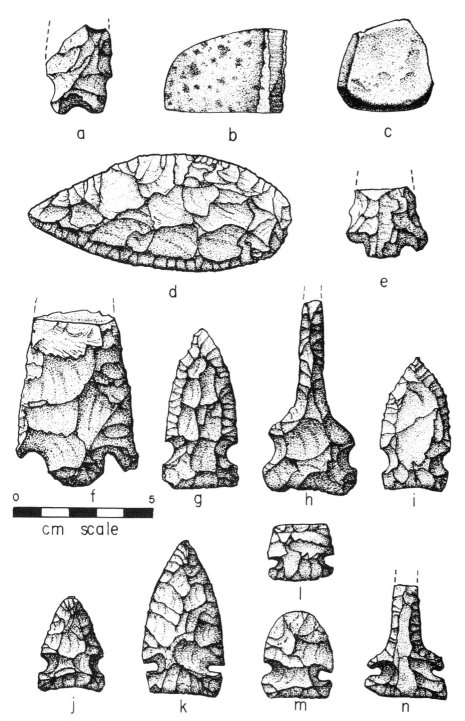

FIGURE 5.3.   Early artifacts found in the Central Valley. (a) Rice point. (b) Crescent-shaped atlatl weight. (c) Hematite rubstone. (d) Oval biface. (e)–(f) Basal-notched points. (g)–(j) Hickory Ridge points. (k)–(n) Cache River points. [(a)–(c), (e)–(n) Courtesy of the Arkansas Archeological Survey; (d) courtesy of Arkansas State University Museum.]

and Lewis 1961). Similar points are rare in the lowlands (Figure 5.3e–f). Basal-notched points are more common in the Ozark Highlands.

The Hypsithermal is interpreted as having become less severe around 4500 B.C., and the hypothesis proposed earlier in this chapter would predict that archaeological debris should increase in the lowlands around 4500 B.C. or shortly afterward. Basal-notched points occur only infrequently in the lowlands. But since there is apparent increased activity immediately after this period, again there is no definite invalidation of the hypothesis. The major problem in the Central Valley is that our sequence is based on extrapolation from outside the valley.

The Side-Notched Horizon (4000–3000 B.C.)

Side-notched points seem to have appeared suddenly in the Plains about 5500–5000 B.C. Most are radiocarbon dated to 4000–3000 B.C. There are similarities to Cache River side-notched, a rare point type found in the Central Mississippi Valley, and to Hickory Ridge side-notched. As mentioned earlier in this chapter, Cache points might conceivably date as early as 7500–6500 B.C., but there is no evidence either way. Until there is more evidence, it is best to identify them temporally with a well-documented side-notched horizon (Figure 5.3g–n).

The Cache point (Figure 5.3k–n) is oval in outline, thin, relatively wide, and of medium length. It is pressure flaked across both faces, and sometimes it is ground. The base is square with a tendency to be concave. The notches are small and expanding. The point is delicate looking and well made. It is of fairly rare occurrence in the valley as a whole but nowhere else is it reported in larger quantities, although the variety exists in a broad geographical area, according to illustrations in regional literature.

In the western portion of the Southeast and in the Midwest, side-notched points that are very similar to Hickory Ridge side-notched (Figure 5.3g–j) became characteristic by around 4000 B.C. Related types are Big Sandy in Tennessee (Lewis and Lewis 1961) and Alabama, Graham Cave in Missouri (Klippel 1971), and Godar in Illinois (Jeffries and Butler 1982). Points are fairly abundant in the lowlands, in contrast to what has been recovered representative of the period 7500–4000 B.C. They are not as abundant as points dated to the post-3000 B.C. Late Archaic.

Essential attributes of the Hickory Ridge type are as follows: The point exhibits wide side notches and is almost triangular in basic outline. Length usually varies between 30 and 60 mm; width is around 25–35 mm, and thickness is about 7–9 mm. Both faces exhibit the relatively large preform flaking pattern. Lateral edges are steeply retouched; the angle of the lateral edge varies around 70–80°. The basic function might have been as a knife. The base is squared with a tendency for a slight concavity. It is normally basally ground. Tips sometimes are needle-like.

COMMENTS ON THE HYPSITHERMAL ARCHAIC

A warmer, drier climatic period existed during a period dating from about 7000 to 3000 B.C. Prairie developed during this period, replacing a significant portion of the lowland mixed oak forest. Human populations evidently responded to this environmental change by shifting permanent settlements to the uplands and major stream valleys, primarily those in the Ozark Escarpment. Most of the valley lowlands became a hinterland that was exploited less extensively than it was before or after the Hypsithermal. The lowlands were not abandoned; they were just used infrequently.

The evidence available for testing these ideas is not conclusive but is supporting. Around 7250 B.C. smaller river channels and fewer recognized artifacts became characteristic. Although Dalton artifacts are plentiful, artifacts dated to between 7500 and 3000 B.C. are rare. Those dated to 6000–4000 B.C. are very rare. Those dated to 4000–3000 B.C. are more prevalent than earlier ones, which correlates positively with a lessening of the severe conditions of the Hypsithermal and population increase in the lowlands. In addition, many point styles are more western than strictly eastern in tradition, which is not surprising given the expansion of prairies into the Central Valley. Yet the adaptive responses continued to be eastern Woodland, not Plains–Prairie. For instance, the Hardin point is a variant of the Scottsbluff tradition. Unlike Scottsbluff, which was designed for penetrating, Hardin was designed for cutting.

Adjustments to changing drier conditions are also documented by archaeological excavations at upland Ozark Highland sites in Missouri. A major shift from a forest habitat to grasslands was shown by pollen cores collected at Rodgers Shelter in central Missouri (McMillan 1976). Human response to this change is reflected in bone remains recovered from the shelter. Fauna changed from forest edge species such as deer to grassland vertebrates such as bison, pronghorn, kit fox, and pocket mouse between 6000 to 4500 B.C. Reinterpretation of data recovered from Graham Cave, Missouri also show deforestation during the mid-Holocene indicated by sedimentological and faunal changes (McMillan and Klippel 1981:237). There was a corresponding shift from an emphasis on forest species such as squirrel and raccoon to forest edge species.

The population in the Central Valley was small, probably not much more than 300 or so, at the beginning of the period. This figure is based on the estimate that only a half dozen or so Dalton bands were present by about

8000–7500 B.C. After the end of the Hypsithermal period the valley population increased significantly, up to 5 and 10 times its earlier numbers, judging from the frequency of Late Archaic remains. Much of this increase may have taken place at the end of the Hypsithermal, since reforestation of the lowlands introduced a new ecological habitat into which to expand for permanent residency.

Two important demographic events, then, evidently took place during this period. One was the population shift from large territories within the valley lowlands into the small territories of Ozark stream valleys. The second was a later increase in population and subsequent expansion of permanent camps and villages into lowland territories of sizes comparable to those in the Ozarks. These latter continued to be utilized.

REFERENCES

Chapman, Jefferson
    1977   Archaic period research in the Lower Little Tennessee River Valley. *University of Tennessee Department of Anthropology Report of Investigations* 18.

Coe, Joffre
    1964   The formative cultures of the Carolina Piedmont. *Transactions of the American Philosophical Society* 54(5).

Frison, George C.
    1978   *Prehistoric hunters of the High Plains.* New York: Academic Press.

Jeffries, Richard W., and Brian M. Butler (editors)
    1982   The Carrier Mills archaeological project: Human adaptation in the Saline Valley, Illinois. *Southern Illinois University, Carbondale Center for Archaeological Investigation Research Paper* 33.

King, James E.
    1981   Late Quaternary vegetational history of Illinois. *Ecological Monographs* 51:43–62.

Lewis, Thomas, and Madeline K. Lewis
    1961   *Eva: An Archaic site.* Knoxville, Tenn.: University of Tennessee Press.

McMillan, R. Bruce
    1976   Cultural change and environmental change at Rodgers Shelter, Missouri. *In prehistoric man and his environments,* edited by W. Raymond Wood and R. Bruce McMillan, pp. 211–232. New York: Academic Press.

McMillan, R. Bruce, and Walter E. Klippel
    1981   Post-glacial environmental change and hunting–gathering societies of the Southern Prairie Peninsula. *Journal of Archaeological Science* 8:215–245.

Mason, Ronald J., and Carol Irwin
    1960   An Eden–Scottsbluff burial in northeastern Wisconsin. *American Antiquity* 26:43–57.

Perino, Gregory
    1971   Guide to the identification of certain American Indian projectile points. *Oklahoma Anthropological Society Special Bulletin* 4.

Saucier, Roger
    1974   Quaternary geology of the Lower Mississippi Valley. *Arkansas Archeological Survey Research Series* 6.
    1981   Current thinking on riverine processes and geologic history as related to human settlement in the Southeast. *Geoscience and Man* 22:7–18.

Webb, Clarence H., Joel L. Shiner, and E. Wayne Roberts
  1971   The John Pearce site (16CD56): A San Patrice site in Caddo Parish, Louisiana. *Bulletin of the Texas Archeological Society* **42**:1–49.
Wright, Henry E.
  1976   The dynamic nature of Holocene vegetation, a problem in paleoclimatology, biogeography, and stratigraphic nomenclature. *Quaternary Research* **6**:581–596.

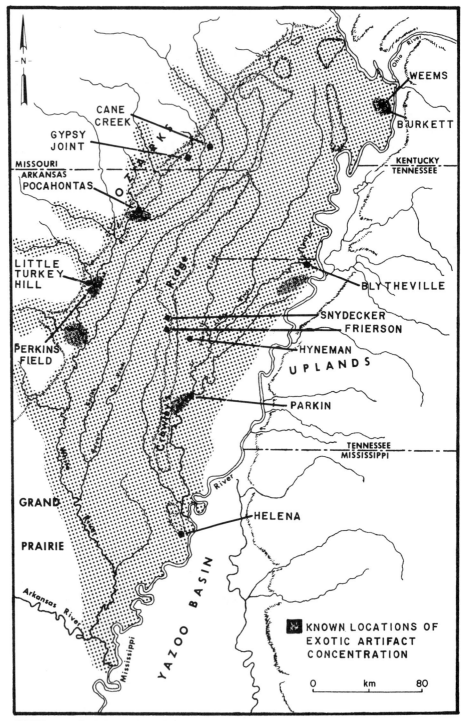

FIGURE 6.1. Distribution of the Poverty Point period population in the Central Mississippi Valley.

6

Archaic Expansion
(3000–500 B.C.)

Geographical expansion out of the uplands began within the latter part of the Hypsithermal (4000–3000 B.C.). Grasslands gave way to more deciduous forests, which was favorable for an increase in game and wild plant foods. This change was associated with less severe drought conditions. Crowley's Ridge seems to have once again become an important upland for settlement.

Human habitation of the lowlands expanded and intensified during the period (Figure 6.1). The development of Meander Belt 4 took place during 3000–500 B.C.. As portions of Meander Belt 3 became isolated, permanent occupation seemingly expanded into those areas. If there was occupation within the active portions of the meander belts, it probably has been buried or destroyed.

This period is known as Late Archaic for most of the eastern United States. Regionally, it is called the Poverty Point period, named after the impressive Poverty Point site located in extreme northeast Louisiana (Webb 1977). This site is around 150 ha in total size and contains a large mound approximately 21 m high and 150 m long, as well as a smaller one. The residential portion of the site is crescent shaped and consists of six ridges arranged in rows in five segments almost like the shape of an amphitheater, with the large mound in back and a stream, Bayou Macon, in front. Extremely elaborate artifacts are known to have been collected at the site, far outshining most of the contemporaneous remains in the Central Valley. Poverty Point objects in the Central Valley, for instance, are not so nearly varied and attractive as those at the Poverty Point site. The characteristic Jaketown microlith industry is completely absent farther north. Fiber-tempered pottery and human clay figurines also are absent in the Central Valley. Although steatite is present in the valley, whole vessels and even decorated steatite sherds have been recovered at Poverty Point sites to the south but not in the Central Valley. Plain and decorated plummets and effigy beads and other ground-stone objects are a southern rather than a northern characteristic. The Central Valley is peripheral to this very exotic culture, but there are definite similarities.

There are no radiocarbon dates from Poverty Point period sites in the Central Valley. The Poverty Point period is normally dated to around 1700–500 B.C. in Louisiana. Recent work in Mississippi at the Denton site, where rich lapidary-industry examples dated to 3000 B.C. and earlier, extends one of the primary characteristics of Poverty Point culture back in time (Connaway 1977). This work forms the basis for the dating used here.

Evidently interregional and intraregional trade in exotic artifacts and material was increasing in intensity throughout the period. Although exotic stone artifacts were made as early as 6000 B.C., the "lapidary industry" is most characteristic of the Poverty Point period in the valley. Nicely made beads, "bannerstones," grooved axes, celts, adzes, "plummets," and other items have been found. Vessels made of steatite also are represented in the latter part of the period. Arkansas novaculite was imported in small quantities from the Hot Springs region, but most of the lithic resources utilized are found in the uplands within or immediately adjacent to the Central Valley. Marine shell is found at sites for the first time during this period.

ARTIFACTS

In the Poverty Point period there was a tremendous increase in artifacts and sites compared with previous periods. This increase may be partly due to the 2500 years making up this period. However, it primarily arose from a significant increase in the lowland population and to seasonal exploitation of the environment by widely dispersed groups.

Indications are that this period was very rich indeed in terms of artifacts. Extrapolation from outside the Central Valley is necessary for identifying specific artifacts. Some of these are also characteristic of Early Woodland and Middle Archaic. Practically every basic artifact class associated with Late Archaic in the eastern United States has been found in the Central Valley. The following discussion highlights the more characteristic artifacts.

Three basic kinds of points date the successive subperiods of the Late Archaic. They are, in order of succession: *Big Creek* (3000–2000 B.C.), *Burkett* (2000–1000 B.C.), and *Weems* (1000–500 B.C.). The latter continues as a type throughout the later Tchula period of 500 B.C.–0.

The Big Creek point is bulbous based, often with a needle-like tip (Figure 6.2a–b). It is a wide corner-notched point and often exhibits prominent barbs and a wide convex base. Size ranges from 3 to 6 cm long, 2 to 4 cm wide, and around 1 cm thick. The overall flaking pattern on better-made points tends to be parallel, lamellar-shaped scars that meet at the central ridge of each face.

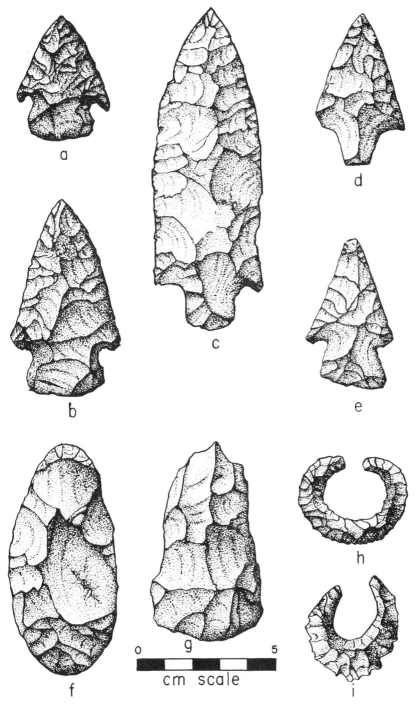

FIGURE 6.2. Chipped-stone artifacts characteristic of the Poverty Point period. (a)–(b) Big Creek point. (c) Burkett point. (d) Gary point of Arkansas novaculite. (e) Weems point. (f) Adz. (g) Celt. (h)–(i) Crescents. [(c) Courtesy of Arkansas State University Museum; (a), (b), (d)–(g), (i) courtesy of the Arkansas Archeological Survey.]

Variations include thicker points that still retain a preform flaking pattern. Since only surface-collected samples form the basis for defining the type, little is known about actual variation of this category. The point is very prevalent and is found almost everywhere in the Central Valley. It was named after a creek that flows near Jonesboro, Arkansas.

The dating of the Big Creek point is based on several considerations. First, it belongs in the Williams point cluster, which is considered a general Late Archaic style (Bell 1960:96). A few Big Creek–like points were found at the Denton site in Mississippi. Radiocarbon dates at this site indicate a time period of around 3500–3000 B.C. Some Big Creek–like points also form part of the Godar assemblage at the Black Earth site in Illinois, radiocarbon dated at around 4000–3000 B.C. (Jeffries and Butler 1982). It is hypothesized that the Big Creek point developed from the Hickory Ridge point around 3000 B.C. It is also apparent to us that it in turn developed into the Burkett point sometime around 2000 B.C.

The Burkett point is named after the Burkett site in the Cairo Lowland (Chapman 1980:306; Figure 6.2c). It resembles points in the Ledbetter–Pickwick cluster of Tennessee and Alabama (Bell 1960:66), which dates it to the general period of 2000–1000 B.C. Another point type that belongs in this general cluster is Etley (Chapman 1975:246), which is prominent in Illinois.

Typical Burkett points exhibit narrow straight stems, prominent shoulders, and recurved body edges. The overall flaking pattern is similar to that of the Big Creek type. Variations include contracting and rounded stems, attributes that merge with varieties of "Gary" points. The latter occur over a wide area but are particularly prominent west of and south within the valley. They probably are essentially contemporaneous with Burkett but are so nebulous in definition and temporality at the present time that they are not very useful in the Central Valley in keying specific complexes (Figure 6.2d). Burkett points range around 4–8 cm long, 2–4 cm wide, and .5–1 cm thick.

Named after another site in the Cairo Lowland (R. Williams 1974:19), the Weems point extends into the initial Woodland (Tchula) period (Figure 6.2e). It is an expanded stemmed, barbed point style. It belongs to a cluster or family of points that include Wade in Alabama (Cambron and Hulse 1964:A-84), Dyroff in Illinois (Emerson 1980), and several formally named styles to the south and west. The period of time indicated is approximately 1000 B.C.–0. Weems points vary around 4–6 cm long, 2.5–4 cm wide, and .5–1 cm thick. The overall flaking pattern is crude, but this might be due to the reworking of broken points. One variation within a Woodland context is a very finely knapped style made on thermally treated chert.

Gary points continue in time, and variations of other points appear to be present. This period seems to be a time of expanding population, possibly resulting in greater variation in basic point styles. Resharpening, due to distance from upland resources, may also be a variable operating against overall stylistic homogeneity at this time. Or, since we lack good temporal control, much of the observed variation may simply result from the plow-zone mixture of samples.

Besides points, the most characteristic chipped-stone artifacts are the adz and celt (Figure 6.2f–g). They tend to be relatively small and occur in large numbers. The term *celt*, from the Latin *Celtis*, chisel, is used by archaeologists to designate ungrooved axes. One strange type of adz is an unifacially flaked cobble. This latter occurs rarely and is restricted geographically.

Small chipped crescent-shaped bifaces are rare but persistent finds at Late Archaic sites (Figure 6.2h–i). The two tips of the crescent are often ground, possibly for hafting. The inner edge is often steeply retouched, as if backed. The curved outer edge sometimes is serrated and evidently was a cutting edge. Most specimens are relatively small, 3–4 cm in maximum dimension. Crescents found in Oregon have been interpreted by Dewey Dietz (1981) as beaked engraving tools used on bone. This explanation is a distinct possibility in the Central Valley, especially since elaborate engraved bone does exist on this time horizon elsewhere in the eastern United States.

A "lapidary industry" is characteristic of most of the eastern United States during Late Archaic. The Mississippi Valley is particularly noted for its stone beads. In particular, the northwest corner of Mississippi and the northeast corner of Louisiana seem to have excelled in the production of plain and effigy beads (Connaway 1977; Webb 1977). In Mississippi carved and polished stone turtle effigies dated around 3000 B.C. have also been found.

Using the term *lapidary* to refer to the nicely made ground-stone artifacts of the Late Archaic is really misleading in several ways. Few were actually made of "precious gems." They were not "cut" and "polished" but most often were chipped and abraded and then polished. They were not manufactured by an "artificer." Rather, they were the product of a basic household economy. There were no skilled specialists involved, only solid craftsmen in most households who could combine skill and patience to make these artifacts. "Bannerstones" and beads represent the best of the art, but axes, celts, adzes, plummets, gorgets, and other items were produced with the same basic technology.

We cannot overemphasize the patience necessary to make bannerstones and stone beads. The drilling process had to be done precisely and would have taken considerable time. There were no true craft specialists in Late Archaic society, but there probably was, as earlier, a lot of leisure time. *Household economy* means that each household had the potential to produce such artifacts. It is possible that only certain persons were best suited by temperament and skill to manufacture beads and bannerstones and that some of these may have been the shamans or "big-men" as well. But it is not expected that an individual only made bannerstones or beads and for this was supported by society. Instead, he would have made beads in addition to his usual tasks of hunting, tool manufacture, quarrying, and house repair. The respect earned by manufacturing such items might have helped make him a big-man, a leader of the tribe.

These lithic artifacts emphasize the large gap that exists in the artifact inventory. In particular, finely crafted objects of wood and fabric would have been present. Good artisans do not limit their craft to only certain materials; rather, we see only what has been preserved (Harrington 1960).

Perforated and polished bannerstones almost certainly functioned as atlatl weights on spear throwers (Figure 6.3a). The bow and arrow were not yet present, and the spear thrower was the major weapon used throughout almost all of the Archaic and Woodland periods. It may even have been present in Paleo-Indian times, possibly brought into the New World by the earliest immigrants. Even bone atlatl hooks are present in the Poverty Point period (Figure 6.3b).

A variety of bannerstone styles exist in the Central Valley and date throughout the Late Archaic and a considerable part of the immediately preceding Hypsithermal Archaic period. These bannerstones are made of local cherts and quartzites and a variety of igneous rock and "claystone." Recognized blanks have been found abraded into shape, and on some even drilling with a cane drill had commenced (Figure 6.3c–d). Whether they were predominantly chipped into preliminary form or made from cobbles that needed little modification is not definitely known.

There seem to be four major kinds of perforated weights found in the Central Valley. It is apparent that major styles succeeded one another through time, but the specific relationships are obscure. Two forms date to the Hypsithermal period. The crescent-shaped weight is dated to generally around 6000–5000 B.C. These are rare in the Central Valley. Tubular weights are thought to date around 5000–4000 B.C. They are very rare in the Central Valley; in fact, a typical early tubular weight has not been recorded for this region.

A unique bannerstone found in northeast Arkansas is essentially tubular with a bird (duck?) effigy mounted upon it. It could date as early as 5000 B.C. but probably dates much later (Figure 6.3g). Many of the bannerstones are stylized effigies of birds, mostly falcon-like, in flight or attack. Presumably this was a magical theme to help ensure the true flight of a spear.

The prismatic or triangular weight category may date as early as 4000 B.C. (Figure 6.3e). The form seems to have persisted up to about 2000–1500 B.C. Variations of the basic form include the "humped," "triangular," "hourglass," and "single face bottle." The basic triangular form is the most common reported. Association outside the valley is with side-notched points in Illinois (Godar) and Wisconsin (Osceola). In Mississippi, this form was found with Denton points and Big Creek-like points. Radiocarbon assays indicate a dating around 3000 B.C. An instance of association with Etley points reported in Illinois could mean that this form persisted later than 2000 B.C.

The rectangular form exhibits less variation than the triangular form, a

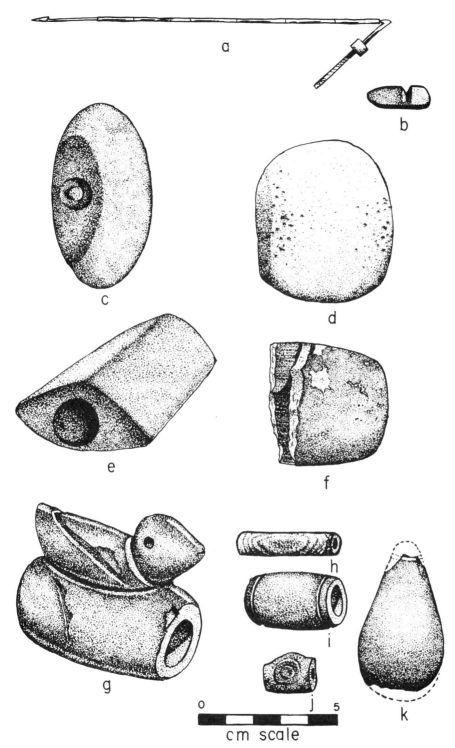

FIGURE 6.3. The Archaic lapidary industry. (a) Atlatl or spear thrower. (b) Bone atlatl hook. (c)–(d) Atlatl weight preforms or blanks. (e) Prismatic or triangular atlatl weight. (f) Rectangular atlatl weight. (g) Effigy atlatl weight. (h)–(j) Stone beads. (k) Hematite plummet. [(b), (c), (f), (h)–(k) courtesy of the Arkansas Archeological Survey; (e) courtesy of Arkansas State University Museum; (g) courtesy of Gordon Rice.]

possible indication of a more restricted period of time (Figure 6.3f). Both forms occur relatively commonly in the Central Valley. The reported Weems site assemblage in the Cairo Lowland contains only the rectangular form, indicating that this form postdates 2000 B.C. However, the rectangular form has been reported associated with Godar points in Illinois, so it could predate 3000 B.C.

There are basically two types of stone beads found in the Central Valley (Figure 6.3h–j). The simplest was made upon the cylindrical core left from drilling a bannerstone. The core was then centrally drilled. A second type was made from scratch, and there are three kinds: One is plain; the second is engraved, sometimes quite elaborately; and the third is an effigy, usually of the cicada. Most beads are made of local chert, but a variety of materials are utilized, and some may be nonregional. We do not know the specific time periods for each of these bead categories.

Effigy beads tend to be cicada effigies. The cicada, noted for its vitamin-supplement properties, is a mysterious insect that burrows into the ground for several years and then emerges to fly in the air and make incredible noise. Anomalies similar to this one were important in historic southeastern beliefs (Hudson 1976) and undoubtedly were already prominent in the ideology of the Late Archaic.

Plummets were usually made of hematite from the Ste. François Mountains or the Ozark Highlands, but occasionally a less heavy igneous stone was used (Figure 6.3k). Shaped like a surveyor's plumb bob, they seem to have functioned as bola stones. The bola is a device whereby stones are attached to individual thongs tied together at their ends and thrown at flying birds. At contact, the stones revolve around the bird, effectively entangling it with the attached thongs. Plummets are very rarely found in the Central Valley lowlands. They are much more common northward in Illinois and in southwest Arkansas and at Poverty Point. If we are correct in inferring their use as bolas for waterfowl, either other bola weights were used or there was another method of capture developed by these Late Archaic peoples.

Grooved axes are probably one of the most characteristic artifacts for the Late Archaic (Figure 6.4a). They are rare in the Central Valley as well as throughout the Southeast. When they occur, they almost invariably are of the full-grooved type and may predate the Late Archaic. Some were made of a chert that subsequent to manufacture has weathered into a chalky substance. Apparently, the basalts of the Ste. François Mountains were not yet being heavily exploited. Archaic ground-stone celts (ungrooved axes) and adzes seem to be rare as well. Heavier cutting implements were knapped for the most part from local cherts and not processed through a final grinding step in manufacture.

Blocked-end tubular pipes that may have functioned as shaman blowers or sucking tubes occur rarely. Gorgets (two-holed pendants) also have been found rarely. Steatite vessel fragments occur very rarely (Figure 6.5). To date, discoveries have been restricted to the meander belt portion of the valley and to the

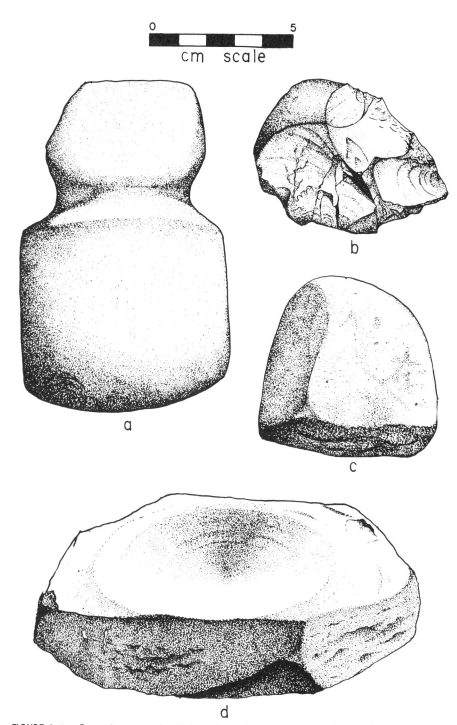

FIGURE 6.4. Ground-stone and cobble artifacts characteristic of the Poverty Point period. (a) Grooved axe. (b) Chopper. (c) Pestle. (d) Mortar. [Courtesy of the Arkansas Archeological Survey.]

FIGURE 6.5. Steatite vessel fragments. [Photograph courtesy of the Department of Anthropology, National Museum of Natural History, Smithsonian Institution.]

White River floodplain in the southern region. No fiber-tempered pottery has yet been reported in the Central Valley. Containers probably were restricted to gourds, wooden bowls, and basketry.

Three very characteristic cobble tools are related to the processing of wild plant foods: a chert cobble modified into a chopper by percussion, and a quartzite or hard sandstone cobble modified into a pestle to be used in conjunction with a quartzite mortar (Figure 6.4b–d). The chopper probably functioned as a vegetable dicer similar to those found in the northwestern United States. Stylistically they range from cobbles with crude working edges at one end to more extensively worked bifaces, usually with a weathered cortex or truncated backing to protect the hand. The typical pestle is a truncated oval cobble with a shallow pitted depression on each face. The truncated end was used for pounding. One face often exhibits striations and polish resulting from grinding. The depressions probably functioned to allow a better grasp of the pestle.

Portable stone mortars, often around 30–40 cm across, are known to date only to this general time period. When one is identified as dating significantly later, the artifact in question is invariably a trough abrader used to grind the final shape of heavy basalt and chert cutting tools. We do not know to how early in the Archaic stone mortars date in the Central Valley.

The most characteristic Late Archaic artifact in the valley, often used as a horizon style, is the "Poverty Point object," named after the type site in Louisiana where they occur in immense numbers (Webb 1977). They are made of clay in a biconical shape as well as a notched or grooved, roughly spherical shape in the Central Valley (Figure 6.6a–f). Poverty Point objects are often around 5–6 cm in size, rarely much larger. Often they are fragmented, from both use and postdepositional disturbance. The variety and frequency here is not on the level observed in Mississippi and Louisiana.

Poverty Point objects functioned as the heating element for earth ovens. The earth oven or cooking pit is a simple device (Driver and Massey 1957: 233). First, a pit is excavated. Its base may be lined with clay and then fired to hold water for steaming or simply to hold the heat better. Heat-retaining elements outside the valley are normally stone, preferably limestone (Morse 1967:15). Sandstone is a fairly good heat retainer, and chert is the least desirable (Figure 6.6g–h). In the valley lowlands south of the Ohio River, small clay objects were substituted for stone, although sandstone and cherts were used as well. The heating elements were heated, then placed into the pit with wrapped food, and the pit was then covered with dirt. Steaming was caused by pouring water on top of the filled pit. This water changed to steam on contact with the heating elements. A fire could be built on top of the filled-in pit to aid heat retention within. This is a significant cultural change in cooking techniques.

Conch shell, gathered in the Gulf of Mexico, was traded over most of the eastern United States at this time, and the Central Valley was included within this network. Shell beads have been found at several sites. A unique specimen is an elaborately incised shell found by Moore (1910:355–357) at Little Turkey Hill (Figure 6.7a).

The "Little Turkey Hill Cup" is normally considered Hopewellian in date (Phillips and Brown 1978:162–163). However, stone and bone Poverty Point artifacts exhibit similar artistic treatment (Webb 1977:Fig. 24, 26). Furthermore, the other artifacts recovered by Moore at Little Turkey Hill are characteristically Archaic. Two possible turtle carapace rattles have been reported (Moore 1910:355), and we recovered a "shaman's sucking tube" made from a human femur (Morse 1977; Figure 6.7b). Deer antler and bone were used for manufacturing a number of items, including antler batons for chipping stone (Figure 6.7c).

TYPES OF SITES

A variety of sites are known for the Poverty Point period in the Central Valley. They range from prominent middens to lithic locations. These latter range from isolated artifacts to long stretches of chipping debris. These sites can be best understood in terms of a seasonally nomadic settlement pattern. In

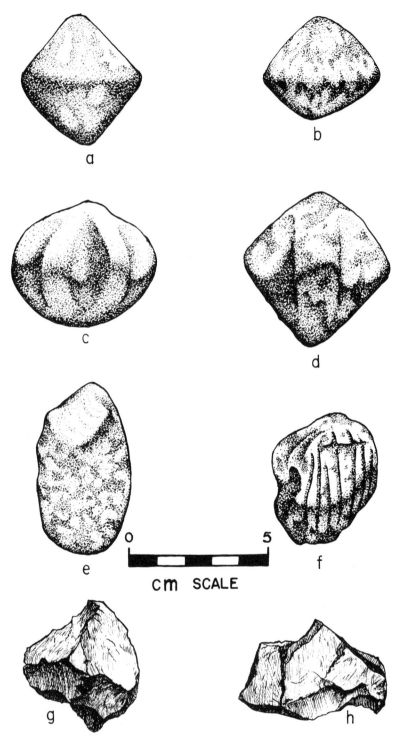

FIGURE 6.6. Earth oven elements found in Feature 7, Hyneman site, Arkansas. (a)–(f) Poverty Point objects. (g)–(h) Fire-cracked chert. [Courtesy of the Arkansas Archeological Survey.]

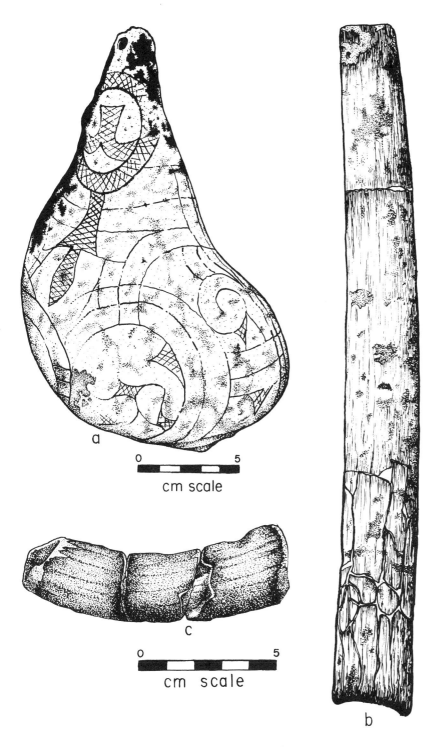

FIGURE 6.7. Bone tube and incised shell dated to the Poverty Point period. (a) Incised shell from Little Turkey Hill, Arkansas. (b) Bone "sucking" tube made from a human femur from Snydecker site, Arkansas. (c) Antler baton found at the Frierson site, Arkansas. [(a) Courtesy of The Academy of Natural Sciences, Philadelphia; (b), (c) courtesy of the Arkansas Archeological Survey.]

all human cultures the year is divided by seasons, which cause fluctuations in the animal and plant populations that comprise food resources. Family groups are expected to have moved seasonally to where resources were most available. Within a small territory older, younger, and infirm individuals would not have had to move with the group. A cyclical seasonal round of activities would have allowed reoccupation of certain sites at times of seasonal nucleation, resulting in large lithic scatters and in deeper midden sites. Dispersal of household units during periods or seasons of sparse and scattered resources would have helped create small lithic scatters, including single, isolated artifacts.

A new type of site, the midden, appeared in the Poverty Point period. Middens are moundlike in appearance and made up of dark, organic, rich soil incorporating numbers of artifacts. Bone and shell have been preserved because of the artificially increased alkalinity of the naturally acid soil. Fire-cracked rock and lithic debitage are present in significant amounts. Little Turkey Hill is an example of a midden site. It is located near the confluence of the Strawberry and Black rivers and was excavated by C. B. Moore in 1910. The dark midden contained flexed burials, points, a turtle carapace (rattle?), conch-shell disk beads, stone beads, a decorated stone tube, and an engraved conch shell. At a nearby site known as Harter Knoll, Moore found a bannerstone and more shell and stone beads. At the Perkins's Field site, located closer to the Black River, he found a stone tubular pipe, a "lancepoint," numerous points, hammerstones, debitage, and four bone artifacts including a bipointed one 14.5 cm long. These artifacts together form a fairly typical Late Archaic assemblage.

These definite midden sites are relatively small, usually around .05 ha (.13 acre), but several may be clustered closely together. At the Frierson site near Jonesboro, four such areas were within 100 m or so of one another (Figure 6.8). These sites tend to be on top of natural knolls, undoubtedly for the better drainage afforded by the silty or sandy soil, in contrast to clayey soils of lower elevations. Test excavations at one of the Frierson knolls indicated the presence of flexed burials and a possible house floor. A bannerstone was also found at Frierson. In Butler County, Missouri, near Cave Creek, Bruce Smith test excavated one of several similar midden sites located near one another and found flexed burials, conch-shell beads, a reel-shaped gorget, hematite, a possible turtle shell rattle or vessel, a full-grooved axe, worked bone and antler, and various points and other lithic debris. Another cluster of sites near Jonesboro was tested and produced a sucking tube made from a human femur. The neighboring Burkett and Weems sites in the Cairo Lowland are multiple component. The Archaic occupations are characterized by Burkett and Weems points, bannerstones, and considerable lithic debris.

A Poverty Point component was discovered at the Gypsy Joint site in Ripley County, Missouri, during the excavation of a Middle period Mississippian farmstead (Smith 1978:31). Five artifacts associated with a human occipital probably represented a burial that had been extensively disturbed. A bro-

(a)

(b)

FIGURE 6.8. Poverty Point period midden at the Frierson site, Arkansas. (a) The midden "mound." (b) Burial at the base of the midden zone. [Courtesy of the Arkansas Archeological Survey.]

ken gray slate reel-shaped gorget, a chert drill, a large uniface, a small biface, and a large point were found there. Pit 1, located nearly, contained a flintknapper's tool kit consisting of a hammerstone, an antler baton, a beaver incisor, and three contracting-stemmed points.

Many midden sites cluster in the lowlands near the emergence of major streams from the Ozarks and Crowley's Ridge. This pattern indicates a basic watershed orientation of the societies involved, which allowed easy access to the uplands for lithic and other resources. James and Cynthia Price completed a survey along the Fourche River near Pocahontas, Arkansas. A total of six Archaic midden sites were recorded within about 80 km². Four are located in the lowlands, one is 3 km beyond the Ozark Escarpment, and the sixth is located 9 km upstream. Their survey suggests that these midden sites are usually in the lowlands but that some are located within the upland valleys.

A pattern of sites located within the lowlands adjacent to the meander belt developed during the Poverty Point period. This is the case with sites in the Cairo Lowland and sites near Blytheville that are situated on the braided stream surface adjacent to the meander belt. In the Parkin area sites exist even within the relict Meander-Belt-3 surface, although there are uplands readily accessible nearby, which differs from the situation in the Cairo Lowland. None of these sites is definitely known to be a midden, but the kinds of recorded artifacts are identical to those normally restricted to midden sites elsewhere.

Midden sites are currently interpreted as winter villages that were reoccupied over a period of several years by a maximum-size social group. Ceremonial activity is evident, manufacturing debris is present, and burials are located in midden sites, all of which support an equation of midden sites with winter villages. In addition, late fall, winter, and early spring constitute the period of maximum lowland resource availability. Communication between villages within the tribe would have been easiest in a lowland setting during the winter.

Winters are not severe enough to necessitate moving to narrow valleys, at least not often. Although the rainfall maximums are in winter and early spring, flooding is usually not a problem until spring when severe storms are characteristic. The winter rainfall maximum equates with the great duck and goose migration down the Mississippi flyway. Many species winter within or just south of the Central Mississippi Valley today. In this general area are "the largest mallard concentrations ever known in North America [Horn and Glasgow 1964:436]." The lowland environment is ideal for duck feeding.

Fishing is another expected economic activity. Flooded backswamps trap fish, and fast waters make catching fish easy. Netting, trotlines, and gigging were probably used. Various game animals are expected to have been hunted, but the white-tailed deer probably provided the bulk of derived protein. Deer are hunted most efficiently during the fall and winter.

Midden sites normally are the sites of exotic artifact discoveries, such as axes, pipes, stone beads, and bannerstones. In particular, there is much evidence of artifact manufacture at midden sites. This type of behavior is expected of winter villages, as evidenced by contemporary societies when this season provided the time and opportunity to schedule ceremonies, manufacture exotic artifacts, and conduct trade.

A variety of site types are classified as lithic scatters. Some are literally kilometers long, whereas others consist of a flake or two. Many can be classified by virtue of the kind of tools recovered. Large lithic scatters exist along ridges bordering streams in both the lowlands and uplands. Much of the debris seems to pertain to the manufacture of bifaces that were transported elsewhere for finishing, and often a great deal of apparent waste is evident. Lowland scatters near Crowley's Ridge are located near streams with gravel deposits. It is quite possible that stone was being rafted to open areas for primary working. Not all of these lithic scatters are necessarily Archaic, but many of the recovered points at lithic scatters are Archaic varieties. The lithic waste often is due to decortication of weathered cobbles or is the shatter of poor-quality stone.

Some upland sites differ. In the Ozarks, lithic debris often is found in small scatters along major streams, although the lithic sources are at the valley bluffs. This workshop activity seems to be associated with good fishing spots. In Crowley's Ridge, upland sites are divisible into those associated with points and scrapers and those associated with mortars, pestles, and choppers. These latter locations are presently interpreted as gathering sites where wild plant foods were processed.

Locations with numerous points and scrapers may be favorite hunting camps. Sites marked only by some sparse debitage may be "bivouacs"—areas occupied only once very briefly by one or a very few persons. Lithic scatters consisting of debitage, a point, or a scraper in swampy terrain can be interpreted as a hunting camp, possibly occupied once during the killing and butchering of a deer.

Along major streams on Crowley's Ridge one often encounters cobbles with a single flake removed to expose the unweathered chert. These apparently were "quarry waste." Nearby will be decortication flakes, perhaps detached from cobbles kept by the knapper. Sometimes other debitage is present, probably due to the knapper manufacturing a preform to decrease weight. Occasionally, one finds a broken preform, signaling an unsuccessful attempt to make a biface. In the Ozark Highlands, workshops exist near quarry areas and consist of all of this debris in much larger concentrations.

Populations may have fragmented into household groups to disperse within the watershed territory during early spring to early fall. Possibly during part of the summer, when resources would have been most scarce, the groups may have reunited at a summer village site. Until we know more about the environment at that specific time and have a better data base of sites and artifacts, including excavated floral and faunal remains, we can do little more than speculate from studies of similar kinds of contemporary societies.

At the confluence of the Strawberry River with the Black River are the midden sites reported by Moore. John House surveyed this area and found small, nonmidden habitation sites, and smaller lithic debitage sites were located here as well as the midden sites. Dan Morse and Sam Smith surveyed the proposed Bell Foley lake some 25 km upstream. They found lithic scatters along the river in places where fishing would have been good and at quarry sites in the bordering hills. Tim Klinger surveyed the headwaters of the Strawberry River and recorded what appear to be limited quarry and hunting locations. The amount of material recovered was much less in this last survey than in the Bell Foley survey, which indicates that fewer people were involved at this distance from the mouth of the river.

The uplands are expected to have been the site of quarry, fishing, and generalized hunting and gathering activities. The lowlands were not abandoned but probably were exploited during the year. As summer progressed, occupation upstream might well have been more desirable in order to escape the heat and insects of the lowlands and to concentrate on a succession of upland plants and turkeys, which flock together at this time. As fall approaches, deer are more vulnerable due to their rutting practices. The loss of deciduous leaves allows easier tracking. Persimmon, grapes, nuts, and other fall fruits become available in quantity even today.

THE DEVELOPMENT OF TRIBAL SOCIETY

Some time during the Archaic tribal society must have developed. After about 3000 B.C. there is evidence of behavior not easily explicable in terms of simple band society. This evidence is similar to that used to interpret the sociology of the Hopewellian tradition after A.D. 1. With the beginnings of the Woodland period, a better case can be made for tribal society because ceramics clearly indicate the presence of large geographical aggregates of otherwise autonomous sites. There is little difference between many of the Woodland and Archaic groups, except for ceramics and the increasing importance of horticulture to some. Hence it is probable that tribal society began within the Archaic. Band and tribal political systems probably did not coexist long within the same ecological zone, so the change must have been fairly rapid.

In contemporary patrilocal tribal societies (Sahlins 1968), the household unit consists of two or more married couples and children. This extended family is often made up of an older couple, married sons, daughters-in-law, children, unmarried daughters, and perhaps a very old paternal relative. This group is a basic economic unit, a diversified labor pool suitable for concentrated labor on a variety of simultaneous tasks.

Bands are made up of nuclear family units, although the entire band network may be viewed as a large extended family. This arrangement allows simple fluidity in a small population. Both bands and primitive segmentary tribes are organized for mobility. Bands may also produce exotic artifacts. The Eskimo and probably most, if not all, of the Upper Paleolithic in Europe are examples. Compared with bands, tribes are more complex sociologically, their household units are more formalized, and with them larger populations are possible.

Two significant demographic events appear to have occurred during the long Archaic period. Population increased and probably finally necessitated the development of a more complex sociopolitical organization. In addition, the Central Valley population was evidently displaced to the more restricted territories of the uplands by the events of the Hypsithermal. This demographic shock could have facilitated the development of tribal organization.

Idiosyncracies of the environment together with adaptation to smaller territories are characteristics associated with the contemporary segmentary tribe. The family is still the basic economic unit of production. It is more formalized and consistent than it is in band society and is also slightly larger in average size. Extended families are grouped into an autonomous community located within a relatively small territory. Families are often in a common village or a neighborhood of residences part of the year and dispersed during the remainder of the yearly cycle. Residential clustering in the Central Valley probably took place during the late fall, winter, and early spring, when most resource clustering takes place in the natural environment. Potential important food resources were ducks, fish, rutting deer, and many flora, from nuts to bulbs. A winter deciduous forest allows easier travel and better visibility, which are important in deer hunting. Winter is also a period of maximum wetness, which is important for net fishing and duck hunting, and is the period of maximum lowland resource availability. The autonomous community would have fragmented into individual extended family households during periods of scarce resources and periods of scattered resources. In contemporary societies exceptions to this rule were infirm people and infants.

The political structure of tribal organization is not very complex. Two important figures are the petty chieftain and the big-man. The first involves little or no authority and is normally an older respected male, often ranked highest in order of descent. The big-man is a male who became prominent by virtue of individual effort and personality. Such an individual does not have authority outside of his ability to convince. The autonomous segments of a segmentary tribe are held together by marriage and a common language. In contemporary examples communities are normally exogamous. Marriage ties between communities are more formal than they are in band society. Often they are guided by a clan system. Clans are also exogamous since clan membership implies common descent and hence incest by definition if marriage is allowed. This system makes marriage an instrument of tribal economies. Marriage ties between communities and between descent groups (clans) provide the threads that hold these groups together. These ties are crucial, as the political autonomy of communities generates tribal fragmentation.

In contemporary tribal societies religious ceremonies, particularly involving curing and purification, are conducted by the shaman, who acquired his or her calling by having a vision. Magic was necessary in a society not blessed with the germ theory of disease, dependent upon the vagaries of climate and edible items, and without any real understanding of modern science. However, all human societies have some knowledge of natural science and are not solely subject to magic.

Central Valley communities within small watersheds probably were autonomous and roughly comparable. They would have been intertwined within a tribal network held together by a descent system probably involving clans. It is not known how many tribes existed at this time. Later, in the ceramic periods, there is evidence of three tribal groups.

REFERENCES

Bell, Robert E.
  1960   Guide to the identification of certain American Indian projectile points. *Oklahoma Anthropological Society, Special Bulletin* **2**.
Cambron, James, and David Hulse
  1964   *Handbook of Alabama archaeology. Part I, point types.* Archaeological Research Association of Alabama.
Chapman, Carl
  1975   *The archaeology of Missouri, I.* Columbia: University of Missouri Press.
  1980   *The archaeology of Missouri, II.* Columbia: University of Missouri Press.
Connaway, John M.
  1977   The Denton site: A middle Archaic occupation in the northern Yazoo Basin, Mississippi. *Mississippi Department of Archives and History Archaeological Report* **4**.
Dietz, Dewey
  1981   More on crescents. *Screenings, Oregon Archaeological Society* **30**.
Driver, Harold, and William Massey
  1957   Comparative studies of North American Indians. *Transactions of the American Philosophical Society* **47**, Part 2.
Emerson, Thomas E.
  1980   The Dryoff and Levin sites: A Late Archaic occupation in the American Bottom. *FAI-270 Archaeological Mitigation Report* 24. University of Illinois Department of Anthropology, Urbana.
Harrington, M. R.
  1960   The Ozark bluff-dwellers. *Museum of the American Indian Heye Foundation Indian Notes and Monographs* **12**.
Horn, E. E., and Leslie L. Glasgow
  1964   Rice and waterfowl. In *Waterfowl tomorrow*, edited by Joseph Linduska, pp. 435–443. Washington, D.C.: U.S. Department of the Interior, Fish and Wildlife Service.
Hudson, Charles
  1976   *The southeastern Indians.* Knoxville, Tenn.: University of Tennessee Press.

Jeffries, Richard W., and Brian M. Butler (editors)

    1982   The Carrier Mills archaeological project: Human adaptation in the Saline Valley, Illinois. *Southern Illinois University, Carbondale Center for Archaeological Investigation Research Paper* **33**.

Moore, Clarence B.

    1910   Antiquities of the St. Francis, White and Black rivers, Arkansas. *Journal of the Academy of Natural Sciences of Philadelphia* **14**:255–364.

Morse, Dan F.

    1967   The Robinson site and shell mound Archaic culture in the Middle South. Unpublished Ph.D. dissertation, Department of Anthropology, University of Michigan, University Microfilms, Ann Arbor.

    1977   A human femur tube from Arkansas. *Arkansas Archeologist* **16, 17, 18**:42–44.

Phillips, Philip, and James A. Brown

    1978   *Pre-Columbian shell engravings.* Part 1. Peabody Museum Press, Harvard University.

Sahlins, Marshall

    1968   *Tribesmen.* Englewood Cliffs, N.J.: Prentice-Hall.

Smith, Bruce D.

    1978   *Prehistoric patterns of human behavior.* New York: Academic Press.

Webb, Clarence

    1977   The Poverty Point culture. *Geoscience and Man* **17**.

Williams, J. Raymond

    1974   The Baytown phases in the Cairo Lowland of southeast Missouri. *Missouri Archaeologist* **36**.

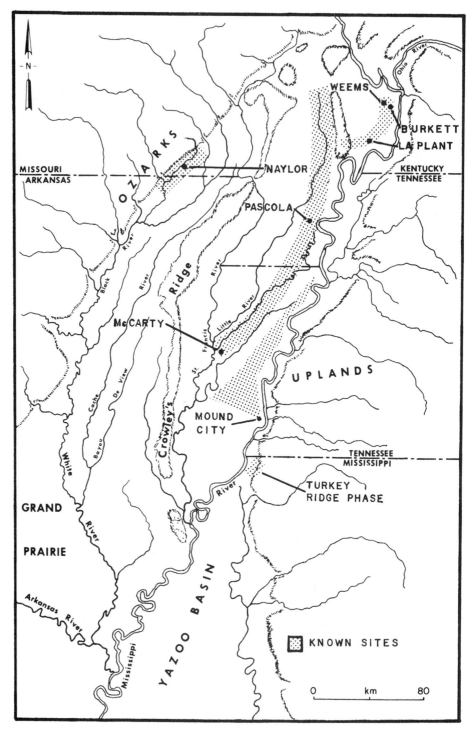

FIGURE 7.1. Tchula period sites and phases in the Central Valley.

7

Woodland Beginnings (500 B.C.–0)

Woodland is traditionally defined as that period when agriculture, burial mounds, and pottery first appear (Willey 1966:267; Griffin 1967:180). However, this traditional definition needs some modification because of recent advances in archaeology. The cultivation of squash and other cultigens began much earlier in the eastern United States (Chomko and Crawford 1978), but agriculture increased greatly in importance at or soon after the beginning of the Woodland period. The addition of a horticultural-based economy signals significant changes in sociological behavior. Burial mounds are most characteristic in the midwestern United States in early Woodland and are actually not prominent until Hopewellian times. They are evidence of a complex level of ceremonial behavior. Fiber-tempered pottery predates the Woodland period (Stoltman 1974:17). However, mineral-tempered pottery is the horizon marker for the Woodland period in the eastern United States. Pottery signals new kinds of cooking techniques and a more sedentary way of life.

The Woodland period in the Central Valley is most noted for the addition of ceramics to the basic trait list described for the Poverty Point period. These ceramics combine elements found northward in Illinois, southward in Mississippi and Louisiana, and eastward in Alabama. No fiber-tempered pottery has yet been recognized in the Central Valley. The earliest pottery is sophisticated, and both grog- (broken sherd) and/or clay-tempered and sand-tempered wares are present. In the Central Mississippi Valley this period is called the Tchula period. One radiocarbon date of 230 ± 290 B.C. was derived at the Burkett site (M–438). Another from the same site might date to this period also: A.D. 60 ± 240 (M–585).

Historical continuity from the local Archaic is evident in artifact styles of the Tchula. No new populations or apparently even significant waves of influence were involved. What did happen for the most part occurred at the same time in the regions surrounding the Central Valley in the Southeast and the Midwest.

There was continuation of the shift in the settlement pattern to a basic lowland orientation, which had begun in the Archaic. By this time, all of the modern lowlands were available for permanent occupation (Figure 7.1). Two coexisting cultural systems primarily associated with the two basic kinds of geological surfaces may have begun to develop. Sandy-paste pottery is associated most with the older braided stream surfaces, whereas clay- or grog-tempered pottery is most characteristic of sites located within or adjacent to the newer meander belts. After the Tchula period the distinction between these two pottery traditions becomes very pronounced. But in the Tchula period a sandy paste makes this Central Valley pottery technologically superior to more southern complexes known as Tchefuncte. True grog in temper may have developed primarily at the end of the Tchula period.

POTTERY MANUFACTURE

Pottery is important to archaeology. Pottery breaks easily and can be collected in large samples, and it reflects temporal change in style and motif. Broken pottery is not commercially valuable to collectors and is well preserved at sites. Archaeological reports dealing with the ceramic period are disproportionately weighted toward ceramic descriptions because of these factors.

Prior to the use of pottery, containers were manufactured of wood, basketry, gourds, skins, shells, and other items. The basic models for early pottery probably were bird nests and baskets and it should be of little surprise that the earliest pottery in the Southeast is tempered with fiber. The thermal alteration of the properties of clay and other substances had been known for a considerable time. After all, hearths are marked by the oxidized (red) clay upon which they were built and used. Earth ovens and their fired-clay Poverty Point objects were sophisticated cooking devices. Careful thermal alteration of chert had been practiced for millennia, and the consequence of being too impatient was well understood.

The essential inventions of pottery manufacture, however, were made outside of the Central Valley. The earliest pottery discovered here is sophisticated and decorated. Slight improvement of the technology was made during the Tchula and succeeding periods until a major breakthrough occurred with the onset of Mississippian, about A.D. 700–800. Until then, pottery identified as Woodland is very distinctive. This distinctiveness is largely technological and not simply stylistic.

Backswamp clay was the main ingredient for all Central Valley pottery vessels. This clay is deposited in slackwater situations such as floodplains beyond natural levees and lakes occupying relict river channels. Backswamp clay is composed of the finest particle sizes available. It exists virtually every-where within the lowlands and was easily available to the Central Valley inhabitants. Attempts to differentiate between the different classes of back-swamp clay by X-ray diffraction analysis have not been successful since the types of clay are all so similar to one another.

The clay may be collected dry by shallow excavation within a floodplain, or it may be collected wet from the bed of a lake. In either case, it must be wet for processing into a suitable pottery clay. Experimentation by Michael Mil-lion (Morse and Million 1980) has shown that dry backswamp clay is prac-tically impossible to process because it is so hard. A first step in processing involves the removal of coarse objects from the collected clay, including twigs, leaves, decomposed organic materials, ice-rafted pebbles, and shells. Many of the shells and much of the coarser vegetation items may be handpicked and the remainder removed by slowly sifting through a fine mesh net. No actual physi-cal exertion is necessary for this sifting. The clay can be allowed to slack naturally through the net into a trough full of water. The inclusions that might cause cracking later are removed while the clay particles are thoroughly wetted to increase workability.

Backswamp clays have a high shrink–swell ratio. Shrinkage is measured at about 12–14%, too high for manufacturing a vessel and allowing it to dry without cracking. The clay is also too sticky to manage effectively. Large amounts of coarse temper are therefore added to the clay to create an efficient pottery clay. In the Central Valley, the coarse inclusions included burned clay fragments, crushed potsherds, and sand. All were readily available within the lowlands. Sand is prevalent in the braided stream regions and was preferred in those regions over crushed sherd or grog temper. A typical sand-tempered sherd is about 25–33% sand by weight. This composition reduces shrinkage to around 9%, allowing a vessel to dry slowly without cracking. However, the weight of the paste is increased considerably by the addition of so much temper, and the clay is stiff and difficult to control, in turn restricting vessel shape considerably. In addition, the increased weight and lack of cohesiveness in the paste dictates that larger vessels be made with flat bases or conical bases so that the vessel will not collapse during manufacture. Conical bases on jars result from manufacturing the vessel at an angle to distribute weight to a larger portion of the vessel (Figure 7.2b). A basic conical shape may have been structurally necessary during the lifetime of the vessel as well. There have not been as many experiments on grog-tempered pottery as there have on sand-tempered ceramics, but very similar shapes are involved, and some of the same technological principles probably are applicable.

The discussion in this section concerns backswamp clays. In Crowley's Ridge and outside the Central Valley better pottery clays are available. As far as we know, the kaolin in Crowley's Ridge was never used, probably because it was not readily available before the extensive gravel removal made possible by mid-twentieth-century technology. No archaeologist can fully understand styl-

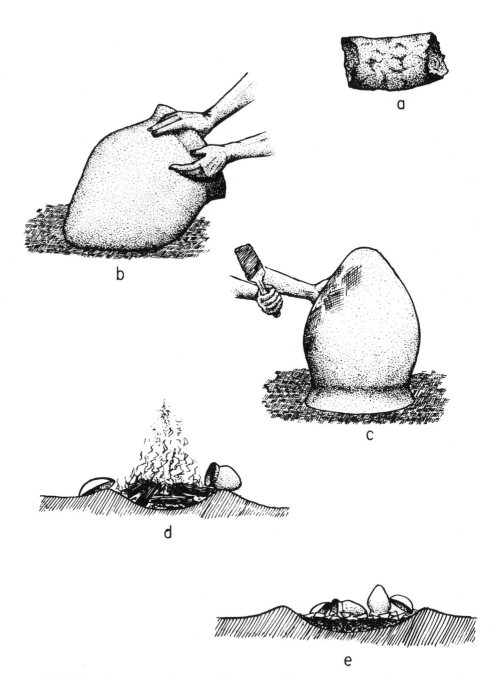

FIGURE 7.2. Pottery manufacture. (a) Pottery coil. (b) Making the jar. (c) Use of the paddle. (d) Starting the firing pit. (e) Vessels stacked for firing.

istic variation in ceramics unless he or she understands the underlying technology of those ceramics. Indians may not have understood the chemistry and physics of what they were doing, but they were well aware of what they were accomplishing and how to get those results.

Probably the most common vessel shape was the food bowl. At the same time, it is the rarest potsherd represented in any sample because it is significantly smaller than any other vessel class except for toy vessels. Food bowls tended to be about .75 liter in capacity, or slightly smaller. Woodland bowls tended to be plain throughout their existence. In addition, they seem to have been made for the most part by molding rather than by welding coils together. Molding without wheel turning restricts size and shape.

Jars were manufactured by the coiling technique. The coils were thick strips squeezed into shape (Figure 7.2a). The base of the jar was molded and the coil strips welded to the increasingly growing jar from the base up to the rim. If not well welded, vessels tended to break along the coil line. Welding was accomplished by using fingertips or a tool made of bone, wood, or cane. Sometimes rim strips were added to help strengthen that part of the vessel. Cord marking was characteristic in Early and Late Woodland times and was essentially restricted to the jar shape. Although a cord-wrapped paddle may have been used during actual construction of larger vessels, the observed cord-marked pattern and the accentuated pointed basal segment are the result of a final finishing step (Figure 7.2c). Cord-marking may have aided in the handling of jars, helping prevent their slipping from one's grasp. Smaller jars would have been used in direct-fire boiling of food, whereas the very large ones may have functioned as storage containers.

Serving bowls also existed. Another class of vessel was the toy pot, invariably in the shape of food bowls or jars. The Woodland potter probably was female, and girls would have learned their craft initially by pinching crude toy pots, although finer toy pots may have been made by their maternal elders. As we know from our field school experiences, one can learn to make a pot within a few weeks. Because of the inherent difficulty involved in manufacturing coarse-tempered pottery, we can conclude that Woodland potters as a group were excellent at their craft.

After the final construction, decoration may be added after the vessel has stiffened slightly. Incising, punctation, and variations of these techniques were applied. A simple wedge-shaped tool made of wood has been used by Doyle Gertjejansen of the Department of Fine Arts of the University of New Orleans to duplicate successfully Tchefuncte motifs. Slipping with a hematite-based (red) substance was also accomplished. Before decoration took place, the surface would have been scraped clean and even, probably with a wooden scraper, although bone or shell tools were also used rarely. Polishing was accomplished by rubbing with a smooth pebble after the vessel was hard.

The final step before firing is one that defeats most experimenters using backswamp clay. It involves a long period of slow and even drying, taking up to a month or more. Patience is a necessary trait. As moisture evaporates, the vessel is first kept in a moist environment before being allowed to dry in the open for short periods. If drying is not accomplished correctly, the vessel will crack during drying or break during firing. Artifact collections suggest that Indians rarely experienced difficulty during this phase of manufacture.

Firing was accomplished in shallow pits defined by a circle of spoil from excavating the pit. During the preliminaries, wood was burned in the pit to create coals to warm the pit and to dehydrate the pots, which were balanced on the spoil bank to prevent spalling of the vessel surface during firing (Figure 7.2d). Sherds probably were placed over the coals, vessels stacked on the sherds, and other sherds placed over the vessels to prevent direct contact with the fire (Figure 7.2e). Thatch and perhaps wood was burned over the whole for about an hour, and the vessels were then ready for use. Firing temperature was about 600°C. Although this procedure has been experimentally done only in conjunction with Mississippian pots, this basic firing technique probably existed during Woodland times as well.

Doyle Gertjejansen has recently experimented with Tchefuncte period pottery replication. According to his findings, these more-southern ceramics were relatively crude. They were not purposely tempered, nor was the clay wedged. The result was a very high attrition rate. The techniques of manufacture severely limited the size and shape of vessels. Small flat and tetrapodal bases were advantageous since there was less cracking of the vessel during drying than there was with larger bases. Many vessels did not survive firing and use after firing, but a firing design that used coals as the medium may be partly responsible. It is obvious that Woodland Tchefuncte pottery manufacture was a fairly difficult craft to master and that attrition was high.

In contrast, Tchula period pottery in the Central Valley was wedged and tempered; at least those sherds from the samples we have collected were so treated. These sherds almost invariably have some or quite a bit of sand inclusions in the paste. Furthermore, the cross sections of sherds do not show the natural lamination that Gertjejansen observed in his Tchefuncte sample. Central Valley ceramics are evidently technologically superior to Tchefuncte pottery.

The typical pottery for the Tchula period is cord marked on the exterior surface. Some fabric-impressed pottery also occurs. The diagnostic–decorated type is Cormorant Cord-Impressed (Phillips 1970:876–878). Punctation is also characteristic (S. Williams 1954:33). There is a great deal of similarity to Alexander pottery in Alabama and to Tchefuncte pottery in the Lower Mississippi Valley.

ENVIRONMENTAL SETTING

At the beginning of the Tchula period the Central Mississippi Valley was essentially modern in appearance. At approximately 800 B.C. the modern Meander Belt 5 system began. As in the previous Poverty Point period, there were two basic environments: meander belt and braided stream. The meander belt environment, however, had increased in total size, almost to its modern extent. Tchula was a period of increased warmth and moisture known as the Sub-Atlantic climatic period, but the precise environmental setting has not yet been reconstructed for the Central Valley.

The uplands became the hinterland for lowland populations during the Tchula period, and this pattern continued thereafter. There is strong cultural continuity from Poverty Point to Tchula and beyond into Marksville and Baytown. In particular, Poverty Point, Tchula, and Marksville constitute a continuum in behavior, and some sites contain components of two or all three of these periods. The Weems, La Plant, and Burkett (also known as O'Bryan Ridge) sites are located in the Cairo Lowland and existed during the late Poverty Point and the Tchula periods; Weems and La Plant also existed during the early Marksville period. During at least the latter part of the Poverty Point period, some groups may have constantly inhabited the lowlands. In the Tchula period this pattern of permanent lowland orientation may have been characteristic of most groups. In particular, it would have been difficult for groups existing adjacent to or within the modern meander belt to include upland regions within a seasonal migratory pattern. This apparent pattern of lowland orientation continued through the Marksville period and became very pronounced in the Baytown period, for which many lithic-poor sites are recorded.

Pottery is a key to our understanding of the Tchula period settlement pattern. Pottery was easy to manufacture, and the necessary materials were readily available wherever backswamp clays occurred. To make pottery, villages would necessarily have been located adjacent to such deposits. The meander belt regions would have become prime occupation locations, but backswamp deposits were present wherever there was a meandering stream or lake. Pottery containers had a distinct advantage over other types of containers, and a whole new cuisine would have been possible, with an emphasis on cooking of soups and stews. We do not know if early pottery was used for cooking, but circumstantial evidence indicates that it was. Pottery also implies some degree of residential permanence. It takes a month or so to allow a vessel to dry sufficiently for firing, if that firing is going to be completely successful. In addition, it would have been difficult to carry a number of pots from place to place.

Horticulture was probably important during the Tchula period. By *horticulture,* we mean an auxiliary economic technology involving cultigens. Marsh elder and sunflower are probable cultigens in the early Woodland elsewhere and were probably known to the inhabitants of the Central Mississippi Valley. Corn may have been added at this time (Yarnell 1976:271), but bone collagen studies indicate that it was not a central economic focus. Squash in the Archaic was primarily hollow, and the edible portion consisted mainly of seeds. Meaty varieties were developed during the Woodland period. Squash is easy to grow, and the meaty varieties are extremely rewarding for the amount of labor necessary to grow them.

Horticulture allowed a greater degree of predictability for plant resources and made summer–fall food readily available to the population. There was less reason to move the village. The adoption of a sufficient variety of cultigens to allow garden plots to be rotated annually would prevent continuity in insect life detrimental to a particular cultigen and depletion of soil nutrients. Fields probably were relatively small and kept up by a small proportion of the population, much as a modern backyard garden is maintained by many households. Small plots of land were cleared and burned most easily in the spring. Large trees shading a potential garden plot were killed by girdling. Last year's vegetation was dead and quickly burned as a low-density fire. Ashes and charcoal were easily mixed into the moist soil, and planting mounds were prepared. The easiest fields to prepare were those that were planted the previous year. Loamy forest soils were the most workable.

Population was concentrated in small dispersed villages during the Tchula period. The identification of definite sites has been a difficult process that is far from resolved. One problem is that a few very rare ceramic decorative types provide diagnostic identification. Cormorant Cord-Impressed is the major marker type. Tchefuncte Stamped is another marker type. Beyond that, a variety of punctated pottery motifs, tetrapodal and other variations of a flat base on jars, and exterior nodes punched into rim sherds with the interior hollows filled with pottery clay are characteristic of Tchula period assemblages. If the pottery collection from a site is small, only cord-marked and, rarely, plain potsherds will be present. This kind of pottery assemblage is also characteristic of the later Baytown period. There are many recorded small "Baytown" sites in the Central Valley, and it is entirely possible that some of these may actually belong to the Tchula period.

Tchula period sites probably exist over much of the Central Valley. The exception seems to be in the central portion of the braided stream surface east of Crowley's Ridge, which evidently did not become permanently occupied until the Baytown period. Certainly the immediately preceding preceramic terminal Poverty Point period is well represented within the Central Valley. Widely dispersed populations and sites, ceramic similarity to Baytown sites, smaller sites, and population mobility all could help disguise a Tchula expression. In addition, Tchula period sites may have been buried or destroyed because of Mississippi River course changes or levee construction.

A group of sites in the Cairo Lowland are classed together as Burkett phase by Williams (1954) and by Phillips (1970). O'Bryan Ridge is a braided-stream feature that extends well into the meander belt of the Cairo Lowland. The Burkett and Weems sites are located on this ridge (Griffin and Spaulding 1951). Both are characterized by clay- or grog-tempered Tchula ceramics. The La Plant site is located on Barnes Ridge, also a braided-stream feature adjacent to the meander belt. This site's Tchula ceramics are also clay- or grog-tempered. Ceramic relationships seem to be with Baumer in Illinois and with the Turkey Ridge phase in Mississippi. Nonceramic artifacts have not been identified.

The Pascola phase consists of sites to the south and west of the Cairo Lowland, along Little River (Williams 1954; Phillips 1970). The Pascola site is located a very few kilometers west of the junction of the braided stream and the meander belt, in the upper reaches of Right Hand Chute of Little River. The ceramics are typical Tchula but, unlike those in the Cairo Lowland, are sand tempered.

The McCarty site, a recently discovered site near Marked Tree, is also regarded as Pascola phase because of its predominant sand-tempered pottery. However, connecting sites in between the Missouri cluster of Tchula sites and the McCarty site have not yet been identified (the following section describes the setting and artifacts of the McCarty site). The site is situated almost twice as far from the meander belt as the Pascola site. Between the McCarty site and the meander belt are a series of relict channels of several abortive attempts by the Mississippi River to change its course, causing considerable confusion in any reconstruction of site setting.

Ceramics from the Mound City site complex just west of Memphis, suggest that it also had a Tchula component. It is difficult in such cases to discern just how much ceramic continuity there was into the Marksville period. Mound City is situated at the edge of the meander belt and adjacent to a large backswamp. Sherds, particularly Cormorant Cord-Impressed, indicative of Tchula components, have been reported from several locations along the meander belt to Missouri and westward almost to Parkin. These sherds are grog or clay tempered and not assignable to the Pascola phase, which is characterized by sand-tempered ceramics. We stress that the Tchula identification here is tentative. Artifacts recovered by surveys in this region may not have been identified correctly and sometimes are no longer available for scientific study. The closest relationship is to the Turkey Ridge phase in Mississippi, just south of Memphis (Phillips 1970).

Tchula sites should be widespread within the Western Lowlands. James Price has recorded a Tchula period occupation called the Grimes phase in the Naylor, Missouri area. The ceramics are similar to those reported for the Pascola phase.

Grog-tempered ceramics are associated with the meander belt, in contrast to sand-tempered ceramics, which are associated with the braided-surface drainages back from the meander belt. It is evident that two traditions of pottery temper are in existence in Tchula times. The McCarty site assemblage indicates that the Pascola phase, at least in the Marked Tree area, was an elaborate expression.

THE McCARTY SITE

In the spring of 1981 Jim McCarty of West Memphis notified us that an archaeological site had been found when a field near Marked Tree was being leveled to plant rice. This site produced the first complete assemblage of

Tchula period artifacts discovered to date in the Central Valley. A second component at the site was represented by a Mississippian "farmstead" dating around A.D. 1000–1050.

The McCarty site is part of a pattern of Tchula villages located near the junction of the braided surface and the meander belt. Modern drainage of this area where the McCarty site is located is to the Tyronza River, a tributary of the St. Francis River, located 3.2 km south. Little River is located about 8 km to the northwest. Between Little River and the McCarty site is Left Hand Chute of Little River, a post-Tchula period stream.

The precise setting of the site is a considerable surprise. It is located within a vast backswamp, probably the most inhospitable place in the lowlands for a permanent settlement. Although the major associated soil is high in natural fertility, there are severe problems with drainage and with maintaining tilth in backswamp clay. There was a small area of soil adjacent to the site on the north, which was more productive and easier to cultivate, according to the farmer. Modern farming in this area has been affected significantly by the New Madrid earthquake sand blows, which make uniform tillage over a large area very difficult. The presence of the Mississippian component is circumstantial evidence that a small area of prime land exists nearby.

The lack of an easily accessible lake or river channel is equally puzzling. Again, circumstantial evidence is necessary to postulate that such a feature once did exist. Fish bone and mussel shell occurred in relatively large numbers at the McCarty site.

The site is on a natural knoll and situated upon a sand substratum. This subsoil may be a sandbar separating two braided channels associated with a much earlier geological episode. A very long sand blow is immediately adjacent to the site and may actually cover the southern extent of the village. The soil is very characteristic of backswamp soil; it is hard when dry and sticky when wet. On the knoll itself, the soil is coarser than is usual with backswamp clays and even sandy, somewhat similar to a low-levee situation.

For the Tchula occupation, the attractions seemed to be: (a) backswamp soil for pottery manufacture; (b) standing water nearby for fish; (c) a small amount of acreage nearby for a garden plot; (d) a higher, better-drained village setting, (e) avenues, mainly waterways, to the ridge for lithics and to the Mississippi River for outside contact; and (f) a hardwood forest region within which to hunt game and to collect wild plant foods. The ecological diversity of this complex geological setting at a time of changing climate would have meant that this region was environmentally rich in vegetation and game.

Much of the site had been removed prior to our investigation, and an unknown portion of the village still exists beneath the earthquake sand blow on the southern end. A cluster of burials were found near the western side of the site. Most probably this represents a cemetery. In the center of the site and to the south were a large number of basin-shaped pits. These would have been storage pits, filled after use with the soil excavated from newer pits. Earth-oven pits were present, but by the time of our initial visit the shallow pits had been largely removed, and no definite intact earth ovens were observed. Fragmented and whole heating elements were of fairly common occurrence at the site.

The method of soil removal and the nature of the soil precluded any possible attempt at an identification of a house pattern. Only the higher central portion of the site was salvaged since this was the primary area leveled. The surface was disked several times by the land leveler, then the loose soil was removed by a scraper mounted behind a tractor. The soil was extremely hard, and hand scraping was not possible. The only identifiable postholes were determined by their content and location to be Mississippian. One probably represented the central portion of a house since the subsoil was burned red nearby; it was inferred to have been the result of its proximity to a hearth. This interpretation means that a Mississippian house was located near the center of the site in the vicinity of most of the Mississippian remains at the site.

There was a total area of approximately 2500 m² of Woodland period remains observed at the site. Mississippian features and Mississippian sherds in undisturbed context were restricted to a total area of only about 500 m². The Woodland occupation minimally covered an area approximately two and a half times larger than that of the later Mississippian component since an unknown portion of the Woodland occupation extended south beneath the sand blow.

Several of the Tchula pit features measured between 1 and 1.5 m in diameter and extended to over .5 m below the base of the disturbed soil. The capacity of these pits might have been somewhere around 400–1000 liters, or much larger, depending upon how much soil is thought to have been removed before their discovery and excavation. Woodland pits in the Central Valley tend to be around .8–1.2 m in diameter, a convenient size to dig, and depth varies considerably. These pits probably functioned to store food. The McCarty site might have been a permanent, year-round residence, but the storage pit sizes do not disprove an interpretation as a seasonal village for little is known of Woodland food storage.

Burials consisted usually of a single, tightly flexed skeleton. Orientation tended to be easterly and westerly. All burials when discovered had been disturbed to a considerable degree. One seems to have been dug up by members of the Mississippian component. Exotic artifact association occurred with three of the eight investigated Tchula graves. These artifact associations were a greenstone celt, a group of copper beads, and a cache including a large point and three small chert adzes. A fourth grave may have had an antler tool in association. Several fragments of a freshly broken Cormorant Cord-Impressed vessel indicated that one grave at the site was associated with a pottery vessel.

The Tchula period ceramics at the McCarty site are surprisingly sophisticated. Most, if not all, were undoubtedly locally manufactured. Paste ranges from very sandy to the chalky feel characteristic of an exclusive grog temper. However, almost all sherds have sand as part of their paste. Only one fabric-

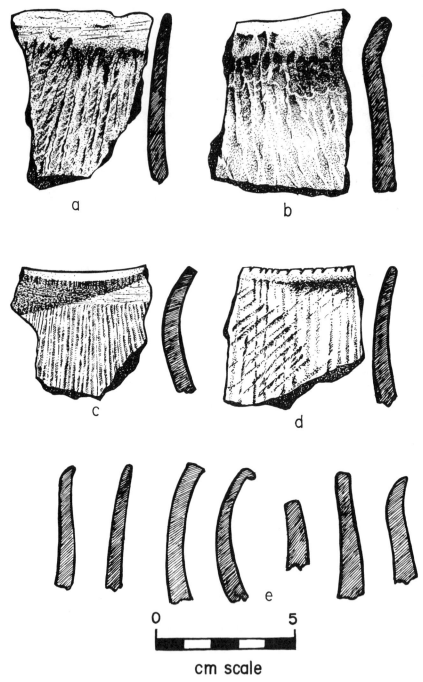

FIGURE 7.3. Cord-marked and plain rim sherds found at the McCarty site, Arkansas. (a)–(d) Cord marked. (e) Plain rim profiles. [Courtesy of the Arkansas Archeological Survey.]

impressed sherd, two check-stamped sherds, and a very few net-impressed sherds were found at the site. Cord-marked sherds predominate (Figure 7.3). Plain-surfaced potsherds appear primarily to be restricted to small food bowls and decorated jars. The utilitarian jar characteristically was cord marked. Variation in cord marking is extensive, ranging from fine to extremely coarse, although most sherds tend to exhibit relatively large cord impressions. Flat bases predominate, but conical bases are also represented in the collection. There are obvious coil breaks, indicating that the complete welding of coils is not being practiced. These obvious coil breaks are a very rare phenomenon in later ceramic assemblages. Cracking during drying, firing, or use may have been a problem, but only one sherd has been noted that had a repair hole drilled into it.

Decorated potsherds at the site are typical of the period. Punctation predominates (Figure 7.4), normally organized in neat rows parallel with and beneath the lip. On many sherds it is evident that a considerable area of the vessel was involved, whereas on others the rows are restricted to the vessel neck. The punctates themselves are adjacent to small hills caused by the penetration of the instrument used for decorating. The deeper and more prominent the punctation, the greater is the extent of the adjacent hill. There is considerable variation, and some vessels were evidently smoothed afterward, resulting in the erasure of areas of punctations. Another observed variation was the use of closely spaced punctations to divide regions of punctates from one another. Yet another was the placement of closely spaced punctations on a ridge just beneath and parallel with the lip. Similarity is to the Tchefuncte type Tammany Punctated (Weinstein and Rivet 1978).

An eroded-surface sherd exhibits dentate-like "stamping" over its surface similar to Lake Borgne Incised. Many of the dentates are actually rows of pointed punctates made at an oblique angle. The treatment then is not a stamp but a "drag and jab" decoration. A single small sherd exhibits small circular punctates zoned by an incised line, somewhat in the manner of Orleans Punctated. This is the only incising noted on the ceramics. Incising is prominent in neighboring Early Woodland complexes, such as Black Sand in Illinois and Alexander in Alabama.

A very elaborate Cormorant Cord-Impressed bowl may have been grave furniture (Figure 7.5a). Only a few freshly broken fragments were recovered. A cord-wrapped stick-notched treatment exists on the inner lip and as zoning in two rows on the exterior. The lip is red filmed. The prominent upper rim has a herringbone cord-impressed design that is similar to cross-hatching in the Marksville period. A lower, indented, region is bounded by two rows of notching and consists of a triangular motif made up of horizontal and oblique cord-wrapped stick impressions.

Rocker stamping constitutes the most popular decoration in terms of numbers of sherds, but many of the recovered fragments are probably from a single jar, and the motif may actually be only second in popularity after punctation

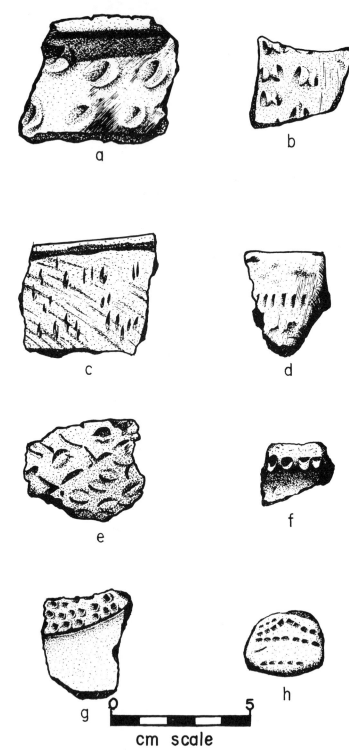

FIGURE 7.4. Punctated pottery found at the McCarty site, Arkansas. [Courtesy of the Arkansas Archeological Survey.]

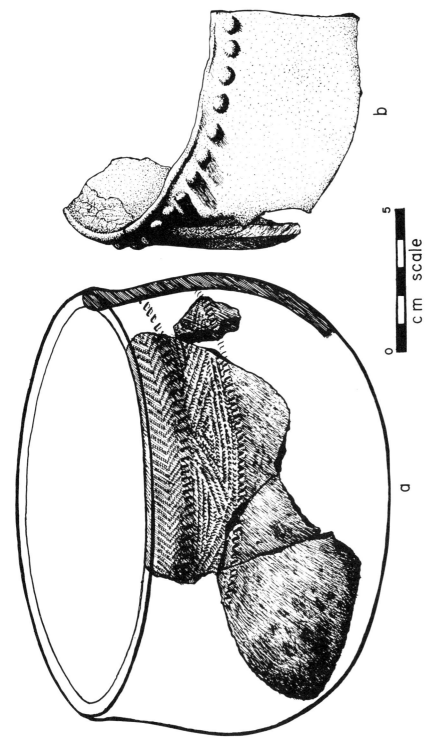

FIGURE 7.5. McCarty site, Arkansas, decorated pottery. (a) Cormorant Cord-Impressed vessel. (b) Exterior embossing on rim sherd. [Courtesy of the Arkansas Archeological Survey.]

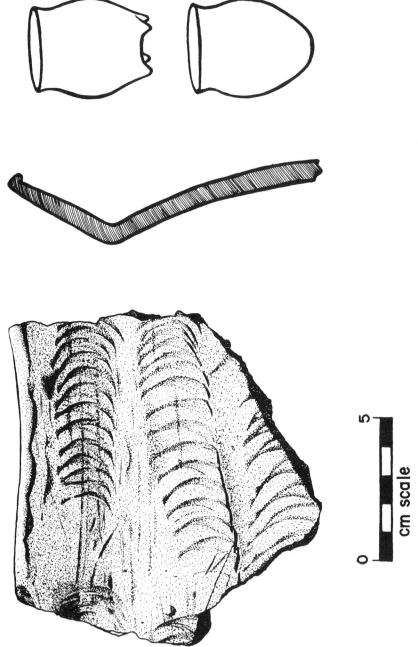

FIGURE 7.6. Tchefuncte Stamped sherd found at the McCarty site, Arkansas, and possible vessel styles for this type. [Courtesy of the Arkansas Archeological Survey.]

cm scale

0   5

(Figure 7.6). The arcs extend for 20–25 mm and are organized in horizontal bands from lip to base. The Tchefuncte type to which this decoration is most similar is Tchefuncte Stamped.

Exterior embossing is another decorative characteristic (Figure 7.5b). A horizontal exterior row of nodes was achieved just beneath the lip by pushing a dowel into the interior surface. Afterward, the interior depressions were covered over with clay. Eroded embossed sherds exhibit the enclosed hollow spaces.

Tetrapodal supports are characteristic of some of the flat-based jars. Some of the footed supports are elaborate. This feature is characteristic in the Tchefuncte of Louisiana and the Bayou La Batre of southern Alabama. Together with the Alexander ceramics of northern Alabama, Deptford of Florida, and, to a certain extent, the Black Sands complex of Illinois, the McCarty site shares distinct similarities in pottery manufacture.

Besides potsherds, a considerable number of burned clay fragments and a number of Poverty Point objects were recovered. The only possible earth oven discovered was Feature 22, which had been completely disturbed by disking associated with land-leveling activities. Artifacts included fire-cracked rock and fragments of biconical Poverty Point objects. The presence of Woodland ceramics within the artifact concentration indicates that the feature dates to Tchula and not to an earlier period. The earth oven continued in use after the adoption of ceramic kitchen utensils.

All of the pottery objects found are biconical in shape (Figure 7.7). Rare specimens are nearly spherical, probably a result of erosion rather than initial design. The variability in object shape noted for the Poverty Point period is not present in this later time period. There is a great deal of variability in size. Diameter is normally larger than thickness, varying from 33 to 74 mm on less-eroded specimens. Most objects measure between about 35 and 50 mm in diameter. The average is 44 mm. Thickness varies between 24 and 44 mm; the average is 35 mm, with most measuring between about 30 and 40 mm in thickness. Pastes vary greatly. Some are very sandy in texture, whereas others seem to lack any sand. Considerable clay particles are evident in most specimens. Most pastes are oxidized completely through, but a few are dark, as if they were never thoroughly heated or were in a reduced atmosphere when heated.

The major point style is Weems (Figure 7.8a). One of the problems in classifying points is apparent in the McCarty assemblage. Fragments and reworked or badly knapped Weems points could well be mistaken for the later but related Steuben (Zebree) point. Weems points essentially are expanded-stemmed, barbed points, whereas Steuben (Zebree) points are basically unbarbed, expanded-stemmed points. The former grades into the latter in appearance as well as in time.

Most other points recovered appear to be variations of Weems. A new point style has been named the McCarty point, in honor of the site's discoverer

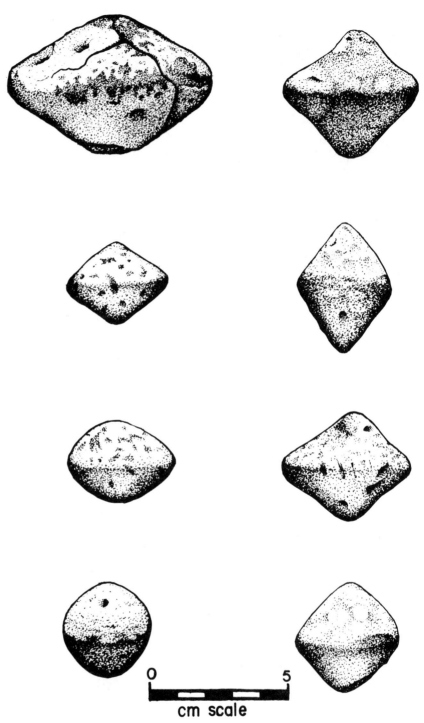

FIGURE 7.7. Poverty Point objects found at the McCarty site, Arkansas. [Courtesy of the Arkansas Archeological Survey.]

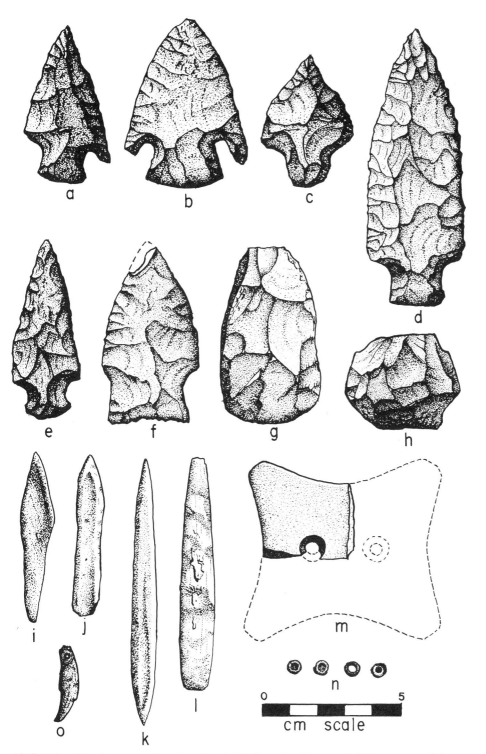

FIGURE 7.8. Miscellaneous artifacts found at the McCarty site, Arkansas. (a) Weems point. (b) McCarty point. (c) "Gary" point. (d) Stemmed point. (e) Side-notched point. (f) Stemmed point. (g) Adz. (h) Hammerstone. (i) Tanged bone point. (j) Bone point. (k) Cylindrical bone point. (l) Bone point or awl. (m) Reel-shaped gorget. (n) Copper beads. (o) Raccoon canine pendant. [Courtesy of the Arkansas Archeological Survey.]

(Figure 7.8b). It is based on the Weems point theme but obviously is a special type. Both examples at the site are made on thermally treated chert oval preforms. The squared notches are unusual and probably serve to make the point look more stemmed than corner-notched. It is possible that these points were grave furniture. They anticipate the well-crafted points found in burial association in the succeeding Marksville period (Ford and Willey 1940:101).

"Gary" points are not well represented (Figure 7.8c). Only one is a good example of a rounded-stemmed style. The others are possible fragmentary examples of "Gary," and one has a squared stem somewhat similar to the Dickson point. A narrow, bulbous-based and side-notched style is represented by several specimens (Figure 7.8e) and may relate as a group to the Motley style, which is characteristic further south around the end of the Archaic. Other points found at the McCarty site (Figure 7.8d, f) are stemmed similarly to the Weems point.

Two tanged bone points are represented at the McCarty site (Figure 7.8i–j). One has a narrow tanged base, and the other is constricted near its midpoint with a wide tang. They are 60 mm and 57 mm long, respectively. Both fall within the categories of typical Archaic bone artifacts called "Pointed base projectile points" and "Notched bone projectile points" in the Indian Knoll, Kentucky, report (Webb 1946: fig. 46A, B, 294–296).

Another typical Archaic bone artifact found widely spread in the eastern United States is also present at the McCarty site. This is a 94-mm-long, bi-pointed, cylindrical point (Figure 7.8k). Approximately 80% of the artifact is a long, tapering, pointed "stem," and the remainder an abrupt pointed "tip." Which was the stem and which was the tip is not actually known. There is a slight swelling at the junction of the two components, presumably where it would hold when fitted within a cane shaft.

An unusual bone artifact that may have been a hafted bone point is over 80 mm long with a missing tip (Figure 7.8l). The base is constricted and thinned as if for hafting in a split-end shaft. These bone points reflect not only a stone-poor environment but also continuity from the Poverty Point into the Tchula period.

Choppers and hammers were made of chert cobbles that were slightly modified (Figure 7.8h). Little difference in these generalized tools exists through prehistory, but their presence is additional evidence that a variety of tasks were accomplished at the McCarty site.

A number of short bifaced chert adzes, chisels, and/or hatchets were also recovered at the McCarty site (Figure 7.8g). These were common Archaic tools and continued to be characteristic into the Baytown period. It is evident from these and other chert tools that a variety of woodworking activities were involved.

The corner fragment of a reel-shaped gorget made of limonite is represented in the collections (Figure 7.8 m). The existing perforation was drilled from one face only, which is an early trait in itself. The reel-shaped gorget is a modification of an earlier Archaic shape with concave sides and convex ends.

The extreme end of this evolving change in shape is the Middle Woodland Copena-style gorget made of copper. The McCarty site's gorget shape is a logical expectation for the Tchula time level.

A stone bead made of chert was also found at the McCarty site. This particular bead is made on a section of the core removed while drilling a perforation in a bannerstone. It measures 22.5 mm long and 11 mm in diameter. The bead perforation measures only 3 mm in diameter. Most probably this was an Archaic artifact that was still being used, an "antique" during the Tchula period.

The skeleton in Feature 8 had a strand of at least nine copper beads (Figure 7.8n). The beads are heavy and thick, characteristic of early copper technology. They were formed by coiling a solid strip around a 2.5-mm-diameter rod. The welded joint was well done on most but more obvious on others. The beads measure 5–6 mm in diameter and 3–5 mm thick. Average weight is .3 gm. Later beads are made of much thinner copper and are not as heavy relative to size.

A minute novaculite chip was also associated with Feature 8. It was discovered during the water screening while the copper beads were being recovered. The chip exhibits a polished surface and may have been detached from the end of a very nicely made bead.

A perforated raccoon canine was discovered in another Tchula feature (Figure 7.8o). This trait is very common in local prehistory, and there are no known time restrictions. Presumably this was part of a necklace or was sewn directly on clothing.

The midsection of a hematite plummet is further evidence of continuity from the Archaic. The most accepted explanation is that plummets functioned as bola stones. Another less popular explanation is that they were attached as a sinker to trotlines.

A basalt adz or "gouge" represents another Archaic trait that continues into the Tchula period (Figure 7.9a). It is 124 mm long, 60 mm wide, and 27 mm thick. The wide working edge is about 60°. The bit is curved and hollowed, with straight striations evident on the convex surface. This is an adz in the traditional sense. Gouges are hand-held chisel-sized tools struck with a wooden mallet. Adzes are hafted and used in a swinging motion. Most adzes are curved or "gouged," particularly bowl adzes. The most common use would have been in the manufacture of dugout canoes and wooden bowls and possibly for sculpture.

An unused celt made of greenstone was found in burial association (Figure 7.9b). The greenstone represents trade from the east—central Alabama area. The unused condition of the artifact allows us to see the pristine shape and size of a Tchula period celt. It is 200 mm long, 62 mm wide, and 42 mm thick. The poll is pointed, and the working edge is constricted to a width of 49 mm. The immediate cutting edge is steep, 80°.

The Tchula period in the Central Mississippi Valley continues many of the practices characteristic of the previous Poverty Point period. In particular,

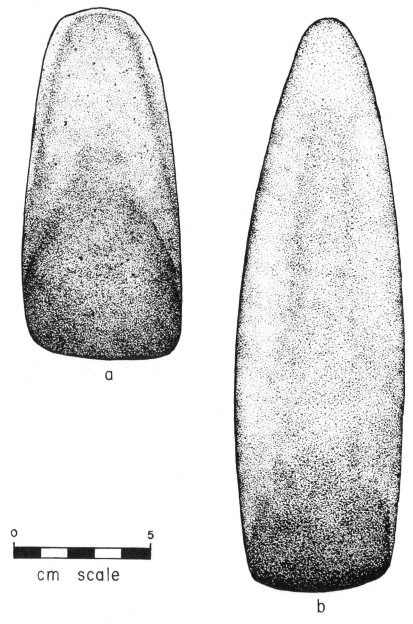

a

b

0   5

cm scale

FIGURE 7.9. Heavy edged tools found at the McCarty site, Arkansas. (a) Basalt adz. (b) Greenstone celt. [Courtesy of Arkansas Archeological Survey.]

there is increasing adaptation to lowland meander belt environments. The new trait of pottery manufacture emphasizes increasing reliance upon the lowlands and an increase in technological competence. Pottery also hints at the development of two separate coexisting traditions in the Central Valley. However, the sandy-paste pottery is part of the technological evolution in the valley, and the distinction between grog-tempered and sand-tempered pottery traditions does not become clear until the next period, Marksville.

REFERENCES

Chomko, Stephen, and Gary Crawford
  1978   Plant husbandry in prehistoric Eastern North America: New evidence. *American Antiquity* **43**:405–408.
Ford, James A., and Gordon Willey
  1940   Crooks site: A Marksville period burial mound in La Salle Parish, Louisiana. *Louisiana Geological Survey Anthropological Study* **3**.
Griffin, James B.
  1967   Eastern North American archaeology: A summary. *Science* **156**:175–191.
Griffin, James B., and Albert C. Spaulding
  1951   The Central Mississippi Valley archaeological survey, season 1950—a preliminary report. *Journal of the Illinois State Archaeological Society*, N.S. **1**:75–84.
Morse, Dan F., and Michael Million
  1980   Biotic and nonbiotic resources. In *Zebree archeological project*, edited by Dan F. Morse and Phyllis A. Morse, ch. 15, 1–30. Final report submitted to Memphis District U.S. Army Corps of Engineers by Arkansas Archeological Survey.
Phillips, Philip
  1970   Archaeological survey in the Lower Yazoo basin, Mississippi, 1949–1955. *Papers of the Peabody Museum, Harvard University* **60**.
Stoltman, James B.
  1974   Groton Plantation, an archaeological study of a South Carolina locality. *Monographs of the Peabody Museum, Harvard University*, **1**.
Webb, William S.
  1946   Indian Knoll. *University of Kentucky Report in Anthropology and Archaeology* **4**.
Weinstein, Richard, and Philip Rivet
  1978   Beau Mire: A late Tchula period site of the Tchefuncte culture, Ascension Parish, Louisiana. *Louisiana Archaeological Survey and Antiquities Commission Anthropological Report* **1**.
Willey, Gordon
  1966   *An introduction to American archaeology, Volume One: North and Middle America.* Englewood Cliffs, N.J.: Prentice-Hall.
Williams, Stephen
  1954   *An archeological study of the Mississippian culture in southeast Missouri.* Ph.D. dissertation, Yale University. Ann Arbor, Mich.: University Microfilms.
Yarnell, Richard A.
  1976   Early plant husbandry in Eastern North America. In *Cultural change and continuity, essays in honor of James Bennett Griffin*, edited by Charles E. Cleland, pp. 265–273. New York: Academic Press.

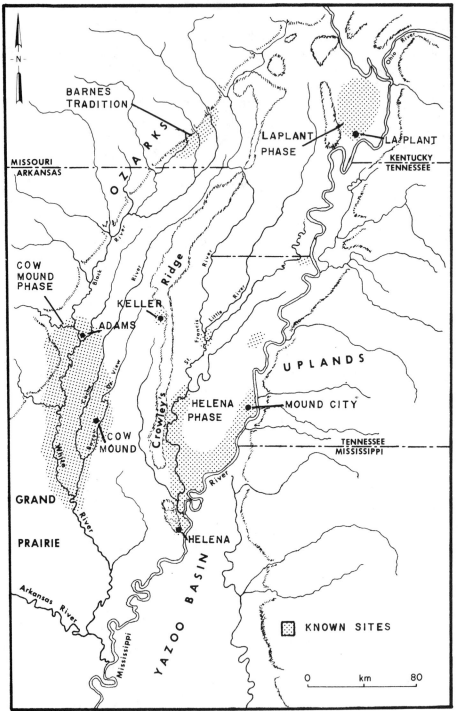

FIGURE 8.1. Distribution of phases and major sites during the Marksville period in the Central Valley.

8

The Hopewellian Period
(0–A.D. 400)

The Hopewellian period, named for the Hopewell Mound Group in Ohio, has provided the fuel for more latitude in scholarly interpretation than probably exists for any other eastern cultural period. The impressive groups of mounds and large geometric earthworks reported by Squier and Davis in 1848 in the Ohio River Valley area were used as evidence by many authors to support theories of migrations and invasions, from the Lost Tribes of Israel to various groups from Mexico. Since archaeological work proved that these earthworks were built by the ancestors of the American Indians, more recent theories on the role of these sites in trade and interaction have been developed (Streuver and Houart 1972). Although the major center of Hopewell culture was in Ohio, mounds covering charnel structures and/or log tombs, exotic artifacts of rare materials, true blades, zoned stamped ceramics, and other traits characteristic of Ohio and Illinois Hopewell are recorded for the Central Mississippi Valley. Brose and Greber (1979) have compiled an excellent synthesis of Hopewell archaeology covering the entire eastern United States.

Each region has its own local name representative of the Middle Woodland Hopewellian. In the Lower and Central valleys, the name is the Marksville period, named after the Marksville site, located in Louisiana (Toth 1974). Early Marksville dates approximately 0–A.D. 200, and late Marksville dates about A.D. 200–400. In discussing the "Marksville connection," Alan Toth (1979) has interpreted the significance of these two subperiods. He feels that early Marksville is more similar to Illinois Hopewell and that late Marksville is more similar to Lower Valley Marksville. Four Central Valley Marksville radiocarbon dates from Helena site samples are 147 ± 184 B.C., A.D. 19 ± 161, A.D. 229 ± 159, and A.D. 350 ± 159 (M–1197, 1199, 1196, 1198).

Horticulture probably became more important during the Marksville period. However, direct evidence of horticulture is rare (Yarnell 1976). Squash and corn probably were present. Beans almost certainly were not. However, C-12/C-13 ratio studies of human bone from sites in the Central Valley dating to different time periods indicate that significant shifts in subsistence did not take place until after the end of Woodland times (Boutton, Lynott, and Price 1983).

Pottery sets apart the Marksville period sites, and it appears technologically superior to Tchula ceramics. Stamped and zoned stamped pottery constitute the basic diagnostic traits signifying that a site contains a Marksville component. Definite grog (broken sherd) temper is characteristic of Marksville ceramics in the meander belt portion of the Central Valley (Figure 8.1). Sand is present in the pastes but usually is very minimal and fine, although grog fragments obviously contain sand. There was a slightly greater variety of vessel shapes than there was in the Tchula period, which may have resulted from use of a lighter paste.

This development of grog-tempered pottery by the beginning of the Marksville period is mostly confined to the meander belt and the White River Valley. Pottery at Marksville period sites on the braided surface is sand tempered, although not to the extent characteristic of braided-surface complexes during the Baytown period. Early Marksville is most conspicuous in the region of Meander Belts 4 and 5, possibly because horticulture had become more important and populations were concentrating on the best soils. In general, the site pattern is one of dispersed, small, autonomous villages. In the braided surface region, late Marksville period sites are the most obvious. Dating is based on the horizon styles of ceramics. For some reason, earlier sites are more difficult to discover. Horticulture may not have been as important on braided stream surfaces, and the population may have been even more dispersed in seasonal villages.

TRADE AND RITUAL IN HOPEWELL

The term *Hopewell* suggests to an archaeologist tombs in mounds, earthworks, platform pipes, copper objects, ear spools, obsidian, mica, zoned decorated pottery, figurines, pearl beads, "Hornstone" preforms, and other exotic ritualistic items. The manufacture and movement of similar artifacts in the Central Valley first become obvious archaeologically in the Poverty Point period and "climax" in the Marksville period. However, the variety of objects traded and the distance from source are unique to Hopewell. The trade stimulus in Marksville was the desire for ritual objects. Consumption of ritual artifacts was by burial with selected individuals, probably mostly big-men, who gained and enhanced their position by the acquisition and distribution of these ritual items. Hopewell is defined by the archaeologist in terms of those ritual artifacts. Ritual, then, was the essence of Hopewell life, according to current archaeological interpretation.

Historic survivals of this big-men trade behavior may have been the traders observed by the De Soto expedition in the Central Valley in 1541 (Varner and Varner 1951:449). Cabeza de Vaca became a trader in 1528 in Texas just so he could move freely among hostile groups and eventually find his way back to a Spanish settlement (Smith 1871:85).

Long-distance trade obviously involves contact between foreign peoples. Such contact permitted the exchange of new ideas. Even if contact was neither frequent nor regular and involved only a few enterprising persons, such trade must have greatly influenced the inhabitants of the Central Mississippi Valley. The presence of such foreign objects as panpipes and ear spools in tombs shows that there were changes in burial practices. The corresponding ritual or ideological changes must also have occurred. A culture does not make these sorts of changes readily, so the impact of this foreign contact in the Central Valley must have been powerful.

Ritual items were probably acquired on trading expeditions conducted by big-men. Objects of copper, galena, silver, and conch shell are the most obvious evidence of interregional trade in the valley. It formerly was thought that Hopewellian copper came only from the Great Lakes area, and any discovery of copper artifacts was used to demonstrate trade with places such as Isle Royale, Michigan, or Green Bay, Wisconsin. It is now known that native copper outcrops were also available in the Southeast, in the southern Appalachians, and even in the Ste. François Mountains. Spectroscopic analysis of artifacts can differentiate between these major sources. Copper artifacts, such as panpipes, from both northern and local sources have been identified at sites in Georgia, Florida, and Alabama (Goad 1979).

Galena is another material frequently found at Hopewell sites. Several potential areas have been suggested as sources where galena was readily available: Missouri, Illinois, Kentucky, and, in particular, the Upper Mississippi Valley region near Galena, Illinois. Spectroscopic analysis of galena found at southeastern sites has shown that all tested specimens could be attributed to the Upper Mississippi Valley area (Walthall, Stow, and Karson 1979).

Silver is occasionally found at Hopewellian sites, most often as an applied strip on copper panpipes. Preliminary analysis shows this source most often to be the Cobalt region of northeastern Ontario. Another source of silver is in Michigan. One site in Ontario and one in Michigan were found to have silver processing centers (Brose and Greber 1979:253).

Artifacts made of conch shell have been turning up in sites in the eastern United States earlier than Middle Woodland (Morse and Morse 1964; Morse 1967). However, cups made of *Busycon* and *Cassis* became one of the most common traits found in Hopewell crypts. Large conch-shell beads, shark teeth, and barracuda jaws also appear in Ohio mounds. No site in Florida or the other Gulf states has yet been definitely identified as a processing center for procuring these objects for trade.

Obsidian is another material that occurs most frequently in Ohio Hopewell and less often in Illinois, Michigan, Wisconsin, and Indiana. Neutron activation analysis of trace elements from potential obsidian sources in the Yellowstone area, California, Oregon, and Mexico demonstrated that the Obsidian Cliff area of Yellowstone National Park was the only location where obsidian was obtained by Middle Woodland Indians (Griffin, Gordus, and Wright 1969). Hopewell traders would have had to make a journey of over 4500 km by canoe up the Missouri River to obtain this obsidian. Other goods such as mica, *marginella* beads, grizzly bear teeth, and freshwater pearls were also desirable trade items. Perishable trade goods, such as brightly colored feathers, furs, and local culinary delicacies, were undoubtedly also involved.

Marksville period sites are interpreted here as essentially autonomous villages. Each village was based on a similar subsistence and technology and was largely self-sufficient. The ceremonies that took place during burial, involving construction of crypts or charnel houses, body preparation, and subsequent mound construction, probably involved a series of feasts given by the family or clan. During these ceremonies the objects from faraway places were exhibited and worn.

An increased importance in horticulture would have brought about a greater uncertainty about the harvest, a small price, perhaps, to pay for the greater predictability and productivity of plant foods. On rare occasions weather may have made it necessary to move foodstuffs from one village to another, but normally there was little economic need for intratribal redistribution. Ideological changes involving planting and harvesting ceremonies occurred as agriculture grew in importance. In addition, rituals emphasize the success of a given society, its ability to endure as a society.

THE PINSON MOUNDS

The Pinson Mounds site, measuring 410 ha (1012 acres) in extent, is located south of Jackson, Tennessee, at the upper reaches of the Forked Deer River (Figure 8.2). Although the major component is Marksville, there was significant occupation at this site before and after the Marksville period. The large size of the site is more an indication of longevity than of a large population. Villages contained within the 410 ha are not all contemporaneous. Nevertheless, the site is very impressive (Mainfort 1980), as 33 mounds are represented. An earthen embankment enclosed one mound, with considerable space inside for ceremonial behavior. Investigation at the site is still in its infancy, but enough has been learned to classify the site as the most important Marksville period location in the immediate drainage of the Central Valley.

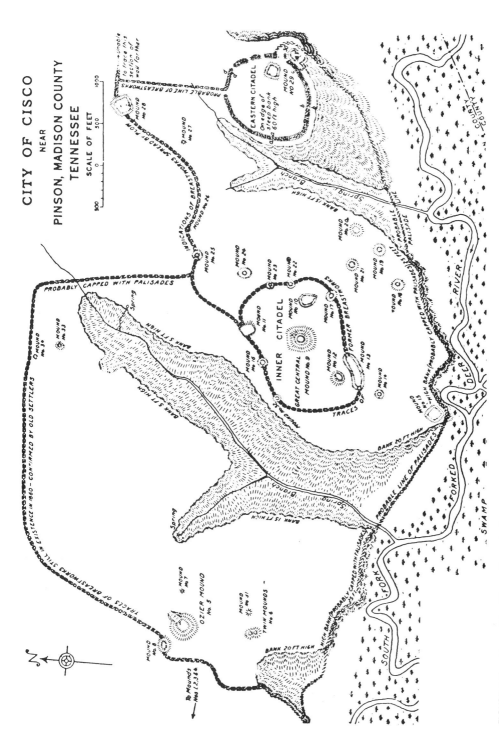

FIGURE 8.2. Map of the Pinson Mounds, Tennessee. [Map courtesy of Robert C. Mainfort, Jr., Tennessee Department of Conservation, Division of Parks and Recreation.]

The mounds are complex and almost certainly contain charnel structures or crypts. Their stratigraphy is complex, and within the fill of at least one a pottery deposit and a disarticulated skull (with mandible) were found. Both flat-topped and conical mounds are present. Some are square in outline. Cremations are reported.

One village measures about .4 ha. Structures defined by circular-to-oval posthole patterns range from 5 to 7 m in extent. Storage pits range between .5 and 2 m in diameter and up to 250 liters in capacity. An earth oven with burned sandstone in its fill was found.

The ceramics at Pinson are most interesting. Most are sand tempered and relate to the northeast Mississippi Miller complex. Cord marking predominates in most samples recovered at the site. Marksville connections include red filming, punctation, zoned cord marking, zoned incising, zoned dentate stamping, and dentate stamping on grog-tempered sherds. Complicated stamped sherds are also present. The characteristic Hopewell prismatic blades struck from specially prepared polyhedral cores are present at Pinson. Expanded stemmed points predominate, along with Copena-like bifaces. Exotic artifacts include quartz crystals, galena, copper, mica sheets, greenstone, and freshwater pearls. Radiocarbon dates mostly fall within a 0–A.D. 400 time period.

The importance of this site to the Central Valley is that, as with the Twenhafel (Illinois) site along the Mississippi River to the north, it may be placed along a route to the east for the passage of exotic ritual artifacts at this time (Myer 1928:Plate 15). To the south, there is not a site comparable to Pinson until one reaches the type site of Marksville in southern Louisiana, where there exists an earthen embankment enclosing five mounds. Other sites and mounds exist outside this embankment. This complex at Marksville is large, but it is still only about one-tenth the size ascribed to Pinson.

THE HELENA MOUNDS

Two of the original five mounds located at Helena Crossing were salvaged by James A. Ford in 1960 before they too fell victim to "progress," symbolized by highway construction, filling stations, and motels (Ford 1963). These mounds, when first discovered in 1940, measured approximately 30.5 m (100 ft.) in diameter and ranged between 4.6m (15 ft.) and 6 m (20 ft.) high. They were located on points of Crowley's Ridge overlooking the Mississippi River a few kilometers south of the mouth of the St. Francis River.

The practice of burial-mound construction in the eastern United States began soon after the advent of the Woodland period and centered in the Adena–Hopewell area of Ohio and Kentucky. The incentive to build mounds not only was to create a permanent visible monument but more importantly was inspired by the need to cover over disintegrating charnel structures. This is obvious in Figure 8.3, a simplified sketch of one of the Helena Mound C profiles.

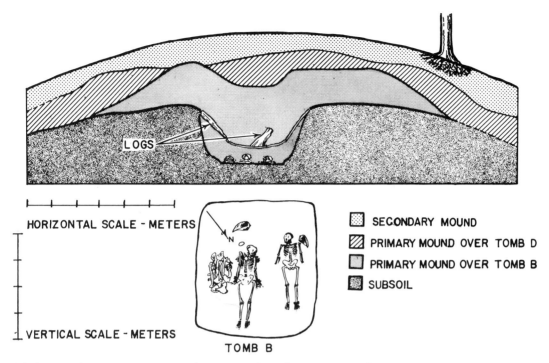

HORIZONTAL SCALE - METERS

VERTICAL SCALE - METERS

SECONDARY MOUND

PRIMARY MOUND OVER TOMB D

PRIMARY MOUND OVER TOMB B

SUBSOIL

TOMB B

FIGURE 8.3.   Profile of Helena Mound C and plan of Tomb B. [Adapted from Ford 1963: fig. 3, 12, courtesy of The American Museum of Natural History.]

The majority of the artifacts recovered from Helena Mounds B and C are strikingly similar to typical Hopewell artifacts from areas north of the Central Valley such as Illinois. The most notable specimen is a copper-and-silver-covered cane panpipe (Figure 8.4d) found on the chest of an adolescent identified as probably female. A large *Busycon* dipper, a necklace, armbands, and wristbands of pearl and conch-shell beads, a belt of drilled wolf canine teeth (Figure 8.4b) and shell beads around the waist, and a set of bicymbal copper ear spools (Figure 8.4e–f) held in the hands were also present with this burial. It is very unusual to find such adornments on young females in Hopewell tombs. Either the sex identification is not valid, or this person had great importance through her kinship connections or marriage ties.

The other four log-roofed tombs in Mound C held burials with a *Cassis* container (Figure 8.5a), other *Busycon* containers (Figure 8.5b), more conch-shell and pearl beads, *olivella* and *marginella* beads, a sheet of mica, and a copper cylinder decorated with cutout designs interpreted as the ferrule for a wooden staff (Figure 8.4g). This latter artifact was laid on top of a bundle burial consisting of an adult female. The lone tomb in Mound B contained two male extended burials with another *Cassis* cup and eight lamellar blades (Figure 8.4a), identified by Ford (1963) as being Harrison County, Indiana, flint. A

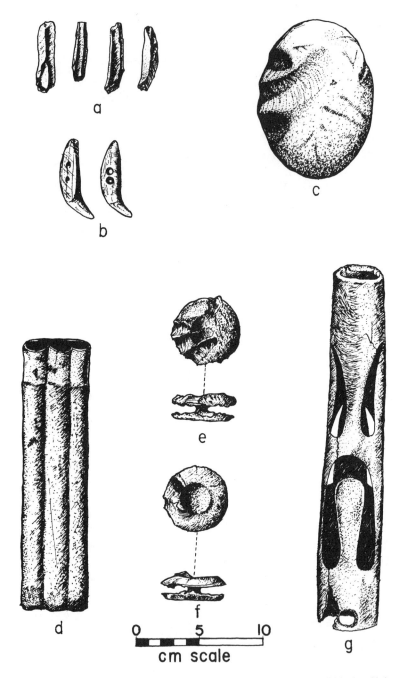

FIGURE 8.4. Marksville period artifacts found in Arkansas. (a) Hopewell blades, Helena site. (b) Drilled wolf canine teeth, Helena site. (c) Hopewell core abrader, White River. (d) Copper and silver panpipe, Helena site. (e)–(f) Copper ear spools, Helena site. (g) Copper ferrule, Helena site. [(a), (b), (d)–(g) drawn from Ford 1963, courtesy of The American Museum of Natural History; (c) courtesy of Arkansas Archeological Survey.]

closer source for this chert is Union County, Illinois. Only one pottery vessel was found in the log tombs: a plain deep bowl accompanied by a mussel-shell spoon. Both extended and bundle burials, with individuals from infants to adults represented, were present at Helena in tombs.

Burial groups placed outside of the log tombs were all extended burials. Many of them were not complete skeletons, including one that was just a skull. More *Busycon* cups, barrel-shaped conch-shell beads, *marginella* beads, two more wolf canines, and another *Cassis* cup were part of the burial furniture. Two Marksville Stamped pottery vessels (Figure 8.5e) were present with the skeleton of an elderly female.

Separate deposits of pottery were found within the mounds. These were interpreted as being included in loads of fill during mound construction rather than as formal offerings. Therefore, these deposits may not necessarily be contemporary with the burials but are possibly representative of an earlier occupation. No evidence of village occupation as a source for these deposits was found on the ridge where most of the Helena mounds were situated. A reconstructable Tchefuncte Stamped jar and sherds of a large Withers Fabric Impressed vessel were found together in one large deposit. Fired-clay balls and charcoal fragments were associated with these two vessels. Another deposit had sherds from only one vessel, identified as Withers Fabric Impressed. Two small Marksville Stamped pots with crosshatched rims and a square, flat base were found together in one area. A deeper deposit near the center of the mound contained two Tchefuncte Stamped tetrapodal jars.

A large deposit with sherds from 17 reconstructable vessels was found associated with ash, charcoal, burned bone, and chert fragments. Two small sheet copper objects of unknown function were also included in this fill. Marksville Plain jars with incised rims, Larto Red Filmed bowls, a possible Troyville Stamped jar, an Indian Bay Stamped or Marksville Stamped jar, a jar resembling Orleans Punctated, a Mulberry Creek Cord Marked jar, and several Marksville crosshatched rims from several vessels were found. The most curious specimen is a U-shaped vessel with two openings (Figure 8.5c). Design motifs included rocker-stamped elements surrounded by rectangular incised lines and three parallel lines forming several bird heads. A similar unusual vessel was found in Florida near Apalachicola. Miscellaneous sherds scattered through the mound fill were of the same pottery types. One Brangenburg-style rim was identified.

Mound C at Helena contained five log-roofed tombs, measuring up to 3–4 m in size. Based on Ford's profile drawing (1963:Figs. 3–6), Tombs A, B, C, and E were in subsoil at the base of the primary mound, which was about 16 m in diameter and 3 m high. Tomb D intruded into subsoil through the primary mound. The burial with the panpipe, numerous beads, wolf canine belt, and copper ear spools was in Tomb A in this primary mound. Typical large Hopewell log tombs, such as Tombs B–E, are currently interpreted not as being dug for primary burial but as structures for the preparation of the dead, who were

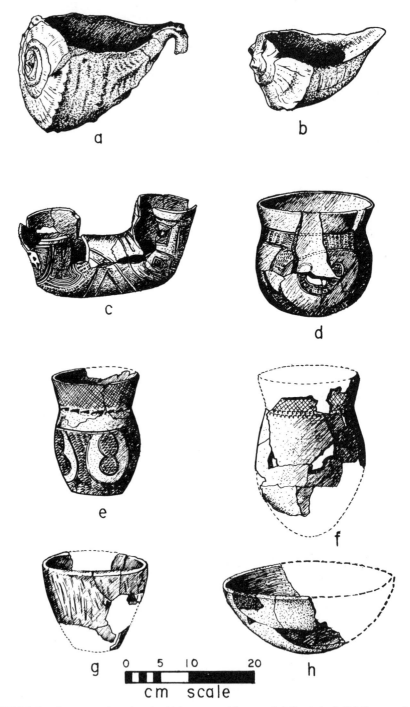

FIGURE 8.5. Containers found at the Helena site, Arkansas. (a) *Cassis* shell. (b) *Busycon* shell. (c)–(h) Pottery vessels. [Drawn from Ford 1963, courtesy of The American Musuem of Natural History.]

then reburied elsewhere. Some of the final burials in the tombs at Mound C are bundle burials, obviously prepared for burial after decay. These crypts or charnel houses are eventually used for burial when the structures are ready to collapse.

Those burials not in log-roofed tombs were laid on the surface of the primary mound before being covered with another mound cap. Mounds were built up with obvious loads of dirt. Definite sags in the fill were present over the tombs where the log roofs had collapsed. Other burials were later placed within these mounds, but none of the burials were bundle burials, although one consisted of only a skull. A final cap of loess, called the secondary mound, was placed on top of the complex series of primary mounds and sag fills and measured about 5 m thick and 42 × 22 m in diameter.

Mound B was much less complex in stratigraphy, containing only one central tomb. It was placed on a lower slope of Crowley's Ridge and was built of clay instead of loess. The tomb was almost 1.5 m (5 ft.) below the original surface of the ground and measured 5 × 3.5 m. Small logs had been placed on the floor, with two larger logs over 1 m in diameter along two of the walls. These supported the large roofing logs. The pit had been lined with split-cane matting, shown by impressions in the clay. One of the roofing timbers had been charred and preserved. Only two adult males were buried in this tomb. Outside the tomb, there were two isolated human skulls and a femur.

It must be emphasized that Helena is only a burial site. The village or villages that brought their dead to be interred here were never definitely located, let alone excavated. The other three mounds at Helena were destroyed before Ford's excavation, diminishing potential data even further. The contents of the tombs and burial groups link Helena definitely with both the North and the South, particularly with Illinois Hopewell and with Marksville. The pottery is primarily southern. The ear spools and panpipes appear to be northern, particularly since the panpipes have a silver plate at the upper end. Silver on Hopewell panpipes is from a Canadian source. Some southeastern copper objects are made from southern sources rather than from Great Lakes copper. The Helena artifacts have not yet been examined for trace elements that may reveal their source.

Big-men are not the only occupants of the tombs at Helena. The inclusion of a cross section of the whole society, from females to infants to older males, demonstrates the existence of an egalitarian society rather than one with ranked lineages.

Helena was located along a major trade artery, the Mississippi River. The St. Francis and L'Anguille rivers also drain into the Mississippi at Helena, linking this area with the interior of northeast Arkansas. Some kind of interchange between the indigenous population and people to the north and south must have taken place, but no actual migrations of new people are proposed to explain the developments at Helena.

MARKSVILLE PERIOD VILLAGES

Tantalizing clues to sites exist, such as large bifaces found near Marked Tree, a Marksville sherd found near Blytheville (Figure 8.6e), and a typical Hopewell core abrader (Figure 8.4c) found along the White River in the Ozarks. There are sites from Blytheville to Memphis that contain fabric-impressed ceramic components. Marksville-related sherds also occur sporadically within the White River alluvial plain from Brinkley to Newport. Various local phases have been defined, mostly from surface-collected data.

The *La Plant phase* is located in the Cairo Lowland, and the associated ceramics are both sand- and grog-tempered (Griffin and Spaulding 1951). A variety of typical Hopewellian decorated sherds are known, including zoned and unzoned dentate stamped, rocker stamped, incised, crosshatched rims, and barred ovoid stamped. The collection from the La Plant site also included typical Hopewell prismatic blades, and a torso of a ceramic human figurine (Toth 1977:180).

At the St. Johns site, located 2 miles (3.2 km) from the present course of the Mississippi River, another small group of sherds diagnostic of Hopewell were found, including Mabin Stamped, Old River Zoned Rocker Stamped, and several crosshatched rims, one of which was limestone-tempered (Toth 1977:189). Tempering pottery with limestone is a trait found in Hopewell ceramics further north in Illinois.

Mounds are possibly associated with the La Plant phase (Adams and Walker 1942:11; Marshall 1965:35—42). The mound excavated by Marshall contained a central sub floor pit but no burials or diagnostic Marksville period artifacts. Those described by Adams and Walker have since disappeared.

The *Turnage phase* is based on sandy-paste fabric-impressed sherds collected in 1940 immediately south of the Missouri bootheel, according to Phillips (1970). All of the fabric-impressed sherds found since then however, have been grog tempered and typical of Withers. Although the sherds probably are Marksville in age, the "Turnage" phase concept should be abandoned unless there is better evidence than now exists.

The *Helena phase* is based on the Helena Mounds excavation by Ford (1963). At Mound City in Crittenden County, Arkansas, fabric-impressed pottery occurs with Cormorant Cord-Impressed, Twin Lakes Punctated, Baytown Plain (predominant), Mulberry Creek Cord Marked, Larto Red Filmed, rocker stamped, and Marksville Zoned Incised and zoned dentate stamped, as well as punctated sherds (Figure 8.6a—b, d, f—g). All were surface collected, and the Tchula period obviously is represented in part. There is little doubt, however, that a major Marksville period component exists here and that this could be a major Marksville site complete with mounds. This site complex (3CT3—5), which is endangered by metropolitan Memphis, may be part of the Helena phase.

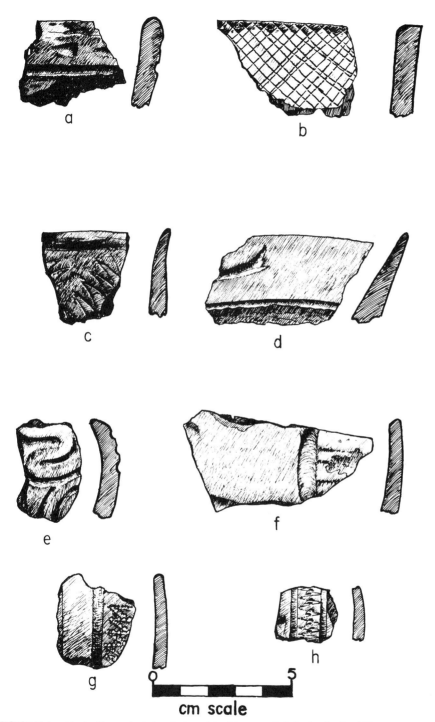

FIGURE 8.6. Marksville period sherds found in Arkansas. (a) Marksville Red Filmed, Mound City. (b), (d) Marksville Incised, Mound City. (c), (h) Marksville Stamped, Adams site. (e) Marksville Incised, site 3MS306, Mississippi County. (f)–(g) Marksville Stamped, Mound City. [Courtesy of Arkansas Archeological Survey.]

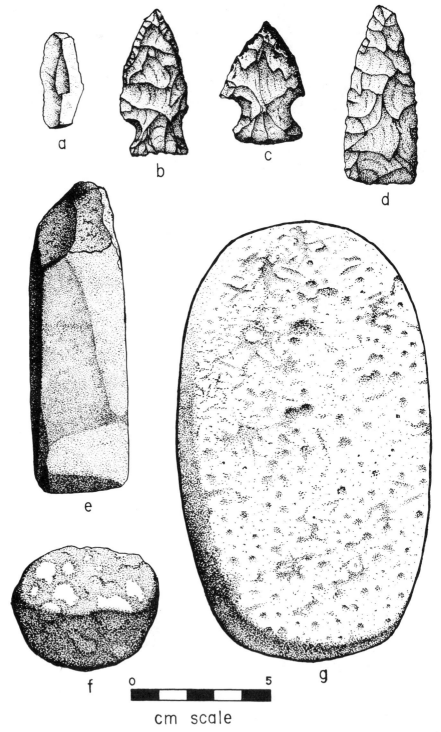

FIGURE 8.7. Artifacts found at the Adams and Keller sites, Arkansas. (a) Blade, Keller site. (b) Steuben-like point, Adams site. (c) Gibson-like point, Keller site. (d) Chipped stone celt, Keller site. (e) Ground-stone celt, Adams site. (f) Earth oven object, Keller site. (g) Mano, Adams site. [Courtesy of Arkansas Archeological Survey.]

The Helena phase includes sites along the St. Francis River up to near Parkin and adjacent to the Mississippi River to above Memphis. Essentially it is a meander-belt phase. How it connects with the La Plant phase is not known. Furthermore, we do not know how either phase relates to late Marksville since both are classified as early. Excavations at Mound City would help clarify this considerably.

The *Cow Mound phase* is associated with an alluvial plain of the White River, in the southwestern corner of the Central Valley, and is based on collections from the Cow Mound and Adams sites. Most probably it is late Marksville in date. Not enough research has been accomplished to investigate for indigenous development. The Cow Mound site is located west of Brinkley, Arkansas. It has a Marksville component, as indicated by the recovery of zoned incised, rocker-stamped, punctated, incised, brushed, and cord-impressed ceramics. The grog-tempered pottery is predominantly plain and consists of flat-based vessels.

Near Newport, Arkansas, is the relatively small Adams site, which was partially salvaged following the employment of deeper cultivation. Besides the remains of a Mississippian occupation, there was an earlier Marksville component discovered at the site. The ceramics are grog-tempered and mostly flat-based vessels. Plain sherds predominate. Adams Cord Impressed is the most common decorated type. Minority types include a zoned rocker stamp, rocker stamp, a crude incised sherd, and Churupa Punctated (Figure 8.6c, h).

Points range around the Gibson and Steuben varieties (Figure 8.7b). Many of the latter have barbed shoulders similar to the Weems point. There are choppers, pestles, and hammers present. A distinctive pestle or mano is oval and flat (Figure 8.7g). Truncated cobble pestles were also collected and together with the Weems-like points probably indicate an Archaic occupation.

Ozark cherts were being exploited. In addition, siltstone and quartzite celts were being made at the site (Figure 8.7e). Preforms, debitage, finished celts, and the distinctive hammerstone variety associated with manufacturing ground-stone artifacts were recovered. The celts are rectangular in shape. An unfinished sandstone bead was also found during the brief salvage period.

A "*Keller phase*" could be based on the Keller site, which is located about 16 km south of Jonesboro and immediately west of Crowley's Ridge near the L'Anguille River. The site was levelled in August 1970, and salvage on the approximately 2000 m^2 that remained when we were notified took place in a single day. Fortunately, the crew excavating the Brand site could be diverted for this sunrise-to-sunset salvage, during which period the site was completely destroyed.

Ceramics consist of both sandy and grog pastes. Most are sandy, but it is a very fine sand and is mostly quite different from the succeeding Dunklin phase texture, although it is in the Barnes tradition and within the braided stream surface region. Cord-marked sherds are rare, making up less than 10% of the small sample recovered. Decorated sherds make up approximately 7% of the

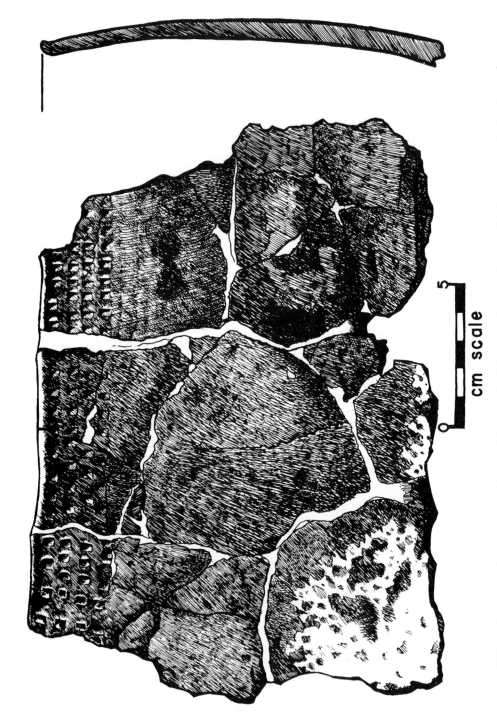

FIGURE 8.8 Late Marksville punctated rim sherd found at the Keller site, Arkansas. [Courtesy of Arkansas Archeological Survey.]

cm scale

sample and include punctation, brushing, crude rocker stamping, cord impression, and notched lipping. No zoned designs were recovered, possibly only because the sample is so small. One rim sherd is similar to the terminal Illinois Hopewell Steuben Punctated (Figure 8.8). This site is dated just at the termination of the Marksville period.

There is one pod from a tetrapod jar present in the collection. Repair holes on either side of cracks are frequent, indicating some difficulty with keeping pots whole. Jar shape is without much shoulder and rim curvature. The overall impression is one of difficulty in the manufacture of pots.

The most common lithic artifact category consists of choppers. There are chert hammers and broken bifaces in the collection as part of the lithic workshop activity associated with Crowley's Ridge gravel exploitation. Other lithic artifacts are an abrader made of ironstone, a uniface made on a true blade (Figure 8.7a), a triangular chipped chisel (Figure 8.7d), and several points. Most points are expanded stemmed, Steuben-like points. One is similar to the Gibson point in Illinois (Figure 8.7b). Deer ulnae awls, splinter awls, and a fragment of turtle carapace that had been made into a container of some sort were also recovered.

Features consisted of postholes, basin-shaped storage pits ranging between .7 and 2 m in diameter, a flexed and a bundle burial, and an earth oven. Only a portion of the base of the earth oven remained, measuring 1.2 × .8 m. The deposits included sherds, fire-cracked chert, and burned debitage plus spherical pottery objects. These clay objects are crude in comparison with the earlier Poverty Point objects and on the average are larger. Figure 8.7f is one of the latest-known earth oven artifacts in the Central Valley. Biconical and spherical pottery objects reminiscent of Poverty Point objects continued to be used throughout much of the Marksville period. They also were being used in earth ovens in Illinois Hopewell (Rackerby 1969).

REFERENCES

Adams, Robert, and Winslow Walker
    1942   Archaeological surface survey of New Madrid County, Missouri. *Missouri Archaeologist* 8.
Boutton, Thomas W., Mark J. Lynott, and James E. Price
    1983   Isotopic analysis of fossil human diet in Southeast Missouri and Northeast Arkansas. Paper prepared for XI International Congress of Anthropological and Ethnological Sciences, Vancouver, B.C.
Brose, David, and N'omi Greber (editors)
    1979   *Hopewell archaeology. The Chillicothe conference.* Kent: Kent State University Press.
Ford, James A.
    1963   Hopewell culture burial mounds near Helena, Arkansas. *American Museum of Natural History Anthropological Papers* 50.

Goad, Sharon
1979 Middle Woodland exchange in the prehistoric southeastern United States. In *Hopewell archaeology*, edited by David Brose and N'omi Greber, pp. 239–246. Kent: Kent State University Press.
Griffin, James B., A. Gordus, and Gary Wright
1969 Identification of the sources of Hopewellian obsidian in the Middle West. *American Antiquity* 34:1–14.
Griffin, James B., and Albert C. Spaulding
1951 The Central Mississippi Valley archaeological survey, season 1950. *Journal of Illinois State Archaeological Society* 1:75–81.
Mainfort, Robert (editor)
1980 Archaeological investigations at Pinson Mounds State Archaeological Area: 1974, 1975, and 1978 field seasons. *Tennessee Division of Archaeology Research Series* 1.
Marshall, Richard A.
1965 An archaeological investigation of Interstate Route 55 through New Madrid and Pemiscot Counties, Missouri, 1964. *University of Missouri Highway Archaeology Report* 1.
Morse, Dan F.
1967 The Robinson site and shell mound Archaic culture in the Middle South. Unpublished Ph.D. dissertation, Department of Anthropology, University of Michigan. University Microfilms, Ann Arbor.
Morse, Dan F., and Phyllis A. Morse
1964 1962 Excavations at the Morse site: A Red Ocher cemetery in the Illinois Valley. *Wisconsin Archeologist* 45:79–98.
Myer, William E.
1928 Indian trails of the Southeast. *Bureau of American Ethnology Annual Report* 42:727–857.
Phillips, Philip
1970 Archaeological survey in the Lower Yazoo Basin, Mississippi, 1949–1953. *Papers of the Peabody Museum, Harvard University* 60.
Rackerby, Frank
1969 Clay bicones, or "Poverty Point Objects," from the Carlyle Illinois region: A request for information. *Central States Archaeological Journal* 16:148–154.
Smith, Buckingham (translator)
1871 *Relation of Alvar Nuñez Cabeca de Vaca*. Smith, New York: Readex Microprint.
Squier, E. M., and E. H. Davis
1848 Ancient monuments of the Mississippi Valley. *Smithsonian contributions to knowledge* (Vol. I).
Toth, Alan
1974 Archaeology and ceramics at the Marksville site. *University of Michigan Museum of Anthropology Anthropological Papers* 56.
1977 Early Marksville Phases in the Lower Mississippi Valley: A Study of Culture Contact Dynamics. Ph.D. dissertation, Harvard University. Cambridge.
1979 The Marksville connection. In *Hopewell archaeology*, edited by David Brose and N'omi Greber, pp. 188–199. Kent: Kent State University Press.
Varner, John, and Jeannette Varner (translators)
1951 *The Florida of the Inca*. Austin: University of Texas Press.
Walthall, John, Stephen Stow, and Marvin Karson
1979 Ohio Hopewell trade: Galena procurement and exchange. In *Hopewell archaeology*, edited by David Brose and N'omi Greber, pp. 247–250. Kent: Kent State University Press.

Yarnell, Richard A.
  1976   Early plant husbandry in Eastern North America. In *Cultural change and continuity, essays in honor of James Bennett Griffin*, edited by Charles E. Cleland, pp. 265–273. New York: Academic Press.

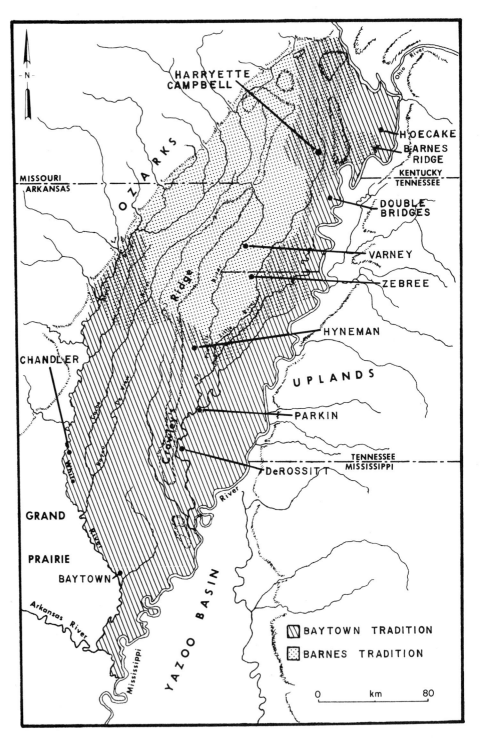

FIGURE 9.1. Distribution pf phases and major sites during the Baytown period in the Central Mississippi Valley.

9

Woodland Conflict
(A.D. 400–700)

The Baytown period is the Central Valley's classificatory niche for Late Woodland (Figure 9.1). Phillips (1970) has designated this period as an interval when "pottery decoration . . . was at a remarkably low ebb [p. 901]." It has been little investigated primarily because of a general lack of exotic artifacts and earthworks. Avocational archaeologists have not been attracted to sites characterized mainly by plain broken ceramics. Professional archaeologists have tended to concentrate on the older lithic complexes, such as Dalton, and upon complex societies, such as Mississippian.

In the Baytown period many of the traits associated with the Marksville period disappeared. They had primarily functioned in a ritual context that evidently was no longer in existence. Exotic artifacts made upon foreign raw materials are absent in Baytown period sites. Before the termination of the Marksville period, such items were not being produced in very significant numbers, and all of those were buried. Marksville pottery, which was diagnostic for the period, was primarily ritual ware and was not very common in the Central Valley except in a context such as the Helena Mounds.

There was cultural continuity, although it is not as obvious as that from Tchula into Marksville. The basic kitchen ceramics constitute an important bridge. Stone tools are also similar, particularly the Steuben expanded-stemmed style point tradition, which is characteristic of both periods. Sites are relatively small, and the basic settlement pattern of dispersed small villages is similar to that evident during the Marksville period.

There is a possible new type of site that is very small in size and interpreted as a single household location. The number of sites that have been recorded suggest that population is much larger than earlier. There is evidence that some populations may have moved seasonally to a greater degree than is speculated for the Marksville period.

There are five northeast Arkansas radiocarbon dates for this period. Two dates on samples from a "Baytown" phase component at the Hyneman site are A.D. 642 ± 138 and 761 ± 151 (M–2112, 2113). Three dates on samples associated with the Dunklin phase component at the Zebree site are A.D. 691 ± 74, 829 ± 70, and 863 ± 84 (SMU–414, 415, 432). These latter dates are thought to date the terminus of the Dunklin phase in northeast Arkansas.

Two dates from southeast Missouri were derived from samples associated with an early Hoecake phase component at the Double Bridges site. These are A.D. 572 ± 150 and 480 ± 140 (GAK–1685, 1686). A late Hoecake phase date from the Hoecake site in the Cairo Lowland is about A.D. 440 ± 150 (GAK–1307). There is a two-thirds chance that the true date falls within one standard deviation (A.D. 290–590) and a 95% probability it falls within two standard deviations (A.D. 140–740). The feature should have dated no earlier than around A.D. 700–800. Another date on a Hoecake site feature is A.D. 1169 ± 150 (GAK–1308), which is later than expected. The date of A.D. 663 ± 184 (M–2212 and 2213 combined) from a mound at Hoecake is a much better fit with the transition from early to late Hoecake phase than are the other dates.

The Scandic climatic episode dates from approximately A.D. 320 to A.D. 740 (Wendlund and Bryson 1974). That these dates are so close to the dates for the Baytown period is a fruitful coincidence to investigate. The problem is that the necessary data to reconstruct the climate in the Central Valley have not been analyzed. As Griffin, Williams, and others have pointed out, there is greater continuity in decorated ceramics south of the Central Valley. In particular, a spectacular discovery of polychrome human-effigy pottery dated to this time period was made in northeast Louisiana at the Gold Mine site (Jones 1979). Whatever adjustments had to be made for slight shifts in climate do not appear to have transpired farther to the south in the Mississippi Valley. This difference between north and south was evident as early as late Marksville times, when plain pottery predominated to the north and decorated pottery predominated to the south (Belmont and Williams 1981).

Two pottery traditions continued to develop in the Central Valley during the Baytown period. The sand-tempered tradition is characteristic of sites on the braided surface. Grog-tempered pottery is limited primarily to sites in the meander belt and along the lower drainage of the White River. Unlike earlier Tchula and Marksville pottery, no clay or grog is typically included in the sand-tempered paste, which is almost the consistency of sandpaper. Grog-tempered sherds, on the other hand, typically have a very chalky feel, denoting a general absence of grit or sand. Evidently, the regional emphasis of temper reflects basic tribal differences. The three named phases that coexisted during the Baytown phase may actually equate with three tribal groups. At least two of those phases were in conflict with each other. The early Hoecake phase expanded at the expense of the Dunklin phase. We think the conflict was physical as well as cultural (Morse 1977).

THE DUNKLIN PHASE

Phillips (1970) has hypothesized that the "question of 'clay' vs. sand-tempered paste . . . may well be the result of purely environmental factors [p. 903]." This hypothesis does not seem to be the case. Barnes Ridge, located in the southern portion of the Cairo Lowland, provided the name *Barnes*, which identifies the sandy-textured pottery known as Barnes Cord Marked and Barnes (Kennett) Plain. Barnes Ridge itself is very sandy. Earlier and later in time Barnes Ridge was occupied by people manufacturing grog-tempered pottery; hence, a sandy environment does not necessarily mean the pottery will be sandy textured. Sand-tempered pottery is a separate ware that should be referred to as Barnes.

The name *Dunklin* is derived from Dunklin County, Missouri, in which is located the Old Varney site, which contained a Barnes tradition component. Old Varney is the type site for the Dunklin phase (S. Williams 1954). Since 1954 a large number of sites with Barnes ceramics have been recorded on the braided surface of the northern half of the Central Valley.

A combination of survey techniques and the excavation of the Zebree site in Mississippi County, Arkansas, near the type site indicates more specifically what kinds of sites are present in the Dunklin phase (Morse and Morse 1980). A .4 km (.25 mile) wide transect has been walked from Little River to the St. Francis River, a distance of 24 km (15 miles). A total of 80 prehistoric loci were recorded within this transect, and a total of 3727 artifacts were collected from them. There were 47 Woodland ceramic components and 23 Mississippian ceramic components recognized (Table 9.1). The Woodland ceramic components probably primarily date to the Baytown period. The Barnes sherds were mostly typed as Barnes Cord marked and only one punctated sherd was recovered.

There is a substantial difference in settlement pattern reflected by these data. There are significantly more Baytown ceramic sites, and they are distributed differently from the Mississippian ones. Only 19 of the 51 locations

TABLE 9.1

Prehistoric Sites Discovered within a .40- × 24-Km Transect between the St. Francis and Little Rivers, Arkansas

Lithics	Ceramics				
	Only Baytown	Only Mississippian	Baytown and Mississippian	Ceramics not present	Total
Lithics present	19	3	16	29	67
Lithic not present	9	1	3	–	13
Total	28	4	19	29	80

were shared. Only 1 of the 29 nonceramic sites involved a Mississippian diagnostic artifact, a Scallorn point. A possible polished chip at a second location could be Mississippian. The point styles and local chert use of the other 28 nonceramic sites suggest that they are mostly Woodland in age. Some are undoubtedly preceramic and Archaic in age. A triangular point was the only recognized diagnostic Mississippian artifact collected from a Baytown period ceramic site.

Mill Creek chert hoe chips were found at three of the sites, and these eight chips plus the Mississippian association with regionally prime agricultural soils clearly indicate at least one difference between the two periods. There is little evidence that during Baytown ceramic sites were located consistently on or adjacent to soils considered the best regionally for gardening. The Baytown period sites seem to be part of a dispersed seasonal occupation of the area. The inferred economy is diversified, and the settlement pattern is an adaptation of a small population to geographical and seasonal variations in the environment. The Baytown period groups evidently were almost constantly moving, whereas the Mississippian groups were relatively permanent and more restricted in site selection.

The surface distributions of artifacts indicate that the size of sites varied enormously. The transect described earlier just barely included the edge of one probable Mississippian village and seems to have included a second village. Otherwise, the sites all appear, based on artifact content and lack of midden, to have been sparsely inhabited ones.

The Baytown period sites probably were mainly single structure sites. The Barnes sherds collected all were badly eroded and small. Most of the sites were less than 300 m², about two-thirds were less than 1000 m², and some of those that were larger contained definite concentrations much more restricted in size. Probably such a site was the location for a minimal kinship unit, an extended family of around 10 individuals. Most of the Baytown period ceramic sites would be such a household. Lithic sites in this transect are probably mostly hunting and/or butchering stations. Some could be the sites of wood procurement or the gathering of wild plants. The most common element was debitage (16 instances); 5 point and 5 uniface instances were present, followed by 3 choppers, 2 hammerstones, a biface, 2 cores, and 1 possible polished chip.

Larger sites are known for the Dunklin phase. Robert Dunnell, Chairman of the Department of Anthropology, University of Washington, Seattle, has been very meticulously mapping Robards Farm in southeast Missouri. The results are being recorded so that special maps called synagraphic computer maps or SYMAPs can be printed. Relatively large Dunklin phase sites with greater amounts of artifacts than found in the Arkansas transect are shown in detail in such maps (Figure 9.2). These sites may be the locations of larger kinship aggregates. However, the total number of recovered artifacts is not very high even in these larger sites. Possibly much of the larger size of these sites is due to scatter from farming.

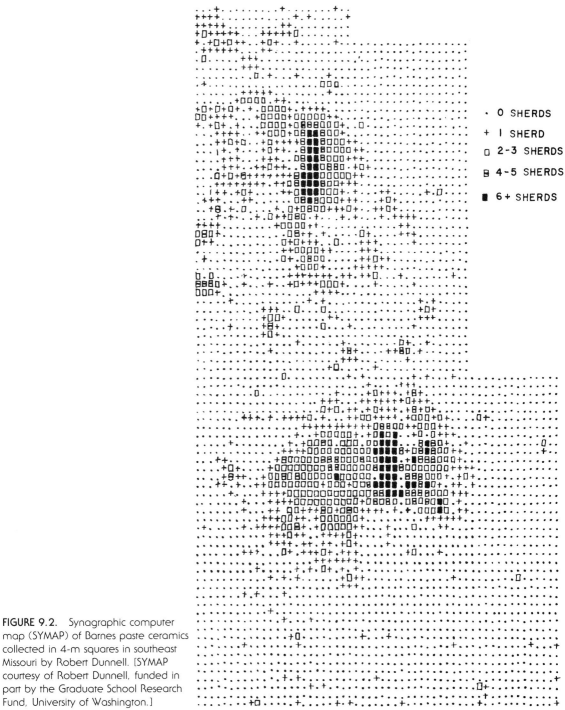

· 0 SHERDS

+ I SHERD

▫ 2-3 SHERDS

▣ 4-5 SHERDS

■ 6+ SHERDS

FIGURE 9.2. Synagraphic computer map (SYMAP) of Barnes paste ceramics collected in 4-m squares in southeast Missouri by Robert Dunnell. [SYMAP courtesy of Robert Dunnell, funded in part by the Graduate School Research Fund, University of Washington.]

The Zebree site includes an example of a relatively large Dunklin phase component with a large number of artifacts. The site is larger than a hectare. The opinion during the subsequent analysis was that approximately 1000 jars were represented by the random square excavation over only half of the site (Morse and Morse 1980). The sand-tempered pottery evidently is fragile and was easily broken. The significantly lesser amounts indicated by surface collections in the transect may mean that fewer pots were in use at these smaller sites. The larger sites such as Zebree are being interpreted as the fall-through-winter villages for several households, in contrast to the single-household spring, summer, and early fall sites. There was a rich Baytown period midden measuring approximately 1200–2400 m², depending upon which ceramic intensity limits are used, at Zebree. Three other less intense and somewhat smaller middens are also indicated by the random squares; one additional midden is indicated by feature clustering outside the random square test area. Intensity results from reoccupation over a relatively long period, estimated to have been about 100 years. Intensity as defined by potsherd count is also probably due to a relatively longer period of seasonal occupation than there was at the smaller sites. The current estimation for the main Baytown period occupation at Zebree during a year is 3–4 months.

A general subsistence base involving almost anything edible is indicated. Two bits of evidence support the absence of horticulture or at least the very small role it plays in Dunklin technology. No cultigens have been identified in Dunklin phase features, and sites are not necessarily located adjacent to acreage best suited for primitive cultivation. Sunflower pollen and seeds and pigweed pollen are associated with the Dunklin phase component at the Zebree site. No corn has been definitely identified as associated. Wild plant foods included wild bean, gromwell, persimmon, grape, acorn, hickory, black walnut, and other seeds not identified to date. Meat was primarily from deer, raccoon, cottontail rabbit, ducks, passenger pigeon, turtle, and fish.

The population evidently was alternately dispersed and nucleated on a cyclical, seasonal basis within minor watersheds. There was little trade, and belongings in general were minimal. The population was sparse. The large amounts of ceramics at some locations such as the Zebree site are due to relative ceramic weakness and to social mobility. The paste was not very strong, and the vessel shape was vulnerable to trauma. The incidence of breakage must have been very high on a relative scale, and larger jars must have been even more vulnerable, resulting in large numbers of sherds. In addition, seasonal mobility encouraged the sacrifice of vessels or at best contributed to the increased potential of breaking vessels.

Jars were increasingly cord marked during the Dunklin period until very little of the surface was left plain (Figure 9.3). Bowls usually were plain and tended to cluster around .75 liter, the normal size of an individual food bowl (Figure 9.3b). They were molded rather than made by the coil method characteristic of the jars. Small jars cluster around 7.5 liters in size and appear to be

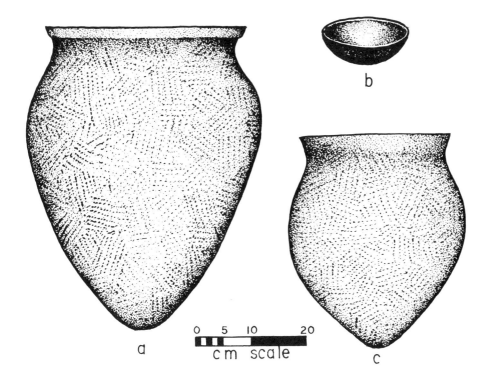

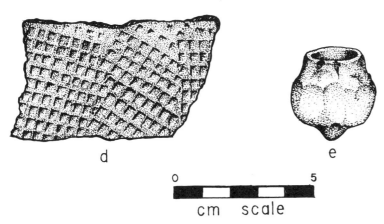

FIGURE 9.3. Dunklin phase ceramics. (a) Large jar (33 l) with reinforced rim. (b) Food bowl. (c) Typical jar (13 l). (d) Check-stamped decoration. (e) Toy jar with nipple base, copying typical jars. [Courtesy of the Arkansas Archeological Survey.]

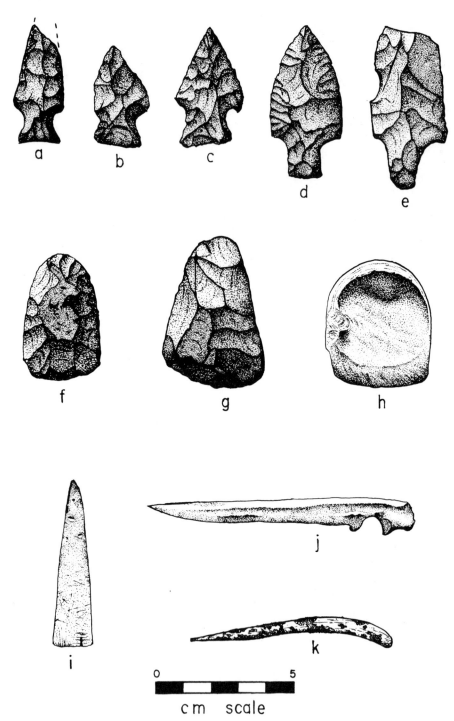

FIGURE 9.4. Baytown period nonceramic artifacts. (a)–(b) Expanded-base (Steuben) points, Zebree site. (c) Expanded-base (Steuben) points, Hyneman site. (d)–(e) Crude stemmed points, Hyneman Site. (f)–(g) Chipped adzes, Hyneman site. (h) Adz made of mussel shell, Hyneman site. (i) Antler point, Zebree site. (j) Raccoon ulna awl, Zebree site. (k) Raccoon baculum awl, Zebree site. [Courtesy of the Arkansas Archeological Survey.]

cooking pots. This size might equate with a household of around 10 individuals. Larger jars may also have been used for cooking (Figure 9.3a, c). If so, their sizes (13–33 liters) indicate the sharing of food for two to five households.

Decorative variations in cord marking included different-size cords spaced at different intervals on the paddle, overstamping of cords perpendicular to one another, and the rare substitution of fabric on the paddle. Very rarely is any other decoration found. Notched lips, parallel incised lines, incision parallel to a rounded lip, punctation, and check stamping (Figure 9.3d) are known motifs. Rim folds are interpreted as attempts to strengthen jar rims rather than as decoration.

Miniature pots were probably toy pots used by girls to practice household duties. They consist of jars and bowls. One jar has a pinched nippled base to represent the conical bases of Dunklin jars (Figure 9.3e). The crudeness of many indicates that little girls were making and firing their first pots.

The basic Dunklin phase point style is an expanded-based one (Figure 9.4a–b). The range in length is 4–6 cm. Shoulders normally are sloping but occasionally will be barbed similar to the 1000 B.C.–0 Weems point style from which it developed. There is a tendency toward a bulbous base on some specimens, and flat-based side-notched forms also occur. Zebree stemmed is a regional variety within the Steuben stemmed cluster or family. In Illinois a large number of point types have been identified, many of which could easily be interpreted as variations of a common theme. The bulbous-based and side-notched variations at Zebree may be part of other contemporary clusters or variations of "Zebree stemmed." These do exhibit older stylistic features, and it is entirely possible that some actually may be reused older points.

If these styles are the only Dunklin phase projectile points, the bow and arrow was still absent from the Central Valley. Small points in the Illinois River Valley indicate the probable presence of the bow and arrow north of here during this period, and its introduction into this part of the valley seems to have been from the direction of the Midwest.

Points recovered at Zebree probably are not representative of the total actually used since lithics were saved. All of the points found at the Zebree site were reused as tools for engraving. Antler points were also used in the Dunklin phase (Figure 9.4i). Raccoon bones (ulnae and baculum) were favorites for the manufacture of awls (Figure 9.4j, k). Bar-shaped pestles may have been used for vegetable processing. Artifacts in total are minimal, further indication of movement by dispersed households.

Houses were circular in shape and made up of poles placed into postholes with a covering of some sort (e.g., skins, grass, or woven mats). Storage pits were small relative to household size, less than 800 liters in maximum capacity. Storage pits are often distinguished by a layer of mussel shells on the basal portion of these basin-shaped pits.

THE HOECAKE PHASE

The Hoecake phase derives its name from the Hoecake site in the Cairo Lowland (Figure 9.5). This site actually seems to bridge the transition from Baytown into Mississippian, around A.D. 700–800, and *Hoecake phase* has been used to refer to both sides of the transition. The solution here is to reference an "early" and a "late" Hoecake phase. The former is Baytown in culture, whereas the latter is Mississippian in culture. We prefer this solution to those of invoking new phase names or redefining older phase names. In this chapter we discuss the early Hoecake phase.

Cord-marked grog-tempered pottery called Mulberry Creek Cord Marked predominates (Figure 9.6). Baytown Plain pottery is also prevalent, both early in the period and later when the transition to Mississippian takes place. Red-filmed pottery is also characteristic of the transition period. There is some incising, punctation, and, rarely, check stamping as decorations on pottery. Expanded stemmed points similar to those associated with the Dunklin phase are most characteristic of early Hoecake phase sites.

FIGURE 9.5. The Hoecake site, Missouri. [Courtesy of the Arkansas Archeological Survey.]

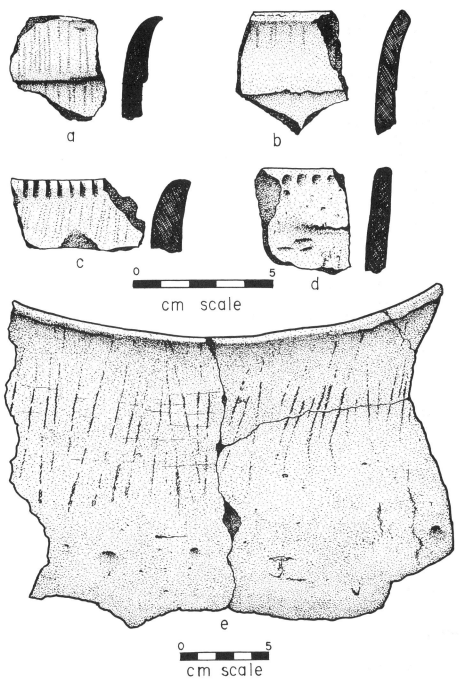

FIGURE 9.6. Early Hoecake phase ceramics. (a)–(d) Hoecake site. (e) Mississippi County, Arkansas site. [Courtesy of the Arkansas Archeological Survey.]

The Hoecake site (J. Williams 1974:56) is discussed in more detail in Chapter 10. Log tombs beneath conical mounds are a trait of the phase but actually may be more characteristic of the late Hoecake phase. The rectangular house pattern with small posts may be restricted to the later period or may be a trait of both the early and late Hoecake phase. The Hoecake site probably owes its tremendous size to a shifting community during both early and late Hoecake phase times. Except for the presence of burial mounds, it is similar in this respect to the Range site in Illinois (Kelly 1981).

Other sites identified to this period in this northeastern portion of the Central Valley are relatively small and similar to the Dunklin phase locations. One exception is the Double Bridges site located south of the Cairo Lowland. Moore (1916:502) counted 23 mounds at this site, but this figure is considered an exaggeration. The site is similar in many respects to Hoecake and together with this site indicates that larger population aggregates may be characteristic of the Hoecake phase, in contrast to the Dunklin phase. The mounds are also important in that they indicate a ceremonial aspect not known to exist in the Dunklin phase.

The Dunklin and Hoecake phases seem to represent two opposite extremes of the segmentary tribe. We cannot be sure of this until we know more of the chronology of the transition of Baytown into Mississippian in the Cairo Lowland. The Dunklin phase is mostly characterized by seasonally dispersed household units in minor watersheds. Maximum social units consisted of two to five or so households. There is no evidence of horticulture, no mounds, and little artifact variability. The Dunklin phase was politically weakly structured. The Hoecake phase, on the other hand, is characterized by burial mounds, which occur at large sites. Implied but not verified is a stronger political organization. Horticulture may be important, but this possibility has not been investigated.

The Hoecake phase expanded at the expense of the Dunklin phase. The coexistence of Barnes and Baytown pottery at sites bordering the two traditions is interpreted as one phase superseding the other within the Cairo Lowland area and immediately west of Sikeston Ridge. Relative to Baytown, Barnes decreases to the east and increases to the west. At the Harryette Campbell site, Ray Williams (1972) reported the stratigraphic priority of Barnes ware under Baytown ware. The initial Mississippian expression within the regions occupied by the Dunklin and Hoecake phases appears to have been essentially the same and primarily of immediate late Hoecake phase derivation.

THE BAYTOWN PHASE

Very little is known about the Baytown phase. The type site, Baytown, is also the name used for the period (Phillips 1970:903). This site also contains a major Coles Creek period occupation, according to current interpretations

(House 1982b:42–43). The Baytown phase as now defined extends over the lower portions of the St. Francis and White River drainages and the lowland portion of the Arkansas River.

Differentiating between Baytown and non-Baytown Woodland sites is difficult. Although the region is noted for a general lack of cord marked ceramics, there is considerable conflict between specific site assemblages. In general, plain-surfaced grog-tempered pottery predominates, although cord marking is most typical during at least part of the Baytown period within the Marksville-to-Coles-Creek sequence.

At Hyneman sites 1 and 2, west of Marked Tree, two major components were recovered during salvage in 1967. One is a Mississippian occupation dating about A.D. 1050. The second is a Baytown phase component with two radiocarbon dates of A.D. 642 ± 138 and 761 ± 151. Vessel shapes are small bowls and jars with flat bases (Figure 9.7). Grog-tempered plain-surfaced sherds predominate; some sherds contain a slightly sandy paste. Cord-marked sherds are rare. Yates Net Impressed sherds, on the other hand, are relatively abundant (Figure 9.7a). Very little actual decoration is present and is limited to crude incising and possibly cord impressing. No punctated or red-filmed sherds were observed in the collections.

Only one site report that describes a Baytown period component from northeast Arkansas is available. Carol Spears used material gathered by the University of Arkansas Museum during a highway salvage excavation in 1965 for her M.A. thesis on the DeRossitt site in St. Francis County. During 6 weeks of excavation under the direction of Jim Scholtz, with both hand excavation and scraping by heavy machinery, 164 pit features and over 500 postholes were found.

Four areas of pit and posthole concentration were found at DeRossitt, indicating four separate areas of occupation by Baytown groups. It is not known if these separate areas are contemporaneous or not. The identifiable floral materials in the pits showed a summer–fall–winter occupation, with such foodstuffs as persimmon, grape, hickory, acorn, and pigweed. No corn was identified in the Baytown features despite flotation of many soil samples carefully collected at the site. The site was located near two oxbow lakes. The small amount of bone preserved showed typical deer, swamp and cottontail rabbit, raccoon, bullfrog, fish, and bird categories present.

A total of 1972 Mulberry Creek Cord Marked sherds and 3446 (64%) Baytown Plain sherds were found in the Woodland pits, whereas only 13 Evansville Punctated and one Indian Bay Stamped sherd were recovered. This is a fairly typical Baytown ceramic assemblage. One Wheeler Check Stamped sherd was also collected from the site. Analyzing large amounts of these very similar sherds causes archaeologists to propose Baytown as a period of either cultural decline or at the least a period of extreme egalitarianism.

Lithics were rare at the site. A very few crudely stemmed points were recovered similar to those from the Hyneman site (Figure 9.4d–e). Small adzlike bifaces were also found (Figure 9.4f–g).

There were 36 pit features carefully measured at the DeRossitt site. The largest was about 1150 liters in capacity. The next largest was only about 300 liters. Ten pits were between 40 and 100 liters. In general, these are very small storage pit figures and seem to reinforce the seasonal nomadic interpretation, which is based on sparsity of artifacts at the site. Spears saw an increased amount and variability of artifacts at the site through time, possibly a reflection of population increase and/or more stable populations.

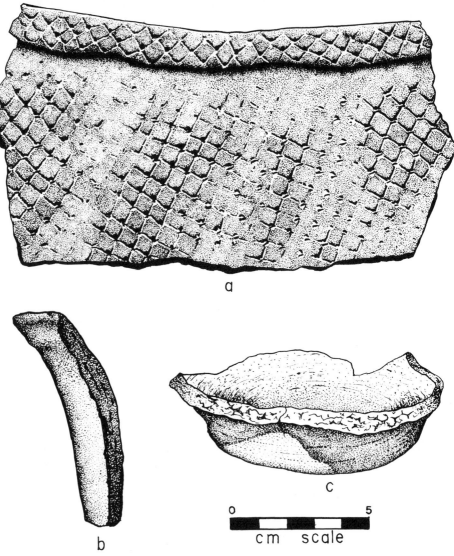

FIGURE 9.7.   Baytown phase ceramics from the Hyneman site. (a) Yates Net Impressed. (b)–(c) Baytown Plain. [Courtesy of the Arkansas Archeological Survey.]

TABLE 9.2
Prehistoric Sites Discovered Immediately Around the Parkin Site, Arkansas

Lithics	Ceramics				
	Only Baytown	Only Mississippian	Baytown and Mississippian	Ceramics not present	Total
Lithics present	13	5	5	95	118
Lithics not present	8	2	0	–	10
Total	21	7	5	95	128

An intensive 1-km survey around the Parkin site in Cross County, Arkansas, provides some additional data on Baytown-site settlement patterning (P. Morse 1981; Table 9.2). During this survey, performed during the brief period in the spring when optimum conditions for the discovery of small sites are present, 26 definite Baytown site locations were recognized. Baytown was defined by the presence of Baytown Plain and/or Mulberry Creek Cord Marked ceramics. Of these locations, 14 consist of only one Baytown sherd, occasionally accompanied by chert debitage. Larger areas of Baytown occupation, measuring 175–2250 m², contained 2–31 Baytown period sherds, as well as lithic artifacts, such as chert debitage, fire-cracked chert, scrapers, choppers, and a few broken chert bifaces.

A total of 128 archaeological locations were recorded immediately around the Parkin site. There were 26 Baytown and 12 Mississippian ceramic occupations represented. Of the total 33 ceramic components, 5 were shared. Of the 95 nonceramic locations, only 2 could definitely be classified as Mississippian. These consisted of isolated finds of a Madison point and a Parkin phase end scraper. Most of the remainder are thought to be Baytown in age, but many undoubtedly are Archaic or preceramic components. These data indicate that Baytown is much more dispersed and less stable in settlement than Mississippian. The general lack of shared locations indicates that horticulture was not as important to Baytown as it was to Mississippian.

Survey area 9, however, located on a slight ridge, had three definite areas of Baytown occupation about 200 m apart, two of which are about 1200 m² in size and the other about 400 m² in extent. Baytown occupation components were also found in areas where there were Middle Mississippian occupations. Although no evidence of Baytown corn agriculture has been recovered in the Central Valley, these particular Baytown site locations are confined to the areas of soils around Parkin that are best suited for hoe agriculture.

The Baytown phase developed into a Coles Creek period culture after about A.D. 700. At the Toltec site, southwest of the Central Valley near Little Rock, Arkansas, excavations show this continuation from Baytown to Coles Creek (Rolingson 1982). This large 40-ha site, enclosed by an embankment, once had at least 18 mounds up to 15 m high. However, there are no thick

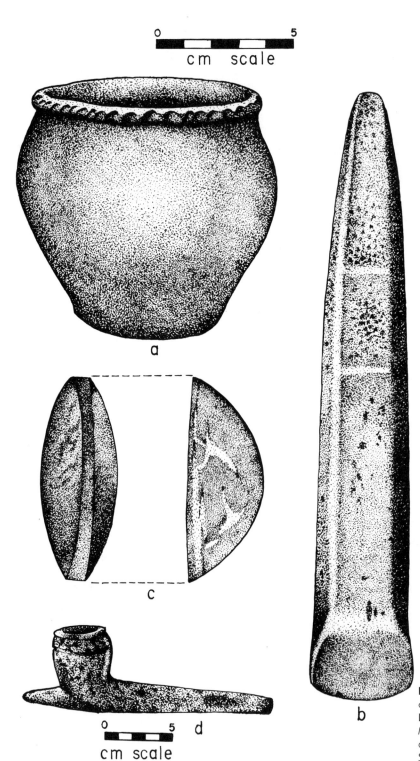

FIGURE 9.8. Coles Creek artifacts found at Chandler Landing, Arkansas. [Drawn from Moore 1910:341–348, courtesy of The Academy of Natural Sciences, Philadelphia.]

midden deposits at the site showing any concentration of population. Over
90% of the ceramics found at the site are Baytown Plain, with some evidence
of a very small later Mississippian occupation. Projectile points, found primarily on the surface, are both late Gary varieties and Scallorn varieties of
arrowpoints. Both boatstones and plummets have been found at the
site.

The lower portion of the Central Valley is characterized by the presence of
Coles Creek ceramics (Phillips 1970:916–917). These ceramics are very evident in the Western Lowlands, mainly because of the excellent survey of the
Cache River basin by Schiffer and House (1975). John House in particular has
worked for many years on the Coles Creek question in this portion of the
valley and to the south. It is apparent that Mississippian remains are not
characteristic in much of the region occupied by the Baytown phase until after
A.D. 1000. A Baytown-like occupation with Coles Creek decorated pottery and
mostly Baytown Plain pottery evidently persisted until that time in the area
concerned, and possibly as late as A.D. 1100 in southeast Arkansas.

There are some very impressive Coles Creek sites present. At Chandler
Landing in Prairie County, Arkansas, C. B. Moore (1910:341–348), mentioned or pictured two "Poole"-style stone pipes, a pottery elbow pipe, two
long narrow chisels, six boatstones, copper, numerous points, a large leaf-
shaped biface, pearl beads, and pottery, including a plain flat-based jar with a
notched or punctated lip (Figure 9.8). In White County, Arkansas, Charles
Figley (1968) has reported significant amounts of Coles Creek Incised pottery,
some of which is shell tempered. Apparently, when Mississippian does begin in
the cultural, or at least artifactual, sense in the southern portion of the Central
Valley, it is very unobtrusive and made up of small sites with plain ceramics
and sparse lithic artifacts. Baytown phase site ties to the central or Ouachita
Mountains, Arkansas, region are evident in the quartz crystals and novaculite
debitage and points, which have been found at several sites.

A draft report by John House on the Powell Canal site summarizes a
typical Baytown period site:

> Beginning at the bayou, there would no doubt be one or more dugout canoes
> perhaps tied to poles thrust in the muddy bank. At the top of a steep path leading
> up the bank would be a house, probably not of very substantial construction. In
> front of the house would be cooking fires and tools and facilities associated with
> varied daily tasks and bare ground strewn with ashes, broken pottery and dis-
> carded food scraps. Behind the house would be an area devoted to another activity
> involving infrequent use of curious round-based pits. Further back, at the edge of
> the woods, would be, in a tightly clustered group, the marked graves of ancestors
> and of contemporaries who died young. At the right season this encampment
> would be one of a number of similar encampments lined up in close proximity to
> one another along this short stretch of the bayou bank [House 1982a:195].

REFERENCES

Belmont, John S., and Stephen Williams
1981 Painted pottery horizons and the Southern Mississippi Valley. *Geoscience and Man* 22:19–42.
Chapman, Carl
1975 *The archaeology of Missouri* (Vol. I). Columbia, Mo.: University of Missouri Press.
Figley, Charles
1968 The Soc site, 3WH34. *Arkansas Archeologist* 7:41–52.
House, John H.
1982a *Powell Canal: Baytown period occupation on Bayou Macon in southeast Arkansas.* Report submitted to Arkansas Highway and Transportation Department by Arkansas Archeological Survey.
1982b Evolution of complex societies in East-Central Arkansas: An overview of environments and regional data bases. In *Arkansas archeology in review*, edited by Neal Trubowitz and Marvin Jeter, pp. 37–47. *Arkansas Archeological Survey Research Series* 15.
Kelly, John
1981 Range site community plans. In *Archaeology in the American Bottom*, edited by Charles J. Bareis and James Porter. *University of Illinois Department of Anthropology Research Report* 6:47–54.
Jones, Reca
1979 Human effigy vessels from Gold Mine plantation. *Louisiana Archaeology* 4:117–121.
Marshall, Richard A.
1965 An archaeological investigation of Interstate Route 55 through New Madrid and Pemiscot Counties, Missouri, 1964. *University of Missouri Highway Archaeology Report* 1.
Moore, Clarence B.
1910 Antiquities of the St. Francis, White and Black rivers, Arkansas. *Journal of the Academy of Natural Sciences of Philadelphia* 14:255–364.
1916 Additional investigations on Mississippi River. *Journal of the Academy of Natural Sciences of Philadelphia* 16:492–508.
Morse, Dan F.
1969 Introducing northeastern Arkansas prehistory. *Arkansas Archeologist* 10:12–28.
1977 The penetration of northeast Arkansas by Mississippian culture. In *For the director: Research essays in honor of James B. Griffin*, edited by Charles Cleland. University of Michigan Museum of Anthropology Anthropological Papers 61:186–211.
Morse, Dan F., and Phyllis A. Morse (editors)
1980 *Zebree archeological project.* Report submitted to Memphis District U.S. Army Corps of Engineers by Arkansas Archeological Survey.
Morse, Phyllis A.
1981 Parkin: The 1978–1979 archeological investigation of a Cross County, Arkansas, site. *Arkansas Archeological Survey Research Series* 13.
Phillips, Philip
1970 Archaeological survey in the Lower Yazoo Basin, Mississippi, 1949–1955. *Papers of the Peabody Museum, Harvard University* 60.
Rolingson, Martha Ann
1982 Public archeology: research and development of the Toltec site. In Arkansas archology in review, edited by Neal Trubowitz and Marvin Jeter. *Arkansas Archeological Survey Research Series* 15:48–75.
Schiffer, Michael B., and John H. House
1975 The Cache River archeological project: An experiment in contract archeology. *Arkansas Archeological Survey Research Series* 8.

Spears, Carol
    1978   The DeRossitt site (3SF49): Applications of behavioral archeology to a museum collection. M.A. thesis, University of Arkansas, Fayetteville.
Wendlund, Wayne, and Reid Bryson
    1974   Dating climatic episodes of the Holocene. *Quaternary Research* 4:9–24.
Williams, J. Raymond
    1972   *Land leveling salvage archaeology in Missouri: 1968.* National Park Service, Omaha, and Archaeological Research Division, University of Missouri.
    1974   The Baytown phases in the Cairo Lowland of southeast Missouri. *Missouri Archaeologist* 36.
Williams, Stephen
    1954   *An archeological study of the Mississippian culture in southeast Missouri.* Ph.D. dissertation, Yale University. Ann Arbor, Mich.: University Microfilms.

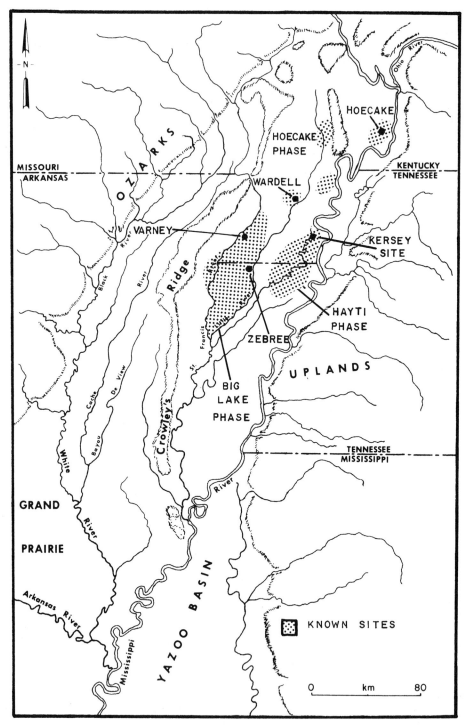

FIGURE 10.1. Early period Mississippian sites and phases in the Central Mississippi Valley.

10

Mississippian Frontier
(A.D. 700–1000)

Around A.D. 700 the Coles Creek culture began in the Lower Mississippi Valley, and the stage was being set to the north for the construction near present-day St. Louis of Cahokia, the largest prehistoric community known in the United States. The development of neither Coles Creek nor the Cahokia Fairmount phase is yet understood in detail. The time period of A.D. 700–1000 in the Central Valley has also been difficult to investigate (Phillips 1970:912). Until recently, a phase hiatus existed for much of the region (Phillips 1970:Figures 445, 446, 447). Slowly but surely, this period in the Central Valley is being put into its proper perspective (Figure 10.1).

Radiocarbon dates indicate that the Mississippian period began around A.D. 700 or shortly afterward and was fully developed by around A.D. 800–850. At the Hoecake site in the Cairo Lowland there is a date of A.D. 663 ± 184 (M–2212, 2213) from a mound thought to date early in this period. Three dates pertaining to the earlier Baytown period Dunklin phase occupation at Zebree were A.D. 691 ± 74, 829 ± 70, and 863 ± 84 (SMU–414, 415, 432). Radiocarbon dates at the Zebree site pertaining to the Early period Mississippian Big Lake phase were A.D. 810 ± 80, 836 ± 84, 838 ± 86, 876 ± 74, 931 ± 57, 941 ± 66, 960 ± 63, 1020 ± 74, 1076 ± 68 (SMU–443, 445, 453, 411, 422, 450, 426, 460, 457). A date obtained by Robert C. Dunnell on a Big Lake phase component in Missouri is A.D. 840 ± 130 (RL–1418). The generally accepted dating, based on these results for the Big Lake phase, is about A.D. 800–850 to A.D. 1000–1050. Radiocarbon dates from Arkansas that are thought to pertain to the end of the Early period Mississippian and the beginning of the next period cluster within or near the eleventh century (see Chapter 11).

Mississippian was not just a period of time characterized by changes in artifact styles. It was a new way of life and embraced new kinds of technology and a new relationship to the environment. It was undoubtedly the closest that the prehistoric Central Valley came to a cultural revolution, as contrasted with the more gradual evolution experienced before about A.D. 700. Although there was continuity from Baytown to Mississippian, the transition was rapid and the consequences were enormous.

ORIGIN OF MISSISSIPPIAN

It is apparent that the Cairo Lowland was central to Mississippian development in the Central Valley. It is also reasonable to assume that proximity to the remarkable site of Cahokia is not coincidental to the beginnings of Mississippian culture in the Central Valley.

Discussions of the possible origins of Mississippian culture almost invariably include migration or diffusion from Mexico. However, Mesoamerican (Mexican) influence on this region was indirect in nature and cannot be seriously hypothesized as causing the development of Mississippian. Corn, squash, and beans are Mesoamerican in origin but probably filtered into the area via the Southwest at different times and not as a complex. There are no known Mesoamerican artifacts in prehistoric context in the Central Valley, nor are there any known Central Valley artifacts in prehistoric context in Mesoamerica. There is no known resource in the Central Valley that the Mesoamerican civilizations would have coveted, and there was no reason, except perhaps curiosity, for Mesoamericans to visit the valley. The development of Mississippian culture must be viewed as indigenous without outside direction.

The Mississippian chiefdom organization probably began when independent tribelets cooperated on a continuing basis by pooling resources to the extent that they became mutually dependent. Ecological diversity within a restricted area must have been an important ingredient in the development of the Mississippian chiefdom system (Smith 1978). Permanent settlements pooled resources from diverse environments and secured themselves against the risk of crop failure by maintaining dispersed farms. The latter helped prevent loss from drought and storm damage. This political system also maintained large surplus-food storage facilities. Population growth and increased reliance upon farming, with its consequential ecological changes, are nonreversible variables that must have been significant. There is mounting evidence that the move to chiefdoms began at several locations within the eastern United States, perhaps even independently of one another.

ENVIRONMENTAL ADAPTATION

Mississippian sites in the Central Valley are found near or within areas of easily worked and well-drained soils with high agricultural potential. Low, seasonally flooded areas and lakes with abundant faunal and floral resources are usually adjacent to these sites as well. Smith (1978) calls the meander belt areas a Mississippian "adaptive niche [p. 480]" (habitat) where the combination of intensive agriculture and seasonal exploitation of selected natural resources made optimum use of the ecosystem. Meandering streams on the braided stream surfaces provided niches that were similar to but smaller than those on meander belt streams. Many sites were located at the junction of different zones in order to provide immediate access to the resources of prairie, upland, braided surface, and meander belt. All sites, however, were near prominent meandering streams, and some were located well within the meander belt region. Annual flooding both enriched the soil and left water for fish and waterfowl. Seasonal protein sources such as deer, raccoon, and turkey were important, but fish and migratory birds may have furnished over 50% of the protein in the diet on occasion. Maize, squash, and, later, beans were certainly important crops, with maize being a major food source. Wild foods were still gathered, in particular, nuts for oil, greens, root tubers, fruits, berries, and seeds.

These sites were not located adjacent to active river channels but were on old or inactive levees, particularly near oxbow lakes full of fish. The most efficient use of agricultural lands was to disperse the population in farmsteads near the best soils, those easily cleared and conducive to hoe agriculture. These areas also were high enough to protect planted fields from late spring floods. Fortified villages served as political and ceremonial centers and for protection when necessary. Most of the population probably was in separate nuclear family farmsteads dispersed around such a village. Mississippian populations possibly even produced a more favorable habitat for deer by clearing and abandoning fields, which created more forest edges, sustaining a larger deer population.

Bruce Smith (1975) has analyzed the exploitation of animal populations through faunal remains recovered from seven Mississippian sites. Over 100 species of vertebrates were found in the collections from these sites, but only a relative few of these were significantly important to the diet when the potential meat yield was taken into account. Deer, raccoon, fish, and waterfowl were the most common, followed by squirrels, rabbits, turtles, wild turkey, beaver, opossum, bear, and elk. Deer was by far the most important meat. Fish were most available in the spring during spawning and in the summer when water in pools and oxbow lakes receded. Backwater areas rather than active streams were usually fished. Turtles were caught most often in the summer. Rabbits were most probably hunted in the summer. Waterfowl were available from about October to April, with some species migrating down the Mississippi flyway and going elsewhere and others spending the winter in the lakes of the Central Valley. There were spring and fall peaks in waterfowl exploitation. The remainder of the animals were more available during winter, from October through March.

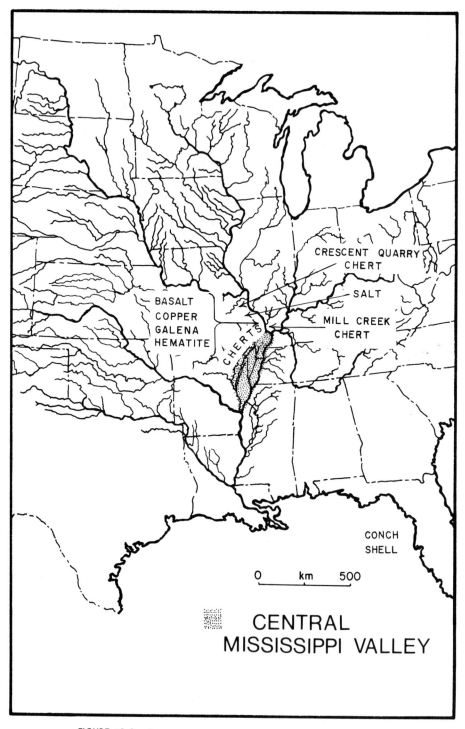

CRESCENT QUARRY
CHERT

SALT

BASALT
COPPER
GALENA
HEMATITE

MILL CREEK
CHERT

CHERTS

CONCH
SHELL

0   km   500

CENTRAL
MISSISSIPPI VALLEY

FIGURE 10.2.   Important outside resources near the Central Valley.

OUTSIDE RESOURCES

Most Mississippian sites in the Central Valley are located where there is not immediate access to certain important resources. The most critical group of such resources is lithic (Figure 10.2). It would be difficult to imagine how this rich alluvial environment could be exploited by Stone Age peoples without stone tools.

Chert debitage is abundant at most sites. The quality of the chert used is excellent, easily on a par with Dalton period use and superior to that of the remainder of the prehistoric sequence. There was considerable exploitation of Ozark cherts, particularly those of the northern Ozark Burlington chert outcrops. The northernmost recognizable chert used in the Central Valley was Crescent Quarry chert, mined south of St. Louis near the mouth of the Meramec River (Figure 10.3). This chert is associated with the entire Mississippian period. A short distance east of the Mississippi River and north of the Central Valley are outcrops of Mill Creek chert, probably the most important outside resource of all. This chert was basic to Mississippian hoe agriculture in the Central Valley. It also was extensively used for the manufacture of ceremonial items including "swords" and "maces" (Figure 10.4). Mill Creek chert ar-

FIGURE 10.3.   Road through one of the quarry pits at Crescent Quarries, Missouri. [Courtesy of Leonard Blake, St. Louis.]

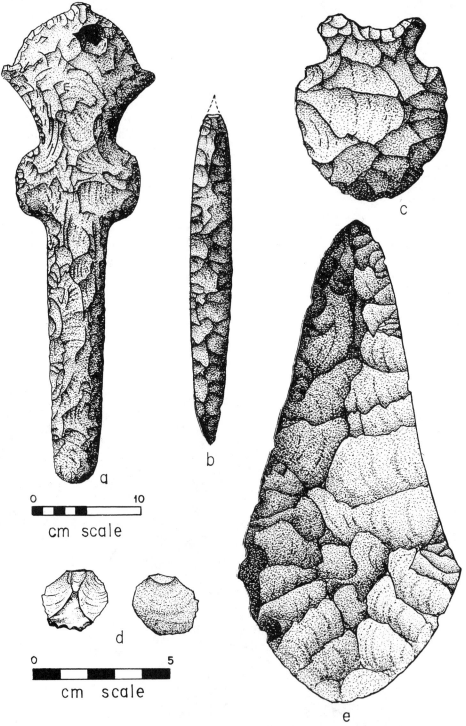

0 ▬▬▬▬ 10

cm scale

0 ▬▬▬▬ 5

cm scale

FIGURE 10.4. Artifacts made of Mill Creek chert found in the Central Mississippi Valley. (a) Mace. (b) Sword. (c) Notched hoe. (d) Hoe chip. (e) Hoe. [(a) Courtesy of the *Missouri Archeologist;* (b), (d) courtesy of the Arkansas Archeological Survey; (c) courtesy of the Department of Anthropology, National Museum of Natural History, Smithsonian Institution; (e) courtesy of Arkansas State University Museum.]

tifacts were traded throughout the Central Valley during the entire Mississippian period.

Another important lithic resource was basalt. We are exercising some freedom in classifying certain igneous rocks together as basalt, much in the same way that different cryptocrystallines are grouped together as chert. Basalt occurs in volcanic dikes in the Ste. François Mountains. It was used extensively in the Central Valley for the manufacture of heavy cutting tools including celts (axes) and adzes.

Copper is also found in the Ste. François Mountains; in fact, this region has produced a considerable amount of copper in contemporary mining. Copper was used for ceremonial objects, including large effigy sheets. Copper is characteristic only in the northern portion of the Central Valley until late in the Mississippian period, when it occurs in some quantity in the central portion.

Hematite and galena are available in the Ozarks, particularly in the area of the Ste. François Mountains. Both were used in paints (red and white). In southeastern ethnography, red symbolized war and white stood for peace. Both mineral paints were used throughout the Mississippian period, but red was particularly common early and late within the period. Probably the importance of war compared with peace was most intensive later in the Mississippian period.

Salt was an important commodity throughout this period of intensive agriculture (Keslin 1964; Brown 1980). It is available in salt springs within a narrow corridor of the Mississippi Valley that connects the Central Valley with the American Bottom opposite St. Louis and in which the Cahokia site is located. Salt springs are located opposite the mouth of the Kaskaskia River, near the mouth of the Meramec, and east of the Mississippi River near Carbondale. Earlier within the Mississippian period, salt was manufactured from a process of burning a lowland plant (American lotus) and leaching salt from its ashes. Apparently, the salt springs were important in the Central Valley only late within the Mississippian period.

Gastropods (*Anculosa*) available in the Ohio River were an important trade item early in the Mississippian period. But the shell that was primary throughout the entire Mississippian period originates in the Gulf of Mexico. Very large specimens of *Busycon* (conch shell) were evidently obtained at the Cahokia site, probably the location of the largest inland concentration of the shell that is known (Parmalee 1958). Whole shells, beads, and, rarely, gorgets (pendants) were traded widely. Speck (1919) provides valuable insight with the following description of wampum in southern New England:

> Briefly we may summarize the following uses assigned to wampum in this area: for ornamentation, as tribute, as a bribe for murder, as ransom for captives or as a compensation for crime, as a fine, as an urger to peace or as an incentive to war, as presents between friends, as a recompense for the services of shamans, as a means of proposing marriage, as conciliation for bereavement, and as the insignia of chiefs [p. 56].

We are not saying, for the record, that shell disk beads in the Central Valley are "wampum," but we are pointing out that beads can have a significant function in a culture. A string of shell beads represents a significant investment in time and energy, and hundreds of thousands, if not millions, of the beads were made.

REVOLUTION IN CERAMICS

Shell temper was the new ingredient in Central Valley Mississippian pottery. Sometimes it was combined with grog and, when done well, produced a very superior ware. But shell temper was not just a fad; its adoption was a true technological innovation that liberalized shape and increased strength. Improvements in the basic cooking jar were an important result.

Michael Million investigated the pottery industry in Arkansas over a period of several years (Morse and Million 1980), aided by the pioneering work of James Porter in Illinois. Million performed microscopic analyses and X-ray diffraction studies of the paste and experimentally replicated the manufacture and firing first of briquettes and then of pottery vessels (Figure 10.5). Interviews with soil scientists, chemists, and artists were conducted throughout the period of experimentation. Recovered by-products of pottery manufacturing included coil sections and "squeezes" of pottery clay duplicating the experimental by-products.

Clay is made up of minute, platelike particles that are so small that ionic charges on their surfaces repel one another, keeping them separated. When calcium carbonate in the form of burned shell is added, these forces are neutralized enough so that the particles tend to stay together. This process is called *flocculation*. The working quality of clay is considerably enhanced as a result. The paste that results is significantly lighter than a paste tempered only with grog, grit, or sand.

The calcium carbonate in mussel shell changes from aragonite to calcite when heated above 100°C. Organic binding is burned off. This shift in the crystalline structure, accompanied by a volume change, significantly enhances the crushing capability of the shell. After burning, it can be easily crushed by hand into minute platelike particles and powder, except for the hinge portions. In fact, if the shell were not burned before being mixed into the paste, the volume change caused by the act of firing would weaken if not shatter the vessel. There is proof that the Indians first burned their shell. An unfired 6-kg ball of shell-tempered processed clay was found at Zebree at the base of a storage pit. The shell had been burned. In addition, deposits at the Miller site included crushed burned-shell lenses identical to experimental results.

The major benefit derived from the adoption of shell temper was increased vessel strength. A lighter paste allowed the manufacture of a globular or spherical shape and this shape is inherently stronger.

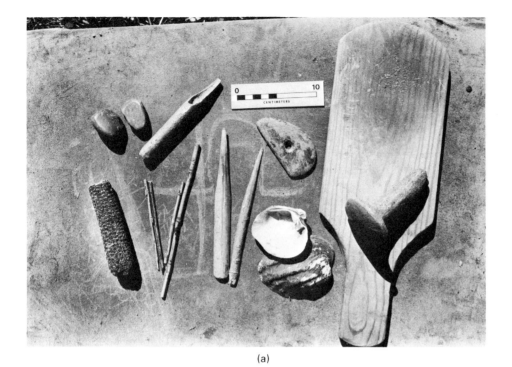

(a)

(b)

FIGURE 10.5. Mississippian pottery replication experiments. (a) Pottery-making tools used in replication experiments. (b) Cooking jar made by Michael Million on a layer of potsherds over coals in a firing pit. [Courtesy of the Arkansas Archeological Survey.]

Another benefit of shell temper and the globular shape is a probable increased efficiency in cooking. More even heating would certainly have resulted. Cooking jars invariably include both powdered shell and 2–4-mm-size shell particles in their paste, the latter presumably allowing an even porosity that might relate to more efficient or more uniform heat transfer.

Shell temper probably was a lowland innovation, as backswamp clay benefits most from the addition of shell. Other clays might not need shell to decrease the shrink–swell ratio characteristic of backswamp clay. The near universality of shell temper in Mississippian ceramics suggests that other benefits were present, such as more efficient cooking. Calcium carbonate is alleged to aid in the digestion of corn, and perhaps Mississippian paste allowed calcium carbonate to dissolve into a corn stew. Lime is used in Mesoamerica to soften dried corn. The B vitamin niacin is freed from corn when the corn is soaked in a hot alkaline solution such as lime water. Otherwise, a steady diet of corn causes pellagra.

Pottery was probably fired in open pits. The Big Lake phase ceramics show a pale brown to light yellowish brown color indicative of an oxidizing atmosphere. The iron impurities were burned out of the clay. Experiments show that a vessel made of backswamp clay has to be dried slowly before firing, usually over a period of several weeks. Spalling will occur where there is excess moisture. The vessel must then be preheated 3 or 4 hours before the actual firing to drive out further moisture. Dry wood is burned in the bottom of an open shallow pit, which was probably placed away from the village houses to prevent fires. After 2–4 hours a thick bed of coals occurs. These are spread out, and the pots that earlier had been preheated around the pit are stacked on top, upside down. Coals and fuel are stacked on top, and a temperature of 600–650°C is achieved. Firing usually takes less than an hour. Two or three dozen pots could have been fired at the same time in a 2-m-diameter pit. A possible pottery firing pit was found at the Zebree site.

Much of the Zebree site pottery is red filmed, characteristically on the interior surface. In order for the vessel to be red rather than black filmed, the painted or slipped surface must oxidize. To allow this, potters elevated vessels on spacers so that oxygen could flow freely into the interior of the vessels. The lips of large vessels often have four evenly spaced black areas where the kiln furniture touched.

OTHER IMPORTANT NEW ARTIFACT TYPES

Arrow points first occur at this time in the Central Valley. The technological advantage of the bow and arrow must have been tremendous, greatly increasing hunting efficiency. One basic style of point is called Sequoyah. It is a stemmed point with serrated edges made on a thin flake. Another is Madison, a triangular shaped point. One spinoff, the bow drill, was of immense impor-

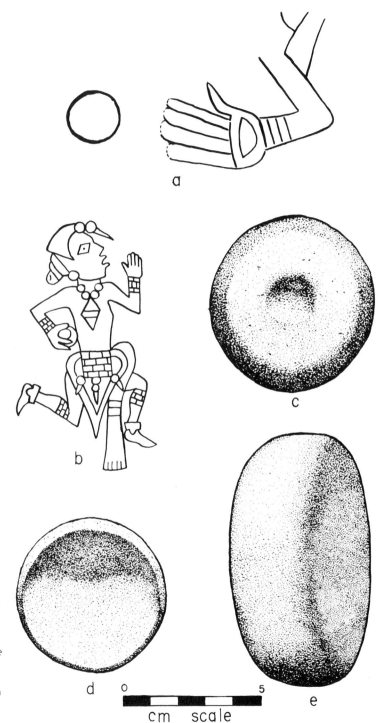

FIGURE 10.6. The chunky or discoidal stone. (a) Releasing the stone, decoration on a stone pipe. (b) Player, decoration on a shell gorget. (c) Typical stone *ca.* A.D. 750–1050. (d) Typical stone *ca.* A.D. 1050–1350. (e) Typical stone *ca.* A.D. 1350–1650. Note that (a) is releasing a stone similar to that shown in (e) and that (b) is holding a stone similar to that shown in (d). [Courtesy of the Arkansas Archeological Survey.]

tance. Without this invention, the large number of shell beads characteristic of Mississippian could not have been manufactured.

The discoidal or chunky stone appears in the Central Valley with the inception of the Mississippian period. The stone is discoidal in shape with rounded convex edges that cause it to fall over on its side (Figure 10.6). George Catlin (in Culin 1907:512) described the chunky game thus:

> The play commences with two (one from each party), who start off upon a trot, abreast of each other, and one of them rolls in advance of them, on the pavement, a little ring of 2 or 3 inches in diameter, cut out of a stone; and each one follows it up with his "tchung-ke" (a stick of 6 feet in length. . .), which he throws before him as he runs, sliding it along upon the ground after the ring, endeavoring to place it in such a position when it stops, that the ring may fall upon it [Culin 1907:512].

SOCIOPOLITICAL CHANGES

Chiefdom organization occupies an intermediate position between the segmentary tribe and the primitive state. Besides Mississippian societies, examples of chiefdoms have existed in Polynesia, central Asia, and large parts of Africa and South America. The development of state organization did not occur in the prehistoric United States, as it did in Mexico and Peru.

Segmentary tribal organization does seem archaeologically complex in some cases. Hopewell is a good example, as exotic artifacts and ceremonial burial sites or mound centers were characteristic. Poverty Point is another example of a segmentary tribal organization characterized by a complex site and exotic artifacts. The main advantages of chiefdom over tribal organization are greater productivity and the ability to support and control larger populations.

Primogeniture is the key to chiefdom organization. The primogenitor or clan ancestor is the basis upon which lineages, villages, and people are ranked relative to one another. No two are of equal rank; even twins are born sequentially. Administrative positions are filled by people entitled to them by virtue of their genealogy. This built-in inequality justifies the political hierarchy. The highest-ranked male normally is the paramount chief, and high-ranking males normally occupy the other administrative niches. Ranking automatically prescribes the rules of succession to an administrative post. In the southeastern United States inheritance was normally through the female line, so the line of succession would have been from the current chief to his sister's eldest son.

Mississippian chiefdom organization was based on agriculture and was characterized by permanent (year round) settlements. The Mississippian population usually was dispersed in farmsteads and villages in order to take the best possible advantage of the environment (Smith 1978:489–491). Farmsteads and hamlets related to villages, which in turn related to a paramount village. Redistribution and storage of surplus took place at the administrative centers. There were large pyramidal mounds arranged around open squares in the major villages.

Consumption of surplus took many forms, such as storage against future crop loss. Another was through feasts when administrative centers were embellished and repaired. Surplus was used to support some craft specialization, as well as the army when it was commissioned. There was commissioning and consumption of surplus foods and crafts by the chiefly lineage for dress and the artifacts of office. Outside trade for raw material and both necessary and exotic artifacts accounted for some consumption of surplus goods. Ceremonies must have taken place at many opportunities, perhaps monthly, if not even more frequently. Ritual would have accompanied planting, harvesting, other religious observations, and—most evident to the archaeologist—burial, particularly of ranked personages occupying administrative niches.

THE AMERICAN BOTTOM

Cahokia is the largest archaeological site in the eastern United States and the best-known Mississippian civic–ceremonial center. It is located north of the Central Valley, within the American Bottom region opposite St. Louis (Fowler 1978). Over 100 mounds occur with a 15.6-km² (6-square-mile) area in the center of this lowland. The multiterraced central mound is 30.5 m (100 ft.) high and covers 6 ha (15 acres). Burials in Mound 72 leave no doubt that there was a powerful chiefdom political system. In addition, there is ample evidence of extensive outside trade, particularly to the south.

The Cahokia site was a dispersed community of mounds and residential areas for several hundred years. It is so complex archaeologically that the origins of the initial Mississippi Fairmount phase are masked. In addition, it is thought that Cahokia as an administrative center was established after the American Bottom Mississippian chiefdom had evolved.

Of the four "second-line" communities (greater than 50 ha or 124 acres) the earliest is the Pulcher site, located in the southern portion of the American Bottom. This 120-ha (300-acre) site is believed to have played an important role in the development of American Bottom Mississippian (Griffin 1977). It very well may have been an administrative center that predated Cahokia, or at least was contemporary with the beginnings of Cahokia. Unfortunately, the site has been little investigated.

The Range site, which is located nearby at the southern end of the American Bottom, typifies the community of this time period and presents evidence of an apparent evolutionary developmental model (Kelly 1982). Communities involved several small structures, similar to those found at Zebree, arranged in an arc around a central square with a post pit. Storage pits were rectangular and circular. Basic Woodland ceramics are associated with shell-tempered types and interior-red-filmed pottery reminiscent of Varney in the Central Valley. The community plan is similar to that at Zebree, except that there is no evidence of a stockade at Range and the earlier Range communities are much smaller.

The American Bottom technically extends from the mouth of the Illinois River to the mouth of the Kaskaskia River, although Cahokia investigators limit its southern extension to opposite the Meramec River. There are about 770 km² (300 square miles) of meander belt lowland in the restricted definition. A large portion of this area is defined as "wet prairies" that were interrupted by significant forested areas including cypress. A mixed hardwood forest zone bordered on the eastern loess bluff slopes, beyond which there were long grass prairies and cedars. The lowlands and uplands provided extremely rich and varied habitats. Some 143 vertebrate species have been identified just from the Cahokia site. The faunal list is similar in many respects to those from Crosno and Zebree in the Central Valley. Ducks, fish, and, most noticeably, the white-tailed deer are significant components.

A growing population and increased dependence upon horticulture complemented each other. Larger populations occupying smaller areas for longer periods of time focused increased attention on local resource exchange and social cooperation. Diverse populations were being drawn into more permanent reciprocal exchange agreements based on real or fictive kinship relationships between tribal chieftains. Each site was situated in a very similar specific environmental location. The same kinds of foodstuffs were immediately available for each site, but materials to procure and process those foods were mostly available only elsewhere. Lithics, Mill Creek chert in particular, were crucial to lowland existence.

In the terminal Woodland period of the American Bottom region, exchange is evident in the ceramics. Crushed limestone became a predominant pottery temper, later replaced by shell. Some Woodland groups seem to have preserved their identity as late as the eleventh century. All of the data from the American Bottom indicate *in situ* transition from the Woodland into the Mississippian period.

The American Bottom and the Cairo Lowland are connected by a narrow corridor within which the Mississippi River flows. The earlier Platten phase and the later Saline phase are the identified Mississippian complexes in this corridor. Platten is characterized by grog- and shell-tempered ceramics. Both complexes are closely associated with the extraction of salt but seem little involved with the developing Mississippian to the north and south.

THE CAIRO LOWLAND

The Cairo Lowland is situated at the junction of the Ohio and Mississippi rivers, an area of extreme environmental diversity, compared with the remainder of the Central Valley. Mountains, highlands, prairie, braided-stream, and meander-belt habitats are present within or immediately adjacent to this fairly restricted area.

The lowland region is approximately 1650 km² (640 square miles). About 15% of the lowland is made up of the centrally located Matthews and East prairies. The rest of the lowland is divided between relict and contemporary meander-belt features (51%) and relict braided stream surfaces (34%). The Mississippi River borders along the south, east, and north. Most of the interior is composed of braided stream surface. An older braided stream terrace makes up Sikeston Ridge, and Commerce Hills is an extension of Crowley's Ridge. Together, they constitute the western border. Beyond Commerce Hills to the northwest are the Ste. François Mountains. Drainage west of the Cairo Lowland is directed south toward Blytheville and the Zebree site.

The Hoecake site is located near the center of the southeastern quarter of the Cairo Lowland. It is the largest site known in the Central Valley. The only other contender is the Rich Woods site, located 65 km to the west, at the edge of the terrace defining the Malden Plain. Both sites would fit Fowler's (1969) "second-line" Cahokia community definition. Rich Woods consisted of 33 mounds stretching over a space of 1450 m. Hoecake was credited with 54 mounds, ranging up to 7.5 m in height at the beginning of the century. The Hoecake site derives its name from the cone-shaped mounds, which resemble southern cornbread cakes cooked on hoes. J. Raymond Williams (1974) accepts at least 31 mounds as originally existing and estimates site size as roughly 80 ha (200 acres). It is a remarkable site.

As with all very large sites, Hoecake probably represents a locally dispersed community made up of residential areas and mounds. It may have been a planned community similar to Cahokia; certainly, some of the mound alignment suggests this. However, Robert Adams and Winslow Walker in 1942, while thinking the site was probably once fortified, did not think it had a plaza or square associated with the large central mound group. Hoecake is located adjacent to the division of the braided stream surface and the meander belt surface. The nearby later sites of Crosno and Beckwith's Fort (Towosaghy) are both located well within the meander belt. The latter site is the major Cairo Lowland phase center, and the former, a lesser center of this phase. Hoecake for the most part is pre–Cairo Lowland phase in date, although it is multicomponent and may encompass a Cairo Lowland phase hamlet. But these sites are not contemporaneous with one another; moreover, Hoecake and Towosaghy seem to be largely sequential through time, as if the local primary administrative site moved closer to the Mississippi River and deeper into the meander belt.

At Hoecake, three widely separated areas were tested, revealing typical Early Mississippian houses and storage pits (J. Williams 1974:55–88). Not enough area was exposed to reveal community plans. Several house patterns were superimposed over one another, and considerable debris is still evident on the surface. There appear to be fairly distinct midden concentrations. The features and structures found are identical to those found at Zebree, but there are important differences in the ceramics and burials.

One mound included several burials, 1 of which was originally associated with a sheet-copper artifact near the neck (J. Williams 1974). Another mound covered three collapsed log tombs with 14 burials. The only artifacts were sherds in the fill. A radiocarbon date of A.D. 663 ± 184 (M–2212 and 2213 combined) was obtained from two of the subsurface tombs. A date of A.D. 800 or somewhat earlier is our interpretation of the actual date.

Triangular points, often serrated, were characteristic. This contrasts with Zebree but is more in keeping with the Fairmount phase. The Kersey plugs for bottles at Hoecake are identical to those from Zebree. One unique feature of the site today is the presence of considerable Burlington chert debitage, much of it primary. No definite microlithic debitage was noted in our one short visit to the site, but the chert suggests this possibility.

The ceramics are similar to those at Zebree in type and to those from the American Bottom in variety. Both typical terminal Woodland and Early Mississippian pottery were evident; furthermore, grog and shell occur together in the paste of some of this pottery. Limestone temper, characteristic further north, is absent. The predominant overall type was Mulberry Creek Cord Marked. It is possible that a Hoecake phase Baytown period occupation accounted for much of this. Baytown Plain is the next most prevalent type; Mississippi Plain and Larto Red Filmed, in that order, were next in frequency. Varney Red Filmed is a minority type. In one of the excavations, Mulberry Creek was a minority type, and Varney Red Filmed and Mississippi Plain occurred in significant numbers.

The reported grog-, grog-and-shell-, and shell-tempered categories are confusing to a certain degree since more specific descriptions were not provided. Wickliffe Thick, usually a shell-tempered type, was reported as "clay tempered" (J. Williams 1974:76). Evidently, there was considerable variation in paste and in surface treatment and shape. Two plain jars found with burials have Fairmount phase outlines, and one has a Big Lake phase outline; both were reported as having a clay and shell paste. There was a moderate amount of red-filmed ceramics present in relation to plain ceramics but not in the numbers that on the basis of Zebree and American Bottom data were expected. The Mississippian component at Hoecake probably predates that at Zebree.

Larto Red Filmed is a minority type wherever it occurs (Phillips, Ford, and Griffin 1951: fig. 9). In the northern half of the northern Central Valley it is usually conspicuous by its absence. It is most prevalent in the eastern portion of the Yazoo Basin (Phillips 1970:99). Yet, it was reported in fair quantity at Hoecake. Red filming apparently occurred as a trait before shell temper developed as the prevalent ware. This trait also occurred in the American Bottom.

Baytown Plain is not an expected late Baytown period type in the quantity reported at Hoecake. Instead, Mulberry Creek Cord Marked (to the lip) was generally dominant around A.D. 700. Plain surfaces may also have developed before shell temper became prevalent.

At Hoecake the following grog-tempered pottery categories were reported (J. Williams 1974:78): incised; red filmed and incised; incised and cord marked; red filmed, incised, and cord marked; incised and punctated; and red filmed, incised, and punctated. Red filmed, plain, incised, and cord marked also occurred in a combined grog-and-shell-tempered paste. Sand-and-shell-tempered paste occurred rarely with plain-surfaced pottery. This latter was typical of Zebree pottery.

At the Kersey site, located some 90 km to the southwest, grog-tempered variations also occurred (Marshall 1965). Cord-marked sherds included some from jars with plain necks similar to those found in early Cahokia. Many of these had the cord-marked border defined by an incised line. Others had crude incisions over cord marking, over the plain neck, or with punctations on the plain neck. There was red filming on some cord-marked sherds. Several rim sherds were incised; some had an incised and punctated motif. Other odd grog-tempered sherds reported at Kersey but not pictured were brushed, simple stamped, incised inverted arcades, curvilinear incised, combed, and part of a Wickliffe funnel.

The Kersey site appears to be multicomponent with a major Mississippian Hayti phase occupation succeeding a late Baytown period occupation. Varney Red Filmed is the prevalent shell-tempered type, even outnumbering Mississippi Plain. The Hayti phase ceramic assemblage is otherwise similar to that of the Big Lake phase. Baytown Plain is of a relatively low frequency and is mostly associated with Mulberry Creek Cord Marked in the lower levels. Larto Red Filmed is just barely present.

THE ZEBREE SITE

The history of archaeological investigation at Zebree parallels the history of the Arkansas Archeological Survey. The Zebree site was discovered in 1967, 2 months after the Northeast Arkansas Survey Station was opened and during a time of intensive regional data gathering. The assemblage at Zebree was immediately recognized as unusual. At the subsequent Southeastern Archaeological Conference Richard Marshall disclosed that he had found a similar assemblage near Hayti, Missouri, which he had classified as Early Mississippian.

The Survey funded tests of three sites near the Big Lake Wildlife Refuge in the summer of 1968. Two of these sites were found to have been disturbed by plowing and building and contained few undisturbed subsurface zone features. However, at the third site, Zebree, several components were found with deep intact midden. A Baytown period Dunklin phase occupation was separated from the Early Period Mississippian level by a relatively sterile layer. Traces of a Middle period Mississippian farmstead and later Euro-American occupation were also found.

The National Park Service provided funds for a major excavation at Zebree in 1969. Two large block excavations were placed in the two higher areas of the site, with a few test pits and auger holes placed in other areas. Over 100 pit features, 8 structures, and 8 burials were dug in 1969. The stratigraphy revealed that there was a sudden change from Woodland to Mississippian. Evidence of the Cahokia microlith industry and bone harpoons like those at Cahokia were found in Big Lake phase levels. Large numbers of Varney Red Filmed salt pan, hooded bottle, and bowl fragments were found, as well as Wickliffe Thick funnel sherds.

The Zebree site was placed on the National Register of Historic Places after this excavation. Subsequently, when the U.S. Army Corps of Engineers planned a drainage ditch that would essentially destroy the site, another major excavation was planned. A multidisciplinary research team and a 20-person field and laboratory crew were assembled in 1975 (Morse and Morse 1980). A zooarchaeologist, ethnobotanist, and ceramics expert were set up in separate labs to analyze material during the excavation. A multistage plan of excavation combined the opening up of large block units, backhoe trench transects, and a stratified systematic unaligned random sample of 1% of one-half of the site. Most material was recovered using water screening or flotation.

A final salvage effort was made during the summer of 1976 with the cooperation of the contractor. Bulldozer transects revealed features in the subsoil, which were quickly excavated. Even a dragline was employed at one point to help excavate an early-nineteenth-century well.

Early Mississippian Ceramics

The recognition of an early "Varney" period (informally used after the main pottery type, Varney Red Filmed, a variety of Old Town Red), was first made by Stephen Williams in 1954. He unintentionally disguised this, however, by including all known Mississippian manifestations in one area into the "Malden Plain phase." The next investigator to recognize the importance of the Varney horizon was Richard Marshall (1965). The excavations at the Zebree site in 1968, 1969, 1975, and 1976 (Morse and Morse 1980) verified Williams's and Marshall's discoveries and provided important new information.

Only three basic shell-tempered wares were found in the Big Lake phase component at Zebree. These were Varney Red Filmed, Mississippi Plain (Neeley's Ferry variety), and Wickliffe Thick (Figure 10.7). A large number (about 40%) of Varney sherds were found at Zebree. About 60% of these are jars (Figure 10.7b). Varney vessel types also included large shallow pans, hooded bottles, and bowls (Figure 10.7d, f, g). The type was originally named by Stephen Williams (1954) and most recently has been established as a variant of Old Town Red since the two types often were indistinguishable. Varney has a typical Mississippian shell-tempered paste with an added thick, often multi-

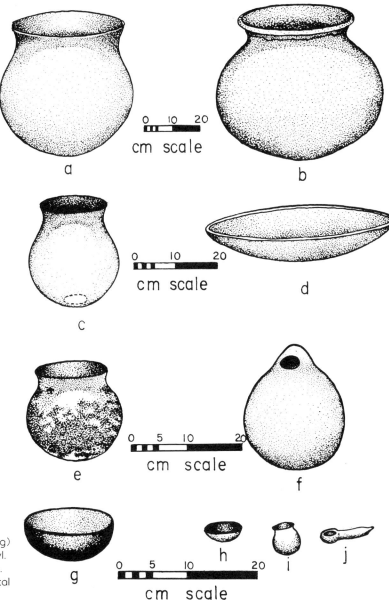

FIGURE 10.7. Basic shell-tempered wares found at the Zebree site. (a) Mississippi Plain large jar. (b) Varney Red Filmed large jar with reinforced rim. (c) Wickliffe funnel. (d) Varney Red Filmed salt pan. (e) Typical Varney Red Filmed cooking jar. (f) Varney Red Filmed hooded bottle. (g) Typical Varney Red Filmed food bowl. (h) Toy bowl. (i) Toy jar. (j) Toy ladle. [Courtesy of the Arkansas Archeological Survey.]

layered, slip of hematite and clay applied to the interior. Bottles were slipped on their exterior. After applications this slip usually was burnished to a high polish, which probably took longer than vessel manufacture. Two 500-gm balls of a red clayey substance that were probably dried red slip were found at Zebree and may have been a trade commodity.

The reason for applying such a thick layer is not known. It is not aesthetic, since it is the interior of vessels (except for bottles) that were red filmed. It may be for strength. Sherds dug at Zebree were both counted and weighed, allowing an index of size to be computed. Red-filmed sherds always constituted the largest sherds, whether in midden, features, or the cultivation zone. The protective filming obviously guarded the sherd against leaching of its shell content, and it may have strengthened the pot as well. Red filming also may have made the pots less porous, although it is difficult to imagine why porosity would have been a problem. Whatever the reason, a lot of care and time was spent applying the red slip, and the reason most probably was a technological one.

The typical Varney jar has a globular body, a round base, and a strongly recurved rim (Figure 10.7e). The interior has a thick red slip, with burnishing marks present. Almost half the exterior sherds are also red filmed, but the film is thinner and not polished. Often only a smear, as if a handprint, is all that is present. Only a very few crude red-filmed loop handles occurred at the Zebree site. The only good association was in one of the latest Big Lake phase features at the site. Handles apparently were not characteristic until after about A.D. 1000–1050.

These jars occur in three sizes. Large jars measure at least 30 cm in diameter at the orifice and are at least 40 cm high. The volume would be 52 liters. The creation of one of these large vessels would be much more difficult for a potter than would the smaller ones, as they had to be made in stages. Reinforcement of the rim with rim strips is characteristic of large jars. Although these large jars took more time and skill to make, they obviously fulfilled a function thought to be necessary in the Big Lake phase. They could have been used to cook large amounts of food at one time. They could also have been used for storage or for soaking dried corn to soften it for cooking.

Measurements showed that a medium-size cluster of jars was also present. Jar height was around 30 cm, and orifice diameter was about 25 cm. Average volume was about 13 liters. These probably functioned as cooking jars. The small jars at Zebree were about 20 cm high and 12 cm in orifice diameter. They held only a little over 3 liters. Ladle damage is obvious on the rim, indicative of use as a cooking jar. The average Pueblo cooking jar for a nuclear family of five contains about 3.1–4.9 liters.

Varney Red Filmed pans were also common in the Big Lake phase (Figure 10.7d). These measure between 50 and 77 cm in diameter and have an average 15-liter capacity. Usually only 12–15 cm high, they are oval in shape with rounded bases, to make a shallow container. Several layers of red filming are usually found on the interior. The exteriors usually have grass impressions, and the pans were held in a mold while being coiled. A pit could serve as such a mold. These pans are well made, with uniform thickness and graduation of walls.

The Varney pans were probably used for the production of salt, either through rapid evaporation or by slower solar evaporation. This shape is often found near saline springs in southeast Missouri (Keslin 1964). There is no evidence of such a spring at the Zebree site ever being present. From an ethnographic model it was hypothesized that salt was derived from the American lotus (*Nelumbo lutea*). The lotus is present at Big Lake today, spreading out over much of the lake's surface during the summer. An atomic absorption test was run on leaves and stems of the American lotus. These were dried and ground, and 1-gm samples were ashed in a muffle furnace at 500°C. The stems in particular yielded very high concentrations of both sodium and potassium, 3800–6600 parts per million (ppm) for sodium and 8500–20,000+ ppm of potassium. The Big Lake phase people could easily have gathered the leaves and stems of the lotus in shallow water, dried and burned them, leached the ash with water through funnels, and evaporated the filtrate in the large, shallow Varney pans. The large jars could have served to collect the water from funnels.

Varney Red Filmed bowls (Figure 10.7g) were found at Zebree. They have simple rounded bases with plain rims. There seem to be four sizes, from small (.26–.89 liter) to one measuring 18.50 liters. Bowls were slipped on both interior and exterior. They probably functioned as food serving and eating containers. The small bowls, which were probably the individual food vessels, averaged about .7 liter.

Hooded bottles, made in the shape of gourds, are another pottery shape found at Zebree (Figure 10.7f) and often even have a dimple in the top where the gourd stem would have been present. One reconstructed hooded bottle has a capacity of 4.4 liters. About two dozen hood fragments of this type of vessel were found. Associated with bottles are "Kersey Clay objects" which are clay plugs that fit the bottle orifice and were used to seal the container. Seed corn could have been stored in these bottles, safe from rodents. Enough seed for several acres can be stored inside a hooded bottle.

Mississippi Plain is the basic utilitarian shell-tempered ware typical of Mississippian cultures. At Zebree, plain vessels were smoothed but rarely polished. Most vessels found at Zebree are large jars (Figure 10.7a). It was estimated that one 52-liter-capacity plain jar could break into about 2500 sherds when smashed. These jars have moderately flared rims and are not recurved. Appendages are not characteristic of the jars at Zebree. These large jars could have been used as cooking jars for large groups, for food storage, or for water storage. Small and medium-size bowls of Mississippi Plain ware were also found.

Wickliffe Thick pottery has only one vessel form, a globular funnel (Figure 10.7c), which is the only pottery shape that has two sets of rim sherds for each vessel. Wickliffe paste is distinctive, being coarsely shell tempered. Sherds are much thicker than they are for other types, usually about 10 mm. There were a variety of surface treatments found at Zebree, including cord marking, incising, and an occasional red wash. Two almost-complete funnels were found at Zebree, measuring 16 cm in diameter and 24 cm high. Capacity is about 5 liters. These funnels tend to break easily along coil lines. They probably were used to process salt from ashes, along with the Varney salt pans.

A few pottery ladles were found at Zebree; three Varney Red Filmed and one Plain. One which may have been a toy is complete and holds 3.4 cc (Figure 10.7j). The largest may have held about 250 cc. There were 14 toy vessels discovered at Zebree; they were in the shape of both bowls and jars (Figure 10.7h, i). Most were plain; 2 were red filmed. These may have been made by girls practicing one of their adult roles.

The Microlithic Industry

The basic Cahokia microlithic industry existed at Zebree. Recovered were 285 microliths, 127 cores, 449 blades, and other associated debitage (Figure 10.8a–g). This is not an incidental occurrence. No other site in the Central Valley has produced over a handful of microlithic elements, which could result from a combination of the very small size of the microliths, inadequate recovery techniques, and lack of recognition. After all, this industry was not recognized until 1959, by Dan Morse when he was a graduate student.

Nearly 90% of the chert used to make microliths at Zebree was obtained from the Crescent Quarries, located 32 km (20 miles) southwest of St. Louis. The microliths made at Cahokia also were manufactured from this chert. Crescent Quarry chert readily fragments with bipolar percussion into blocky fragments suitable as preforms for cores.

Over half of the cores are columnar in shape, with blades having been removed from both ends. About 10% are bipolar, including some very small exhausted examples. Other cores tend to be pyramidal or just "amorphous" in shape. Usually between two and five blade scars exist on all cores, with columnar ones averaging higher figures. Platform preparation involves edge retouch and battering over the striking surface of the core rather than down the multiple-fluted blade surface (Morse 1974).

Microliths can be divided into tabular (40%) and cylindrical (60%). The former were made on blades chosen for natural working areas and underwent a minimum of retouch. The latter were retouched into narrow awl and needle-like drill points. Cylindrical microliths exhibit either rounded and worn tips or beaked and worn tips. Sometimes they are polished. The rounded tip microliths are probably drill bits for perforating shell beads. Beaked tips probably functioned as gravers for grooving shell or bone preparatory to splitting, similar to the process of cutting glass. Experiments in drilling and graving produced breaks identical to recovered examples.

The unmodified blades were the knappers' castoffs. These had been discarded after selection of blades suitable for microliths. Comparison with the microliths clearly showed that a narrow thick blade that could be retouched into a cylinder shape was wanted. The cross section was triangular or rectangular.

Michael Sierzchula (1980) conducted experiments replicating and using microliths. Nodules collected from road cuts near the Crescent Quarries

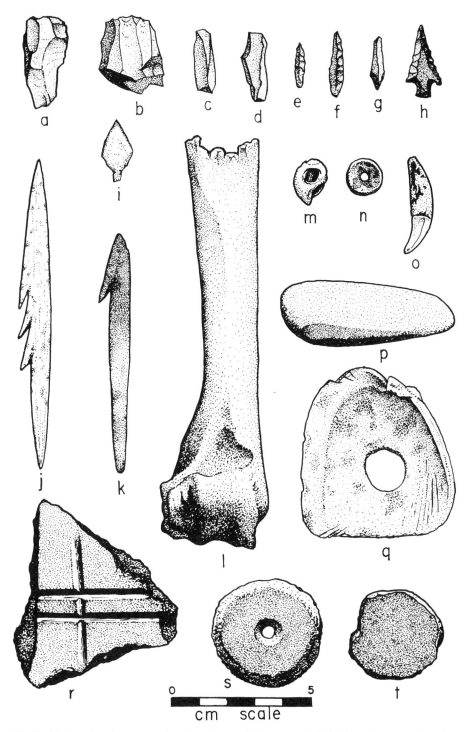

FIGURE 10.8. Miscellaneous artifacts found at the Zebree site. (a)–(b) Microlith cores. (c)–(d) Microlith blades. (e)–(g) Microliths. (h) Sequoyah–Scallorn point. (i) Gar scale point. (j)–(k) Bone–antler harpoons. (l) Deer-humerus flesher. (m) *Anculosa*-shell bead. (n) Conch-shell bead. (o) Raccoon canine pendant. (p) Pottery polishing stone. (q) Mussel-shell hoe. (r) Potsherd abrader. (s)–(t) Pottery disks. [Courtesy of the Arkansas Archeological Survey.]

(which is on the National Register of Historic Places) were reduced using bipolar percussion. Striking platforms were created from which blades could be struck, and prominent core ridges to allow thick blades to be removed were made. Direct percussion of a hammerstone with the core encircled by a fore-finger was by far the most effective technique tried. The core could be easily positioned, and there were few broken blades. The selected blade was best retouched by pressure with an antler tip on the blade held in a wooden vise, which was a small wooden slab with a central groove suitable for the blade, which was held in place with a thumb. The abortion rate was only about 10%. The drill bit then had to be abraded to remove platforms; otherwise, the point rounded and could not drill.

The cylindrical microlith was then hafted in a freshly cut cane, cut near a joint to stop the drill bit from pushing too deep. The cane held the tool fast. A bow drill was found to be very effective using these bits. A shell was drilled in 10 minutes. After 12 holes, the two microliths were still functional. Wood, green bone, and teeth also were drilled. For instance, it took less than 2 minutes to drill a hole in a fresh dog canine.

The time spent making shell beads, the quantity of serviceable drill bits still extant, and their distribution throughout the Zebree site indicate that bead making (at least drilling) must have been a basic household activity. A lot of bead makers had to be involved. It would have been difficult for one specialist to produce large quantities of beads. The relative lack of shell debris at Zebree may be due to the complete use of the conch shell. At Cahokia, where the shell was extremely plentiful, there was a great deal of waste in the sense of discarding those parts most difficult to make into beads.

Other Artifacts

The point style most common at Zebree was the serrated Scallorn or Sequoyah type (Figure 10.8h). Points were fairly rare, and possibly nonlithic tips were on arrow shafts. For instance, a small gar scale at Zebree had been modified into a stemmed point.

Fishnet impressions in accidentally burned clay and bone fishhooks were expected finds. An unexpected find consisted of four bone harpoons, the first ever reported from the Central Valley (Figure 10.8j, k). However, harpoons have been found at Cahokia in association with the Fairmount phase. The four harpoons from Zebree measure 7–11 cm long and include three with single barbs and one with triple barbs.

Perforated and unperforated pottery disks were common at the Zebree site (Figure 10.8s, t). Less than 10% were perforated; two were multiple perfo-rated and probably functioned as strainers in gourd or wooden bottles, or possibly in the pottery funnels. The others were probably used in a dice or guessing game (Culin 1907:45, 227).

Several ceramic discoidals were recovered at Zebree, but a sandstone specimen best exemplifies the nature of the earliest style of discoidal. Measuring 6 cm in diameter and 4 cm thick, it has a convex side and flattened faces, each of which contains a small central depression only 1.7 × 1.2 × 0.2 cm deep. The convex side of the circumference allows the disk to fall over after being rolled on the ground.

Beads were made of clay and conch shell. In addition, possible tubular beads made of the long bones of birds and small mammals 1–4 cm in length were recovered, but the most unusual and numerous beads were made of the gastropod *Anculosa* (Figure 10.8m). Except for one reported Archaic association, these are not known to occur before this time period in the Central Valley.

Mill Creek chert artifacts were fairly common at Zebree. Most of the 35 polished hoe chips, a biface made on a broken hoe, and even a small percentage of the elements of the microlith industry were Mill Creek. This chert outcrops in Union County, Illinois, as extremely hard, flat boulders suitable for manufacturing into hoes. It must have been a tremendous technological advantage to have those superior hoes. The trade in Mill Creek chert artifacts (not raw material) becomes characteristic of a significant portion of the Mississippi Valley, including all of the Central Valley.

Pottery-polishing pebbles constitute a newly recognized tool (Figure 10.8p). Those found at Zebree differ from later types, although no two are alike. Most are edge abraded, and some are single-face abraded. Later Mississippian polishing stones are small pebbles polished over portions of the surface but rarely on edges. Polishing pebbles are readily identified by striations identical to experimental ones.

Grooved pottery sherd abraders are pretty much limited to the Central Valley. They first appear during the Early period Mississippian. Most are made on the earlier sand-tempered Barnes pottery (Figure 10.8r). Between 20% and 25% are made on Mississippian pottery, a statistic that increases with time during the Mississippian period.

A strange group of artifacts that occurred at Zebree and may well be unique to it involved an orthoquartzite industry. The stone outcrops on the other side of Crowley's Ridge almost due west of Zebree. Artifacts manufactured were choppers and backed knives lightly to heavily ground on the working edges. They possibly could have functioned to cut up conch shells into bead blanks or even to groove sherds for use as abraders. Approximately 3.5 kg of orthquartzite was recovered, mostly small debitage. There were seven "choppers" and 26 "backed knives."

Less is known about woodworking tools at this time than is known for later periods, but apparently the basic Mississippian technology of tool manufacture was present. Chipped and ground adzes and chisels were being made of chert and basalt. The trough abrader, indicative of basalt celt manufacture, is present. Basalt debitage is not present, and possibly only the final stages of manufacture were accomplished at the site. A ground-stone tool was first chipped into basic shape, roughly abraded with specialized end-abraded hammerstones, and then ground into its final shape with trough abraders. A large variety of sandstone abraders were also being used.

All of the Mississippian elements of knapping were present and probably differed little, if at all, from earlier techniques. Hammerstones, deer antler batons, and deer antler tips are not uncommon finds. In addition, quartzite pebbles with polished and striated surfaces probably were used to grind the edges of bifaces during the knapping process.

Bone, antler, and shell manufacture characteristic of, but not unique to, Mississippian is well represented at Zebree. These items include examples of grooved-and-snapped bone ends, longitudinally grooved mid-shaft portions, longitudinally sawed bone and antler for strips to make into awls and other artifacts, mussel-shell hoes and spoons, turtle-shell containers, deer-humerus fleshers, retouched bone scrapers, various kinds of awls, bipointed bone "gigs," and raccoon canine pendants.

Artifacts associated with painting were also found: a "paint palette" made on a flat cobble; cubes of hematite, galena, and kaolinite; and two spheres of prepared hematite-based paint. A fragment of mica was also recovered.

Zebree Site Environment

A number of approaches were used to reconstruct the particular past environment around the Early period Mississippian Zebree site in Mississippi County, Arkansas, in order to test the hypothesis of conscious selection of a particular adaptive niche by Mississippian peoples. The General Land Office surveyors' notes and maps, which were made from the 1820s to 1840s, were used as basic data by Suzanne Harris (1980) to delimit the past microecological zones. The area of the Big Lake phase, between the Little and St. Francis rivers, is now completely cleared of trees and farmed by modern agribusiness methods. The early surveyors in the area were ordered to blaze four witness trees at the corner of each section and two trees in each quarter section and to note the species. With the notes from a 310-km² (120-square-mile) area, over 1000 particular trees could be cross-tabulated with other environmental data to discern subtle habitat changes. Modern soil studies, older soil maps, quadrangle sheets showing modern contour lines, geological surveys, and the early nineteenth-century surveyors' comments on the topography all were used in recreating the past environment around the Zebree site. The faunal data collected during the excavations and analyzed by Eric Roth were added to this. Attempts were also made to use tree-ring dating and pollen analysis. Botanical specimens from the excavation were collected and analyzed.

The most immediate habitat is the Zebree site located just west of Big Lake. The site was located on sandy loam and is adjacent to prime agricultural land. The site area was selected, cleared, and settled by people who recognized the superior agricultural potential of this specific location. Remains of both

12- and 14-rowed corn constitute the only cultigen identified. Pigweed and gromwell seeds, possibly from cleared fields, were recovered as well.

One of the diverse environments immediately available to the Zebree inhabitants was the aquatic community of Big Lake itself. This lake is much larger (3200 ha) and shallower than the usual Mississippian-associated lake. Largemouth bass, flathead and channel catfish, gar, suckers, drum, walleye, and buffalofish bones were identified in Big Lake phase middens. In fact, 66% of the bone fragments found during the initial investigation were fish. The method of data recovery makes a great deal of difference when interpreting the importance of fish in the diet. The finer the screen size used, the more fish remains are recovered for study. The use of one-eighth in. (.3 cm) screen and flotation of selected levels greatly added to the numbers of fish found at Zebree. Identification of mussel shell species also reflected the presence of a lake environment. A riverine zone, the Right Hand Chute of Little River, also existed near Zebree.

The numerous species of waterfowl found at Zebree are indicative of either a lake or swamp environment. Ducks prefer open water in good weather, but this open water would be present in both areas. The mallard was the most common bird found at Zebree, just as it is today. The sandhill crane, Canada goose, teal, pintail, merganser, shoveler, and cormorant were other migratory fowl that were also found. The wood duck, a more permanent resident, was also present.

The littoral biotic community, on the edge of permanent standing water, includes lakes, ponds, and sloughs. Many edible plant species exist in this ecological zone; they include knotweed, water millet, cattail, floating leaf vegetation such as the American lotus and yellow water lily, and free-floating vegetation such as duckweed.

The swampland habitat was dominated by the cypress–hardwood and cypress–tupelo communities. Overflow was as much as 2.5–3 m in some of these areas in the winter; some peripheries were dry during the summer. Semiaquatic fauna including swamp rabbit, raccoon, marsh rabbit, otter, beaver, muskrat, rice rat, and mink have been identified at Zebree and were obtained from this habitat. Fish were present here after spring flooding and would have been caught easily as the waters receded. Deer would have lived here during the drier seasons.

A deciduous bottomland forest habitat included a lower elevation sweetgum–elm–hackberry association and a higher white oak–sweetgum association. There was occasional overflow of about 30–60 cm in places. Mammals including deer, bear, rabbit, and squirrel were commonly found. The lower sweetgum association was the most common habitat in the 310-km² area. Oaks were numerous as well, particularly on the ridge on which Zebree was situated. Hickory trees often are associated with oaks, and the hickory nut was the most common nut found in the excavations, followed by acorns and walnuts.

The white oak–sweetgum association, located 25 km west of Zebree, near the St. Francis River, would have produced the greatest number of acorns and therefore seasonally would have attracted deer, wild turkey, bear, and squirrels in great numbers. This area possibly was seasonally used as a hunting ground by the Zebree inhabitants, but other Big Lake phase sites in that region had more immediate access.

An intermediate zone, the cottonwood–willow–sycamore plant community, also was present in a large area west of the Big Lake highlands. Nuts, grapes, hackberry, mulberry, and persimmon were present. Raccoon and opossum lived here, as well as semiaquatic mammals and deer.

A prairie also existed near the Zebree site during the Big Lake phase. Both the prairie chicken and the thirteen-lined ground squirrel were identified in fauna from the site. There is a prairie just north of Zebree in Missouri that could have produced these species.

These microenvironments, all available within a short distance of the Zebree site, provided a great diversity of both fauna and floral resources. There would also have been a great number of forest edges present where ecotones met; these are particularly attractive to deer. Exploitation of faunal resources was still heavily weighted by the presence of the larger mammals such as deer, which provided by far the most potential meat yield. However, if one uses weight tables with a heavy average fish weight for larger specimens, the lake–seasonal-swamp habitat would donate at least as much protein as would the forest and forest edge habitats.

Settlement Pattern

Mississippian settlements usually are oriented east of north. Cahokia, for instance, fits this model (Fowler 1969:15). Mississippian villages are well planned and were probably built under the direction of a village chief.

The Big Lake phase village at the Zebree site seems to have been built quickly (Figure 10.9). A large pit feature in the center of the site probably was a post pit similar to those identified at Cahokia. These pits were dug so that a large and heavy log such as cypress could be pushed into the pit, then raised to a vertical orientation. This feature is the central axis of two 114-m-long transects whose ends define the four corners of the village. These transects probably originally were oriented along true north–south and east–west axes (based on a knowledge of solstice positions). This arrangement created a square village plan. However, if these transects are rotated slightly to adjust to the slough bank (15° east and 5° south, respectively) the village plan is rectangular, but more importantly, the known village is nicely defined. The actual measured area is 11,550 m² or 1.15 ha (2.84 acres).

A ditch existed around the perimeter of much of the village, but its exact nature could not be ascertained. Possibly a stockade or, more probably, just a fence of some sort was built just inside the ditch, but evidence of a fence could

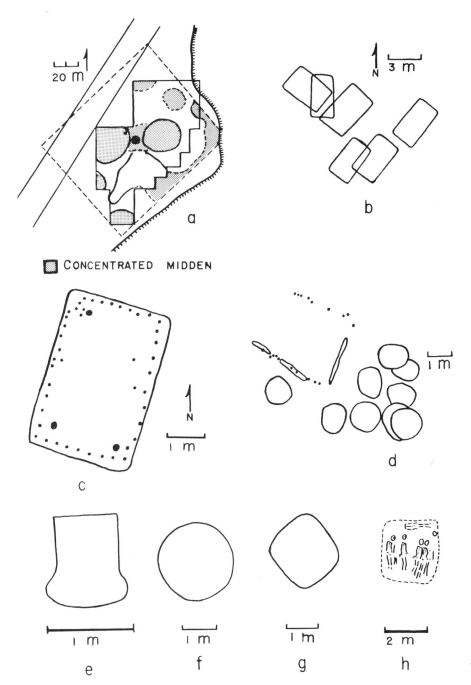

CONCENTRATED MIDDEN

FIGURE 10.9. Hoecake and Zebree site features. (a) Zebree site midden concentrations. (b) Cluster of house patterns at Hoecake site. (c) Hoecake site house pattern. (d) Zebree site house and storage pit patterns. (e) Cross section of storage pit at Hoecake. (f)–(g) Zebree site storage pit outlines. (h) Zebree site burial. [(a), (d) based on Morse and Morse 1980; (b), (c), (e) based on J. R. Williams 1974; (f)–(h) based on Morse 1976.]

not be discovered because of the nature of the deposits. Soil was moved around on the site, apparently to help level it, and this ditching system probably functioned primarily for borrow. Movement of soil across the site began with construction. For instance, Baytown period check-stamped sherds, probably from the same vessel, were found at two widely spaced locations, one of which was Mississippian fill.

The nature of the interior residence pattern is not absolutely clear. House patterns were difficult to discover; it is clear, however, that the site was not made up of pan-village rows of houses. The distribution and intensity of artifacts, particularly kitchen ceramics, storage pits, and house patterns clearly show that the site was made up of residential subareas. Midden concentrations were readily apparent. Up to a maximum of seven middens were present (Figure 10.9a), although they differed considerably in artifact density. The most probable pattern is an arc of middens from the southern corner around along the west and north to just beyond the eastern corner, with an open area in the southeast quadrant. These middens overlapped and probably shifted through time, making precise identification difficult.

All middens contained artifact debris, storage pits, and evidence of structures. A midden probably averaged about four houses and ranged between two and six structures. Individual houses were rectangular in shape (Figure 10.9d). Small postholes, 6–8 cm in diameter and spaced 20–30 cm apart for the studs, defined structures; in one instance shallow wall trenches were present. Size varied between 6.6 and 11.4 m² and averaged about 8.5 m². Walls were probably constructed of interwoven split cane and small tree limbs. This same type of house occurred at Cahokia and at the Hoecake site in the Cairo Lowland. There were no interior hearths or central roof-support logs at Hoecake, where the houses averaged about 9.2 m² and floors were sunk 8–50 cm into the sterile soil (Figure 10.9b, c). The roof was apparently supported by slightly larger corner posts. No daub (plaster) was present, and the walls were probably finished with mats of cane that could be rolled up in the summer. The depressed floor and cane walls would probably have provided adequate insulation against the cold.

Associated with each house at any one time was a storage pit. Actually, several were found, since a pit would be used for only 1 or 2 years. The typical Big Lake phase pits, of which 68 were found, were cylindrical in shape with flat bases and were slightly to moderately bell shaped at the base (Figure 10.9f, g). Two were rectangular in shape. The pits ranged from 1.36 to 3.9 cu m in capacity and averaged around 2 cu m, indicating they could have held on the average about 57 bushels of shelled corn and up to 110 bushels in the largest ones.

Pit storage took advantage of carbon dioxide produced by the respiration of grain (Coles 1973:39–45). Grain on the exterior might have been damaged, but the contents were preserved. Numerous fabric-impressed burned clay fragments indicate that the pits were sealed on top with a fabric or rush mat caulked with clay. Burrowing animals and moisture would have been a nuisance but probably not a significant one.

The minimum-size cooking jars indicated that a nuclear family of around 5 made up a household. An average pit held about 2 metric tons of shelled corn, more than sufficient for a household over the year. A cylindrical pit evolved into a bell-shaped pit when it was cleaned for reuse or left open to erosion. Microflora were removed by scraping the sides. Bases are harder to scrape and tend to become belled out. In addition, the upper portions are held intact by roots while lower portions collapse. Larger pits will result from the upper portions finally collapsing from natural erosion.

Households were responsible for pottery manufacture and their lithic and bone tools. Microlith production and, presumably, shell bead manufacture was the responsibility of the household or at least the household cluster. Similarly, salt-manufacturing debris was found throughout the site; this distribution does not indicate specialization.

Households were not completely egalitarian. Mammal bones (mostly deer) in contrast to other fauna remains concentrate in one midden, roughly centrally located along the northwest side of the village. Trace element analysis of skeletal remains indicates that red meat (not fish and fowl) was not as significant to the diet as nonred meat foods. It is possible that red meat was largely restricted to the ranking lineage. The midden which produced the mammal bones also contained most of the exotic artifacts and a large grave. However, the inhabitants of this grave did not eat a significant amount of red meat either, according to the trace element analysis.

Dog burials and bones were frequent, which is unusual for Mississippian sites (Smith 1975:102–110). Their value would have been high as sentinels, since Zebree apparently was on the Mississippian frontier. There was no evidence at Zebree that dogs were eaten, although Bruce Smith (1975) includes dogs as possible Mississippian food.

Human burials occurred in the midden, near the houses. Usually, the rectangular grave contained a skeleton extended full length on its back. In one grave, a second skeleton in the flexed position lay on the legs of the primary interment. The remains of 27 skeletons and an additional 26 locations of isolated human bones were recorded. No grave furniture was included. The females, as expected in a frontier situation, were relatively tall and healthy and tended to outlive males.

In the midden that was thought to be the location of the ranking lineage was a burial consisting of eight skeletons (Figure 10.9h). The grave measured 1.8 × 1.65 m, and the four males and four females had been buried in the flesh. Seven were buried with skulls oriented to the north, and the eighth was oriented to the west.

At the Kersey site in Missouri, Marshall (1965) reported the discovery of

10 bundle burials within a circular posthole and wall trench structure about 2 × 3 m (10 × 7 ft.) in extent. The actual area covered by bone was approximately the same size as the Zebree grave. Both features indicated the presence of charnel houses at the villages, possibly exclusive to or maintained by the ranking lineages. At the Hoecake site in the Cairo Lowland, the Story Mound location reportedly contained log-lined tombs with multiple skeletons that appear to date to this initial Mississippian period. The very elaborate burials at Cahokia date at the end of or after this period.

Cahokia is 1500 ha in size, whereas Hoecake may be 80 ha in extent. Hoecake, of course, is a multiple-component site, and it is not known how the Early Mississippian component was patterned there. Zebree is only a little over a hectare and probably was typical of a major village. Based on a variety of evidence, including the skeletal population, estimated total of storage pits, cooking jar sizes, midden sizes, number of middens, and other calculations, it is thought that the maximum population at Zebree was around 130–140. The radiocarbon dates indicate a period of occupation of about 200 years, and this figure was used in the calculation of population. It is supported to a certain extent by evidence of rebuilding, shifting middens, and the enormous amount of debris. The midden, however, is generally relatively shallow at Zebree, as the 1-m depth in part of the site is mostly due to vertical disturbance, such as the excavation of overlapping storage pit features. Thicker midden at later Mississippian sites is due to a practice of carrying in soil to cover demolished heavily plastered houses. Many of the sites mapped in southeast Missouri in the nineteenth century were covered with house mounds built up in this manner. Another argument against a 200-year time period is lack of obvious change in the ceramics. However, basic kitchen ceramics changed little during the Mississippian period. There are subtle changes in handle attachment and rim profiles of jars, but the best possibility for change through time is in grave furniture simply because there are a greater variety of possibilities for change. There is no known grave furniture for the Zebree Big Lake component.

The relationship of Zebree to the other sites in the Big Lake phase is not known. Immediately adjacent to the site was a ceramic scatter probably indicative of a household or hamlet. Another nearby site was a microlith scatter with very few sherds. This same situation exists at Cahokia but on a much grander scale. Other possible sites in the Zebree site area were destroyed by ditching before they could be surveyed. Beyond Zebree a number of household sites presumed to be farmsteads, hamlets, and small villages are known. Stephen Williams's (1954) Old Varney River site is included within the Big Lake phase. Northward into the Cairo Lowland are a large number of sites with early components. Many are multiple component. None except Hoecake is known to be larger than Zebree. To the south and west of the Big Lake phase are similar sites, but none are dated earlier than about A.D. 1000–1050. It is expected that Mississippian sites dating at least as early as A.D. 900 should exist in that area.

The Big Lake phase is a full-blown Mississippian expression and probably was roughly contemporaneous with the Hayti phase. Similar sites exist between Zebree and Kersey and beyond into the Cairo Lowland. There is a prominent Hayti component at the Wardell site, for instance. The Big Lake phase certainly did not develop at Zebree, and the Hayti phase probably did not develop at Kersey.

The Big Lake phase component at Zebree was superimposed directly upon a Dunklin phase occupation. The radiocarbon dates indicate that the initial Mississippian occupation may have moved into a Baytown period seasonal village still in use. The superior technology, political system, and numbers of people would have guaranteed success in any such venture. Most probably this exemplifies how the Mississippian chiefdom organization was able to spread so quickly within a region. Such a model has the added attraction of helping to explain the distribution of the Siouan language family (Griffin 1960).

The American Bottom and the Cairo lowland experienced a similar roughly simultaneous development into Mississippian culture. There is absolutely no evidence of a migration of an independent chiefdom into the Cairo Lowland. Lesser-ranked lineages of a complex chiefdom tend to break away into new habitats where they can be equal or even superior. Local indigenous populations become amalgamated into the new order as lower-ranking lineages. The only way to combat amalgamation into the chiefdom organization is to change before amalgamation can take place. This expedient may have occurred in the Cairo Lowland. However, both regions may have developed together to coordinate the exploitation of important resources located between them.

These early sites were not large civic–ceremonial centers; those evolved later. The sites were farmsteads, hamlets, small villages, and larger villages characterized by a distinctive Varney Red Filmed pottery or a close relative. The spread of a chiefdom is initially characterized by relatively egalitarian populations. Complex hierarchies develop with time.

REFERENCES

Adams, Robert, and Winslow Walker
  1942   Archaeological surface survey of New Madrid County, Missouri. *Missouri Archaeologist* **8**:1–23.
Brown, Ian W.
  1980   Salt and the Eastern North American Indian, an archaeological study. *Peabody Museum, Harvard University, Lower Mississippi Survey Bulletin* **6**.
Coles, John
  1973   *Archaeology by experiment.* New York: Scribner's.
Culin, Stewart
  1907   Games of the North American Indians. *Bureau of American Ethnology Annual Report* **24**:1–811.
Fowler, Melvin (editor)
  1969   Explorations into Cahokia archaeology. *Illinois Archaeological Survey Bulletin* **7**.

Fowler, Melvin
   1978   Cahokia and the American Bottom: Settlement archeology. In *Mississippian settlement patterns*, edited by Bruce Smith, pp. 455–478. New York: Academic Press.
Griffin, James B.
   1960   A hypothesis for the prehistory of the Winnebago. In *Culture in history*, edited by Stanley Diamond, pp. 809–865. New York: Columbia University Press.
   1977   The University of Michigan excavations at the Pulcher site in 1950. *American Antiquity* **42**:462–488.
Harris, Suzanne E.
   1980   Reconstruction of the nineteenth century environment. In *Zebree Archeological Project*, edited by Dan F. Morse and Phyllis A. Morse, ch. 13, pp. 1–14. Report submitted to Memphis District, U.S. Army Corps of Engineers, by Arkansas Archeological Survey.
Kelly, John E.
   1982   Annual report of investigations at the Range site. In *Annual Report of Investigations 1981 FAI-270 Archaeological Mitigation Project*, pp. 7–19. Illinois Archaeological Survey, University of Illinois, Urbana-Champaign.
Keslin, Richard O.
   1964   Archaeological implications on the role of salt as an element of cultural diffusion. *Missouri Archaeologist* **26**.
Marshall, Richard A.
   1965   An archaeological investigation of Interstate Route 55 through New Madrid and Pemiscot Counties, Missouri, 1964. *University of Missouri Highway Archaeology Report* **1**.
Morse, Dan F.
   1974   The Cahokia microlith industry. *Newsletter of Lithic Technology* **3**:15–19.
Morse, Dan F., and Michael G. Million
   1980   Biotic and nonbiotic resources. In *Zebree Archeological Project*, edited by Dan F. Morse and Phyllis A. Morse, ch. 15, pp. 1–30. Report submitted to Memphis District U.S. Army Corps of Engineers, by Arkansas Archeological Survey.
Morse, Dan F., and Phyllis A. Morse (editors)
   1980   *Zebree archeological project*. Report submitted to Memphis District, U.S. Army Corps of Engineers, by the Arkansas Archeological Survey.
Parmalee, Paul W.
   1958   Marine shells of Illinois Indian sites. *Nautilus* **71**:132–139.
Phillips, Philip
   1970   Archaeological survey in the Lower Yazoo Basin, Mississippi, 1949–1955. *Papers of the Peabody Museum, Harvard University* **60**.
Phillips, Philip, James Ford, and James B. Griffin
   1951   Archaeological survey in the Lower Mississippi Alluvial Valley, 1940–1947. *Papers of the Peabody Museum, Harvard University* **25**.
Sierzchula, Michael C.
   1980   Replication and use studies of the Zebree microlith industry. M.A. thesis, Department of Anthropology, University of Arkansas, Fayetteville.
Smith, Bruce D.
   1975   Middle Mississippi exploitation of animal populations. *University of Michigan Museum of Anthropology Anthropological Papers* **57**.
   1978   Variation in Mississippian settlement patterns. In *Mississippian settlement systems*, edited by Bruce Smith, pp. 479–503. New York: Academic Press.
Speck, Frank
   1919   The functions of wampum among the Eastern Algonkian. *American Anthropological Association Memoir* **6**.

Williams, J. Raymond
  1974   The Baytown phases in the Cairo Lowland of southeast Missouri. *Missouri Archaeologist* **36.**
Williams, Stephen
  1954   *An archeological study of the Mississippian culture in southeast Missouri.* Ph.D. dissertation, Yale University. Ann Arbor, Mich.: University Microfilms.

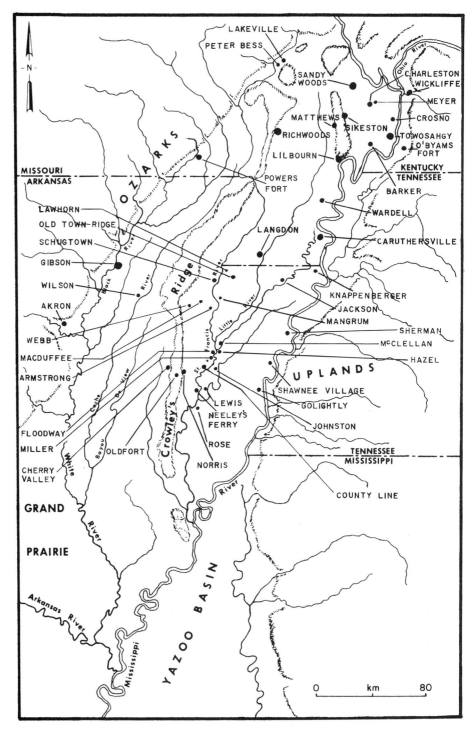

FIGURE 11.1. Known major Middle period Mississippian sites in the Central Valley.

11

Mississippian Consolidation
(A.D. 1000–1350)

By about A.D. 1000–1050 independent Mississippian chiefdoms were distributed throughout the Central Mississippi Valley. Present were many contemporaneous phases that are often hard to separate out geographically. It is easier to detect temporal change in artifacts than to define subtle regional variations. Data furnished by modern extensive excavations and reports provide much more information for the Middle period Mississippian than was often the case for other time periods. The population and cultural center was in the Cairo Lowland, where a majority of the most exotic artifacts and most of the largest sites and mounds occur.

· During this period there was increasing attention to the protection of the civic–ceremonial center. There is little direct evidence of warfare, however, and raw materials as well as exotic artifacts were traded throughout the region. Phases are more easily defined in the later portion of the period, possibly because of a process of consolidation that led to a decrease in the number of independent chiefdoms and to unoccupied buffer zones around phase regions.

A considerable amount of work has been accomplished at sites dated to the Middle period Mississippian, particularly in the Cairo Lowland. Because much of this work has concentrated upon complex major sites, change during this period has been difficult to reconstruct. It has been investigated at less intensively occupied sites in the central portion of this region, resulting in the reconstruction of events used here. The most difficult problem is the comparison of burial (ceremonial) ceramic and kitchen (domestic) ceramic assemblages. Another difficulty is that most ceramics are plain, and thus small samples tend not to contain good examples of diagnostic pottery. A recently recognized complication is that sites in the Cairo Lowland may date no later than about A.D. 1350–1400 (Williams 1977). In contrast, many major sites in the central and southern portions of the Central Valley were occupied by complex later settlements. These have masked the presence of earlier components and also often caused the destruction of earlier features.

Figure 11.1 shows the distribution of known major sites. Larger sites exist in the north, particularly within the Cairo Lowland. To the south, Middle Mississippian sites are considerably smaller. There are more sites known than are plotted, on Figure 11.1, but in the meander belt, Middle period components are almost only recognizable from formal test pitting. A Middle period dispersed population essentially exists everywhere. But the most complex centers are in the north, closest to the major important outside resources.

The events at Cahokia are still important to our discussion. Cahokia reached its peak of florescence from the terminal Fairmount phase through the Stirling phase (1050–1150) and into the Moorehead phase (1150–1250) (Fowler 1978). Caddoan vessels and point styles from east Texas or Oklahoma were traded to Cahokia during these periods, so Cahokia was far from being an isolated community. There are artifact similarities to Cahokia in the Central Valley, but to date only a few artifacts possibly manufactured at Cahokia have been recovered. Yet contact with, knowledge of, and trade with the Central Valley certainly was involved. In addition, there probably was a basic linguistic relationship.

TRANSITION FROM EARLY TO MIDDLE PERIOD MISSISSIPPIAN

A predominance of Varney Red Filmed ceramics is probably the single most easily recognized trait for sites classified as Early period Mississippian. About A.D. 1000–1050 red filming decreased quickly. Vessel shapes continued as before in kitchen pottery, so there is no need to invoke new population shifts. However, burial and hence ceremonial ceramics had important innovations. They seem to have evolved locally rather than to have been representative of a movement of styles or people from outside the Central Valley.

At the Mangrum site (3CG636), located near the St. Francis River in Arkansas, two radiocarbon dates were obtained: A.D. 978 ± 69 and 1039 ± 61 (TX–3074, 3073) (Klinger 1981). The site seems to have existed during the transition from Early to Middle period Mississippian. The dates pertain to a feature that contained a large percentage (almost 40%) of Varney Red Filmed, but the site assemblage as a whole is characterized by a relatively low percentage, about 10%. It is possible that the site has two or more Mississippian components, but a single-component Mississippian occupation about A.D. 1050 is the easiest interpretation. The site is relatively sparse in terms of artifact intensity and seems to have been a hamlet located near the St. Francis River as part of a dispersed population pattern.

Other sites echo the situation at Mangrum. One is the McCarty site east of Marked Tree, which contained a Mississippian component similar to that at Mangrum. The kitchen ceramics are basically Big Lake phase in nature, but red-filmed pottery is not common. This site was an isolated household site, probably a single-family farmstead. An unusual find was a small pear-shaped gorget of conch shell, the earliest known Mississippian "shell mask" gorget (Figure 11.2l). Thin sherds, both red filmed and plain, occur. Smaller jar rim sherds are characteristically exaggerated in the exterior rim curvature.

At the Hyneman site (3PO52), west of Marked Tree, an assemblage of pottery was recovered from a hamlet or small village location. The pottery is not so much like the Big Lake phase in appearance as the Mangrum assemblage was. For the most part, the pottery is thin walled. It includes jars with exaggerated exterior rim curvature, red filming, notched rim lips, and a sandy shell-tempered paste (Figure 11.2d, e). Shapes are fundamentally simple jars and bowls with little variation.

A burial at the Mangrum site was associated with a ceramic assemblage different from that recovered from the general hamlet midden. The burial consisted of a small jar and bottle and some human bone representative of two individuals. The jar had been fitted with loop handles, only one of which had been preserved. Loop handles are usually round in cross section. They were riveted into the wall of the vessel (Figure 11.2f). This technique ensured that the handle would not be lost during firing. The practice of appliqued handles did not become universal until much later in time. Wood shavings associated with two similar jars found at or near the Rose Mound site were radiocarbon dated at A.D. 1050 ± 65 (CWRU-172; Brose 1976). The bottle found with the burial at Mangrum is very significant. It represents the earliest known appearance of the true bottle form in the Mississippian of the Central Valley. The Mangrum bottle is spherical with a relatively long neck and a flat base.

At the Banks Mound 3 location east of Wapanocca Lake, an extraordinarily important ceramic assemblage was recovered (Perino 1967:72–87). A radiocarbon date of A.D. 1079 ± 87 (M–1162) was obtained on a sample from the central portion of the Mississippian stratigraphy. In the early mantle three crudely shaped bottles with short, wide necks were found. One was missing its neck, possibly a firing mishap and an indication of difficulty in welding. Also in the early mantle was a bowl with a rim effigy (turkey?) opposing a rim tail flange, the earliest example of this type of vessel known in the Central Valley. Rim effigy bowls probably copy wooden effigies. Thin red-filmed and plain sherds, both grog- and shell-tempered variations, were in the mound fill.

The middle mantle included a loop-handled jar, a triangular point, one plain bottle, one red-filmed bottle, and a bowl. In the final mantle were several burials with vessels, including bottles, jars, and bowls. One of the bottles had a dimpled base. There was a constricted rimmed bowl with incised design. A jar had a "rolled" rim; one jar had no handles, whereas some had loop handles. There were also two beaker fragments and part of a plate form. In addition, black polished sherds, angular-shouldered jar sherds, and a Ramey Incised sherd were recovered. A variety of incised decorations were present in the assemblage, but decoration of any kind was very rare.

Both grog and shell temper were characteristic throughout the Mississip-

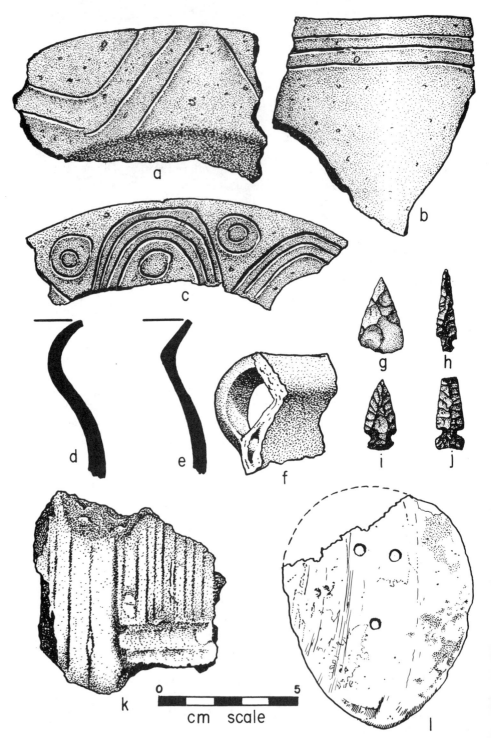

FIGURE 11.2. Artifacts recovered from the earlier Middle period Mississippian occupations in northeast Arkansas. (a)–(c) O'Byam Incised plate rims, Hazel site. (b) Mound Place Incised beaker rim, Hazel site. (d)–(e) Jar rim profiles, Hyneman site. (f) Loop handle showing technique of riveting to vessel wall. (g)–(j) Madison, Scallorn, and Schugtown arrow point styles. (k) Daub fragment, Hyneman site. (l) Shell mask gorget, McCarty site. [Courtesy of the Arkansas Archeological Survey.]

pian mound stratigraphy. The pottery has not been examined microscopically to see if the grog is crushed-shell-tempered sherds. Grog here is not indicative of a transition from Baytown or of Caddoan influence; rather, it existed contemporaneously in Tennessee at Obion and Pinson, up river in the Cairo Lowland, and at Cahokia. Grog reflects the development of Middle period Mississippian pottery. There was a great deal of ceramic innovation occurring in a relatively short period of time, and grog was part of it. The new forms were handled jars, the bottle, the beaker, the plate, and rim effigy bowls. The ceramic innovations seem to have been restricted primarily to the development of a ceremonial ware, found by archaeologists in graves, which were the normal final repository of ceremonial items.

The second mantle of Banks Mound 3 was associated with a complex charnel-house structure interpreted by Perino (1967) as a crematory. The structure, which unfortunately had been badly damaged by earlier pot hunting, was circular in shape, 3.6 m in exterior diameter, and defined by 20-cm posts 75 cm apart. There was a hard-packed dirt stairway on the eastern slope that narrowed from 120 to 90 cm in width where interrupted by the pot hunting.

The Golightly site, north of Wapanocca Lake, is a ceremonial center with two mounds. Excavations in one mound in 1932 by the University of Arkansas exposed a central burned structure associated with plain Mississippian pottery and numerous burials, which appears to be the same type of situation as is at Banks Mound 3. Near the mounds is a small village, which was probably contemporaneous.

A dispersed settlement pattern of farmsteads and hamlets is present around the Golightly site. An intensive survey of part of the Wapanocca Lake Refuge resulted in the discovery of more than 15 such isolated house sites and hamlets, characterized mainly by plain Mississippian pottery. Additional sites are represented by single potsherds.

THE CHERRY VALLEY PHASE

The Cherry Valley site is situated upon the western apron of Crowley's Ridge in Cross County, Arkansas, overlooking the Western Lowlands. Five mounds were present in the Cherry Valley group in 1958. No village was associated with these mounds, although some Baytown and Mississippian pottery was found in the mound fill. The mounds were 4–4.5 m tall and 18–20.5 m in diameter. Pot hunting had created numerous pits and tunnels. Many of the vessels acquired by the amateur diggers were of shapes previously unreported in Arkansas. Three of the mounds were salvaged by Gregory Perino for the Gilcrease Institute of Tulsa, Oklahoma (1967).

Primary and secondary mound-building stages were identified at Cherry Valley, associated with bundle, extended, and rare cremated burials. Bone preservation was poor, and often just tooth caps and grave goods indicated the presence of an interment. Perino (1967) recovered at least 467 burials, accompanied by 64 bottles, 59 bowls, 130 jars, 7 plates, 42 beakers, 4 pipes, 2 conchshell vessels, and numerous shell and seed (possibly gromwell) beads. Probably as many artifacts were recovered by collectors in the upper parts of the mounds.

Mound 1 had three large postholes at the base, associated with bundle burials. Mound 3 covered a 4-m square house pattern at the base. Mound 2, the central mound of the Cherry Valley group, covered a large structure built on the original ground surface: a circular building 10 m in diameter with an entryway 6 m long (Figure 11.3). This building had a level floor with a large rectangular fire basin in the center, 1 m deep and 1.1 × 2.2 m in size. Four 40-cm postholes were 3.6 m apart around this basin and served as roof supports. Walls were made of clay, 1.5 m wide at the base and 1 m wide at a height of 1 m. The entryway walls were 70 cm apart, made of 16 15-cm cedar posts placed in two long rows.

Three radiocarbon dates were obtained on samples from the Cherry Valley site: A.D. 722 ± 137, 933 ± 160, and 1102 ± 120 (M–917, 918, 1486). The first and last dates are on charcoal associated with the main charnel house in

FIGURE 11.3 Structure at the base of Mound 2 at the Cherry Valley site. [Courtesy of Gregory Perino.]

Mound 2. The middle date is a combined charcoal and charred-bone sample from a burial in Mound 3. The A.D. 1102 date probably represents a best guess, with A.D. 1050–1150 being the current general dating of the Cherry Valley phase.

The most common artifact found preserved with Cherry Valley burials was pottery, with jars being the most usual form (Figure 11.4a). This characteristic is particularly interesting because the typical Mississippi burial in the Central Valley contains a bottle and a bowl. These jars were often small, under 12 cm in diameter, thin, and with rounded shoulders, and can usually be typed as Mississippi Plain. An occasional pair of lugs on the lip served as decoration. One jar had a single row of nodes around the shoulder. Nodes are appliqued and indicate increasing confidence in pottery making. Rims on jars were rounded on the edges, vertical or rolled slightly, and occasionally everted. Handles, the most distinctive feature of these jars, are all loop handles, riveted through the vessel wall below and attached above by welding to the rim. Those jars with handles have only two. Some handles looped up above the rim, some had projections above the area of attachment on the rim, and some had projections on the lower end of the handle. There is a jar with rare frog-effigy handles in the assemblage, as well as a "crow foot" handle with appliqued outspread "toes" on the vessel shoulder. An occasional handle is grooved in the center. Burnishing marks are apparent on Cherry Valley jars.

Bottles of many forms were found at Cherry Valley (Figure 11.4e). A hooded human effigy bottle and a stirrup-necked bottle with an annular base came from the upper part of Mound 2 and probably date to a later period. The same is true for a tetrapod bottle with fat round legs, a high neck, and a raised ring applied where the neck joins the body. Four painted bottles were also recovered from upper levels, three of these by collectors. One from upper Mound 2 was a Carson Red on Buff design, with red crosses inside circles painted on the body. Two painted bottles are from the upper portion of Mound 3. One, a Nodena Red and White vessel, was painted with a step design. The other, recovered by Perino, was badly decomposed and crusted with manganese but appears to be a negative-painted red-on-white cross and circle design, with the lower portion painted red. Another vessel, from the upper levels of Mound 1, may be negative painted with red, black, and white but was very badly decomposed and encrusted with manganese. It had a carinated body, and the design appears to be starlike circles. Three additional vessels were a solid red color and would be typed as Old Town Red.

Incised decorations were found on three bottles. One wide-mouthed bottle had a Mound Place Incised–like decoration on the shoulder. Another had a curvilinear shoulder design, and a third was decorated with a series of "parallel straight lines" on the shoulder. One bottle had six nodes on the shoulder. Another long-necked bottle had a noded fringe at the neck base. Most Cherry Valley bottles had dimpled or flat bases.

Bowls were a common vessel form at the site. These were usually plain, with convex or vertical walls and flat or convex bases. A few had constricted

a

b

c

d

e

f

0   5
cm   scale

mouths. Bowls were medium to small in size and were wider than they were deep. A few had rim effigies, such as one with a large rattle-head owl effigy and an opposing tail tab with V-shaped lines incised on the upper surface. A human rattle head rim effigy was reportedly found by collectors. Other bowls had rudimentary bird heads and were occasionally red filmed. Some bowls were noded, with several large bowls having nodes on the rim edge. One smaller bowl had constricting sides and a row of nodes on the shoulder. Some bowls had suspension holes near the rim, and two had square openings. Two other large bowls with convex bases and vertical sides had a pair of flat horizontal lugs 5–8 cm long placed below the rim.

Beaker-like bowls were also present. These have a beaker-shaped body with concave or recurved sides but lacked the beaker handles that define this shape. They occasionally have a pair of small lip lugs on the rim. One beaker bowl even has a bird-head rim effigy and a beaker handle. Another beaker bowl had a broad lip lug and a long, broad handle placed below the rim on the opposite side.

The beakers themselves are what makes the Cherry Valley site discovery so unusual. Beakers had not been previously described for the Central Valley (although a number had been collected by the Smithsonian in the 1880s from near Bay, Arkansas). The beaker is a vessel with parallel, vertical, or slightly constricting sides and a flat or slightly convex base (Figure 11.4c–d). Most had a long projecting handle attached below the rim. A great variety of beaker forms were present at Cherry Valley and were actually more diversified than those found at Cahokia. Most were small, and many had lip lugs. If there was only one lug, it opposed the handle. Otherwise, the second lug was placed over the handle. Both round and oval tapered handles are found, either projecting out straight or curved. One beaker even had a loop handle on one side and a small lug on the other, resembling a modern measuring cup.

A few Cherry Valley beakers were decorated, with either Mound Place Incised lines or something like "Ranch Incised" on both red-filmed and plain burnished vessels. One beaker form was without handles, with small perforation holes near the rim. Occasionally, small perforated lug handles were found on red-filmed beakers.

Plates constitute another new vessel form for this period in the Central Valley (Figure 11.4b). These were from 2.5 to 9 cm deep and had flat bases with rounded corners and a flat rim. The plates were all polished. Only two were decorated. One was red filmed, and the other was a deep plate with an O'Byam Incised design on the upper wide rim. Several small clay dippers similar to those associated with Big Lake and other phases were found at Cherry Valley.

FIGURE 11.4. *Cherry Valley phase pottery. (a) Jar. (b) Plate. (c)–(d) Beakers. (e) Bottle. (f) Beaker over bottle. [(a)–(e) photographs of Cherry Valley site ceramics, courtesy of Gregory Perino. (f) photograph of Floodway site ceramic, courtesy of the Arkansas Archeological Survey.]*

A clay ear spool, pulley shaped and perforated through the center, was recovered. Shell-tempered clay pipes with the common equal-arm shape with biconical perforations were present. One pipe was a large frog effigy, which resembles those found elsewhere that are usually made of stone. Two discoidals were found, one made of stone and one of clay. These are biconcave with sharp rims, typical of Middle period Mississippian discoidals. Thin and with a shallow concavity, both were perforated in the center. Similar discoidals have been recovered at other sites in Arkansas and Missouri and probably date to this same time period.

Very few points were found in the mounds. Two small triangular points were discovered with a burial in Mound 2. One interesting find was a 10-cm-long Dalton point that had been included with a burial in Mound 2. It had apparently been found by the Indians and included as a grave offering. Another point resembling a "Ramey knife" was with a burial in Mound 3.

Numerous mussel-shell spoons, both plain and decorated, were included either near or inside vessels. One shell was made into a canine-tooth-shaped pendant. Conch-shell disk beads were present. There were two conch-shell vessels deep in Mound 3. The columella had been cut off, and one vessel had been painted red. *Marginella* beads with ground perforated shoulders were found in parallel rows, some of which were probably on a headdress.

Other Cherry Valley phase mound sites have been excavated. Two located north of Harrisburg, Arkansas were excavated by the Arkansas State University Museum. The Smithsonian sponsored a dig in 1883 at Jonesboro, at or near the Webb group or Bay mounds (Thomas 1894). Another mound, part of a group of five, was salvaged by Dan Morse just west of Marked Tree. This mound covered a circular structure with a series of central hearths and/or ash pits, probably indicative of the different times it was used ceremonially as a charnel house. The structure had been buried beneath a primary mound. Bundle burials, interred over the structure, either originated in a neighboring structure or represent the bundles kept inside the charnel house before it was abandoned. Other mantles were added and associated bundle and primary burials were interred before the mound was terminated as a burial place. One beaker was found positioned over a bottle (Figure 11.4f). The Cherry Valley phase burial ware probably was used in libation ceremonies of some sort.

The large number of burials at the Cherry Valley type site is unusual in that interment at the ceremonial center apparently was widely available. Other Cherry Valley phase mounds seem to have been more restrictive but still contain numerous burials. Death is apparently this society's major excuse for ceremonial gathering.

AFTER CHERRY VALLEY

At the base of the Hazel site, near Marked Tree, a Middle period Mississippian component was discovered. Radiocarbon dates are A.D. 848 ± 92,

1084 ± 111, 1093 ± 74, 1111 ± 92, and 1186 ± 74 (TX–700A, 845, 844, 704, and 878A). Archeomagnetic dates collected and run by Dan Wolfman ranged from A.D. 1170 to 1240 and were in the proper order on a stratified series of burned house floors (Wolfman 1982:286). The component is thought to date about A.D. 1150–1250.

A basal feature at the Hazel site contained O'Byam Incised plate fragments as a predominant decoration (Morse and Smith 1973; Figure 11.2a, c). In addition, Mound Place Incised and Old Town Red were represented. The Mound Place sherd and two plain sherds appear to have been from broken beakers (Figure 11.2b). Plain plate fragments were present as well. Jar rims are excurvate, similar to those in the Cherry Valley phase. A strap-shaped handle was of the riveted variety. O'Byam Incised sherds were found on the partially leveled mound located near the village, but only one sherd was recovered from a house floor. House floors at Hazel were aligned in rows indicative of a major village. Large plain jars with strap handles were on the floors. A stylized bird-head rim effigy bowl was also collected off a floor. The jars have straight to slightly incurved profiles. House patterns consisted of wall trenches and burned daub. A Duck River–style "ceremonial sword" made of Mill Creek chert was recovered from one of the wall trenches (Figure 10.4b). The sword had been placed adjacent to the wall, as indicated by wall posts, and the house burned before it could be retrieved. The pottery is less spherical than that in the Cherry Valley phase, particularly the jars, which have high shoulders. Strap or appliqued handles signify better control, or at least more confidence, in working with a shell-tempered paste. Decoration still seems to be largely confined to ceremonial ware, or what we interpret to be ceremonial ware.

The predominance of plain kitchen ceramics for much of the Middle period Mississippian frustrates archaeologists' attempts to seriate site pottery collections. A trend at Hazel, where absolute dates exist, is extremely important: The village had increased in size, and houses were oriented in rows. A large mound was closely associated with the village. A series of isolated house sites (farmsteads) existed immediately outside the village and beyond. The population was apparently becoming more consolidated around a civic–ceremonial center, and sites were becoming more obviously part of a hierarchical system of sites.

The discovery of a few ceremonial artifacts from Middle period Mississippian sites in the Central Valley showed participation in the networks of trade and exchange of objects used in what is called the Southeastern Ceremonial Complex (Waring and Holder 1943) (Figure 11.5). The material is not nearly as abundant as that from the Spiro area in Oklahoma, Etowah in Georgia, or Moundville in Alabama. However, the use of certain motifs on decorated shell and copper objects certainly shows some awareness of and contact with these other societies by Middle Mississippian peoples.

The Snell gorget from the McDuffee site shows two chunky players in reverse, or court card, positions (McGimsey 1964; Figure 11.5a). These players are wearing typical bellows-shaped aprons and have forelock beads and

a

b

c

d

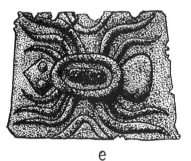

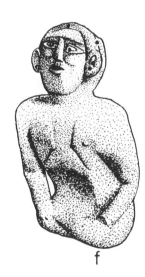

f

e

FIGURE 11.5. Artifacts found in the Central Valley identified as belonging to the Southeastern Ceremonial Complex. (a) The Snell gorget. (b) The Potter gorget. (c) The Douglass gorget. (d) Repoussé copper anthropomorphized hawk Wulfing plate. (e) Repoussé copper spider from the Parkin site. (f) Statue from the Schugtown site. [(a) courtesy of the *Arkansas Archeologist;* (b), (c) adapted from *Pre-Columbian Shell Engravings* (Phillips and Brown 1978, Peabody Museum Press, Paperback edition, Part I, figs. 299, 230), copyright 1978 by the President and Fellows of Harvard College; (d) adapted from the *Bureau of American Ethnology Bulletin;* (e) adapted from the *Missouri Archaeologist;* (f) courtesy of the University of Arkansas Museum.]

conch columella pendants. They are clearly related to depictions of the chunky player found on gorgets at Spiro; Eddyville, Tennessee; and St. Marys, Perry County, Missouri.

The Potter gorget was recovered in the late nineteenth century from a mound in southeast Missouri, probably in the Cairo Lowland region (Phillips and Brown 1978:176–177). A priest–chieftain is carrying a severed head and a staff (Figure 11.5b). He has a bellows-shaped apron, forelock beads and beaded arm and leg bands. The Douglass shell gorget, from New Madrid County, Missouri, depicts a long-nosed figure carrying an ax, with a mace stuck in his belt, a bilobed arrow hair ornament, an unusual headdress with long braids, and a severed head or rattle in the other hand (Phillips and Brown 1978:177; Figure 11.5c).

Among the most widely known artifacts from the Central Valley are the Malden or Wulfing plates, a group of eight embossed copper plates reportedly found in a stack in a field near Malden, Dunklin County, Missouri (Fowke 1910). Stephen Williams (1954) interviewed the widow of the original discoverer and visited the area where the plates were plowed up. Only two thumbnail-size shell-tempered sherds were found here. The plates may have been cached at that spot for some reason. These are obvious examples of the art motifs connected with the Southeastern Ceremonial Complex. Seven of these plates represent hawks, and one shows a hawk–man (Figure 11.5d). The hawks have a forked eye and curved talons. The hawk–man has a human head with ear spools, a forked eye, a human mouth, and forelock beads, but the same hawk body. These most closely resemble plates found at the Spiro site in Oklahoma (Hamilton, Hamilton, and Chapman 1974).

Another partial hawk dancer plate has been reported from the Peter Bess site in Bollinger County, Missouri (Hamilton *et al.* 1974:161). It has a typical forked eye and four crest feathers. This plate continued to be used after it was broken and was found on the forehead of a female burial. It most closely resembles the Malden hawks, found to the south of Peter Bess.

Spiders are also a common motif in the Central Valley. One of copper was found at the Parkin site (Hamilton, Hamilton, and Chapman 1974:164–165; Figure 11.5e). It probably dates at the end of the Middle period Mississippian (see Chapter 12).

The Duck River-style sword at Hazel is an element of the Southeastern Ceremonial Complex (Figure 10.4b). Its appearance at this time may be an indication that chiefdoms in the Central Valley were evolving politically into more complex entities and that conflict between independent chiefdoms was intensifying. Another sword was reported from near Forrest City. A Mill Creek chert mace was discovered on the chest of a male at the Lilbourn site (Chapman *et al.* 1977; Figure 10.4a). Radiocarbon dates on charcoal thought to relate to a contemporary burial were about A.D. 1100 (N–1233, 1232). Other dates from the Lilbourn site suggest a general dating of around A.D. 1150–1200 to 1350. Other chert maces are reported from Old Town Ridge, and four were found at an unknown location in Mississippi County, Arkansas.

A stone figurine or statue (Figure 11.5f) in the University of Arkansas Museum is from the Schugtown site, north of Jonesboro near the St. Francis River. A slate spud was also found at Schugtown. This site was first reported by the Smithsonian in 1883, when it had four mounds. Today, only one potted mound and the remnant of a second one exist. A plaza area is apparent, and residential areas exist around it. The site is shallow, and the remains are sparse; yet, it has been visited by many collectors. Ceramics are mainly plain surfaced and similar to those found in the early levels at Hazel. The next most prevalent pottery type is Old Town Red on a variety of vessel shapes but most notably on jars with constricted straight rims similar to Cahokia Cord-Marked rim profiles. Smoothed black pottery and Mound Place Incised continue from earlier complexes. A new pottery type is Carson Red on Buff, which also occurred at the Hazel site. Fragments of a hollow rim head effigy (owl?) with notched applique strips were recovered during a test dig. The hollow effigy contained very small clay balls so that it could rattle. A very wide strap handle, also characteristic at Hazel, was recovered.

A pot filled with beads was discovered at isolated house locations near both sites. In the Hazel situation, the 1400-plus beads were both finished and unfinished (Figure 11.6a–d). All were from a single conch shell and probably represent a basic household industry. The only portion of the conch shell not accounted for was the outer spiral, which was probably removed to manufacture a gorget. A shell found west of Jonesboro is complete except for this portion (Figure 11.6e). At the Hazel site an abrader with a sizing groove was recovered (Figure 11.6f). After the beads were blocked out and drilled, they were tightly strung and rolled on an abrader. This process resulted in an exact diameter dimension. The sizing groove ensured equal sizes in groups of beads.

The National Register Webb or Bay Mounds site near Jonesboro was dug by the Smithsonian in 1883 (Thomas 1894). One mound nearby contained typical Cherry Valley phase pottery. The site itself today consists of two prominent mounds and a sparse village area. A number of mound centers similar to Webb and Schugtown exist in the central part of the Central Valley and seem to represent the shift to greater control by a chiefdom administration over populations, with protection of the civic–ceremonial center and the population evidently becoming a greater concern than they were earlier.

The same process seems to have occurred to the south and to the west as well. In part of the Western Lowlands, however, there was a slightly different ceramic tradition characterized by "flowerpot"-shaped pots (Figure 11.7). Some flat-based jars have strap handles. Middle period Mississippian sites occur deep into the Ozarks. The Guion site in Izard County, Arkansas, contained shell-tempered "flowerpot" and jar rim sherds with wide and narrow strap handles, a lug, a deeply notched lip, and a normal vertical profile. A quantity of corn was found at Guion. Other sites along the White River near Batesville present the same general picture: a typical Middle period Mississippian assemblage with the addition of the "flowerpot" shape. These sites may

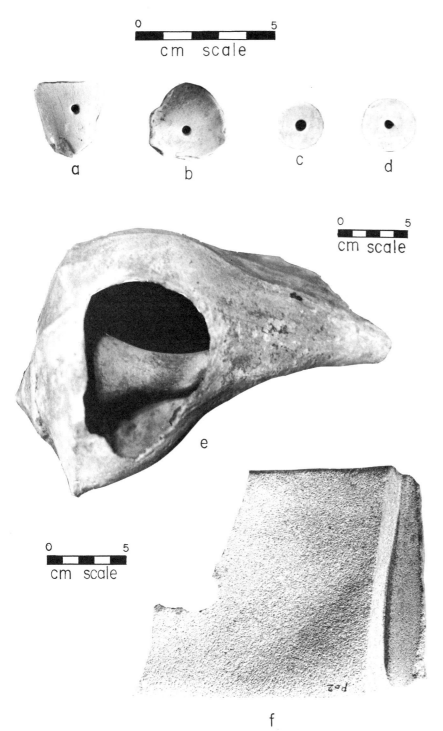

FIGURE 11.6. Shell bead industry. (a)–(b) Unfinished beads from 3PO213 near Hazel. (c)–(d) Finished beads from 3PO213 near Hazel. (e) Conch shell from which gorget blank has been removed from 3CG453. (f) Abrader with sizing groove from Hazel. [Courtesy of the Arkansas Archeological Survey.]

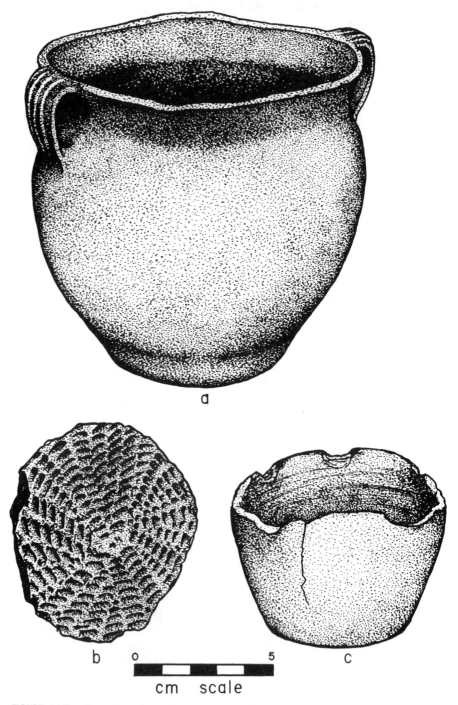

FIGURE 11.7. Examples of vessel shape in the Western Lowlands of Arkansas. (a) Strap-handled jar. (b) Base showing textile impression of mat used during manufacture of vessel. (c) Bowl. [Courtesy of the Arkansas Archeological Survey.]

be multiple component, and the flat-based vessels may represent a strange Early period Mississippian acculturation of Baytown–Coles Creek people to shell tempering their pottery, but the current interpretation is that the Baytown-like shape is coincidence.

Middle period Mississippian farmsteads and hamlets constitute the most common type of site recorded when intensive surveys are done. At the Zebree site a wall trench and small post house measured 5 × 4.2 m, with an interior living space of 17.8 m² (Morse 1975). A second adjacent structure, reconstructed mostly from artifacts plotted on a level, measured 5.2 × 4.1 m in maximum dimension, with an interior living space of about 18 m². A third probable house existed several meters away, but only a hearth and a few postholes were preserved. Four associated graves were discovered, but others apparently had been disturbed by pot hunters. One grave contained a Neeley's Ferry Plain bottle and conch-shell beads. Another contained a fish effigy bowl (Figure 11.8e). Other features were corn concentrations and possible storage pits, which were shallow and irregular in shape.

The total area of this component at the Zebree site was around 400–500 m². If all three houses were occupied at the same time, approximately 15 people were present. House floor ceramics included a Carson Red on Buff bottle and a Matthews Incised jar with strap handles. A plate fragment was recovered, but the most common pottery was cooking jars and food bowls. Matthews Incised and Manly Punctated were common decorations and suggest an A.D. 1250–1350 time period (Figure 11.8a). Notched jar lips and scalloped rim bowls were also common. Mound Place Incised was rare, and a single instance of a possible rudimentary "Haynes Bluff" rim treatment was found. Strap handles predominate over loop handles 52 to 10; of the latter, 7 may actually date to an earlier component. Other artifacts included a turtle-shell rattle found on a house floor, a Dover chert adz, small corner-notched, side-notched, and triangular points, and other relatively nondiagnostic Mississippian debris. An archeomagnetic date for this component at Zebree is A.D. 1210 ± 50 (ZB49). The probable period of occupation is about A.D. 1250–1300.

The Zebree site Middle Mississippian component may be part of a hierarchical system involving the Langdon mound and village site to the north and the Old Town Ridge large village and Lawhorn small village or hamlet to the west. Aerial photographs revealed Old Town Ridge to be a large rectangular village defined by a stockade ditch and containing rows of houses. The Lawhorn site was excavated by avocational archaeologists under the general supervision of Carl Chapman (Moselage 1962). Scallorn points were predominant, and Madison points were infrequent. The artifact assemblage is basically similar to that of the Powers phase, described in the following section. Houses were almost identical in construction details. No daub was found, although plastered houses were built throughout this Middle period elsewhere in the Central Valley (Figure 11.2k). Some differences in traits compared to the Powers phase

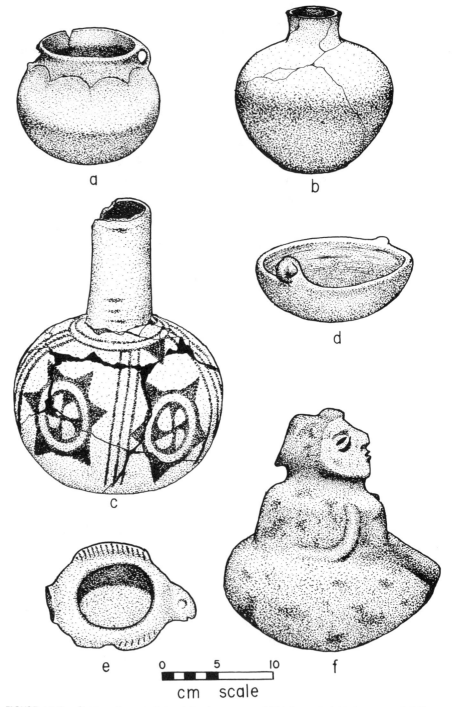

a

b

c

d

e

f

cm   scale

0   5   10

FIGURE 11.8. Pottery characteristic of the later part of Middle period Mississippian. (a) Matthews Incised jar, Zebree site. (b) Mississippian Plain bottle, Zebree site. (c) Carson Red on Buff Bottle, Hazel site. (d) Stylized bird effigy bowl, Hazel site. (e) Fish effigy bowl, Zebree site. (f) Human effigy hooded bottle, Matthews site. [(a)–(e) courtesy of the Arkansas Archeological Survey; (f) drawn from *The Archaeology of Missouri II* by Carl H. Chapman by permission of the University of Missouri Press. Copyright 1980 by the Curators of the University of Missouri.]

were "ash pits" adjacent to puddled clay hearths, stone mortars and pestles near the hearth, a hewed charred log on one floor, and only a very few storage pits in the site. A total of 35 graves, 3 houses, and almost 10,000 potsherds were discovered in this dig. Three radiocarbon dates were A.D. 1194 ± 160, 1308 ± 160, and 1536 ± 162 (M−1158, 1156, 1157). The probable date is within the A.D. 1250–1350 period.

One notable characteristic of Middle period sites is the large concentration of hoe chips. Mill Creek chert hoes occur throughout the Central Valley. One alleged find was a cache of 108 hoes in northeast Arkansas from a site near Big Lake. Normally, only a very few occur at a single site. Dover chert (Tennessee) hoes were being traded into the area as well. To date, no evidence of hoe manufacture has been found in the region, suggesting that the hoes were traded as finished tools. Basalt celts and adzes occur sparingly over the Central Valley. Since trough abraders for accomplishing the final grinding of these and similar tools exist over the region, apparently the final phase of manufacture was a valley-wide activity. Basalt debitage is absent; apparently, therefore, the trade involved either basalt preforms ready for finishing or the finished tools themselves. Other trade was in hematite, galena, quartz crystals, Crescent Quarry (Missouri) and/or Kaolin (Illinois) chert, copper, whole conch shells, and other items. Salt was not being manufactured in most of the Central Valley and probably was being traded from within and near the Cairo Lowland.

In the Arkansas Western Lowlands considerable occupation is evident. One remarkable find near Batesville is the Akron Shell, found by the Smithsonian in the 1880s (Thomas 1894) and dated by James Brown, Northwestern University (personal communication) to this period, although the site seems to postdate A.D. 1350. Apart from that discovery, investigation has been limited to salvage but shows the extent of the Mississippian adaptation. At the Campus site (3CG629) on Crowley's Ridge, just south of Arkansas State University, a large typical wall-trench house pattern 42 m² was uncovered. Evidence for two other possible houses nearby was present as well. The Campus site is central to a 1.6-km stretch of prime agricultural land adjacent to a stream. A corn kernel was recovered from the deposit. West, within the lowlands along the Cache River but on ridges lateral to the flood plain, are Mississippian sites ranging from at least one village with a mound, villages without mounds, hamlet-size villages, and isolated house sites. A portion of a ridge was salvaged, revealing some partial house patterns at the Johnny Wilson site. Site 3LW106 included a wall trench house that was rebuilt twice. Adjacent to it was a cemetery and storage pits. Rebuilding increased the house size from 17.6 to 33.6 m², reflecting either an increasing household size or an increasing need for more space by a given household.

One of the most interesting isolated house sites was found much further to the south. The Wampler site (3CS118), located north of Brinkley, involved 2 structures, 11 pit features, and 225 m² of debris. One structure was probably residential, and the other, for storage. The 22 m² house features were wall trenches, a doorway on the east, central support posts, central hearth, sleeping platform (?) postholes, and a mud wall. Since the house was not burned, the daub did not fire. The 17 m² storage shed was marked by narrow wall trenches and mud walls. Like the house, it had been abandoned and allowed to decay. Hunters used the shelter on several occasions, as evidenced by a stratified interior fireplace used as the walls decomposed but not before the clay daub washed onto the floor.

There is another type of site not often thought to be associated with Mississippian culture; the petroglyph or pictograph. Recent investigation in the Arkansas Ozarks has revealed dozens of previously unrecorded specimens of rock art (Fritz and Ray 1982). Several of these rock art sites are located in the White River drainage in the foothills of the Ozarks. Pecked sandstone slabs with sun symbols, footprints, arrows, and human figures are found here. These may be associated either with Middle or Late period Mississippian settlements in the White River Valley.

POWERS PHASE

A group of closely related Mississippian sites are associated with a tight cluster of sand dunes located essentially in the Little Black River drainage and adjacent to the Ozark Escarpment in the Western Lowlands of Missouri and Arkansas (Black 1979; Price 1978; Price and Griffin 1979; Smith 1978a; Figure 11.9a). A total area of almost 250 km² is involved, of which an intensively surveyed 120-km² Missouri portion encompasses most of the 80 sites identified as Powers phase. Some sites are located in the nearby uplands, and others (not counted) are located southward in Arkansas.

There are 30 radiocarbon dates available for the Powers phase on samples from five sites: Powers Fort, Snodgrass, Turner, Flurry, and Gypsy Joint. A considerable variation in temporal latitude (twelfth into sixteenth centuries) is evident in the results, but this variation is partly because of the large number of samples. Most of these uncorrected dates (18) are between about A.D. 1300 and 1400; if corrected, they would cluster between 1275 and 1375.

The Powers phase exemplifies the extent of Mississippian consolidation on this time level. Mississippian populations were more dispersed throughout this general area during the previous 3 centuries or so. The "sudden" appearance of the Powers phase probably results not from migration from afar but rather from a regional nucleation of populations into a recognizable system of fortified sites.

The largest site is Powers Fort, which is 4.6 ha (11.5 acres) in extent (Figure 11.9b). This rectangular site is defined by a fortification ditch and includes a square and four mounds, one of which was recorded as 6 m high in 1894 by Thomas. The site is the only known location for regionally reported exotic painted, polished, or engraved ceramics. More is known about the grave

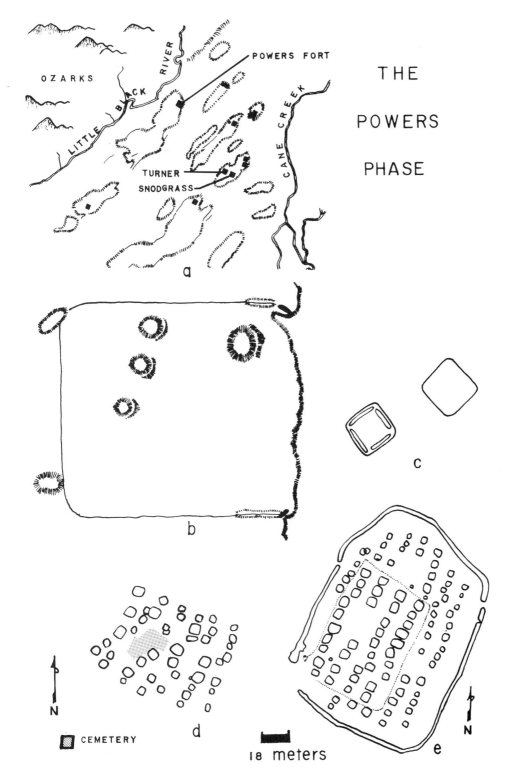

FIGURE 11.9. Powers phase sites, Missouri. (a) Location of sites. (b) Powers Fort. (c) Gypsy Joint. (d) Turner. (e) Snodgrass. [(a), (c)–(e) drawn from Price 1978; (b) drawn from Thomas 1894.]

pottery at the contemporaneous Gibson site, located to the south on a separate cluster of sand dunes. Jars decorated with Matthews Incised with or without the associated variety Manly Punctated; elaborate hooded owl effigy bottles; a red-filmed simple bottle with a hooded human-head effigy rim; kneeling and squatting human effigy bottles with the face appliqued to a traditional bottle neck; and a Mound Place Incised bowl with double bird-head rim effigy can serve as an indication of the variety of ceramics expected at Powers Fort. However, C. B. Moore (1910) was not impressed with the Gibson site: "All vessels from this place seemingly were the work of potters without artistic ambition and lacking in care or skill [p. 361]." Moore described this site as extending for .8 km and consisting of six mounds. Like Powers Fort, Gibson was evidently the civic–ceremonial center for a phase whose people lived mainly in villages, hamlets, and farmsteads.

There are 10 other villages recorded for the Powers phase ranging in size from .6 to 1.2 ha (1.5–2.85 acres). They are not distributed evenly within the region but are situated according to sand dune distribution and probably on the soils most suitable for agriculture. There are three groups of paired sites, possibly reflecting a single community in each case. In at least two cases, one site in the pair is significantly larger than the other. One of these paired communities has been almost completely excavated, an extraordinary feat in the history of archaeological work in the Central Valley.

The Turner and Snodgrass sites are separated from each other by only approximately 160 m. The most logical interpretation of their relationship is that they are sequential in time. The mean of the 8 radiocarbon dates for Turner is A.D. 1325 (corrected date of 1308), and the mean of the 15 radiocarbon dates for Snodgrass is A.D. 1364 (corrected date of 1343). Turner evidently was built first (Figure 11.9d). It measured almost .6 ha (1.5 acres) in extent and consisted of a tight cluster of 44 or so structures in six rows. Pits, presumably for storage, are associated with many of the structures and are particularly noticeable on the eastern half of the site, that portion of the site closest to Snodgrass (Black 1979). Two to four of the structures may have been rebuilt (48 in total were recorded). There probably was a square in the center of the western half of the site at one time. When the move to the Snodgrass site took place, the square was used as a cemetery. A total of 118 individuals were represented in this cemetery; they were interred in rows. Infants less than 1 year in age were absent. Elderly persons were not conspicuous. The 118 skeletons were in only 54 graves. Several bundle burials, involving only adults in multiple burials, occurred, suggesting that adults were retained in a charnel house until the appropriate period for burial. It is most interesting to note that this practice, dating as early as the Cherry Valley phase, was still in vogue at this later date.

It appears that the Turner site was occupied for nearly a generation before the Snodgrass site was constructed. Occupation may have continued in some structures, but the site seems to have been recycled from a village to a mortuary complex. Since there are two other paired sites that have cemeteries in the smaller of the pair, this pattern might have occurred throughout the phase.

The Snodgrass site is considerably larger than Turner (Figure 11.9e). The total extent of the site, including the surrounding ditch, is approximately 1.3 ha (3.25 acres). The existence of this ditch is part of the evidence of the well-planned layout of the site (Price and Griffin 1979). Turner did not have a ditch but must certainly had been fenced since the remains fit a neat rectangular pattern. The Snodgrass site has an inner ward defined by a post-and-clay wall that was plastered. The inner ward is nearly the same size as the Turner site, as if the Turner inhabitants moved into the inner ward of Snodgrass. The remainder of the Snodgrass site is composed of houses that evidently were occupied only by temporary tenants. In Table 11.1 the categories of artifacts that have been described for the Snodgrass site are listed (Price and Griffin 1979). A very large majority of the portable artifacts and an unknown majority of the pit features occur within the inner ward, despite the fact that the majority of structures occur outside the inner ward.

The Snodgrass site accommodated a population that was dispersed in hamlets and farmsteads around the site. The site provided protection for this dispersed population. The approximately 450 individuals who related to the Snodgrass site retreated there for protection and for ceremony, particularly in connection with the burial of dead in the Turner cemetery. The 118 children and adults in that cemetery are nearly what is expected in mortality in a

TABLE 11.1
Major Artifact Categories at the Snodgrass Site, Powers Phase[a,b]

Artifact category	Inside inner ward		Outside inner ward		Total
	Count	Percentage	Count	Percentage	
Structures	38	42	52	58	90
Pit features (probably for storage)	Many more	—	Many less	—	?
Projectile points	174	84	34	16	208
Sherd abraders	17	59	12	41	29
Pottery trowels	11	92	1	8	12
Pottery disks	85	89	10	11	95
Ceramic ear plugs and ear spools	31	86	5	14	36
Wickliffe thick sherds	23	100	0	0	23
Effigy appendages	22	81	5	19	27
Scalloped rims from bowls	37	86	6	14	43
Matthews incised sherds	75	94	5	6	80
Noded sherds	22	92	2	8	24
Notched rim sherds	46	85	8	15	54

[a] Figures from Price and Griffin 1979.
[b] There are no other artifact categories quantified.

population of 450 in a generation. Protection was apparently a key factor in site placement (Figure 11.9a). The villages are all on ridge tops, where defense was easiest. Powers Fort itself is situated so that it is encircled by the other villages, particularly toward the east and southeast, where the Parkin and Nodena phases were developing. The settlement pattern is different from the typical Mississippian model developed by Bruce Smith which was based on ecological considerations (Smith 1978b). The pattern is defensive. Two burials contained individuals who had died as a result of having been shot with arrows. These sites are situated on soils classified as only moderately productive, although they are so defined because of problems with erosion and drought. Evidently, a dispersed population pattern, in existence for several centuries, shifted to a more nucleated one in stages but over a short period. The region was then abandoned, so evidently the settlement shift was not a successful strategy.

All of the structures in the Snodgrass village had been burned, and good evidence of house construction techniques was recovered. The house floors were originally built below ground level, 20–60 cm deep. Wall trenches were dug along the edge of the floor, except in the corners, and posts were set into them. A horizontal pole was lashed to these wall supports at the edge of the floor. Cane mats were hung on the inside of the wall posts from the ceiling to the floor. Grass thatch was placed on the roof. Doorways were probably on the west side. No evidence of the use of daub on the walls was found. Clay was used around the smoke hole in the roof to protect the thatch. There were usually nine support posts in three rows in each structure.

It is supposed that the 90 structures at Snodgrass were primarily family dwellings. Their size varied from 1.8 m^2 to 42.5 m^2. The patterning of houses, courtyards, and walls indicates that there were three separate residential areas at the site. One large area of the site, in the southwest center, was surrounded by a wall defined by some postholes and white clay. There were 38 houses within the wall, lined up in four rows. There was a plaza or courtyard in the center about 506 m^2. The only apparent opening to this separate area is in the southwest corner. The houses here tended to be larger than 21.5 m^2, averaging 30 m^2.

Price (1978) defined two other segments in the site. One, on the north end around another 405-m^2 courtyard, was bounded on three sides by the fortification ditch and on the south by the white wall and a row of structures thought to belong to another segment. Its 28 houses averaged 15 m^2, and only 4 were larger than 21.5 m^2. There are seven rows of houses here. The third area, two long rows of structures, was placed on the eastern and southern side of the site, with a small 16.5- × 15-m courtyard near the wall. It was also bounded by the fortification ditch. Most of these houses were also smaller than those in the central area, averaging 17.4 m^2 in size. The boundary between these segments is admittedly arbitrary and is based on a deviation in orientation of houses.

The entire village is surrounded by a fortification ditch that ranges from 1.2 to 2.4 m in width and was over 60 cm deep. There is an obvious entryway on the southwest corner, where a gap is present. There was probably a protective bastion in this western corner. Three bastions were found on the eastern edge, formed by semicircles of upright logs. They were placed about 22.5 m apart. Numerous pits were associated with structures, both within and without their walls. Six adult burials were oriented along the east–west axis in an extended posture and were accompanied by small jars and bowls. Infant burials were found under some structure floors.

Most of the projectile points appear to be variants of the Scallorn point, a typical Middle period Mississippian point. Eight triangular points are probably the typical Mississippian Madison points. The two willow-leaf points are not typical Nodena points but fall within the published range for the type. They may represent prototypes of Nodena, variants of Madison, preforms, or Nodena points lost by later hunters.

Only effigies, lugs, handles, and decorated sherds are analyzed in the Snodgrass report (Price and Griffin 1979). There are 23 sherds of Wickliffe Thick from the site, probably representing four vessels. There were 27 effigy appendages recovered, including 2 human heads from bowls, 2 hooded bottles interpreted as human effigies, 6 bear effigies, 11 bird forms, 1 deer, 1 frog, and 1 conch-shell effigy. Small scalloped-rim bowls were present, as were perforated and bifurcated strap handles from jars. Incised decorations were found on both large and small jars. Three lines in a chevron design on the shoulder exemplify a type called Matthews Incised (Phillips 1970). A few sherds were punctated, again on jars and once on the interior of a bowl. The type Manly Punctated has been classified by Phillips (1970) as a variant of Matthews Incised and is often found in combination with it at Middle period Mississippian sites. Some nodes are found on small bowls with incurving rims and on small handleless jars. Small groups of two or three nodes are placed opposing one another on these vessels. Rim notching at the Snodgrass site is often found on small and large flaring-rimmed bowls and on jars.

The Gypsy Joint site is a small farmstead site dating to the Powers phase (Smith 1978a; Figure 11.9c). Two structures, one burial, one maize concentration, and eight pits were discovered. The Powers phase component at the site measured about 360 m². One structure was placed in the center of a dune, and the other features were arranged in a circular manner around this structure. It was a rectangular house basin measuring about 5.1 × 4.8 m (24.5 m²), built with single-wall-post construction techniques. Almost 300 artifacts were plotted *in situ* on the house floor during excavation. Chert debitage was the most common artifact class found. Two hammerstones, a "mortar," two scrapers, a deer mandible, several cores, and a minimum of three large pottery jars were recovered from this floor. One jar had an incised chevron design on its shoulder, typical of the Powers phase and of the type Matthews Incised. Deer, squirrel, and beaver bones were found in the structure. Other subsistence evidence included hickory nuts, acorns, black walnuts, maize, marsh elder, knotweed, grapes, plums, and wild beans. No interior cache pits or hearths were identified.

A second structure was buried deeper than the first one. Only 11.3 m² of living space was enclosed within wall trenches. An internal hearth was found, and one shallow pit was present near this hearth. Three Scallorn projectile points were recovered, two of them unfinished. At least six vessels were present: three large jars, one small jar, one bowl, and one large short-necked bottle. Five large lumps of hematite were found in the structure. Deer, turkey, and box turtle remains were present.

Analysis of faunal and botanical remains showed that the site was occupied year round, and typical household activity is implied. There is considerable evidence of plant processing. A concentration of maize kernels was found 3 m (10 ft.) southeast of the first structure. The corn was small and of the 10- and 12-rowed variety typical of other Powers phase sites. Over 1200 gm of charred hickory nutshells were associated with two pits, suggesting that the area was probably used to boil nuts for their oil.

A lithic manufacturing area was indicated by cores, debitage, and aborted projectile point preforms. In another area about half of a deer and a chert knife were recovered. A minimum of 12 animals were present, with at least 6 white-tailed deer represented.

Smith (1978a) concluded that the Gypsy Joint site was occupied for less than 3 years, on a year-round basis. Five to seven adults and subadults, who were probably a nuclear family, lived there. Males probably constructed both a warm- and a cold-weather house, hunted during the fall and winter, butchered, and made lithic tools. Females collected wild plants and prepared them for eating. Males probably cleared land for farming, with both males and females working the subsequent cultivation. Maize may have been stored in a crib. The group took tools such as adzes and hoes with them when they moved away. This group was essentially self-sufficient. Galena and ocher at the site show some evidence of linkage to outside trade, probably through Powers Fort, which is 3.2 km away. Gypsy Joint probably represents the bottom end of a hierarchy of sites within the Powers phase.

THE CAIRO LOWLAND PHASE

Phillips (1970) stated: "The best Cairo Lowland site collections are from Matthews (5–R–3), Sandy Woods (5–S–4), Crosno (5–T–1), and Lilbourn (6–R–1) [p. 926]." He also comments that "the best description of a Cairo Lowland site in print [p. 925]" is O'Byam's Fort in Kentucky, also known as the McLeod Bluff site (Webb and Funkhouser 1933). Ceramic characteristics of the Cairo Lowland phase listed by Phillips (1970:925) are Bell Plain (variety New Madrid), Matthews Incised (variety Matthews, Beckwith, and Manly),

Old Town Red, O'Byam Incised, Kimmswick Fabric Impressed, Wickliffe Thick, Mound Place Incised, and Nashville Negative Painted (variety Sikeston), plus occasional finds of Nodena Red and White, Walls Engraved, and Nashville Negative Painted (variety Angel). The Cairo Lowland phase extends over a relatively long time period; in fact, it dates during much of the Middle period Mississippian. Radiocarbon dates indicate a general dating around A.D. 1150–1350.

The development of Mississippian in the Cairo Lowland after the Hoecake or Varney period must have been similar to those developments just described to the south within the Central Valley. However, the Cairo Lowland phase is more difficult to interpret because sites are larger, multicomponent, and more complex. None have been completely excavated.

The earliest portion of the Middle period Mississippian is not clearly evident here. Populations were probably dispersed, and prominent civic–ceremonial sites apparently had not yet developed. No spectacular site such as Cherry Valley or artifacts such as beaker-style vessels are known. However, there are isolated mound sites, some of which are quite prominent. None of these seems to have been professionally excavated, nor is it known if they have been dug into by treasure seekers. The closest reported discovery is at a site burdened with several names, including Canada, Beckwith, Charleston, and Hearnes. The site complex is multicomponent, but at least one portion seems to be earlier than most known sites and is somewhat similar to early Arkansas finds. At the Hearnes site (Klippel 1969), crudely spherical jars with loop handles or no handles, bottles including one with a prominent high shoulder, hooded bottles, simple noded jars, steep-sided bowls, and the typical contour-sided bowls were recovered in mounds with fragmentary and definite bundle burials. One mound included part of a posthole pattern, possibly a charnel structure.

Adams and Walker (1942) claim that Towosahgy (also known as Beckwith's Fort) is "perhaps the largest and most spectacular mound group in the bottomlands of Missouri [p. 6]." Remains were scattered within an area of 120 or 160 ha (300 or 400 acres), according to Houck in 1908; over 20 mounds were then present. The main portion of the site was marked by an embankment and ditch combination. Remnants of a fortification wall that enclosed 10 ha (25 acres) and 7 mounds have been found. The extension of Mississippian remains outside the wall has been verified. Of the remaining mounds, 2 are truncated; one was 7 or 7.5 m high and the other 3 m high at the turn of the century. Four of the seven radiocarbon dates from the site range from around A.D. 1000 to 1250; three are significantly earlier. The presence of O'Byam Incised and Matthews Incised in Stephen Williams's (1954) collection from the site indicates a maximum possible time period of about A.D. 1050–1350. Healan (1972) conducted a carefully controlled surface collection of the site. The collection included O'Byam Incised as the predominant decorative type; Matthews Incised was not mentioned. Polished Bell Plain was frequent. All these data indicate a dating within the twelfth and thirteenth centuries. The surface collection revealed three residential areas within the fortification and demonstrated that the black polished pottery was restricted in location to the southeastern portion of the site. This latter discovery emphasizes the presence of complex behavior at the site, perhaps ceremonial versus nonceremonial or chiefly versus nonchiefly.

Towosahgy probably is a result of the following events: A ceremonial center developed after the Hoecake site was largely abandoned and the population concentrated more upon the meander belt soils of this portion of the Cairo Lowland. Towosahgy at this time was a dispersed site of mounds and residential areas over an area of perhaps up to several hundred hectares. At some time during the twelfth century a fortified civic–ceremonial center that was much more restrictive in area was constructed within the dispersed mound area. At Cahokia (Fowler 1978) a similar situation existed. During the twelfth century a fortification wall with bastions was constructed around the central portion of the site, 80 ha (200 acres) of the 15.5 km² (6 square miles) of remains. Protection of the civic–ceremonial center is a development that took place over a large portion of the Mississippi Valley. Such a center would have provided refuge to the population dependent upon the center.

Other fortified town sites also developed as subsidiaries to the paramount one. The Crosno site is evidently such a site (Williams 1954). Crosno was a 7.4-ha (18.5-acre) fortified site with four mounds, one of which was truncated and 9 m high at the turn of the century. In 1952 the main mound was 5.5 m high. Aerial photographs showed a possible wall and ditch around the site. A plaza probably existed to the southeast of the mound but was destroyed by levee construction before it could be verified.

Three kinds of structures were found at Crosno. Rectangular buildings with wall trenches, interior hearths, and roof-support postholes were about 4.2 m square. They were of wattle and daub construction. Rectangular small post structures measuring only about 7.2 m² in extent are reminiscent of the earlier Hoecake-type house. A circular wall trench structure measuring 6.5 m in diameter may have been a sweat-house used for ceremonial purification or a charnel structure.

Points at Crosno were usually triangular or side-notched. Scallorn points are rare in the Cairo Lowland. The Scallorn point, which seems to be an adaptation to cane hafting, is more typical of regions to the south; however, cane shafts were readily available throughout the lowlands of the Central Valley. Williams (1954) was able to define two Mississippian components, Early Crosno and Late Crosno. The former includes O'Byam Incised and a cord-marked type from jars with outcurved rims, whereas the latter characteristically included Matthews Incised and the more exotic painted and engraved pottery. Kimmswick pans and Wickliffe funnels are characteristic throughout the period of the Crosno site and indicate that salt was being locally manufactured in the Cairo Lowland phase.

The first zooarchaeological analysis of faunal remains in the Central Mississippi Valley was done under Williams's direction at Crosno. Not surprisingly, deer was by far the most common mammal, although 17 other mammals included raccoon, rabbits, dog, beaver, mink, bobcat, and cougar. An impressive list of 30 birds included many migratory fowl expected to be in the Mississippi flyway. The most common was the sandhill crane. Passenger pigeon was the only species that is now extinct. Wild turkey, prairie chicken, and bobwhite quail were local year-round residents. Large fish like gar, catfish, and drum were also found.

The environment of the Cairo Lowland has already been discussed in connection with the development of Mississippian in the Central Valley in Chapter 10, but it should be reviewed here. The center of the lowlands is the location of a prairie, which accounts for approximately 15% of the 1600-km^2 (640-square-mile) area. About 51% of the lowlands is made up of meander belt surface, adjacent to the modern Mississippi River. The remaining 34% of the lowlands is braided stream surface. Sikeston Ridge is an older terrace of braided stream surface that includes prairies. Commerce Hills is an upland remnant, part of the Crowley's Ridge complex. The immediate environment consists of five distinct land surfaces. Major sites, defined by size and number of mounds, are distributed around the prairie. Most major sites are situated adjacent to or within a meander belt region. Sandy Woods to the north is on the interface of the meander belt and the braided stream surfaces. Lilbourn to the south is on the interface of Sikeston Ridge with the meander belt surface. Towosahgy is within the meander belt to the southeast. The next major site is Sikeston, which is situated on the interface of Sikeston Ridge and the more recent braided stream surface, in the west-central part of the Cairo Lowland. The Wickliffe site in Kentucky is located near where, based on this pattern, a major Cairo Lowland phase site is expected. However, it is not known if Wickliffe is a Cairo Lowland phase site.

Sandy Woods measured approximately 22 ha (55 acres) in extent, was fortified, and included nine mounds. A large number of pots from here exist in the collections at Harvard and Yale. Lilbourn measures at least 16.2 ha (42 acres) within the fortification, with eight mounds inside and a spectacular mace-shaped mound located outside the wall. Sikeston is approximately 16 ha (40 acres) in extent and includes five mounds inside the fortification and several others outside. The nearby Matthews site is somewhat larger than Crosno (9 ha, or 22 acres), with seven mounds located within its fortification system. The sizes of other sites in the Cairo Lowland are not known, mainly due to partial destruction before they could be examined; however, many appear to be major sites but are probably more on the order of Crosno and Matthews rather than Lilbourn or Towosahgy.

Lilbourn's 10 mounds included 5 pyramidal ones, 2 in the center, and 3 in the northern portion of the site (Chapman *et al.* 1967). The largest measured 6.3 m high, a second measured 3.3 m high, and the third and fourth, 2.7 m high; a fifth was 2.5 m high in the late nineteenth century. The mace-shaped mound outside the main site was prophetic since a nicely chipped chert mace was discovered on a burial during salvage operations at the site before much of it was destroyed by construction. Radiocarbon dates number 16, with two clusters of dates: A.D. 1100–1180 and 1230–1370. There was one date higher and one lower than any of these. Dates of 1180 and 1370 were obtained from the same burned structure; otherwise, dates on the same feature tend to be very close or at least within the same date cluster.

Specific components relating to these two clusters of dates are not identified in the Lilbourn report; there was too much material to analyze in the relatively short period between salvage and report. However, the dates and the general nature of reported artifacts indicate that, as for other Cairo Lowland complex sites, there was development of the fortified civic–ceremonial center throughout the period of the Cairo Lowland phase, beginning in the twelfth century A.D. and terminating somewhere within the second half of the fourteenth century A.D.

SUMMARY

Middle period Mississippian began around A.D. 1000–1050 with a sharp decrease in red-filmed ceramics. New forms began as a ceremonial or burial ware. Experimentation took place in grog- and shell-tempered paste along with the development of handles, rim effigies, and lugs, plus innovation in new forms, including the beaker, plate, and true bottle.

Primary or bundle burial was often associated with a charnel structure, which ultimately became mounded over. The earliest ceremonial–burial sites do not usually have associated villages. The population was dispersed in farmsteads, hamlets, and small villages in most of the region until about A.D. 1150.

Villages became increasingly associated with the ceremonial center, which became a "civic–ceremonial center." Villages became stockaded with rows of houses and the ceremonial component inside. Protection of the ceremonial center and the population became increasingly important.

By A.D. 1250 a clear hierarchy of sites had come into being: a civic–ceremonial center with mounds, associated with palisaded villages, in turn associated with a dispersed farmstead pattern. The farmstead population had houses in appropriate villages to which they could retreat for protection or major ceremonial activities. Wattle and daub wall trench houses developed but were not constructed universally. Above-ground storage probably developed during this period.

Pottery became fairly standardized and well made. A variety of effigy and painted forms were being made but were still largely restricted to ceremonial–burial use. Decoration became fairly prominent in the northern two-thirds of the Central Valley. O'Byam Incised gave way to Matthews Incised as the plate form disappeared. Carson Red on Buff, Nodena Red and White, and negative painting appeared. Bell Plain became an established paste for decorated and smoothed ceremonial pottery mostly in the northeast. Mound Place Incised and Walls Engraved appeared. Most kitchen pottery was plain and consisted of cooking jars, food bowls, and water bottles. Some jars had large strap handles and capacities of 80 liters or more.

Trade intensified, particularly in exotic items but also in useful tools such as Mill Creek hoes and basalt celts and adzes. Numerous prominent civic–ceremonial centers date from this period. Many appear to have been short-lived. Catastrophic events ended this period: "All major village and town sites of the phase were consumed by fire, bringing the cultural activities to an abrupt and instantaneous halt [Price and Griffin 1979:7]." This event in the Powers phase is documented by radiocarbon dating to have occurred at about A.D. 1350–1375. The sites seemed to have been fired by members of the Powers phase themselves, therefore flight was, in part at least, voluntary. No really useful tools seem to have been left behind. Pots remain but would have been easily replaced and cumbersome to carry in quantity. No people are known to have been trapped by the firing. The fire at Snodgrass began at one corner and quickly moved through the village. Permanent Mississippian occupation of the Powers-phase region ceased.

Powers was not the only phase to terminate or the only region to be abandoned. Large portions of the Central Valley suffered a similar fate. Apparently, the gradually increased attention toward protecting populations and civic–ceremonial centers somehow reached a critical point. Yet Mississippian culture in the Central Valley as a whole flourished.

REFERENCES

Adams, Robert, and Winslow Walker
   1942   Archaeological surface survey of New Madrid County, Missouri. *Missouri Archaeologist* **8**: 1–23.
Black, Thomas
   1979   The biological and social analyses of a Mississippian cemetery from southeast Missouri: The Turner site, 23 BU 21 A. *University of Michigan Museum of Anthropology Anthropological Papers* **68**.
Brose, David
   1976   Some Mississippian ceramics from Arkansas, in the Cleveland Museum of Natural History. *Kirtlandia* **21**:1–11.
Chapman, Carl, John Cottier, David Denman, David Evans, Dennis Harvey, Michael Reagan, Bradford Rope, Michael Southard, and Gregory Waselkov
   1977   Investigation and comparison of two fortified Mississippi tradition archaeological sites in southeast Missouri: A preliminary compilation. *Missouri Archaeologist* **38**.
Fowke, Gerard
   1910   Antiquities of central and southeastern Missouri. *Bureau of American Ethnology Bulletin* **37**.

Fowler, Melvin
    1978   Cahokia and the American Bottom: Settlement archeology. In *Mississippian settlement patterns,* edited by Bruce Smith, pp. 455–478. New York: Academic Press.
Fritz, Gayle, and Robert Ray
    1982   Rock art sites in the southern Arkansas Ozarks and the Arkansas River valley. In Arkansas archeology in review, edited by Marvin Jeter and Neal Trubowitz. *Arkansas Archeological Survey Research Series* 15:240–276.
Hamilton, Henry, Jean Hamilton, and Eleanor Chapman
    1974   Spiro Mound copper. *Missouri Archaeological Society Memoir* 11.
Healen, Dan M.
    1972   Surface delineation of functional areas at a Mississippian ceremonial center. *Missouri Archaeological Society Memoir* 10.
Houck, Louis
    1908   *A history of Missouri.* Chicago: R. R. Donnelley.
Klinger, Timothy
    1981   The Mangrum site, mitigation through excavation and preservation in Northeast Arkansas. Report submitted to Memphis District U.S. Army Corps of Engineers by Arkansas Archeological Survey
Klippel, Walter
    1969   The Hearnes site: A multicomponent occupation site and cemetery in the Cairo Lowland region of southeast Missouri. *Missouri Archaeologist* 31.
McGimsey, Charles R. , III
    1964   An engraved shell gorget from the McDuffee site. *Arkansas Archeologist* 5:128–129.
Moore, Clarence B.
    1910   Antiquities of the St. Francis, White, and Black rivers, Arkansas. *Journal of the Academy of Natural Sciences of Philadelphia* 14:255–364.
    1911   Some aboriginal sites on Mississippi River. *Journal of the Academy of Natural Sciences of Philadelphia* 14:367–478.
Morse, Dan F.
    1975   Report of excavations at the Zebree site, 1969. *Arkansas Archeological Survey Research Report* 4.
Morse, Dan F., and Sam Smith
    1973   Archeological salvage during the construction of Route 308. *Arkansas Archeologist* 14:36–78.
Moselage, John H.
    1962   The Lawhorn site. *Missouri Archaeologist* 24.
Perino, Gregory
    1967   The Cherry Valley mounds and Banks Mound 3. *Central State Archaeological Societies Inc., Memoir* 1.
Phillips, Philip
    1970   Archaeological survey in the Lower Yazoo Basin, Mississippi, 1949–1955. *Papers of the Peabody Museum, Harvard University* 60.
Phillips, Philip, and James A. Brown
    1978   *Pre-Columbian shell engravings* (pt. 1). Cambridge, Mass.: Peabody Museum Press, Harvard University.
Phillips, Philip, James A. Ford, and James B. Griffin
    1951   Archaeological survey in the Lower Mississippi Alluvial Valley, 1940–1947. *Papers of the Peabody Museum,* Harvard University 25.
Price, James E.
    1978   The settlement pattern of the Powers phase. In *Mississippian settlement patterns,* edited by Bruce D. Smith, pp. 201–231. New York: Academic Press.

Price, James E., and James B. Griffin
  1979   The Snodgrass site of the Powers phase of southeast Missouri. *University of Michigan. Museum of Anthropology, Anthropological Papers* **66**.
Smith, Bruce D.
  1978a   *Prehistoric patterns of human behavior: A case study in the Mississippi Valley.* New York: Academic Press.
  1978b   Variation in Mississippian settlement patterns. In *Mississippian settlement systems*, edited by Bruce Smith, pp. 479–503. New York: Academic Press.
Thomas, Cyrus
  1894   Report on the mound explorations of the Bureau of American Ethnology. *12th Annual Report of the Bureau of American Ethnology for 1890–1891.*
Waring, Antonio J Jr., and Preston Holder
  1945   A Prehistoric ceremonial complex in the Southeastern United States. *American Anthropologist* **47**:1–34.
Webb, William, and W. D. Funkhouser
  1933   The McLeod Bluff site. *University of Kentucky Reports in Archaeology and Anthropology* **3**:1–33.
Williams, Stephen
  1954   *An archeological study of the Mississippian culture in southeast Missouri.* Ph.D. dissertation, Yale University. Ann Arbor, Mich.: University Microfilms.
  1977   Some ruminations on the current strategy of archaeology in the Southeast. Paper presented at Southeastern Archaeological conference, Lafayette, La.
Wolfman, Daniel
  1982   Archeomagnetic dating in Arkansas and the border areas of adjacent states. In *Arkansas archeology in review*, edited by Neal Trubowitz and Marvin Jeter, pp. 277–300. *Arkansas Archeological Survey Research Series* **15**.

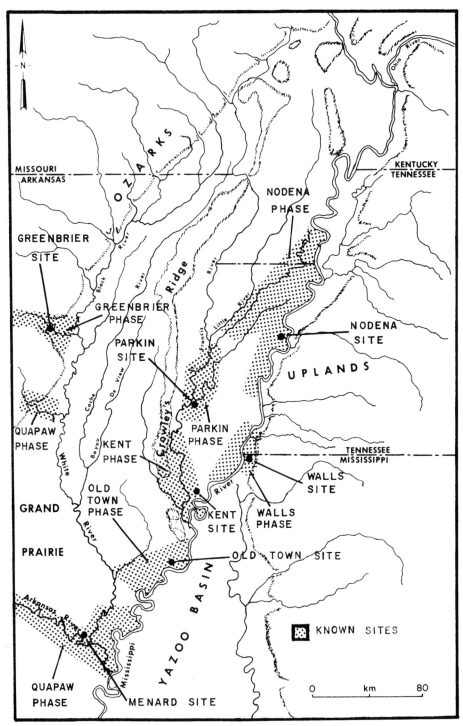

FIGURE 12.1. Location of Late period Mississippian phases and selected sites in the Central Valley.

12

Mississippian Nucleation
(A.D. 1350–1650)

Beginning in the twelfth century there was an increased emphasis upon protecting the civic–ceremonial center and the population with which it was associated. The actual process of uniting formerly independent chiefdoms into larger aggregates may have begun in earnest after about A.D. 1250. The Powers phase is an example of this process.

Suddenly—that is, in terms of 50–100-year time units—large portions of the Central Valley became uninhabited (Figure 12.1). The dating of this happening is around A.D. 1350–1400, definitely prehistoric in origin. The areas not abandoned experienced significant population increases at about the same time, an extraordinary population nucleation. During this process of chiefdom consolidation a critical point must have been reached that resulted in a severe demographic adjustment. That it could happen at all is a tribute to Mississippian political organization.

HORIZON MARKERS

The main difficulty in looking at this period developmentally is one that plagues all investigations of higher societies. Sites are complex, and many are multicomponent. Scientific sampling, compared with the amount of data available, has been minimal, and much of the contemporary interpretation has been based on the "loot" obtained by treasure seekers.

A primary horizon marker is the Nodena point (Figure 12.2a). These points have convex sides, resemble willow leaves, and range in length from 1.5 to 5 cm. An obvious hypothesis is that the Nodena point was a specialized arrow point developed for warfare. It must also have been effective for hunting

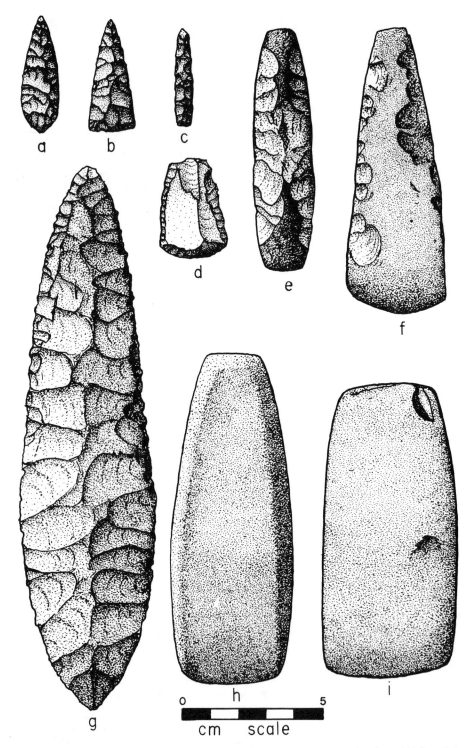

FIGURE 12.2. Stone artifacts typical of the Late period Mississippian in the Central Valley. (a) Nodena point. (b) Madison point. (c) "Pipe drill." (d) End scraper. (e)–(f) Chisels or adzes. (g) Biface. (h) Basalt adz. (i) Basalt celt. [(a)–(e), (h) courtesy of the Arkansas Archeological Survey; (g) courtesy of the Department of Anthropology, National Museum of Natural History, Smithsonian Institution.]

deer because this point style is widely distributed at locations thought to be hunting camps. Its sudden appearance and the sudden disappearance of the Scallorn point coincided with population nucleation. The Nodena point was part of the reaction to the need to consolidate population in more restricted areas. It is basically unique to the Central Valley and immediate environs.

The earliest reported context for Nodena points is at the Banks site in Crittenden County, Arkansas (Perino 1966:33–35). The date should be around A.D. 1400, although the radiocarbon date is A.D. 1490 ± 162 (M-916). But the Nodena points from the Banks site vary considerably from the later traditional examples. They tend to be laterally serrated on the basal portion, and many have truncated bases in addition to lateral serration for attachment to a shaft. Most probably their antecedents were the triangular points of the Cairo Lowland phase. No Scallorn points were found at Banks, an unusual situation for a site that is characterized mostly by Manly Punctated and Matthews Incised ceramics and that has produced four complete negative-painted vessels. Negative painting is more characteristic of the Cairo Lowland, lower Ohio River, and the Nashville, Tennessee, regions than of northeast Arkansas and is normally dated to an earlier time period than its Banks site context.

A burial at the Parkin site included similar serrated Nodena points plus other artifacts including a copper repoussé plate and a long copper awl (personal communication, Stephen Williams, Harvard University). The plate is a typical Middle period Mississippian spider design (Figure 11.5e). This burial should date about A.D. 1400.

The Madison point (Figure 12.2b), in contrast to the Nodena point, was part of a wide geographical tradition of triangular arrow points that date almost as early as the bow and arrow. However, Madison points date from only around A.D. 1000–1200 in the Central Valley, except for the Cairo Lowland, and were fairly rare until after about A.D. 1350–1400. Triangular arrow points continued to increase in popularity, compared with the Nodena point, during the sixteenth and seventeenth centuries and emerged within the eighteenth century as the prominent, if not exclusive, point type.

Artifacts called "pipe drills" occur in this period as well. They are small narrow bifaces (Figure 12.2c) that may have functioned as drills. Similar artifacts have been found in earlier contexts and are not unique to the Late period Mississippian.

Antler tip points are also characteristic of the Late period. Although they did occur in earlier contexts, they were more common during the late period. Several instances of unfinished point caches are known. Typically, antler tip points exhibit a single basal "barb." Presumably, they were adapted for fish spearing (see Figure 12.4k). The only known bow and arrow outfit found in the Central Valley contained antler-tipped cane arrow shafts (Nash 1957).

A diagnostic artifact that may date to later stages of the Late period Mississippian is the "thumbnail" end scraper (Figure 12.2d). It occurs in large numbers, as at the Rose and Blytheville Mound sites. None was reported from the Banks or Hazel sites, which are dated early in this period. End scrapers occur with Nodena points at base settlements for hunters and at hunting campsites. They appear to have functioned in the preparation of deerskins. The De Soto accounts mention hunters concentrating on white-tailed deer (Bourne 1904:29–30). Presumably, the high incidence of end scrapers reflects an increasing attention toward the processing of deerskins. In the eighteenth century the deerskin trade with the French was firmly established, but it is evident that its roots go back at least over two centuries.

Chisels and adzes made of chert became more common in the Late period Mississippian (Figure 12.2e, f). Some are double bitted. Usually manufactured from yellowish cobbles typical of Crowley's Ridge chert, the ground portions are often red, as if oxidized from some sort of thermal reaction with the iron mineral components, perhaps due to the friction from abrasion. Woodworking obviously was an important industry. The De Soto accounts described large canoes (Bourne 1904:113). Sandstone abraders proliferated in shape and texture, and craftsmen kept their tools in good working order.

Larger bipointed bifaces were apparently used in butchering (Figure 12.2g). They are rarely found complete; usually, resharpening flakes and fragments are recovered. Sometimes laterally beveled to the midpoint, these specimens appear to have been dulled by use on one end and then reversed so the opposite end could be used.

Basalt is thought to have become a resource monopoly of the Nodena phase (Figure 12.2h, i). On sites near Blytheville, the closest to the source in the Ste. François Mountains, primary basalt debitage is common. In addition, the trough abraders (Figure 12.3f, g) and ground beveled hammerstones (Figure 12.3e) used to manufacture basalt celts and adzes tend to be exclusively associated with the Late period Mississippian sites in this Blytheville area.

Copper sheets of the nonrepoussé type in the effigy forms of hawks, snakes, and humans are known, the former from several sites (Figure 12.4a). Copper is exceedingly rare in most of the Central Valley, except in the Late period sites, where it is infrequent. It was more common earlier in the northern part of the Central Valley. Traders may have brought copper into the Central Valley along with catlinite from the Upper Mississippi Valley. The copper sheets tend to be extremely uniform in thickness, and it is possible that much of it may be European. However, the De Soto expedition obtained native copper here, and it is likely that copper was mined by the Nodena phase in the Ste. François Mountains.

Decoration is normally limited to pottery vessels. Exceptions include a bone gorget carved into a turtle effigy (Figure 12.4c) and a deer phalange carved into an owl effigy (Figure 12.4b). Engraved shell "buttons" are another diagnostic but rare trait (Figure 12.4m).

Pottery human figurines are rare. Occasionally, there will be one on a vessel appendage (Figure 12.4g). Nonhuman effigies made of fired pottery occur at many sites (Figure 12.4e, f, h).

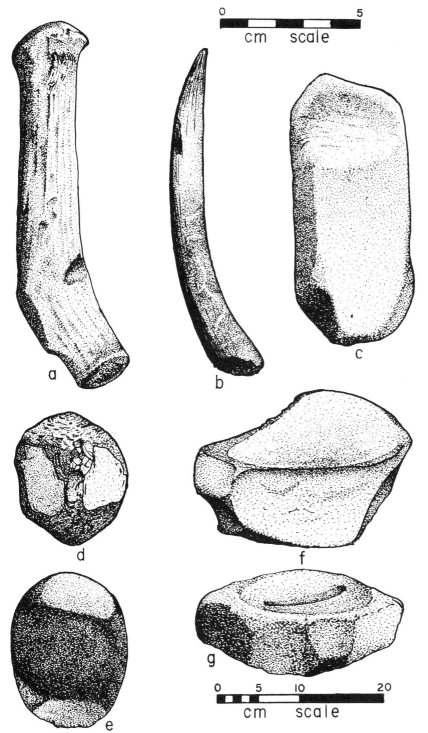

FIGURE 12.3. Mississippian knapping tools. (a) Antler baton. (b) Antler punch. (c) Quartzite preform abrader. (d) Battered-edged hammerstone. (e) Abraded-edged hammerstone used to make basalt tools. (f)—(g) Trough abraders used to finish basalt tools. [Courtesy of the Arkansas Archeological Survey.]

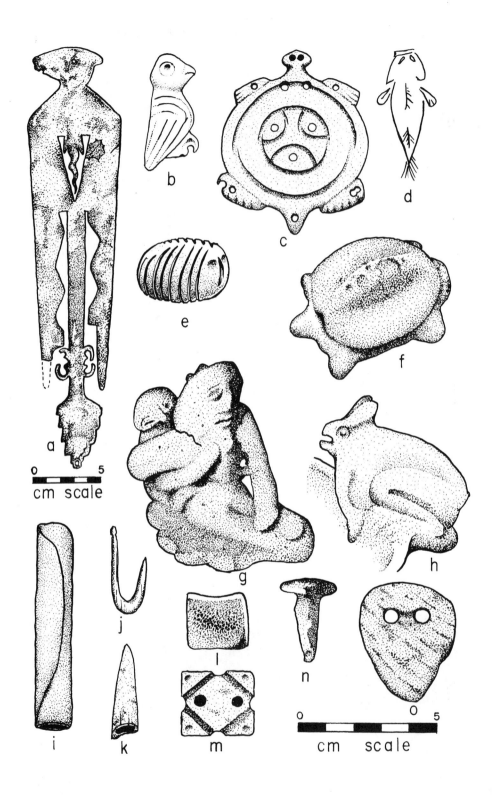

a

0   5
cm scale

i   j   g   h

k   l

m   n
0   0   5
cm   scale

Decoration of the hair may have been more important in the Late period Mississippian. Bone tubular beads are characteristic earlier and copper ones later (Figure 12.4i). At the Banks site there were several instances of conch-shell beads across the forehead of skeletons from side to side. Copper disks have been found at the Parkin, Banks (as ear spools), and Hazel sites. "Shell mask" gorgets are found but are known to exist in earlier context as well (Figure 12.4o). Mushroom-shaped shell ear plugs are characteristic. An intriguing custom was the placement of bird wings (fans?) in some graves.

Bone fishhooks (Figure 12.4j) were in existence long before this Late period but at this time became fairly common. They usually occur in groups of four or six. Most probably they constitute trotlines and could have been used as vertical lines attached to a tree limb or a float. An engraved bottle from the Parkin site seems to depict intestine floats with attached lines. Trotlines also could have been anchored to a shore and laid on the bottom of a slough. All kinds of fish were caught, but catfish and suckers were plentiful in refuse deposits and as decoration on pottery and bone.

Late period Mississippian discoidals are very distinctive (Figure 10.6). They are flat on one face and convex on the opposite face, possibly reflecting an increasing complexity in the chunky game since the two faces are distinct from each other. Astragalus dice were usually made from the bones of white-tailed deer and sometimes of elk (Figure 12.4l). Very rarely a die will be recovered that is made of a buffalo astragalus. These may have been used in a gambling game or have been artifacts used in oracles.

Catlinite is a new trait in Late period sites. Beads are reported from one site, but the usual artifact of catlinite is the "Siouan" disk pipe (see Figure 13.3b). These are made of catlinite aboriginally mined at Pipestone, Minnesota. Catlinite disk pipes were possibly similar to the "Calumets" used by the French as emblems for safe passage in the Mississippi Valley. These were in use before the French first penetrated the Central Valley in 1673. At the time of the French exploration each village had its own calumet, which was used in the calumet ceremony occasioned by diplomatic visits. The French complained as early as the late seventeenth century that they had to endure a calumet ceremony at each village, sometimes lasting all night.

The catlinite disk pipe may be an important link to Siouan speakers in the Upper Mississippi River Valley. The Quapaw are Siouan speakers, but it is not

---

FIGURE 12.4. Miscellaneous nonlithic artifacts typical of the Late period Mississippian in the Central Valley. (a) Nonrepoussé copper hawk effigy. (b) Bone owl effigy. (c) Turtle bone turtle effigy. (d) Catfish engraved on bone. (e) Cicada pottery effigy. (f) Pottery turtle effigy. (g) Mother and child pottery effigy. (h) Rabbit pottery effigy. (i) Copper tube. (j) Bone fishhook. (k) Antler point. (l) Bone die. (m) Shell button. (n) Shell pin. (o) Shell mask gorget. [(a), (n) drawn from Moore 1910, courtesy of The Academy of Natural Sciences, Philadelphia; (b), (c), (e), (h)–(m), (o) courtesy of the Arkansas Archeological Survey; (d) courtesy of the Henry Clay Hampson II Memorial Museum of Archeology; (f) courtesy of the Department of Anthropology, National Museum of Natural History, Smithsonian Institution; (g) courtesy of Ralph Olson.]

known precisely with which language within the Siouan language family Quapaw is affiliated. It has been suggested that the dispersal of the Siouan language family (established by 1000 B.C.) was related to the spread of Mississippian culture out of the St. Louis–Cairo Lowland area (Griffin 1960). Catlinite pipes or fragments have been reported from five sites in the Central Valley including Upper Nodena.

Historic artifacts, mostly sixteenth-century Spanish, include brass hawk bells (Clarksdale bells), chevron glass beads, blue glass beads, Nueva Cadiz glass beads, various unidentified iron objects, a brass scabbard part made into a pendant, and a possible matchlock rifle support. A "non-Indian" skull found at Middle Nodena had an arrow point embedded in it. An Indian skull from another site had a musket ball inside. A pipe stem and stoneware (Rhenish) fragment were found at Upper Nodena, but there is some uncertainty about their precise dating. An extraordinary human effigy vessel found near Batesville seems to be wearing a pair of glasses on its forehead.

The major ceramic marker types are Parkin Punctated and Barton Incised, often occurring together on the same cooking jar (Figure 12.5). Parkin is a body design, whereas Barton is a rim motif. Again, the earliest known context is at the Banks site. Interestingly, Manly Punctated and Matthews Incised, often occurring together as shoulder designs, are different in execution on Banks-site pots than on earlier pots from southeast Missouri. At the Banks site, the incisions are sharper and narrower, more like Barton Incised. The Parkin and Barton motifs are not very prominent in some areas, making it difficult to specify stylistic shifts exactly through time.

Barton Incised may have come into existence before the Late period but Parkin Punctated almost certainly did not. The Banks site assemblage suggests that they developed out of Matthews Incised and Manly Punctated. Parkin Punctated became increasingly popular as a body treatment on Barton Incised jars. As a consequence, there was an increased sherd ratio count, which peaked and then subsided. Barton Incised then predominated over Parkin Punctated at the very end or shortly after this period of A.D. 1350–1650. By this time Wallace Incised, a spinoff of Barton Incised, began to become dominant over Barton.

On jars such as these, handles were of the applique strap variety. Normally two to four handles and/or lugs were characteristic. A later development was an increase in the number of handles, which because of their small size were no longer functional. In fact, "handles" ranged from arcaded to appliqued strips ("Campbell" type) to simply incised lines (Smith 1969). The handle tended to disappear altogether on jars some time after A.D. 1600.

Much of the pottery found is Mississippi Plain (variety Neeley's Ferry), which is characteristic throughout the Mississippian period. However, Bell Plain is an important horizon marker, particularly in sites near the Mississippi River. Actually, Bell paste came into existence much earlier but did not become prominent in the south until after about A.D. 1350–1400. Bell Plain is another

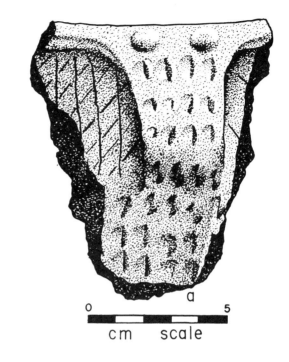

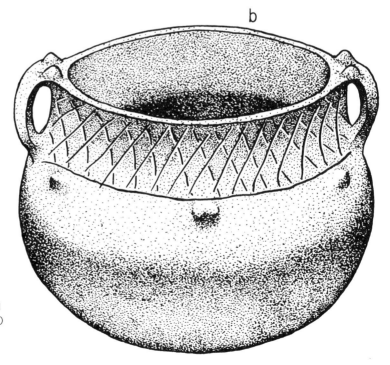

FIGURE 12.5. Parkin Punctated and
Barton Incised motifs. (a) Rim sherd
with Barton Incised rim treatment and
Parkin Punctated body decoration. (b)
Barton Incised jar. [Courtesy of the
Arkansas Archeological Survey.]

development of the Cairo Lowland phase that was apparently transferred south with population movement. Shell particles average .5–2 mm, in contrast to 3–5 mm in Mississippi Plain (also called Neeley's Ferry Plain). In addition, very fine grog made of crushed potsherds was added to the paste. Since grog was already fired, its presence reduced the thermal shock of a vessel being fired, also resulting in a darker, often black, surface color and a harder paste. Most importantly, however, the clay's working quality was greatly improved. The fine-grained paste allowed the forming of more exotic shapes, the creation of a smooth, high-luster surface finish, and the easier application of pigmented slips and engraved designs. Mostly bowls, bottles, and effigy vessels were involved. Bowls characteristically exhibit a notched horizontal applique strip immediately beneath the lip and are plain. Bottles are often painted and engraved. Effigy vessels, sometimes adapting the basic bottle and bowl form, are plain or painted. Bell-paste vessels tend to be grave furniture.

Rare marker ceramic types include Walls Engraved, Vernon Paul Applique, Rhodes Incised, Ranch Incised, Nodena Red and White, Avenue Polychrome, and Fortune Noded. Fortune Noded and crude versions of Walls Engraved occurred at Banks. An unnamed red-on-white decoration also was present at that site. Painted pottery increases in proportion through time.

Distinctive effigy forms are numerous (Figure 12.6): the "serpent–cat" rim effigy form, the severed human leg effigy, painted human beings, head pots, most complete quadruped effigies, and "tail riders" (effigy on a rim extension or "tail" usually opposite another rim effigy). The "teapot" is a stylized effigy of some sort of quadruped and gourd combination. It is not a copy of an early French teapot. The head pot is almost certainly protohistoric and is the most elaborate of the ceramics known for the Late period Mississippian.

Compound vessels, both horizontal and vertical, are present. Jars are joined by straps, and bottle forms are superimposed on jar forms, or vice versa. These existed as well in earlier periods. Tripod-footed bottles are also known; sometimes the individual broken foot is mistaken for a toy vessel. Occasionally, the feet are human foot effigies. The stirrup-neck bottle is also present but is rare. Tetrapod vessels, mostly effigy bowls, are also characteristic.

POPULATION NUCLEATION

Around A.D. 1350–1400 almost all of the braided stream surfaces and the Cairo Lowland were abandoned as permanent settlements (House 1975; Price *et al.* 1976; Williams 1977). However this area was far from vacant in the sense of a complete lack of occupation. Indeed there is considerable evidence of activity within the abandoned regions.

Abandonment of southeast Missouri, for instance, did not seem to have interrupted the continued exploitation of the Ste. François Mountains for

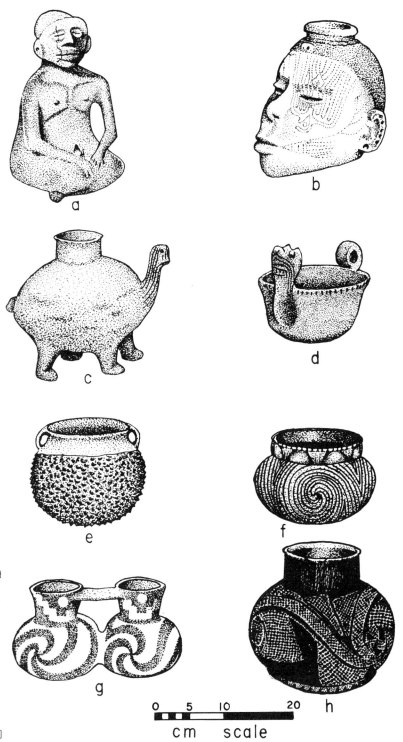

FIGURE 12.6. Some typical Late period Mississippian pottery styles. (a) Human effigy bottle. (b) Head effigy vessel. (c) Turtle effigy tetrapod bottle. (d) Serpent effigy bowl. (e) Fortune Noded jar with strap handles. (f) Rhodes Incised jar with arcaded handles. (g) Nodena Red and White compound bottle. (h) Walls Engraved bottle. [(a), (c)–(h) courtesy of the Arkansas Archeological Survey; (b) courtesy of the Henry Clay Hampson II Memorial Museum of Archeology.]

critical natural resources including salt, basalt for heavy edged tools, copper for ornaments, galena and hematite for paint, and cherts for a variety of edged tools. For example, primary basalt debitage is present at some of the Arkansas Nodena phase sites in substantial quantity, a clear indication of easy access to the outcroppings in the Ste. François Mountains. Goods were passing through this vacant quarter either by direct exploitation or indirectly through the trader system noted by early Spanish explorers (Varner and Varner 1951: 449; Smith 1871:85–86).

In addition, a rare but persistent artifact found in Arkansas sites is the catlinite disk pipe. These pipes are evidence that despite the vacant quarter, communication with the inhabitants of the Upper Mississippi Valley took place. There is evidence of trade between the Central Valley and the Caborn-Welborn phase in southwestern Indiana, dated to A.D. 1400–1700 (Green and Munson 1978).

But perhaps the most persistent evidence of occupation within the vacant quarter is the Nodena point. These diagnostic points are present virtually everywhere within the Braided Stream Surface area, but they are rare. However, two sites have been recorded where they are particularly numerous along with end scrapers. A minor amount of Late period pottery is found at these two sites but for the most part the pottery is datable to the Middle period and particularly to A.D. 1250–1350. Both sites were important civic–ceremonial centers of that time period (Moore 1910: 359–361). Our interpretation of these data is that these are the archaeological residue of hunting activity within this Braided Stream hinterland. The two concentrated sites were probably base settlements for hunters (and possibly their families) and the occasional scattered Nodena points the sole recognizable leavings from temporary hunting camps. This hunting behavior was recorded by the early Spanish explorers who first penetrated this region (Phillips, Ford, and Griffin 1951:358–359).

The persistence of permanent occupation in the Cairo Lowland beyond the A.D. 1400 date line is argued by some investigators (Lewis 1982). However, the artifacts found at some of these sites, radiocarbon dated as late as A.D. 1500 and 1600 (Lewis 1982), indicate a very basic Middle period Mississippian assemblage. The similarity of some of the plate shapes and guilloche design motifs in the Cairo Lowland (Lewis 1982) to those characteristic of the Protohistoric Alabama River phase (Sheldon 1974:207, 209) does indicate some occupation after A.D. 1400. But, based on the evidence presented to date, there was no substantial permanent population in the Cairo Lowland after *about* A.D. 1400.

This population did not simply disappear. It shifted into the meander belt areas of the Mississippi and St. Francis rivers, the Little River–Pemiscot Bayou crevasse channel of the Mississippi, and the alluvial soils of the White River. These particular regions experienced significant increases in population. Trying to determine which particular site population went where specifically is not really possible at this time. The Cairo Lowland population almost certainly went south to Mississippi County, Arkansas, and the immediate environs to help form the Nodena phase. Many of the other Eastern Lowlands populations presumably nucleated together as the Parkin phase. Probably, many of the Western Lowlands populations nucleated to form the Greenbrier phase.

The abandonment of sites presents an interesting problem. At the Snodgrass site, and indeed at all the Powers phase sites, the sites were deliberately fired. The indigenous population seems to have set those villages on fire since few useful and easily portable artifacts were left behind and no accidental human casualties seem to have resulted. The abandonment seems to have been not only quick for the phase as a whole but also well planned. Chapter 11 details the defensive nature of the Powers phase settlements.

Many of the sites in the Nodena phase are single Mississippian component sites, probably an indication of a sudden increase in population. Although many Parkin phase sites involve the resettlement of older civic–ceremonial centers, there appears to be a temporal gap between the two populations. At the Hazel site, there is evidence that earlier features were leveled, although it is not known if the Parkin phase population did the leveling. Important civic–ceremonial centers north of the Hazel site were never resettled except by hunters.

There are possible ecological reasons for the population shift. There are two major regions of contrasting soils with distinct geological origins responsible for their makeup. One is the older Braided Stream Surfaces of most of the Western Lowlands and portions of the Eastern Lowlands. The other is the Meander Stream Surface adjacent to the Mississippi River plus the major alluvial portions of the Little River in the Eastern Lowlands and the White River in the Western Lowlands. Populations shifted away from the Braided Stream Surfaces and nucleated on the Meander Stream Surfaces.

An important distinction between these two major regions is the distribution of silty and sandy loams which constitute the prime agricultural soils in northeast Arkansas (P. Morse 1981:81). Braided Stream silt and sandy loams do not normally occur in large concentrations while Meander Stream silt and sandy loams do occur in quite extensive concentrations. Both distributions can accommodate a dispersed settlement pattern, characteristic of Early and Middle period Mississippian sites. But only the Meander Stream Surface can accommodate the nucleated populations in fortified villages thought to be characteristic of the Late period Mississippian sites. This was clearly demonstrated during the Parkin Project of 1978–1979 (P. Morse 1981). Most, if not all, of the Parkin phase population was concentrated in compact, probably fortified villages located within specific habitats involving substantial hectares of arable land immediately adjacent to the villages.

The Central Valley population was nucleated not only into specific areas but also, for the most part, into fortified villages or towns, representing a complete break with the previous pattern of farmsteads dispersed around a civic–ceremonial center. It seems obvious that the population was nucleated for protection. The Nodena phase seems to have been the main reason for this nucleation, as it apparently was expanding at the expense of other phases.

During this period there was a real florescence. Crafts were superbly produced, especially ceramics. Numerous woodworking tools indicate that wood artifacts were also well crafted, and the few examples of carved bone reinforce this inference. Elaborate ceramics are found interred with the dead. As such pottery was not made quickly, these ritual pots reflect a complex ceremonial life considerably beyond a life-after-death belief. Continuous association within a closed fortified village may have contributed to this ritualistic florescence. Undoubtedly, the control needed for such a population contributed significantly to ritual behavior. The onset of the Protohistoric period, about A.D. 1500–1550, coincided with an increased ritualism more obviously centered upon death. All of the Central Valley except for the Lower Arkansas River was visited by the De Soto expedition in 1541 and the inhabitants were directly impacted by carriers of new diseases. The deaths of half the men, most of the women, and most of the children could have resulted, as occurred after the first French contact with the Quapaw. Drastic population decrease would have constituted a kinship crisis, particularly in high-ranking niches. Individuals not previously expected to occupy high ranks would have become next in line. Head pots may be a reflection of chiefly deaths on a large scale. Ritualism may have peaked in the protohistoric, much as it did in the Northwest Coast in a similar situation.

Continuous indirect (and possibly direct) contact with Europeans may have kept the Central Valley weakened by diseases. The accounts of the Quapaw indicate that immunity was not building up, but it is always possible that different diseases were involved. The Quapaw phase seems to be a final Central Valley expression of the protohistoric. Elements of southwest Arkansas Caddo but primarily northeast Arkansas Mississippian were present. The historically documented Quapaw Indians constituted a very small portion and the latest period of the Quapaw phase. Tremendous population decreases and cultural changes had taken place by then.

THE NODENA PHASE

Moore (1911:367–373) thought much of the pottery from Holmes's "Middle Mississippi Valley region" (1903) was inferior. Yet in the center of this region and particularly from the site of Pecan Point, he collected many pots that he obviously was proud to describe. This collection forms the nucleus of what eventually was to become known as the Nodena phase.

Phillips, Ford, and Griffin (1951:445) called this the Memphis subarea. Griffin (1946:81) first named the complex the Alpika Focus; later (1952:233–238), he named and described the Walls–Pecan Point "Complex," shortened in his description to Walls Focus. Stephen Williams, who had been working with the collection accumulated by James Hampson from Upper Nodena and related sites, proposed that the Walls–Pecan Point "Focus" be split into the Nodena and Walls phases. This idea gradually became accepted, and the Nodena phase was described by Phillips (1970:933–936), including a ceramic quantification with cumulative curves. Stephen Williams (1980) has also proposed the Armorel phase to include what other investigators call "late Walls" and "late Nodena."

Dan Morse (1973) edited a volume describing the Upper Nodena site and the Nodena phase. It was an attempt to bring together the available data pertaining to the phase before initiating fieldwork. Subsequently, Morse directed field schools in archaeology at two Nodena phase sites, Upper Nodena and Armorel. During one field school, Tim Klinger (1974) tested the Knappenberger site. An attempt in 1980 to perform an investigation similar to that of the Parkin phase was short-lived because of lack of funds.

The advantage of using the term *Nodena* to describe this phase is that the Upper Nodena site still exists and three museum collections are available for study. Evidence indicates that Pecan Point was the major site and possibly the capital; however, this site was completely washed away by a flood. Nodena phase sites are distributed along the meanders of the Mississippi River from north of Memphis into Missouri and inland along Left Hand Chute of Little River and Pemiscot Bayou.

The main distinction of the Nodena phase ceramics is a high frequency of Bell Plain, although it is not as high as in the Walls phase. The frequency ranges around 25–35% of the total decorated and rim sherds. Mississippi Plain ranges around 45%. Painted ceramics are relatively rare except for Old Town Red. Barton Incised and Parkin Punctated are fairly common at some sites and rare on others. Fortune Noded, Walls Engraved, and other decorations are fairly uncommon.

Nodena phase sites occur in three geographical clusters. Six sites are recorded in the immediate vicinity of Wapanocca Lake, in Crittenden County north of Memphis. The most spectacular one was the Bradley site. When C. B. Moore visited the site in 1911, one of the four mounds, up to 6 m (20 ft.) high, had already been incorporated into a levee. Some of the pottery recovered during construction of this levee had been donated to the Cossitt Library in Memphis and was later transferred to the Memphis Pink Palace Museum. Moore described a large areal concentration of debris associated with the mounds. He also describes remains as being almost continuous along Wapanocca Bayou for a considerable distance, about 8 km (5 miles). Bradley Ridge is a prominent relict natural levee of the Mississippi River, and Wapanocca Bayou, which occupies the abandoned channel, drains Wapanocca Lake. It is an ideal setting for Mississippian occupation, and the recovered data reflect a long period of Mississippian development and habitation.

The Bradley site appears to have been a classic late Nodena phase village or town. Actually three sites (3CT7, 9, and 43) exist almost continuously over a 2-km stretch. One burial found by Moore at 3CT7, a young child, had an unusual necklace of 36 shell beads, a conch-shell columella pendant, two tubular beads of copper or brass, two copper "bracelets," and two "glass beads" (Moore 1911:431). Moore made the following statement without further discussion: "At the Bradley place was abundant evidence of aboriginal intercourse with the whites [p. 435]."

Although the remains on Bradley Ridge date to much of the Mississippian period, most seem to cluster within the latest division. The Banks site seems to be the earliest Nodena-phase site known. It is located at the opposite end of Bradley Ridge from the Bradley site and was reported by Perino (1966) to be almost 4 ha (10 acres) in extent. A plaza about 52 m² was recorded, but no mounds are known to have been present. It is not known if the site was palisaded. Houses were square in shape with upright post studs in individual holes or in wall trenches. Split cane and cane or small-tree-limb lathing (wattle) provided a strong woven wall, which was then plastered with mud (daub) 5 or more cm thick. The roof was then shingled with thatch. Houses ranged in size from 12 to 41 m². Each house had a central hearth and two or three "ash pits." Some houses had interior sleeping benches. In one case five houses had been constructed on one construction site, an event that could indicate up to 100 years of occupation. This length of occupation is also indicated by the 60 cm of midden buildup. No storage pits were found, and it is evident that by A.D. 1400 grain was stored above ground in specially built granaries.

Perino (1966:151–159) spent considerable time following leads for isolated house sites or hamlets. Finally, 1.2 km from the Banks site he discovered a cluster of house patterns and graves. Within an area smaller than the Banks site were at least 10–15 houses and associated graves. Dwellings were widely separated from one another, 60 m apart in one instance. The presence of end scrapers might indicate that the hamlet was roughly contemporaneous with the Bradley site. It was certainly later than Banks, since no Matthews Incised or Manly Punctated pottery was found.

A Nodena phase village, 3CT139, perhaps measuring between .8 and 1.6 ha (2 and 4 acres), exists on the opposite side of Wapanocca Lake. Ceramics indicate a relatively early dating, and it appears to overlap in time with the Banks site. No other Nodena phase sites have been recorded to the north for several kilometers, but this area has not been investigated intensively.

In southeastern Mississippi County, Arkansas, is a cluster of at least 21 Nodena phase sites. The largest and most spectacular was Pecan Point. There is little doubt that Pecan Point was a prominent late Nodena phase site. In 1911 nine head pots were known to be from this site. Collections exist at the Smithsonian Institution, Putnam Museum in Davenport, Iowa, and the Museum of the American Indian, Heye Foundation.

The site was described as large but was never completely measured. Nearby, a 4.5-m-high mound, 45 × 24 m in extent, was a prominent feature. The site portion investigated by Moore (1911:447–475) was approximately 1.2 ha

(3 acres) in size; the remainder had already been incorporated into levees. The depth of midden was usually at least 1 m and in places extended to beyond 1.5 m. Moore found 349 graves, despite the earlier heavily concentrated pot hunting and excavations. The earlier Smithsonian investigation in 1883 also involved a small area (about 1.5 ha or 4 acres?), which Thomas (1894:220) described as a large cemetery. He felt that this was "evidence that there was formerly an extensive village here [which] may have been swept away by the Mississippi." Pecan Point possibly was the Pacaha described by the De Soto expedition in 1541 (see Chapter 13).

Upper Nodena provides some insight into the makeup of a Nodena phase village (Figure 12.7b). This 6.2-ha (15.5-acre) site was palisaded and includes a plaza with associated domiciliary or temple mounds and a second plaza or square (Morse 1973). Numerous houses effectively fill the remainder of the rectangular midden. Burials tend to be clustered, as if in family plots near the houses. Possible small hamlets exist just outside the palisade walls; these represent either the beginnings of sister villages or earlier hamlet occupations before the village was established. Test excavations were accomplished along the eastern edge in 1973. Midden was no deeper than .4 m. At least two house construction episodes in one site were demonstrated. All in all, the eastern portion of the site seemed to have experienced a relatively brief period of occupation, perhaps only a half century. The more central portion of the site, where previous investigation was concentrated, probably was occupied for no more than a century.

Before the village was constructed, considerable farming took place. This farming practice caused the annual erosion of a higher area on the north, with subsequent deposition of charcoal-mottled lenses nearby. The charcoal presumably resulted from the burning of fields prior to spring planting.

The Upper Nodena site probably was occupied around A.D. 1500–1550, although the radiocarbon date is somewhat earlier (1300 ± 135; M-385). End scrapers are absent. The ceramic assemblage, however, is primarily late Nodena phase in makeup. Head pots are missing. One complete and one broken catlinite disk pipe are present. Two possible early historic items, a pipe stem and a Rhenish stoneware sherd, have been found on the surface. An urn burial of an infant found at Upper Nodena is unique west of the Mississippi; it is a very late trait even east of the river.

In Mound 5 at Upper Nodena were found 314 male and 2 female skeletons and few associated artifacts. This discovery is extraordinary, if the sex determinations are valid. Males are generally the least likely of the population to be affected by an epidemic, so this situation remains a mystery.

The Upper Nodena site, nevertheless, may be an example of a site abandoned soon after the beginning of the protohistoric. The abandonment of sites should have intensified during that latest period of the Nodena phase. It is possible that several sites in this cluster terminated about the same time or shortly afterward. Descriptions of the Quapaw describe the combining of two

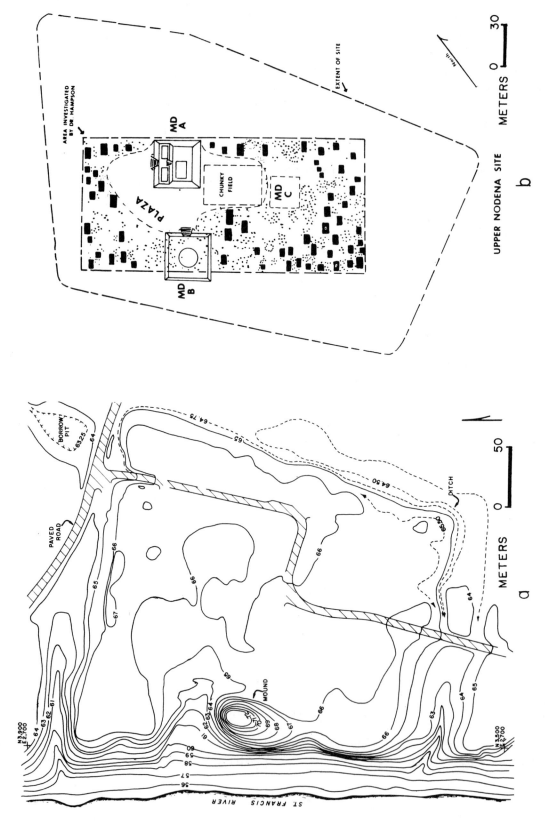

FIGURE 12.7. Late period Mississippian sites. (a) The Parkin site. (b) The Upper Nodena site. [Courtesy of the Arkansas Archeological Survey.]

former villages into a single village because of smallpox deaths (see Chapter 13).

Other sites in the southeastern Mississippi County, Arkansas, cluster are similar to Upper Nodena. Shawnee Village is a good example and the closest in size to Upper Nodena. Other sites tend to cluster around approximately 2.8–4 ha (7–10 acres) (seven sites) and about .8–1.6 ha (2–4 acres) (nine sites). The lack of an associated mound with any site may not be significant because mounds tended to disappear quickly in the Central Valley lowlands for levee, railroad, and highway construction. Two apparent hamlets or small villages are about .1 ha (.25 acre) in extent. No isolated household sites have been recorded.

Cultigens were recovered from the Upper Nodena site and examined by Leonard Blake and Hugh Cutler (1979). Corn, of course, was prevalent. Interestingly, corn recovered from the general village midden was relatively small compared with that recovered from a burned-crib assemblage. The latter was larger. Cupule width, for instance, was significantly larger, and the proportion of 12-rowed cobs, greater. Apparently, smaller ears were used first, and larger ones were put in storage for later consumption or for seed. The corn remnants from sites in the Central Valley tend not to be the more stress-resistant eastern 8-row, and these Upper Nodena data emphasize the ideal conditions that must have been present for corn cultivation.

Another cultigen recovered was the bean, found at nine different locations in the site. Beans are present fairly late in the eastern United States. Wild plant food at Upper Nodena included hickory nut, persimmon, black walnut, pecan, wild cherry, hazelnut, and pawpaw.

A total of at least 34 sites cluster together in Arkansas and Missouri, primarily along Pemiscot Bayou–Little River. A major site is at Blytheville and is associated with a prominent mound. Mounds tend to be absent at most sites. A mound at the Campbell site was alleged to have covered a 5-m-deep (16 ft.) shaft grave with considerable artifact content, including a large catlinite disk pipe, a glass bead (Nueva Cadiz), several brass hawk bells, and such other items as fabrics and a wood effigy. Whether this intelligence is valid, there is no doubt that a considerable number of European artifacts existed at the site. Blue glass beads, iron tubular beads, and other fragments of iron had been discovered associated with graves at the site by Leo Anderson (Chapman and Anderson 1955). Both at Campbell and at Blytheville end scrapers are of common occurrence.

Site size of 19 Arkansas locations is not well known. At least 3 sites range around 4.4–5.6 ha (11–14 acres). Two larger sites have more restricted Nodena phase occupations of unknown extent. There are 4 sites around 2.8–3.6 ha (7–9 acres), and 9 sites, about .4–1.6 ha (1–4 acres) in extent. One site may be a hamlet, but the situation is confused by a large scatter of multiple-component debris. In addition to these, a possible single isolated household site has been recorded. There are an additional 14 major sites in Missouri, none of which have been accurately measured. There has been considerable commercial digging within this cluster of sites. A tremendous number of commercially valuable ceramics have been removed. It is evident that a viable population existed here to a very late date.

Both Parkin phase and Nodena phase sites exist along Little River between Marked Tree and Blytheville. A gap in Late Mississippian sites exists within the area between the towns of Lepanto and Etowah. Another gap exists within much of the area between Lepanto and Marked Tree. The number of Bell Plain ceramics decreases sharply upriver from Etowah, and it is possible that the three sites near Etowah and the three near Lepanto are Parkin phase sites. For the present, however, the Etowah area sites are classified as Nodena phase, and the Lepanto area sites are classified as Parkin phase. A brass pendant made from a scabbard part was found at the Wildy site near Etowah (Morse 1971). With these sites, there are a total of 60 major Nodena phase sites known in Arkansas and Missouri.

Across the Mississippi River in Tennessee are four sites included by other investigators in the Nodena phase. These are Richardson's Landing, Bishop, Johnson's Place, and Hales Point. They are all linked by an unusual mode of interment: the urn burial. One from Hales point actually looks very much like a casket. Furthermore, a "teapot"-style vessel has been reported from Richardson's Landing. These traits indicate that there is a very late unnamed phase here that shares some characteristics with groups to the south and southeast into Mississippi and Alabama (Sheldon 1974).

THE PARKIN PHASE

The Parkin phase is composed of sites located near the St. Francis and Tyronza rivers. The existence of a distinctive regional expression of Mississippian has been recognized throughout much of the present century. In 1910 C. B. Moore described the St. Francis pottery using terms such as "great monotony," "general inferiority," "commonplace form," and "trivial decoration [pp. 260–261]." After this daunting introduction to the region, Moore described visits to 21 sites, from which he collected 1415 pots.

Phillips, Ford, and Griffin (1951) defined a "St. Francis-type" site as a rectangular planned village with a plaza, surrounding mounds, and evidence of a large population. They commented on the characteristic deep refuse, as much as 4.5 m, which elevated these sites above the surrounding areas. Later, Griffin called this complex of sites the St. Francis focus (1946: Fig. 12.7a) and subsequently changed this name to the Parkin focus in a detailed description (1952:231–233). Stephen Williams in 1954 was the first to reference the culture as the Parkin phase. Phillips (1970:930–933) described the phase and furthermore quantified the distinctiveness of the Parkin phase with a cumulative curve.

Phillips's (1970) cumulative frequency graph plus an assemblage of almost 16,000 sherds tabulated at the University of Arkansas from the Parkin site constitute the basis of a ceramic characterization of the Parkin phase (P. Morse 1981: Fig. 7). Sites in the Parkin phase do contain pottery types similar to those in other contemporary phases, but the frequency of these types differs. Mississippi Plain predominates, whereas Bell Plain is rare. Parkin Punctated is the most common decorated type, being four to five times as prevalent as the second most common decoration, Barton Incised. This predominance of Parkin punctated occurs partly because Barton Incised and Parkin Punctated often occur together on the same pot, with the punctated body involving significantly more area than the incised rim. Fortune Noded, Ranch Incised, and Old Town Red are minority decorated styles, and other late decorations are very rare.

Most of the whole vessels found with burials in the Parkin phase appear to be utilitarian food bowls and water bottles rather than special vessels made just for ceremonies. Some more-elaborate forms do occur, with at least three head pots and one engraved vessel traced to the Parkin site. Nodena points, pottery disks, stone hoes, small end scrapers and marine shell beads are other typical Parkin phase artifacts.

There are at least 21 sites known to have Parkin phase components (P. Morse 1981:46). Three sites on the Little River and a number of sites on the lower St. Francis were not included in the Morse study because either they could not be personally examined or there was some question of whether they were actually Parkin phase. Four categories of sites have been defined, with site size as the major criterion.

The Parkin site was by far the largest site, measuring almost 7 ha. It is strategically located immediately below the junction of the St. Francis and Tyronza rivers. Parkin is defined as the major ceremonial center of the Parkin phase. The Parkin site is enclosed by a wide ditch on the northern, eastern, and southern perimeters. The western border is the St. Francis River. Major features of the site include the ditch, a 6.5-m-high temple mound with an apron or extension on the southern end, the enclosed village area, which rises as much as 3 m above the surrounding plain, and a borrow pit on the northern edge outside the ditch (Figure 12.7a). The temple mound is in the center of the western edge of the site, on the left bank of the St. Francis River. This typical flat-topped pyramidal mound probably functioned as the foundation for either a temple or a chiefly residence. The 1.5-m-high apron or extension on the southern end of the temple mound supported one or more houses, as shown by a row of postholes found during test excavations (Klinger 1977).

The ditch surrounding the site is extremely well preserved, being 1 m or more deep in many places. It probably functioned as part of a protective system, with a corresponding palisade between the ditch and the village area. An entryway to the village may have been present in the northeast corner. Soil from the ditch was used by the site inhabitants to build the temple mound and help raise the habitation level of the site. A large artificial pond area opposite the northeast corner of the site is a borrow pit, which also furnished soil for construction purposes. Parkin phase sites were built up quickly. Houses seem to have been leveled by burning, with the house debris buried beneath soil brought to the site from outside before a new house was constructed. The longevity of a house is estimated at around 20–30 years. A century of rebuilding could build up a significant midden. Upward of 400 houses could have existed at one time at the Parkin site.

Six smaller mounds, measuring from .6–1.2 m (2–4 ft.) in height, were mapped at the Parkin site in 1940 (Phillips, Ford, and Griffin 1951:331). These may have been major house mounds, supporting the residences of important persons. Five of the small mounds were located near the large temple mound on the edge of the plaza.

Other recorded village sites are smaller than the Parkin site. Sites in the Parkin phase are patterned relative to one another, in terms of distance from one another. They also are patterned in relationship to two rivers, the St. Francis and Tyronza. Sites are literally strung like beads, with the two rivers representing the connecting cord. Four sites are spaced about 8 km away from the Parkin site and from one another, and each measures about 3 ha in size. These include Neeley's Ferry, Barton Ranch, and Rose Mound. In between these, about every 4 km, are eight villages about 2 ha in size, such as Hazel, Miller, Taylor's Shanty, Big Eddy, and Cummings. Small villages under .8 ha, such as Fortune and Togo, exist between these sites. All but one site appeared to have been palisaded.

Another site category, the dispersed isolated farmstead or homestead, was expected in the Parkin-phase settlement pattern. An intensive survey within 1 km of the Parkin site recorded 128 separate artifact loci or sites, with 133 components (see Chapter 9). Only one, an isolated find of an end scraper, could be attributed to the Parkin phase. Both Baytown and Middle period Mississippian farmsteads were found, but no sites with typical Late period Mississippian artifacts, such as Nodena points and Parkin Punctated pottery, were located. The closest known Parkin phase village is 4 km from Parkin. To date, there is not one Parkin phase isolated household site recorded as such in the site files of the Arkansas Archeological Survey.

It was concluded from those data that it was necessary for Parkin phase folk to live within fortified villages, safe from attack behind palisades. More people were concentrated in less space for protection. This pattern is significantly different from previously known Mississippian settlement patterns.

According to the De Soto expedition accounts (Varner and Varner 1951:430–431) the villages in the province of Casqui were relatively small (15–40 homes) and large (up to 400 houses). No household or hamlet sites were described.

The Parkin phase location is possibly the province of Casqui; if so, the Parkin site is probably Casqui itself (see Chapter 13). The description of Casqui is similar to what Parkin seems to have been like, even to the large mound, upon which the Spanish erected a large wooden cross. The University of Arkansas excavated a large charred post on the summit of the mound in 1966, and two sixteenth-century Spanish artifacts have been recovered at this site.

The Spanish related how the province of Casqui had been at war with Pacaha for "many centuries," with the Casqui being in general "pushed . . . into a corner [Varner and Varner 1951: 434–435]." The paramount chief of Pacaha warned the paramount chief of Casqui that the Spanish would not be there to help him the next time there was a conflict (p. 445). The future of Casqui as a power did not seem bright. It is not surprising that the population was concentrated into fortified villages and towns.

A basic problem for such a tightly nucleated settlement pattern must have been food. Various ecological zones with differing biotic communities were present in the Parkin phase area. Most obvious is the fine agricultural soil. The topography in the Parkin phase area is dominated by changes in the course of the Mississippi River. Parkin is located on a clay plug, a filled-in oxbow lake associated with the Meander Belts 3 and 4 of the Mississippi. The river left the area about 2500 years ago, and the St. Francis runs in an old Mississippi River channel. Linear bands of high, well-drained, silty and sandy loams deposited by the river constituted prime crop soils. Other linear bands of less productive silty clay and backswamps provided variety for wild plants and animals. There were also numerous lakes containing many species of fish and attracting ducks and geese.

People in low-energy societies establish their residences in accordance with primary economic resources. The closer a given resource is to a village, probably the more important that resource is to the village for its existence. The natural resource most important to Parkin phase people seems to have been arable land suitable for hoe agriculture. Corn, beans, squash, and other cultigens, such as sunflowers, were probably grown and stored in large quantities. De Soto found sufficient stored food throughout the Central Valley to feed his army even though their journey took place during the growing season and before the period of major harvest (Varner and Varner 1951:430,450; Bourne 1904:123).

Phyllis Morse (1981) used the technique of site catchment analysis (Roper 1979) to analyze the soil types around each Parkin phase site within a 1-km radius. It was assumed that this 1-km area immediate to a site would be used most intensively. By using recent Soil Conservation Service maps three classes of soil productivity, measured in metric tons of corn per hectare, were defined. The resulting productivity figures were used to compare all the Parkin phase sites with Parkin and with one another (P. Morse 1981:87). This is not a complete site catchment analysis, since resources other than agricultural soils were not examined in detail.

The Parkin site is the only Parkin-phase site that theoretically was unable to provide sufficient corn to feed its inhabitants by planting within its 1-km catchment. Enlarging the catchment, decreasing the household need of 1 metric ton per year, and other manipulations could change this situation, but the fact remains that given certain assumptions, all sites except Parkin could provide their own food. Thirteen sites could theoretically provide sufficient corn for their own needs by using only one-half or a little over one-half of the arable land within 1 km of each site. Parkin is the only site without a positive correlation between site size and soil productivity. The estimated 400 households residing within the site had to get half of the estimated needed 400 metric tons of corn that were necessary per year outside of their basic catchment. The strategic location of Parkin, in effect controlling two rivers, might have been more important than mere productivity in its selection as the major ceremonial center of the phase. Other sites could have produced a surplus and contributed tribute to the major center in the form of food and labor. This situation is not unusual with known advanced chiefdoms, but it is difficult to demonstrate archaeologically.

The development of the Parkin phase is an unsolved problem mainly because only very typical components have been investigated. Certainly, the demographic shift around A.D. 1350–1400 complicates this kind of inquiry. Fortunately, the sites are deep, and important Middle period and early Late period Mississippian components are still preserved for future investigation.

The University of Arkansas Museum excavated at the Hazel, Neeley's Ferry, and Barton Ranch sites (Dellinger and Dickinson 1940). At the Parkin site, the University of Arkansas Museum and Arkansas Archeological Society conducted a 9-day test excavation in 1965 (Davis 1966). A University of Arkansas archaeological field school was held at the site in 1966 (Klinger 1977). Phillips, Ford, and Griffin excavated a test pit at Rose Mound (Phillips, Ford, and Griffin 1951). At the Hazel site, a University of Arkansas field school was held in 1964 and 1969, and highway salvage was accomplished in 1969 (Morse and Smith 1973). Excavations at Neeley's Ferry, Barton Ranch, and Miller have not been analyzed or reported upon, as is also the case with some of the work accomplished at Hazel.

Parkin phase sites tend to be located upon earlier Mississippian sites. At Rose Mound, a 2-m test demonstrated a sequence of three occupations: Baytown, Middle period Mississippian, and Parkin phase. The Parkin phase made up 1.2–1.4 m of the 2.5 m of midden, and the middle component occupied approximately .6–.8 m or slightly more of the deposit. Adjacent to and upon the Parkin site are Middle period Mississippian artifacts, yet stratigraphic tests that have revealed at least 1 m of Parkin phase midden have not yet uncovered an earlier Mississippian deposit. At the Neeley's Ferry site, the Parkin phase component is superimposed upon a prominent Middle period Mississippian component. At Miller, the approximately 1-m basal portion of the midden is earlier Mississippian, with some 2 m of Parkin phase superimposed midden (Figure 12.8). The Hazel site contains a very prominent Middle period Mississippian deposit upon which the Parkin phase component is superimposed.

FIGURE 12.8. Excavation test at the Miller site showing depth and nature of Parkin phase midden. [Courtesy of the Arkansas Archeological Survey.]

The total eroded deposit is 1.7 m deep, at least 1 m of which contains numerous pre-Parkin phase architectural remains.

Abandoned Middle period Mississippian sites may have been prime locations to choose for villages, especially if they had been civic–ceremonial centers. These locations would have been among the best available along established trails. Some may actually represent the sites of Parkin phase development, but to date test excavations at sites such as Hazel have indicated that a disconformity exists between the two time periods.

Several radiocarbon dates were obtained from samples collected by the University of Arkansas in 1933 from the Hazel site. The results of those that probably pertain to the Parkin phase occupation were A.D. 1330 ± 102, 1421 ± 94, and 1540 ± 191 (TX–848, 877, 847, 846). These indicate a basic fifteenth-century date, although occupation could be interpreted as having extended from near A.D. 1350 to almost A.D. 1550. Exotic ceramics found at other Parkin phase sites are noticeably absent at the Hazel site. This absence argues for termination of occupation at Hazel by around the early part of the protohistoric, certainly within the early sixteenth century, if not earlier.

THE WALLS PHASE

Brown (1926:288–319) described the ceramics from the vicinity of Walls, Mississippi, located just south of Memphis. His description forms the basis of what is known today as the Walls phase. Stephen Williams suggested in 1954 that the Walls phase be separated out of the Pecan Point–Walls complex of Griffin's classification, but this proposal was only gradually accepted (Perino 1966; Rands 1956). The most complete published description of the Walls phase is by Phillips (1970:936–938), complete with cumulative curves quantifying the ceramics.

Walls phase sites are plotted on both sides of the Mississippi River by Phillips (1970:Fig. 447). However, since the Mississippi River is a prominent geographical barrier, we expect it to be a cultural barrier as well. In addition, the De Soto accounts describe the two provinces at Quizquiz and Aquixo on opposite sides of the Mississippi River at or near this location (Bourne 1904:111, 116). Quizquiz was vassal to the province of Pacaha (Bourne 1904:25). The similarity of the grave ceramics in the Walls phase sites to each other and to the Nodena phase sites makes sense in light of the De Soto descriptions. Our interpretations are that the Nodena phase was a mega-chiefdom, expanding at the expense of downstream independent chiefdoms, which is precisely what the De Soto expedition seems to have described.

The Walls phase is plotted mainly east of the Mississippi River by Phillips (1970). The Walls phase sites west of the Mississippi River, probably can be classified with several of the nearby sites classified by Phillips as Kent phase, especially since these sites were formerly classified as Walls–Pecan Point (Phillips 1970:936). The Phillips (1970) classification was deliberate in order "to preserve the purity of the Walls formulation [p. 936]." Kent phase sites cluster within the drainage of the lower St. Francis, except for these, which are located closer to the Mississippi River.

In Mississippi and Tennessee 8 sites and in Arkansas about 12 sites are recorded as Walls phase. They include small (.4 ha, or an acre or so) and large (up to 4–8 ha or "10–20 acres") sites with mounds that appear to have been palisaded. A complex network of sites exists between the Mississippi River and the St. Francis River within a classic wetland environment. The Belle Meade and Beck sites could have been about the first encountered by the De Soto expedition after it crossed the river (see Chapter 13).

The site of Chucalissa, 14.5 km from downtown Memphis, is included in the Walls phase. The site is located on a ridge top at the edge of a steep bluff, by Nonconnah Creek. A central plaza 52 m² has a higher residential ridge area 15–30 m wide on the west, south, and east, a 4.5-m-high pyramidal mound on the north, and a smaller pyramidal mound on the western edge of the plaza (Nash 1972). Four radiocarbon dates of A.D. 1410 (2 dates), 1550, and 1560 (M–584, 787, 788, 789) date the Walls phase component. A number of excavations have taken place at Chucalissa over the last 40 years, and various features have been left exposed *in situ* for educational purposes. A cemetery area with skeletons and grave goods is a prime attraction. Excavations in the large temple mound have found at least four building stages, with accompanying structures. Chucalissa is located high above the floodplain, and Bruce Smith (1975:155) found less use of such species as fish, migratory waterfowl, and swamp rabbit at Chucalissa in comparison with Mississippian sites located by oxbow lakes.

Bell Plain ceramics predominate on Walls phase sites. This variety comprises about 20–25% of the total rim and decorated sherds in excavated samples from several sites. The discrepancy between excavated and surface samples probably results from treasure seekers tossing broken plain pots found in graves out onto the ground surface. The ratio of Bell to Mississippi Plain is about 2 to 1, even higher than in the Nodena phase. In a stratigraphic test at the Walls site, Bell Plain increased slightly over Mississippi Plain through time. Bell Plain is a prevalent type only in the Nodena, Walls and Kent phases.

The most common decorated types are Parkin Punctated and Barton Incised, and Old Town Red is fairly common. Rare types include Kent, Ranch, and Rhodes Incised, Walls Engraved, Nodena Red and White, Avenue Polychrome, and Fortune Noded. Variations between sites indicate that chronological control based on ceramic style change through time is very possible with this phase. The lithic assemblage of the Walls phase includes Nodena and Madison points. Moore (1911:415) found "one tubular bead of blue glass" at the Rhodes site in Arkansas.

Robert Rands (1956) looked at over 1100 vessels from Walls–Pecan Point phase sites, mainly those from Mississippi. He was looking for evidence of Southern Cult motifs as decorations on this pottery. He found a considerable divergence from the classic cult motifs described by Waring and Holder (1945). Motifs used on pottery were an occasional cross, usually enclosed in a circle; the forked eye; the ogee symbol on bottles around the neck; and a death motif of skull and bones. A version of the horned rattlesnake was also present. Symbols lacking were the bilobed arrow, sun circle, hand and eye, and barred oval. It is not surprising that these motifs do not correspond exactly to classic Southern Cult symbols, as they may be 200 or 300 years later in time. The horned serpent might have been a mythological creature retained in Central Valley folklore through time.

THE KENT AND OLD TOWN PHASES

These phases were named and described by Phillips (1970:938–989), who places the Kent phase on both sides of the Mississippi River and along the lower reaches of the St. Francis River and the Old Town phase south of Crowley's Ridge and west of the Mississippi River. Probably three or four phases are actually represented. The De Soto accounts described a series of independent chiefdoms downstream: "To the south, or down the river, there were large towns, and the Caciques governed wide territories, with numerous people [Bourne 1904:132]." There is very little known scientifically about these sites, despite that many of them are still being actively dug for their treasures. We restrict the Kent phase to the approximately 21 sites situated near the lower St. Francis River and the Old Town phase (as Phillips does) to 4 sites located further downriver, including Baytown. This entire cluster of sites may be within the province of Quigate, described by the De Soto expedition, with a capital said to be the largest town seen in Florida.

The Kent place was 8 km (5 miles) from the Mississippi, on an old river channel. A mound 5.4 m high and 54 × 36 m at the base was observed by Moore, (1911:406–410) with two broad ridges that were probably residential areas nearby. A burial in the top of the mound had a "rude" sheet copper ornament with three suspension holes and both shell and glass beads at the neck. One small area of the site produced all of the artifacts of interest. Four teapot-shape vessels were found at Kent. One bottle had wide horizontal stripes of red and white; other bottles were decorated with red and white oval painted sections and one had red and white crosses painted on its body.

Many sites in the Kent and Old Town phase area measure 1 ha (2.5 acres) or slightly larger in size. They were palisaded and contained deep midden deposits, and several have temple mound and plaza components. Burials were numerous and included a high percentage of "bundle" or secondary interments. Red-filmed vessels and exotic shapes, such as stirrup and "teapot" shapes, have been recovered. Bell Plain ceramics are characteristic of Kent but not of Old Town. European artifacts have been found at two sites (Kent and Clay Hill) and included glass beads (Moore 1911:409) and a Clarksdale bell. The latter was found in a grave with a nonrepoussé copper "eagle" similar to those from two Parkin and Nodena phase sites. Nodena points and "thumbnail" end scrapers are also characteristic.

THE GREENBRIER PHASE

This phase, centered within the White River basin near Batesville, Arkansas, is located at and just beyond the Ozark Escarpment. Little is known about this phase, which has never been formally described; only occasional references to a Magness or Greenbrier phase are in the archaeological literature (Morse 1982). The phase is now named after the Greenbrier site, since this was the first site recorded in Independence County, Arkansas.

When at Pacaha, the De Soto expedition sent a reconnaissance party to the northwest, where "large settlements" were reported. The trip through swamps and canebrakes took 8 days. Rather than large villages, the party found the province of Caluç or Caluça:

> collections of huts, covered with rush sewed together. When the owner of one moves away, he will roll up the entire covering, and carry it, the wife taking the frame of poles over which it is stretched; these they take down and put up so

readily, that though they should move anew every hour, they conveniently enough carry their house on their backs. We learned from this people that there were some hamlets of the sort about the country, the inhabitants of which employed themselves in finding places for their dwellings wherever many deer were accustomed to range [Bourne 1904:29–30].

Several apparent contradictions are evident in this account. The existence of a nomadic group of hunters some 4 (or 8) days travel from a powerful chiefdom is unexpected. In addition, the expedition was following a lead to large settlements but found the hamlets of hunters. These apparent contradictions can be resolved with archaeological data and interpretations and give valuable insight into Mississippian behavior.

Northwest of Pecan Point at a distance of about 120 km (75 miles) is the Gibson site, which is adjacent to the Black River. This very large multiple-mound site, first reported by C. B. Moore (1910:359–360), was apparently the capital of the Gibson phase, which is similar in settlement pattern and artifact content to the more northern Powers phase. By the time of the De Soto expedition the site had been abandoned by its original inhabitants. However, Nodena points and end scrapers are prominent at the site, whereas late ceramics are very rare. This evidence suggests that the Gibson site was being used by Mississippian hunting parties after about A.D. 1400, which may be essentially what the De Soto expedition described. The town sites of the Greenbrier phase are actually located 48–64 km (30–40 miles) to the southwest. The Gibson site is not a unique example of reuse by later hunters. North of the Parkin phase is a similar situation at the Old Town Ridge site. The Hickman site in the Cairo Lowlands also may follow this pattern (personal communication, Barry Lewis, University of Illinois).

We do not know, of course, if the Gibson site is Caluça but circumstantial evidence is impressive. In between the Pecan Point and Gibson sites are numerous prairies and swamps, which were uninhabited after 1400. Also, Caluça is similar to the Muskogean word *Okalusa*, which means "black water" (Phillips, Ford, and Griffin 1951:380), and the Gibson site is located next to the Black River. At the least, this account together with archaeological observation gives us insight into hunting behavior and sites.

Greenbrier phase village sites range up to 2 ha (5 acres) or more in size. No mounds have been recorded for the late sites, and it is not known if the sites were palisaded, although they tend to be distinct and essentially rectangular. Most ceramics are plain; Bell Plain is not characteristic. Barton Incised and Parkin Punctated are the major decorated categories. Old Town Red is frequent, and most of the ceramics characteristic of the Parkin phase are present. Nodena points predominate; Madison points are relatively infrequent. End scrapers and chert chisels are common artifact finds. A copper tubular bead and a stylized human effigy made on sheet copper have been reported. Human effigy pottery is characteristic but rare. One such vessel possibly exhibits a pair of glasses resting on its forehead. Similar glasses were being worn in Europe before the De Soto expedition. Weeping-eye "face mask" shell gorgets are also characteristic.

THE QUAPAW PHASE

C. B. Moore (1908:481–482) recognized that the sites near the mouth of the Arkansas (and White) River existed during the historic period and referenced Marquette's description of the aborigines found there. This discovery was better treated in a brief paper by S. C. Dellinger and S. D. Dickinson in 1940 and expanded admirably by Phillips, Ford, and Griffin (1951:392–421). The most important paper probably is Ford's Menard site report (1961). The "Menard" or "Wallace" complex was finally named the Quapaw phase by Phillips (1970:943–944). Despite a considerable amount of discussion in the scholarly literature, there is a surprising lack of information available for the Central Valley's only ethnographically known indigenous seventeenth- and eighteenth-century culture, the Quapaw. The pre-seventeenth-century Mississippian sequence has not been developed to date in the lower Arkansas River valley area. Most probably, the "Quapaw phase" covers a longer time period than the historically described "Quapaw tribe." Although only a few Quapaw villages were described by the French in a very limited area of the lower Arkansas River, over a dozen major Quapaw phase archaeological sites have been recorded along the Arkansas River to above Little Rock. Even Quapaw phase hunting sites have been tentatively identified in south-central Arkansas. The Quapaw phase is a significant archaeological manifestation that begins within the protohistoric and extends into the seventeenth and eighteenth centuries as the historic Quapaw tribe.

Quapaw phase sites are varied in size and nature. Major villages with or without plazas, temple mounds, and house mounds are present. Smaller sites made up of a cluster of house mounds have also been recorded. Apparent hunting stations have been identified on the basis of the presence of Nodena points, end scrapers, and a very few shell-tempered sherds. Shell-tempered pottery is predominant, and stone discoidals are characteristic. Shell-tempered pottery is normally plain. Wallace Incised is the major marker style. Painted pottery is frequent. Most of the styles known in the Parkin and Nodena phases are also present. The Quapaw phase is as Mississippian as the Parkin and Nodena phases.

Caddoan-like traits occur more often as one goes upstream (Hoffman 1977). Keno Trailed is a shell-tempered Caddoan-related type that is prominent near Little Rock, for instance. Along the Little Red River, a main tributary of the White River out of the Ozarks, are sites closely related to the Quapaw phase. Keno Trailed and Natchitoches Engraved together with red-filmed and plain ceramics and Nodena points are present. Yet this cluster of sites is located on the other side of the Grand Prairie from the Arkansas River upstream grouping. The Oliver phase east of the Mississippi River is closely related to the Quapaw phase of the late seventeenth and early eighteenth centuries. John Belmont's work with this material indicates that chronological control of these data is possible (Phillips 1970:941–942).

When the De Soto expedition left Quigate (Kent phase), it headed northwest toward the mountains and the province of Coligua. Bison were hunted nearby, and salt was available but apparently was not mined here. The De Soto description might apply to the Greenbrier phase except for the statement that the Coligua differed considerably from those provinces seen up until then. This description also indicates that the Little Red River complex was Coligua. At any rate, De Soto skirted most of the Quapaw phase; ironically, the Quapaw Indians were the only group left to greet Marquette. Although the Quapaw probably were composed of remnants of the greatly reduced Central Valley population, one wonders how many would have been present in 1673 if De Soto had not crossed the Mississippi River in 1541.

SUMMARY

Around A.D. 1350–1400 a significant demographic shift took place within the Central Mississippi Valley. The reasons appear partly political and partly environmental. The politics of the thirteenth century revolved around the development of a very major chiefdom, known as the Cairo Lowland phase, characterized by large fortified sites and evidently the monopolization of major upland lithic and copper resources and salt. Whatever the specific causes, fortification and defense became a predominant concern by most or all Central Valley inhabitants. This reaction to political evolution nucleated formerly dispersed households into fortified villages. Braided stream surfaces could not support large nucleated populations dependent upon agriculture. Nucleation of these populations near the end of the fourteenth century had to take place in favorable alluvial environments where soils best suited for hoe agriculture were clustered.

One such soil cluster was near Batesville, where the Greenbriar phase developed. Another more major cluster, a meander belt, was on the St. Francis and Tyronza rivers where the Parkin phase appeared. Other phases are known farther downstream from the Parkin phase. The Nodena phase appeared in the major meander belt region. The Nodena phase core appears to have been the older Cairo Lowland phase shifted downriver into a larger meander belt surface and adjacent to its traditional enemies, now incorporated as the Parkin phase. By 1541, the date of the De Soto expedition, Pacaha (the Nodena phase) had enlarged its control over at least two other chiefdoms (the Walls phase) and was the predominant chiefdom in the Central Valley. This period was one of florescence. By 1673, when the French first visited, all of the societies visited by the De Soto expedition were extinct. Remnants of the former great chiefdoms of the Central Valley were joined together as the Quapaw, known as the "downstream people."

REFERENCES

Blake, Leonard, and Hugh Cutler
1979   Plant remains from the Upper Nodena site (3MS4). *Arkansas Archeologist* **20**:53–58.
Bourne, Edward G.
1904   *Narratives of the career of Hernando De Soto.* New York: A. S. Barnes.
Brown, Calvin S.
1926   *Archeology of Mississippi.* University: Mississippi Geological Survey.
Chapman, Carl, and Leo O. Anderson
1955   The Campbell site: A Late Mississippi town site and cemetery in southeast Missouri. *Missouri Archaeologist* **17**.
Davis, Hester
1966   An Introduction to Parkin prehistory. *Arkansas Archeologist* **7**:1–40.
Dellinger, S. C., and S. D. Dickinson
1940   Possible antecedents of the Middle Mississippian ceramic complex in northeastern Arkansas. *American Antiquity* **6**:133–147.
Ford, James A.
1961   Menard site: The Quapaw village of Osotouy on the Arkansas River. *Anthropological Papers of the American Museum of Natural History* **48**.
Green, Thomas, and Cheryl Munson
1978   Mississippian settlement patterns in Southwestern Indiana. In *Mississippian settlement patterns*, edited by Bruce D. Smith, pp. 293–330. New York: Academic Press.
Griffin, James B.
1946   Cultural change and continuity in eastern United States archaeology. In *Man in northeastern North America*, edited by Frederick Johnson. *Papers of the Peabody Foundation for Archeology* **3**:37–95.
1952   Prehistoric cultures of the Central Mississippi Valley. In *Archeology of eastern United States*, edited by James B. Griffin, pp. 226–238. Chicago: University of Chicago Press.
1960   A hypothesis for the prehistory of the Winnebago. In *Culture in history*, edited by Stanley Diamond, pp. 809–865. New York: Columbia University Press.
Holmes, William H.
1903   Aboriginal pottery of the eastern United States. *Bureau of American Ethnology 20th Annual Report:*1–237.
Hoffman, Michael
1977   The Kinkead–Mainard site, 3PU2: A late prehistoric Quapaw phase site near Little Rock, Arkansas. *Arkansas Archeologist* **16, 17, 18**:1–41.
House, John
1975   Summary of archeological knowledge updated with newly gathered survey data. In *The Cache River Archeological Project*, assembled by Michael B. Schiffer and John H. House. *Arkansas Archeological Survey Research Series* **8**:153–162.
Klinger, Timothy C.
1974   Report on the 1974 Test excavations at the Knappenberger site Mississippi County, Arkansas. *Arkansas Archeologist* **15**:45–72.
1977   Parkin archeology: A report on the 1966 field school test excavations at the Parkin site. *Arkansas Archeologist* **16, 17, 18**:45–80.
Lewis R. Barry
1982   Two Mississippian hamlets: Cairo Lowland, Missouri. *Illinois Archaeological Survey Special Publication* **2**.
Moore, Clarence B.
1908   Certain mounds of Arkansas and of Mississippi. *Journal of the Academy of Natural Sciences of Philadelphia* **13**:477–592.
1910   Antiquities of the St. Francis, White and Black rivers, Arkansas. *Journal of the Academy of Natural Sciences of Philadelphia* **14**:255–364.

1911   Somes aboriginal sites on Mississippi River. *Journal of the Academy of Natural Sciences of Philadelphia* **14**:367–478.
Morse, Dan F.
1971   An historic Indian grave near Blytheville, Arkansas. *Arkansas Archeologist* **12**:56–60.
1982   Regional overview of northeast Arkansas. In *Arkansas archeology in review*, edited by Neal L. Trubowitz and Marvin D. Jeter. *Arkansas Archeological Survey Research Series* **15**:20–36.
Morse, Dan F. (editor)
1973   Nodena. *Arkansas Archeological Survey Research Series* **4.**
Morse, Dan F., and Samuel D. Smith
1973   Archeological salvage during the construction of route 308. *Arkansas Archeologist* **14**:36–77.
Morse, Phyllis A.
1981   Parkin. *Arkansas Archeological Survey Research Series* **13.**
Nash, Charles H.
1957   A burial with bow and arrows. *Tennessee Archaeologist* **13**:96–97.
1972   Chucalissa: Excavations and burials through 1963. *Memphis State University Anthropological Research Center Occasional Papers* **6.**
Perino, Gregory
1966   The Banks village site, Crittenden County, Arkansas. *Missouri Archaeological Society, Memoir* **4.**
Phillips, Philip
1970   Archaeological survey in the Lower Yazoo Basin, Mississippi, 1949–1955. *Papers of the Peabody Museum, Harvard University* **60.**
Phillips, Philip, James Ford, and James B. Griffin
1951   Archaeological survey in the Lower Mississippi Alluvial Valley, 1940–1947. *Papers of the Peabody Museum, Harvard University* **25.**
Price, James E., Cynthia R. Price, and Suzanne E. Harris
1976   An assessment of the cultural resources of the Fourche Creek watershed. Report submitted to the USDA-SCS, Columbia, Missouri by American Archaeology Division, University of Missouri, Columbia.
Rands, Robert
1956   Southern Cult motifs on Walls–Pecan Point pottery. *American Antiquity* **22**:183–186.
Roper, Donna C.
1979   The method and theory of site catchment analysis: A review. In *Advances in archaeological method and theory* (Vol. 2), edited by Michael Schiffer, pp. 119–140. New York: Academic Press.
Sheldon, Craig T. Jr.
1974   The Mississippian-historic transition in Central Alabama. Ph.D. Dissertation, Department of Anthropology, University of Oregon. University Microfilms, Ann Arbor.
Smith, Bruce D.
1975   Middle Mississippi exploitation of animal populations. *University of Michigan Museum of Anthropology Anthropological Papers* **57.**
Thomas, Cyrus
1894   Report on the mound explorations of the Bureau of Ethnology. *12th Annual Report of the Bureau of American Ethnology for 1890–1891.*
Waring, Antonio J. Jr., and Preston Holder
1945   A Prehistoric ceremonial complex in the Southeastern United States. *American Anthropologist* **47**:1–34.
Williams, Stephen
1977   Some ruminations on the current strategy of archaeology in the Southeast. Paper presented at Southeastern Archaeological Conference, Lafayette, La.
1980   The Armorel phase: A very late complex in the Lower Mississippi Valley. *Southeastern Archaeological Conference Bulletin* **22**:105–110.

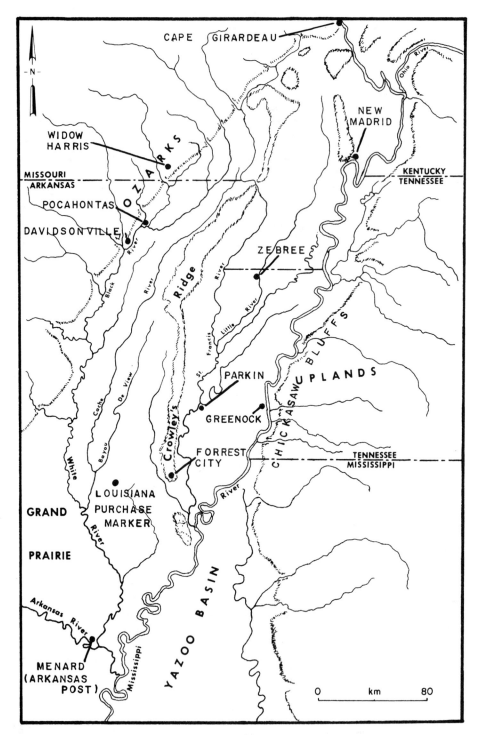

FIGURE 13.1. Some Central Valley historic sites.

13

Epilogue: Historic Archaeology

Archaeology in the United States is not simply an investigation of prehistoric Indian remains. There are almost 500 years of the Historic period represented in the Central Valley that can also be studied using archaeological techniques (Figure 13.1). The Protohistoric is the earliest Historic period. It is restricted to that period of time after initial Spanish artifacts are possible but before the recognition of ethnographically known native groups such as the Quapaw. We use the date 1650 to separate the two earliest Historic periods, although technically the Quapaw were not seen by the French until 1673. After the French contact period, there were several native American Indian groups in the Central Valley. As far as we know, only one, the Quapaw, was indigenous. Around A.D. 1800 there was a period of settlement by Euro-Americans or "pioneers." The Central Valley was the hinterland of both St. Louis and New Orleans in the late eighteenth and early nineteenth centuries. This book ends with a discussion of a case of twentieth-century deception, which underscores the gullibility of the general public in archaeological interpretation.

THE PROTOHISTORIC–SPANISH PERIOD (A.D. 1500–1650)

One brief glimpse of Late Mississippian chiefdoms is available to researchers. The accounts of the De Soto expedition, which entered the Central Valley in 1541, give us our only ethnological description of these complex flourishing societies. Hernando De Soto acquired great wealth when he accompanied Francisco Pizarro during the conquest of Peru. He was appointed the governor of Cuba and Florida (the southeastern United States) by Charles V of Spain and was commissioned to conquer these new lands at his own expense.

Announcement of this enterprise brought numerous volunteers, as the previous success of both Hernando Cortes and Pizarro made some participants extremely wealthy. Four narratives, which differ in length, detail, and quality, were left by survivors of the expedition (Ranjel, Elvas, and Biedma, in Bourne 1904; Garcilaso, in Varner and Varner 1951).

The expedition arrived at Tampa Bay on May 31, 1539, complete with horses, a large drove of pigs, camp followers, priests, supplies, and some vicious dogs. The search for gold led the Spanish through the modern states of Florida, Georgia, Tennessee, Alabama, and Mississippi before their arrival in the Mississippi Valley on May 8, 1541. A Spanish gentleman rescued in Florida translated through an increasing line of interpreters as their journey progressed. They captured servants and bearers as needed, keeping them controlled with the dogs.

Pinpointing the route of the De Soto expedition is a frustrating exercise. The narratives are brief and to a certain extent supplement each other. But there are important contradictions and variations in the interpretation of the meanings of given passages. The usual method of reconstructing the De Soto route is to locate archaeological sites that may have been described in the accounts and correlate these with geographic descriptions and numbers of days of march (Swanton 1939; Phillips, Ford, and Griffin 1951; Brain, Toth, and Rodriguez–Buckingham 1974; P. Morse 1981). "De Soto visited here" folklore exists virtually throughout the Central Valley. Almost anyone who has lived along the Mississippi River, however, knows that there is a low probability of actually finding a specific site after 4 centuries of erosion and flooding.

For the Central Valley, there are two major hypothesized routes in contention. One is called the Commerce Landing route (Phillips, Ford, and Griffin 1951; P. Morse 1981) and is adopted in the following discussion. The other is called the Sunflower Landing route (Swanton 1939; Brain, Toth, and Rodriguez–Buckingham 1974). The Sunflower Landing route has considerable merit (Brain, Toth, and Rodriguez–Buckingham 1974). The narratives describe crossing a swampy lowland area east of the Mississippi River interpreted as the northeast portion of the Yazoo Basin. The expedition would have followed an eighteenth-century trail between the Chickasaw villages and the Mississippi River. The site of the actual crossing is marked on a 1796 map. There are archaeological sites that date around 1541 in the region of the crossing.

However, one narration has the army marching north for 3 days within the lowlands, which would take it off the Chickasaw trail to near Commerce Landing. The first town was caught by surprise, an indication that an established trail was not followed at that point. There are also archaeological sites that date around 1541 in the Commerce Landing area.

Brain, Toth, and Rodriguez–Buckingham (1974:244) state that "events on the other side of the river in Arkansas hold the key to the correct identifica-

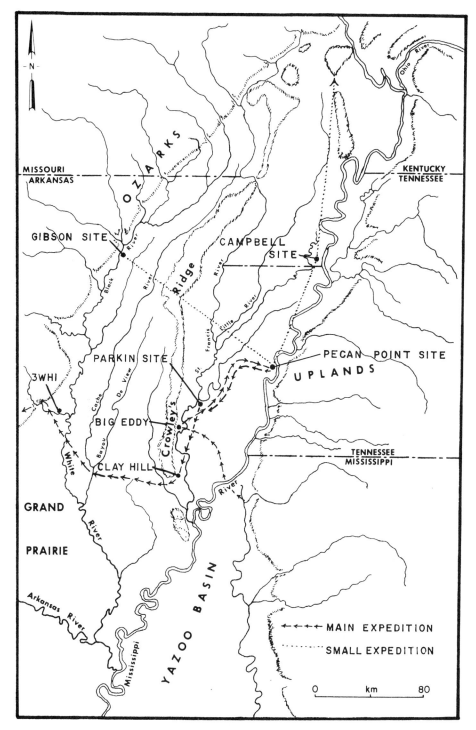

FIGURE 13.2. Proposed route of the De Soto expedition in the Central Mississippi Valley.

tion [of the crossing]." We will emphasize in the following discussion why we feel circumstantial evidence based on the narratives on the Arkansas side favors a Commerce Landing crossing. Mainly, the evidence is: (a) uninhabited regions west and north of the contacted phases; (b) nomadic hunters in the western Lowlands; (c) copper and salt in the Ste. François Mountains; (d) similarity of the Parkin site with the capitol of Casqui; (e) similarity of the Parkin phase settlement pattern with that described for the Province of Casqui; (f) equating the Province of Pacaha with the Nodena phase; (g) identification of the Walls phase, once classified with the Nodena phase as Walls–Pecan Point, as Quizquiz and Aquixo, both vassals of Pacaha; and (h) identification of a dense and flourishing population north of the region selected by Brain, Toth, and Rodriguez–Buckingham, which, according to the De Soto narratives, was sterile and poorly populated.

The Spanish were looking for gold. They evidently felt gold was to be found in mountainous areas because their reconstructed route has them checking mountains at every opportunity. The Spanish expedition has always to be interpreted in terms of that quest for gold. They did not move haphazardly around the countryside. There were advance search and foraging parties, and the route taken, although largely impromptu, has to have been deliberate.

The Spanish entered the Central Valley after an exhausting winter fighting off the Chickasaw. After an 8- or 9-day march through deserted country in northern Mississippi, they surprised the province of Quizquiz and captured one of their towns. After 4000 warriors assembled in a few hours, the Spanish returned their captives and stolen goods and made peace with the chief of Quizquiz. Three villages of Quizquiz were described as about a league apart, located near the great river, the Mississippi. Quizquiz was described as vassal to the "lord of Pacaha." Three such sites containing Late Mississippian ceramics exist near Commerce Landing, Mississippi: the Hollywood, Indian Creek, and Commerce Landing sites.

After several days of rest and provisioning, De Soto moved his army to a place along the Mississippi where they built shelters on a plain and began making barges to cross the river. The recognition of this crossing point is crucial to all theories of the exact route of the Spanish in Arkansas. Commerce Landing, Mississippi, is a suitable low spot where an army could descend from the bluffs of the river and build the necessary boats.

It took almost a month to build four vessels, which held 60–150 soldiers and 6–30 cavalrymen and horses each. While they were busy sawing planks and making nails they were visited by the chief of Aquixo, from the opposite shore of the Mississippi. He was accompanied by 200 canoes filled with armed men. The ochre-painted warriors wore great plumes of feathers and carried feathered cane shields to protect the oarsmen. The chief's barge even had a canopy. The Spanish were regularly harassed by arrows from canoes full of warriors every day at 3 o'clock while building their barges but were luckily left alone on the day chosen for crossing.

The river was crossed on June 18, 1541, with two trips being necessary to carry everyone over. The Spanish then went upstream to an Aquixo village, where they dismantled the barges and retrieved precious iron. The towns of Aquixo province were all deserted, and the Spanish did not linger. Several contemporary Walls phase sites such as Belle Meade (3CT30) and Beck (3CT8) in Crittenden County, Arkansas, are located on a large oxbow lake near the Mississippi above the Commerce Landing location and may be where the boats were dismantled after the crossing.

The Spanish wished to visit powerful Pacaha, located upstream. The easiest route was northwest toward Crowley's Ridge, as there was a tremendous backswamp directly to the north. They had already heard of the province of Casqui and made their way there, away from the Mississippi, spending several days traversing what was described as the worst tract of swamp and water they had seen in all Florida. They eventually arrived at some high hills and saw a village of 400 houses, surrounded by numerous fields of corn and a number of fruit trees. What they described as the worst tract of swamp between Aquixo and Casqui could easily have been the south edge of that very large backswamp between the Mississippi and the present course of the St. Francis River. The high hills are actually a rare phenomenon in the Central Valley. Such a location is present at the Parkin phase Big Eddy site (3SF9), at the base of Crowley's Ridge along the St. Francis River. At least two head pots, dating to the protohistoric, are known from this site.

This village by the high hills was one of the towns of the province of Casqui. The Spanish were welcomed in peace. They stayed there several days and then proceeded up the River of Casqui to the village of the chief of the Casqui. The River of Casqui is interpreted as the St. Francis River, and the village of the chief probably was the Parkin site (P. Morse 1981). On the way they saw fields thickly set with great towns. De Soto was offered the residence of the chief, on a high mound on one side of the town. After being fed for 3 days, De Soto was asked by the chief to petition his obviously powerful god to make it rain. A cross, which took more than 100 men to move, was built of the largest and thickest "pine" (probably cypress) in the whole region. It was placed on the top of a tall mound in the village. Spanish priests held an appropriate ceremony while 15,000 Indians watched from across the river. A heavy rain began to fall that night and lasted for 2 days, greatly impressing the Casqui natives.

The Parkin site, located upriver from the Big Eddy, is interpreted as the capital of the province of Casqui. Casqui had a large mound that held the chief's dwelling, and Parkin contains such a mound and an apron or extension on the mound where his wives' and retainers' houses could have been placed. This same mound would have held the large cross erected by the Spanish. These ceremonies would have been visible from the opposite side of the St. Francis River, just as described. Two Spanish artifacts that have been found at Parkin date to this time period: a Clarksdale-style bell and a seven-layered

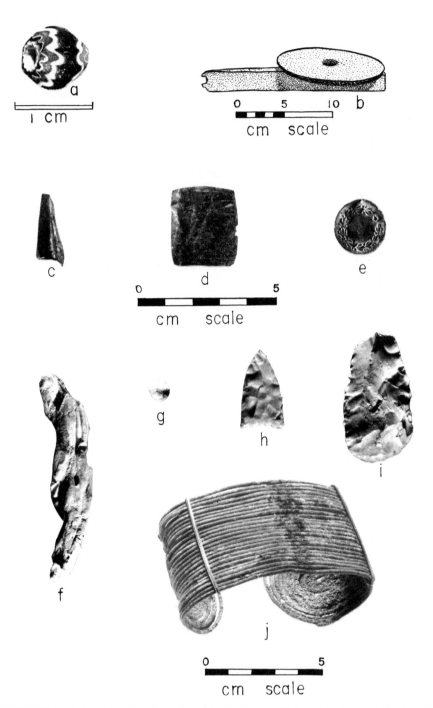

FIGURE 13.3. Typical historic artifacts found in the Central Valley. (a) Chevron glass bead (sixteenth century). (b) Catlinite disk pipe (sixteenth century). (c) Brass tinkling cone (eighteenth century). (d) Preform for tinkling cone (eighteenth century). (e) Brass button (eighteenth–nineteenth centuries). (f) Lead lump (eighteenth–nineteenth centuries). (g) Lead bullet (eighteenth–nineteenth centuries). (h) Triangular point (eighteenth century). (i) End scraper (eighteenth century). (j) Copper wire bracelet (seventeenth–eighteenth centuries). [(a)–(i) Courtesy of the Arkansas Archeological Survey; (j) courtesy of the Department of Anthropology, National Museum of Natural History, Smithsonian Institution.]

chevron glass bead (Klinger 1977; Figure 13.3a). These styles of beads and bells are both limited to the sixteenth century (Brain 1975; Smith and Good 1982). University of Arkansas archaeologists found a large charred post in the top of the mound at Parkin, causing speculation that this was where the cross was erected.

The people of Casqui had been at war with the neighboring province of Pacaha for a long time and were near surrender. They were afraid to leave their boundaries in case they offended the more powerful Pacaha. Taking advantage of their new Spanish allies, the Casqui volunteered to help De Soto enter Pacaha and provided guides, 5000 warriors, and 3000 food bearers. They followed the river of Casqui toward Pacaha, spending several nights in or near Casqui villages. The Tyronza River, which joins the St. Francis just above Parkin from the east, is interpreted by us as appearing to the Spanish as part of the River of Casqui. It leads toward the Nodena phase. There are several Parkin phase villages, such as Barton Ranch, along the way where the Spanish and the accompanying Casqui warriors could have spent the night. A great swamp divided the two provinces. A swampy area still exists beyond Barton Ranch, which may be the swamp that the Spanish crossed to get to the province of Pacaha.

Several days travel took them to the principal town of Pacaha. There were 500 houses on a man-made island, stockaded by a palisade with towers. A wide moat surrounding the town was fed by a canal that led to the Mississippi. Despite messages of friendship sent by De Soto, the chief of Pacaha retreated to an island fortress. When the Casqui entered the town, they looted it and smashed the wooden chests filled with bones of the ancestors of the Pacaha chief located in a temple in a large public plaza. De Soto prevented them from burning the town.

The capital of Pacaha possibly was the Pecan Point site in southern Mississippi County, Arkansas. It was on one of the most elevated points along the river and dates to the Nodena phase. It was dug extensively by both the Smithsonian (Thomas 1894) and C. B. Moore (1911), producing nine known head pots. At least one large mound was present at the site. Its total size can never be determined, for this site was washed into the Mississippi during a flood. It obviously was once able to contain a large population and is located near the Mississippi, where the island retreat described by the De Soto expedition could have been situated.

A fleet of Casqui canoes arrived, and the Pacaha island retreat was attacked. After the Pacaha fought off the first attack, the Casqui tried to flee, abandoning the Spanish. The Pacaha chief then spared some Spanish warriors and made peace with De Soto. Orders were given to do no more looting, and De Soto tried to make peace between the Casqui and Pacaha chiefs. At a banquet given by De Soto, the Pacaha chief refused to accept any place except at the right hand of De Soto, citing the prominence of his ancestors over those of Casqui as the main reason. The Casqui chief acceded to this demand, acknowledging the genealogical superiority of Pacaha. The classic hierarchy in chiefdoms, the ranking of lineages relative to one another with an emphasis on primogeniture, is reflected in this description.

The Spanish spent about a month at the capital of the province of Pacaha, being fed from the Indians' stores in the middle of the summer. They sent out exploratory parties to reconnoiter the surrounding country. A great amount of fine salt was reported in mountains 40 leagues (170 km) away, along with a great deal of yellow metal. Two Spaniards were sent out with traders to explore this area, carrying such trade goods as pearls, chamois skins, and beans. After an 11-day journey, they returned with six loads of salt and a load of copper. The land they traveled through was observed to be sterile and poorly populated.

Such a trip from Pecan Point could have reached the Ste. François Mountains in southeast Missouri. In mountainous Ste. Genevieve County, Missouri, there are both numerous salt springs and the largest surface copper deposits in Missouri. Numerous Spanish trade goods, including glass beads, iron, and Clarksdale bells, have been found at the Campbell site in southeast Missouri, which is situated along this proposed route to these mountains. Much of the area in southeast Missouri beyond Campbell actually was very sparsely occupied during Late Mississippian times, thus being sterile and poorly populated, as the Spanish described.

An expedition to the northwest from Pacaha headed for some reported large settlements. An 8-day journey took the explorers through large ponded swamps and wide plains overgrown with high plants, which were hard to break through even on horseback. From Pecan Point, a route through a buffer zone between the Parkin and Nodena phases would cross many swamps and several prairies including Maumelle Prairie. They encountered some Indians living in portable rush huts that could be rolled up and moved easily. These hunters camped near areas where deer and fish were easily obtained and moved frequently. This province of Caluç did not look promising, and the Spanish returned to Pacaha. This province could have included the Gibson site, a Middle period Mississippian site reoccupied by hunters of the Greenbrier phase as a hunting base camp. The Greenbrier phase could have been the reported large settlements sought by the Spanish, and the rude hunters could have been Greenbrier members out on their summer hunt. Greenbrier phase towns are located south of the Gibson site, near Batesville.

These Spanish expeditions investigated the mountains to the north and to the northwest. As the northern areas looked unpromising in their search for gold, they decided to go west. They left Pacaha and traced their steps back to Casqui. After a 5-day rest, they spent 4 days following the River of Casqui down through this "fertile and well populated" land. The Spaniards reached the border of the Province of Quigate on August, 1541 and were helped across the river by some Casqui canoes. They then slept the first night in a burned village. The next day they found a village with abundant pumpkins, corn, and beans. The capital of Quigate was reached the next day and was reportedly the largest town they saw in all of Florida. Quigate was on the River of Casqui and was divided into three wards, with one containing a high mound upon which was the chief's residence.

The journey back down the River of Casqui to Quigate is archaeologically not as clear. There are many sites in the Kent phase that can be dated to the protohistoric, such as Kent, Soudan, and Clay Hill. But none of these has been recently surveyed or professionally excavated. This area was certainly densely populated and abundant with food, although the "largest town" has not yet been identified. Several artifacts that date to the sixteenth century, including a Clarksdale bell and a nonrepoussé copper eagle, have been found at the Clay Hill site.

After spending a few days at Quigate, skirmishing with the Indians and burning half the town, the Spanish learned of a province called Coligua or Colima, to the northwest, that was near the mountains and where people lived by hunting cattle. Still hoping for gold and a passage to the South Sea, they crossed through four swamps in 4 days and finally found the River of Coligua, which could be the White River, finding a pretty village between some ridges on the gorge of the river. They were received peacefully by the inhabitants of Coligua, but the populace fled after 2 days of contact. The Spanish then turned south, possibly following what is now called the old military road, and left the Central Valley.

Between the province of Coligua and Quigate there are four rivers beyond the St. Francis in the vicinity of the Clay Hill site—L'Anguille, Big Creek, Bayou De View, and Cache—which easily could correspond to these four swamps. A protohistoric site (3WH1) on the Little Red River identified with the protohistoric Quapaw phase could be in the province of Coligua visited by the Spanish. It is near the Natchitoches Trace on an old trail that leads along the Ozark Escarpment southwest to Little Rock and beyond.

To summarize, the De Soto expedition crossed the Mississippi near Commerce Landing in the province of Quizquiz (east Walls phase), crossed to Aquixo (west Walls phase), went inland to Casqui (Parkin phase), back east to Pacaha (Nodena phase), visited the Ste. François Mountains and the Greenbrier phase, retraced their steps to Casqui, and went south to Quigate (Kent and/or Old Town phases) and then farther west to the Ozarks (Quapaw phase) before turning south toward Little Rock.

The De Soto expedition accounts provide only a brief glimpse through the eyes of treasure seekers of the period May 8–September 7, 1541. The different accounts often conflict, and the cultural descriptions are minimal. The effect that this expedition, suddenly appearing upon tall horses, seizing bearers and servants, and requisitioning large amounts of food, must have had upon the various native populations can only be compared to the impression an invasion of strange beings from outer space would have upon our culture today. The disruption of existing political alliances must have been considerable. Leaving behind an occasional lost pig as a new food resource could even have been beneficial. But one legacy of the Spanish, the spread of new virulent diseases, must have been overwhelming in impact.

There is a striking contrast between the areas of dense population encountered by the Spanish and the few small towns near the Arkansas River found by the French 130 years later. The thousands of warriors, towns of 400–500 houses, paramount chiefs, and highly developed societies were gone. One area in the Southeast in which a highly developed sociocultural organization remained was the lands of the Natchez people. The De Soto expedition never penetrated this area of Mississippi. Epidemic disease spread by the Spanish has long been suggested as the ultimate cause for this change in population density and culture.

Milner (1980) has proposed an epidemic disease model for the Southeast. Crowd infections, such as measles, smallpox, and influenza, with a pattern of epidemics and subsequent immunity, require a large host population for maintenance. In "virgin-soil" populations, there is potential for a devastating death rate upon first contact with these diseases. A large portion of the population will probably become infected. Spread of disease to other settlements, poor health care, and the interruption of nursing of children because of parental illness increases the death rate.

The De Soto expedition described great towns that were dispeopled and overgrown with grass at Cofitachequi, in South Carolina. A plague had appeared there 2 years earlier. Spanish goods, which probably were from the Ayllon settlement of 1526 on the Carolina coast, were found in a charnel house at Cofitachequi. The spread of similar diseases by De Soto's men is an expectation.

One good description of the effects of a European disease upon a native population is that of the smallpox epidemic that hit the Mandan in 1837. A trader's boat arrived at Fort Clark on the Missouri River on June 19 with three diseased Indians aboard. By August 22, 35–50 men were dying every day (Meyer 1977:93). By September, 800 were dead, and when the disease had run its course, at least seven-eighths of all the Mandan were dead. Many of the survivors were Old Ones, who had already had smallpox once. George Catlin (1967) estimated 2000 Mandan in 1832; after the epidemic only 120 or 130 were left. The dead were left unburied in one village when survivors fled. Suicides of lone survivors of families were recorded. The remaining Mandan dispersed themselves among several neighboring tribes except for one small village that remained separate. Adjoining tribes such as the Hidatsa began catching the disease. Warnings by traders to stay away from infected villages and a belated attempt to vaccinate other tribes prevented complete population decimation of the Plains.

One can assume that the longer the time of contact between De Soto and the "province" visited, the greater was the potential for a resulting epidemic. The spread of disease by those fleeing infected villages would more likely be to other villages of kinsmen in the same society, not to those seen as enemies. The most hospitable groups such as Casqui and Pacaha, who entertained De Soto and his army for over a month, were probably the most likely to be decimated by this contact. The practice of having everyone in the society live within a fortified village also made these groups far more susceptible to such infections. Many more persons would die in a tightly nucleated settlement than in dispersed farmsteads.

Milner (1980) suggests that archaeological proof of such epidemics can be found. In particular, mass burials of individuals without their usual mortuary offerings are an expectation. Evidence of acute disease affecting bone growth and tooth development will be present in skeletons. Analysis of age and sex in graves may show an unusual number of the young and the old present. If there was a subsequent infection, the older persons would be immune and only those born after the last epidemic would die. In this case, there would be an unusual number of children buried.

Epidemic diseases are not the only ones assumed to be left by the De Soto expedition. Other lingering infections such as tuberculosis and various venereal diseases could also take their toll. A study of skeletal remains reported to have spinal tuberculosis showed most cases not to be tuberculosis (Morse 1978). However, one of the few cases that was most probably tuberculosis was found at Chucalissa, near Memphis, and could be postcontact in date.

There are no further recorded contacts of the Spanish going inland into the Central Valley, therefore it is possible that only one intensive contact between these alien cultures took place. Some Spanish trade goods were certainly brought into the Central Valley after De Soto left. Trade of indigenous goods from the north in the form of catlinite, particularly as pipes, indicates knowledge of events occurring outside the area (Figure 13.3b). There were large numbers of Spanish in the Caribbean and along the Gulf Coast. Other Spanish in the Southwest were linked to the Central Valley by the Arkansas River. By the end of the seventeenth century all Indian groups had access to European artifacts on a continuing basis.

THE FRENCH IN THE MISSISSIPPI VALLEY

On the 7th, whilst we halted on the Bank of a River to eat, we heard the tingling of some small Bells; which making us look about, we spied an Indian with a naked sword-blade in his hand, adorned with Feathers of several colours, and two large Hawks Bells, that occasion'd the noise we had heard. He made signs for us to come to him, and gave us to understand, that he was sent by the elders of the village, whither we were going, to meet us, caressing us after an extraordinary manner. I observ'd that it was a Spanish Blade he had, and that he took Pleasure in ringing the Hawks Bells [Joutel 1714:144–145].

There is no further written description of the Central Valley until May 1673, when Father Jacques Marquette and Louis Jolliet traveled down the Mississippi from Canada with five other Frenchmen in two canoes (Thwaites 1900). Their purpose was to discover if the river flowed toward the Gulf of California and also to spread the word of God to the Illinois and beyond. Marquette was greeted warmly by the Illinois and provided with a calumet, a highly respected pipe made from a red stone on a 60-cm (2-ft.) stem, adorned with colorful feathers. This calumet served as a passport between Indian nations and safeguarded his entry into unknown territory.

Below the mouth of the Ohio the explorers saw some natives armed with guns. They also had hatchets, hoes, knives, beads, and glass powder flasks, which they had obtained from Europeans to the east. When shown the calumet, these Indians were friendly and fed the French. Near the thirty-third degree of latitude they found a village on the waters' edge called Mitchigamea, whose inhabitants began to attack until, again, they saw the calumet. These people did not understand any of the six languages known by the French. One old man was found there who could speak Illinois. They were told there was another large village called Akamsea 8 or 10 leagues (34 to 42 km) downriver. They reached this village the next day.

At Akamsea they learned that they were only 10 days' journey from the sea. Hostile nations armed with guns prevented the Akamsea from trading with Europeans to the south, but the Akamsea (Quapaw) acquired hatchets, knives, and beads from other Indian groups to the east and west. They did not yet possess guns. They welcomed the French with a great deal of feasting, feeding them corn cooked in "very well made" great earthern jars, served on plates of baked earth. Their long and wide houses were made of bark, with sleeping platforms at two ends. They spoke a language considered very difficult by Marquette. Having ascertained that the Mississippi did flow south to the Gulf, the French decided not to explore its entire length and returned to the north. Marquette left a map, which shows not only Mitchigamea on the west bank and Akamsea on the east bank but also eight more villages to the west inland below Mitchigamea, probably along the Arkansas River. The Arkansas is not indicated on this map, although the Ohio, Missouri, and Illinois rivers are shown. This report is the first mention of the Indians who later were called the Quapaw.

René-Robert de La Salle came down the river 9 years later, in 1682. Below the Ohio he saw a few lodges on the bank, but no larger villages were noted. His expedition built a temporary fort near the Chickasaw Bluffs (Memphis area), where one of their number was lost while hunting. They were contacted by some Chickasaw, whose villages were too far away to visit easily. They reached the village of Kappa 50 leagues (210 km) downward. Again, a calumet served as an introduction. The inhabitants of Kappa were enthusiastically described as well made, well proportioned, nimble, modest, and honest. The French erected a post marked with the arms of France, taking possession for the French king. Two other "Akansa" (Quapaw) villages on the Mississippi were visited, and they told the French about the village of Osotouy, on the Arkansas. Lodges thatched with cedar or cypress and cypress canoes were described. The natives already had both peaches and chickens, important European additions to their diet. No guns are mentioned.

La Salle planned to cut the Iroquois domination of the fur trade by using the Mississippi as a new trade route. His plans for building a colony went awry 2 years later when he missed the mouth of the Mississippi and was wrecked on the Texas coast. Henri de Tonti traveled down the Mississippi to rescue La Salle in 1686. He again found three villages of Quapaw on the Mississippi River. He also left a party of 10 Frenchmen at the river "Akansas," thus beginning Arkansas Post, the first European settlement in the whole Lower Mississippi Valley. A small remnant of the La Salle colony made their way from the Texas coast to the Mississippi River in 1687 (Joutel 1714). All the tribes contacted along the way were already familiar with European trade goods, being equipped in particular with knives, hatchets, and beads. One tribe even had watermelons. Several Frenchmen were also found living among the tribes on the Ouachita. Nearing the Mississippi, they met a native work party who were about to cut bark to cover their houses. The Indians led them to a river, across which they saw a great cross and a French-style house on the opposite bank. They learned they were in the nation of the "Accancea," and the French garrison at Arkansas Post had built this cross and residence there.

A more detailed description of the four villages of the Accancea (Quapaw) was given by Joutel, a member of this La Salle expedition remnant. He stayed in a house in one of the villages made of cedar, or cypress, rounded at the corners, on a small mound. There was a plain full of game near the village. Some of the cottages in the villages were reported to be very large, holding up to 200 persons. They were covered with bark and rounded at the top. Their "moveables" were earthen vessels and oval wooden platters, so neatly made that they were used in trade with other groups. The people were well shaped and handsome. Their canoes were made from one piece of wood. The usual calumet or pipe ceremony was held, and the French gave the Indians a firearm, 100 charges of powder and ball, two axes, six knives, and some beads. They got in return four guides, one from each village, to take them back to the French settlements to the north.

The first French settlement, at Arkansas Post, was apparently occupied only intermittently. Many French traders deserted to the English, and Thomas Welch led an expedition in 1698 from Charleston, South Carolina, to the Quapaw at the mouth of the Arkansas. Indian trade was of great importance to the English settlers of South Carolina, surpassing even rice as a source of export goods (Crane 1929:115). They made large profits and kept Indian friendships at the same time. The English traditionally paid higher prices for deerskins than did the French or Spanish, giving them a great advantage. Trade in Indian slaves was also practiced by the British.

In 1698 a smallpox epidemic hit the Quapaw. It was estimated that fewer than 100 men were left at one village, all the children died, and only a few women survived. Two villages were then combined into one. The survivors were too weak even to hunt for meat. The next village, at the mouth of the Arkansas, had more population surviving with some children left. The culture of the Quapaw must have been changing even more rapidly after this population loss.

The village of Osotouy, the first location of Arkansas Post founded by de Tonti and described by the survivors of La Salle's colonization effort, has been identified as the Menard site (Ford 1961). Menard is situated on a low escarpment on the edge of Little Prairie, the nearest location 5–6 leagues (21 to 25 km) above the probable mouth of the eighteenth-century Arkansas River, which would be free from flooding. The site has one large mound 10.5 m high, a connecting large domiciliary mound, and at least four other smaller mounds. A late pottery complex was discovered at Menard, accompanied by European trade goods. C. B. Moore (1908) described 159 shallow burials there, often only 30 cm (1 ft.) below the surface. They were accompanied by 211 pottery vessels, some glass and brass beads, rusted iron, and a discoidal. The most interesting pottery shape found here by Moore is the so-called teapot form (Figure 13.4b). These spouted vessels are seen as a horizon marker type, dating to the French contact period. They are not copies of French teapots. A "Conway-style" head pot (Figure 13.4a) and a deep animal effigy bowl were also recovered by Moore, as well as Avenue Polychrome bottles, Carson Red on Buff bowls, and various Caddoan ceramic types.

Ford found at Menard one complete house plan with associated burned daub. The irregular posthole pattern measured 6 × 9 m (20 × 30 ft.) and included a partition interpreted as a sleeping bench. There was a packed yellow-clay floor over an older floor and three possible fireplaces, two of which were adjacent to the house walls, which is not a very reasonable location. Four burials were located around this house, one with trade goods. Fired clay daub showing impressions of split-cane matting was abundant. Nodena points, large triangular points, and thumbnail scrapers were also found. The presence of numerous small thumbnail scrapers is interpreted as evidence of hide or deerskin preparation. The described house is fairly large, but not nearly large enough to hold the 200 persons described by Joutel.

A collection and notes made in 1932 by University of Arkansas excavators at the Quapaw phase Kinkead–Mainard site north of Little Rock was recently analyzed by Hoffman (1977). In five clusters, 57 burials were recovered, accompanied by 137 vessels. These groups are of particular importance because they combine pottery types thought to be representative of the Caddo area to the west with types from northeast Arkansas and new types thought to be solely Quapaw. Avenue Polychrome, Carson Red on Buff, Old Town Red, Parkin Punctated, and Rhodes Incised from the Central Valley are combined with Natchitoches Engraved, Hodges Engraved, Keno Trailed (Figure 13.4c)

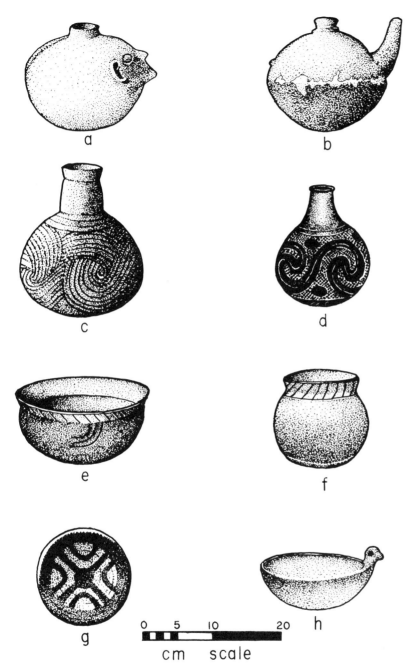

0   5   10   20

cm   scale

FIGURE 13.4. Quapaw phase pottery probably dating to the French period. (a) Late Mississippian-style head effigy vessel. (b) "Teapot" vessel. (c) Keno Trailed bottle. (d) Natchitoches Engraved bottle. (e) Wallace Incised "German Helmet" bowl. (f) Wallace Incised handleless jar. (g) Carson Red on Buff bowl. (h) Old Town Red effigy bowl. [(a), (c)–(f), (h) Drawn from Hoffman 1977, courtesy of the Arkansas Archeological Society; (b), (g) drawn from Ford 1961, courtesy of the American Museum of Natural History.]

and Wallace Incised (Figure 13.4e–f). A few copper beads, a copper nugget, Nodena points, a greenstone spatulate celt, and shell beads were also included in graves. New shapes such as the "German Helmet bowl" (Figure 13.4e) were present. The continuing use of the Nodena point shows its efficiency in hunting.

Evidence from excavated Quapaw phase sites such as Menard and Kinkead–Mainard shows relatively egalitarian burial groups clustered around houses. No obvious high-status burials have been found at any Quapaw site. There are more Quapaw phase sites known than the few indicated by the early French maps. Marquette's map shows 10 villages, but he did not visit most of them. Henri de Tonti definitely limits the Quapaw to only 4 villages. Quapaw phase graves with trade goods such as glass beads are known far up the Arkansas River beyond Little Rock and Pine Bluff. A site identified as a possible Quapaw hunting camp has been found in the Felsenthal wildlife refuge in south Arkansas. It is possible that the Quapaw had a larger population at some time before the period of direct French contact.

The question of the origin of the Quapaw is not completely solved. Their own tribal legend has them coming from "upstream," interpreted by many as from the Ohio River. Actually, when the Cairo Lowland phase became the Nodena phase, there was a population shift from near the mouth of the Ohio River to just north of Memphis. It is likely that the Quapaw are an amalgamation, the remnants left after European disease hit, of groups such as the Casqui, Pacaha, and Aquixo. There was not an immediate and complete collapse of these chiefdoms. Those left alive after the first impact consolidated, kept old religious rituals going, and contended for political offices now more open than before. There probably was a period of phase consolidation. The missing 130 years between De Soto and Marquette can be filled in only by future archaeological research. Unfortunately, the commercial value of the pottery at these sites is causing increased destruction. Three sites thought to have been visited by De Soto are being dug with heavy machinery in order to recover pots as this book is being written.

EIGHTEENTH-CENTURY DISRUPTION

There are only three aboriginal groups documented for the Central Valley area at the beginning of the eighteenth century. The Osage laid claim to southeast Missouri and northeast Arkansas as a hunting territory. The Chickasaw dominated the area east of the Mississippi, spreading out from their original territory near Tupelo, Mississippi, to control a large part of western Tennessee, Kentucky, Mississippi, and even part of Alabama. The Quapaw, near the Arkansas River, occupied the lower reaches of the Central Valley. These various groups were manipulated by the world political situation, with France, Spain, and England all trying to gain and keep control of the New World.

Toward the end of the eighteenth century the American Revolution added further pressure on these groups. Other tribes began moving across the Mississippi because of Euro-American population pressure, a practice politely called "removal." It is rather difficult to give a balanced picture of this process because most histories have not only an anti-Indian and pro-European bias but also a pro-English bias. Both French and Spanish sources have been neglected by many historians, and the achievements of English-based colonies have been disproportionately glorified.

The amount of ethnographic data on the Quapaw is paltry compared with that available for many other southeastern groups. They apparently had patrilineal clans and moieties and probably reckoned descent patrilineally, in contrast to most southeastern matrilineal tribes. The Quapaw language is classified as Siouan rather than being included in the Muskogean or Gulf language family more typical of the Southeast. Both the Ofo and Biloxi farther south in Mississippi and the Catawba of the Eastern Seaboard are also classified as Siouan speakers. The Osage, Quapaw, Kansas, Ponca, and Omaha are often grouped together as Dhegiha Sioux and seen therefore, as closely related, in opposition to other Siouan languages such as Winnebago and Ioway. However, there is not enough phonological data available to categorize the Quapaw so precisely (Griffin 1960:813). The Quapaw are probably derived from the Middle and Late Mississippian cultures of eastern Arkansas and southeast Missouri rather than being recent migrants either from the Ohio Valley or the Plains.

France, and later Spain, maintained fairly constant contact with the Quapaw through the small garrison stationed at the constantly changing location of Arkansas Post. At the ill-fated John Law colony, established on the Arkansas beyond the Quapaw village of Osotouy by the French in 1721, 200 German immigrants were reduced to one-fourth that number in less than a year. French soldiers were stationed at Osotouy at that time. Arkansas Post ended up at the present location of Arkansas Post National Memorial after 1752. The Quapaw were soon reduced in number to three villages after initial French contact. There were as many as 6000 Quapaw in 1682, but in 1750 it was estimated that they had only 400 warriors.

In the 1720s the French discovered a considerable amount of lead on the upper St. Francis River area, and ephemeral occupation by enterprising miners began. In 1735 the French founded Ste. Genevieve on the west bank of the Mississippi as a shipping point for this lead. Most French farming settlements, however, remained on the eastern side of the river.

The British gave firearms to the Indians for more efficient hunting, a policy that the Spanish disapproved of. Trade goods such as guns, brass kettles, knives, bells, and beads were exchanged for skins and slaves. As Indians became dependent upon these trade goods, their cultures were altered and destroyed. The practice of urging Indians to capture members of other tribes to be sold as slaves kept old tribal enmities alive, weakening any political power that pantribal alliances could have created. The Chickasaw remained allied to the more generous British traders, leading many slave raids across the Mississippi. An alliance of Chickasaw and Natchez tried to drive out the French in 1729. The Chickasaw occupied Chickasaw Bluffs, a strategic position for harassing traders on the Mississippi. As British allies, they also became involved in the American Revolution but signed a peace treaty in 1783.

Recorded contact with the Osage is slightly later than that with the Quapaw. The Osage resided mainly along the Missouri River, although they hunted widely in both the summer and winter. At contact they were composed of at least three bands, which probably at one time were separate tribes. A French map dating to 1686 shows 17 Osage villages. The French soon involved the Osage into the fur trade after Marquette's voyage down the Mississippi (Baird 1972). After acquiring both guns and horses, the Osage also participated in the slave trade, raiding groups farther west, such as the Pawnee and Caddo. They were treated with deference by the French, who frequently gave them gifts. The French tried to stop the slave raiding after 1719, finding it disruptive to commerce. The Osage dominated all trade on the Red, Arkansas, and Missouri rivers. When the Spanish tried to bypass them and develop trade with the Southwest, the Osage blocked them by frequently capturing their traders. Near the beginning of the nineteenth century over half the Osage moved to Oklahoma on the Arkansas River to be near their favorite French traders.

Spain acquired Louisiana in 1762. Its policy was to keep the Indian allies of the French under its influence while trying to alienate those under British influence. Most French officials were retained by the Spanish, and there is little evidence of Spanish culture in the Central Valley. Eastern tribes were attracted to the Arkansas Post area to conduct hunts and trade. For instance, the Peoria from Illinois moved near Arkansas Post in 1766 but later moved back to their homeland. Other groups such as the Kaskaskia and Delaware also moved back and forth across the Mississippi River. Philip Pittman in 1770 spoke of an annual rendezvous of European hunters from New Orleans who would winter on the lower St. Francis and make a provision of salted meats, suet, and bear oil for New Orleans. At this time there was no settlement on the banks of the Mississippi between Arkansas Post on the Arkansas and Kaskaskia on the Illinois.

Spain tried to attract settlers to upper Louisiana. It required immigrants to be Catholic and to swear allegiance to the Spanish ruler. Spain also tried to control all traffic along the Mississippi, even after 1776. During the American Revolution Spain opposed the British, seizing outposts such as Natchez and Baton Rouge in 1779. A 6-year summer drought forced many tribes to appeal for food at various Spanish posts, eventually causing the Chickasaw and Choctaw to make peace with Spain in 1783.

Delaware and Shawnee began permanently moving to the western side of the Mississippi at the end of the Revolution. A British sympathizer with a

Delaware wife moved to the Ste. Genevieve area just above Kaskaskia in 1780 and attracted 1200 Shawnee and 600 Delaware to the Apple Creek region nearby (Morrow 1980). These Indians lived in the watersheds of the St. Francis, Black, Current, and White rivers. Tribes retained separate but nearby villages and always traveled together. The Indians raised cattle and corn, trading meat to the whites. The Spanish formally allotted them land in 1793.

New Madrid became an important trade center after 1788, when a colony of Americans moved there. They moved away however, when they were denied promised land grants. Spain changed its stringent citizenship requirements at the end of the eighteenth century, and rapid immigration by Americans began. The French and Spanish economy continued to focus on trading with Indians instead of developing the land for agriculture. The French traditionally lived in towns and laid out long narrow fields, whereas Americans preferred to live in isolated farmsteads. Some Cherokee asked Spain for land and began moving to the St. Francis River drainage in 1795. By 1800 over 500 Cherokee families had moved there, and others moved to the White and Arkansas rivers.

Sites that are representative of the eighteenth-century occupation, either Indian or Euro-American, are simply not well known in the Central Valley. Farther up the Mississippi evidence of French settlement dating back to 1735 is represented at the well-preserved town of Ste. Genevieve, Missouri. The French long-lot system of fields can still be seen there in some aerial photographs. Many French and Spanish land claims appear on the original survey maps of the Central Valley area, those made by the General Land Office, but many of these may never have been occupied.

Some clues to eighteenth-century Indian activity in the Central Valley do exist. Catlinite and other artifacts found near Forrest City and Parkin, for instance, may date to this century. The previously discussed kaolin pipe stem and stoneware fragment found at Upper Nodena might also date to that time. Perhaps one of the most spectacular clues consists of a pair of copper wire bracelets (Figure 13.3j) in the Smithsonian collections. The two bracelets are from an unknown location in Mississippi County, Arkansas. They appear to be identical to an iron bracelet found at the Lasanen site in Michigan (Cleland 1971: fig. 18E). Cleland also references three similar bracelets made of copper from New York, suggesting that the style is fairly widespread. The Lasanen site is dated by Cleland to between 1670 and 1715. Triangular points, end scrapers, brass tinkling cones, and catlinite beads constitute some of the artifacts found at the Lasanen site that also occur in the Central Valley.

One site, which has produced brass tinkling cones and preforms to make into cones (Figure 13.3c–d), has been found near Pocahontas, Arkansas. These were surface finds. The tinkling cones and larger janglers were often found on buckskin jackets of both Indian and Euro-American hunters. No European ceramics were found at this site, although shell-tempered ceramics are present. A glass pendant, triangular arrow points, and end scrapers have also been recovered (Figure 13.3h–i). This site might date to this eighteenth-century period. Pottery burial urns found on the eastern side of the Mississippi such as at Richardson's Landing, may date to the Protohistoric but may be as late as the seventeenth or eighteenth centuries (Sheldon 1974:66).

North of Jonesboro in Greene County, Arkansas, two early Historic sites were located. An early nineteenth-century map identified them as Delaware and Shawnee. A visit to the Delaware location resulted in the recovery of a few historic artifacts, including a lead lump and a lead bullet (Figure 13.3f–g). These two sites probably date at or soon after A.D. 1800.

THE JEFFERSON PURCHASE AND THE NINETEENTH CENTURY

The French secretly acquired Louisiana back from the Spanish and almost immediately relinquished it in 1803, when Thomas Jefferson purchased millions of acres of land west of the Mississippi. Settlement of the area was hampered by the need for a legal survey and the existence of old French and Spanish land grants. The General Land Office began operations in 1815, setting out the present system of sections, townships, and ranges from a point near Monroe County, Arkansas, and surveying all the land to the Canadian border.

After the American Revolution the question of title to Indian land came to a head. Previously, the Spanish had a stated policy wherein the Indians held full rights to land that they were using but not to unoccupied lands or uninhabited areas (Thomas 1899). These waste lands belonged to the crown. The French considered lands in their domain to be theirs by conquest but had an active policy of assimilation, wherein Indians would become participants in French culture. The British originally had no formal Indian policy, leaving this to the various separate colonies. In 1761 a specific policy was drafted instructing colonists not to interfere with Indian land rights. The U.S. Supreme Court considered the question of Indian land claims in 1823 (Thomas 1899:537). It concluded that conquest gave title and that the European claims of title to territories by right of discovery were passed on to the United States after the Revolution. Congress reserved the right to acquire and give title to Indian lands and began treating tribes as distinct nations during treaty negotiations. As pressure for more land grew with expanding Anglo-American populations from the east, land cessions reducing tribal territories became common (Royce 1899). Exchanges for lands farther west also became more usual.

In 1808 the Osage ceded much of their land, over 21 million ha (52 million acres), in return for promised tools, implements, an annuity of $1500, and payment of claims against them. This cession provided an area for dispossessed tribes to move to. Many Cherokee moved to this Arkansas land in 1809. However, the Osage continued to harass these emigrants, and further cessions and payments were necessary. By 1825 they relinquished title to all lands in

Missouri and Arkansas Territory. More Delaware, Kickapoo, Shawnee, Miami, Piankanchaw, and Wea moved into the Central Valley area.

The fur trade continued after the United States took possession of its new territory. The factory system had originated in 1795, with official U.S. traders dealing with the Indians at cost, driving out private traders. One purpose of this system was to get Indians in debt to the factories and then take land in trade to pay off these debts. Factors were usually the Indian agents who distributed annuities and medals. Many of the trade goods were of English and German manufacture when the superintendent of trade thought these articles to be superior.

Various lists of trade goods are still extant. Articles such as guns, powder, flasks, pipes, beads, axes, traps, calico, blankets, window glass, hoes, plows, and seed were stocked at the trading posts. No liquor was supposed to be traded. Silver peace medals showing various presidents were presented to chiefs. Deer hides were the preferred southern commodity traded for, with muskrat, mink, bear, buffalo, and beaver fetching lower prices. Arkansas Post became the site of one of these government factories in 1805. A trader's house, a warehouse, a skin room, and a stable were part of the factory. Quapaw, Cherokee, Choctaw, Delaware, Chickasaw, and Osage all traded there, but trade was considered sparse. Essentially, all Indians had been pushed out of the Central Valley by the 1840s.

Emigration of Americans to the Central Valley was temporarily halted by the New Madrid earthquakes of 1811–1812. A series of landslides into the Mississippi River threatened boat traffic for most of the year. The epicenter of this earthquake was the southeast Missouri–northeast Arkansas area. Its intensity was apparently equivalent to the more famous San Francisco earthquake. The creation of sand blows throughout the area somewhat altered the landscape. Reelfoot Lake in Tennessee was probably created by being dammed by landslides during the earthquake. Although loss of life was very slight, most residents of the New Madrid–Little Prairie area in southeast Missouri were given the opportunity to trade their land claims for others up the Missouri River and did so.

In 1819 Arkansas Post became the capital of Arkansas Territory. It contained only about 60 families. When Thomas Nuttall saw it 1 year later, he was impressed by the number of lawyers, doctors, and mechanics who had moved there. The post had a brief building boom before the capital was moved to Little Rock in 1820. John Audubon visited after the move and found the post nearly deserted. A branch of the Bank of Arkansas was built there in 1840, but the village dwindled in population. Later the site of a Civil War battle, Arkansas Post is now a National Monument.

On June 30, 1830, the Indian Removal Act was signed by President Andrew Jackson. This legislation required the southeastern Indians to move west of the Mississippi. Many Cherokee were already living in Arkansas. A formal treaty allotting them land from the Arkansas to White rivers was signed in 1817. This was changed in 1828, when lands were exchanged for those in Indian Territory. The forced removal of the Cherokee from Georgia in 1838–1839 caused the death of over one-fifth of the tribe along the infamous Trail of Tears. One branch of this trail went through southeast Missouri and Arkansas.

The Chickasaws ceded the last of their eastern lands in 1832. The money received from the sale of their lands east of the Mississippi financed their trip west. Many of them traveled by steamboat up the Arkansas River, with 4000 people taking 5000 horses with them. Relatively few died on their way west.

The Quapaw signed a treaty in 1818 giving up 12 million ha (30 million acres), almost all their land in Arkansas. They ceded the remaining 800,000 ha (2 million acres) of the reservation near Arkansas Post in 1824 and moved over to live with the Caddo. Later, they were given a reservation in the northeast corner of Oklahoma, and many later moved in with the Osage. The tribal roll listed only 215 persons in 1892 (Baird 1975).

Some archaeological investigation has taken place at the various locations of Arkansas Post, providing data to augment the scanty historical documentation. Test excavations by Preston Holder at three locations of the post dating 1755–1796 revealed articles, such as a tin-glazed English delftware sherd, Rhenish stoneware, French faience, and even Mexican majolica (Walker 1971:11). John Walker conducted excavations at the site of the Bank of Arkansas, which was destroyed during the Civil War. The foundations of the bank were excavated, and considerable brick rubble was found. The dig confirmed that the building was used as a Confederate hospital and that it was burned with artifacts such as window weights, square-cut nails, butt hinges, flathead screws, and window glass present. Use as a hospital was verified by medicine bottles, a metal frame from a doctor's bag, and urine bottles (Walker 1971:29). Refined earthenware sherds of many different patterns were present, including blue and green shell edge, several colors of transfer print, a very small amount of ironstone, and stoneware jugs and jars.

Other work has been done at the site of a building housing a trading post dating to 1804–1807 and a tavern dating about 1814–1821 at this final Arkansas Post location (Martin 1977). A palisade-type fence and a cypress-lined well were found, as well as several trash-filled pits. Two lists of goods purchased by traders at Arkansas Post were compared with items excavated. Beads, lead, gunflints, knives, scissors, thimbles, pipes, wampum, mirrors, bridles, spurs, buttons, and hawk bells formed part of both inventories.

Later use of the building as a tavern was recognizable. Almost 5000 wine and liquor bottle sherds were found, including some from bottles of Bordeaux wines. Over 24,000 ceramic earthenware sherds were excavated, many more than would be expected in a one-family household. Knives, forks, spoons, and glasses were also found. The ceramics included some tin-glazed earthenware typical of a French occupation, over 8000 creamware sherds, and over 13,000 pearlware sherds. The few marked pearlware sherds are almost all from the Davenport factory of Longport, Staffordshire, England (Martin 1977:47; Figure 13.5d). One Davenport marked fragment is also imprinted with the name of a New Orleans importer. The New Orleans area was probably the main source of merchandise for the Central Valley in the early nineteenth century.

The accidental discovery of a mid-nineteenth-century occupation at the Zebree site in Mississippi County, Arkansas, gave us some evidence of what a typical isolated subsistence farmer–hunter occupation would have been like in the nineteenth century (P. Morse 1980). A cypress-lined well at least 4 m deep was found here. Pearlware sherds typical of the early nineteenth-century English ceramics exported from the Staffordshire potteries at this time were present, such as blue shell edge (Figure 13.5a), underglaze hand painted, spongeware, and transfer-print sherds. Both salt-glaze stoneware and yellow-ware utilitarian wares, parts of a metal bucket, a scimitar-shape bone-handled knife with brass rivets, a bar of lead stock, a clay pipe, a pegged shoe heel, buckles, a hook and eye, small lead shot, an iron skillet sherd, square-cut nails, glass buttons, gunflints, strips of leather, stone marbles, window glass, and whittled wood scraps were all found in the well. Much of this was preserved by being below the water table. Food remains found by flotation included corn, peaches, plums, watermelons, muskmelons, peanuts, grapes, hickory nuts, pig and chicken bones, and eggshells.

An American settlement pattern of dispersed isolated settlements and wider dispersed towns is typical of many frontier families in the early nineteenth century. Henry Schoolcraft (1821) described such families in Arkansas in his journal of 1818. Some focused principally on hunting, living in small cabins and moving frequently to better hunting grounds. Others were more permanently established, with outbuildings such as smokehouses, barns, and fences. The Zebree inhabitants appear to have been comfortably established, digging a well and planting an orchard.

Contact with the outside world is shown by the preponderance of English goods in the well. Traders probably went up the St. Francis and other rivers in keelboats, trading for skins. The majority of the trade goods probably were acquired in New Orleans. No documentary evidence is present for the pioneers who lived at Zebree, as they never made a claim on the land or paid taxes on it.

It is usually claimed that the Euro-American settlement of Arkansas and Missouri took place principally in the Ozarks and that lowland settlement was later (House 1977:247). The Ozark Highlands and uplands were supposed to attract populations, whereas the drainage problems of the lower elevations discouraged settlement. This picture may be changed when more surveys are done in lowland areas. The Zebree pioneers are one example of a lowland population, with their cabins on a natural levee of the Little River. Also, during the surface collection of all known Parkin phase sites, it was observed that most of these had evidence of early nineteenth-century occupation. Barry Lewis (1974) also noticed that the locations of large Mississippian sites in

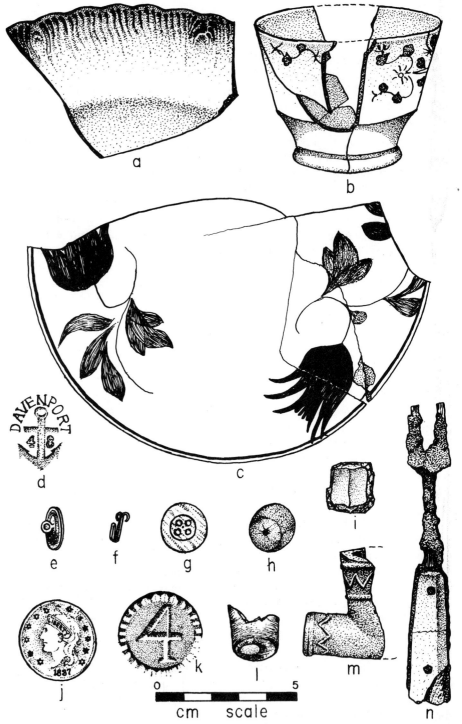

FIGURE 13.5. Early nineteenth-century artifacts typical of the Central Valley. (a) Shell-edged pearlware plate rim. (b) Hand-painted porcelain cup. (c) Hand-painted pearlware plate. (d) Davenport factory mark. (e) Brass button. (f) Brass fastener. (g) Bone button. (h) Blue glass bead. (i) French gunflint. (j) American penny. (k) Stoneware mark. (l) Free blown bottle base with pontil scar. (m) Earthenware pipe. (n) Two-prong fork. [Courtesy of the Arkansas Archeological Survey.]

southeast Missouri were used by pioneers. Modern roads often parallel ancient trails dating back to pioneer Anglo-American and Indian periods.

James and Cynthia Price have been conducting an archaeological investigation of the early nineteenth-century Widow Harris residence for several years (Price 1979). This site is located on the highland edge of the Ozark Escarpment, by the old Natchitoches Trace. Several early travelers including George Featherstonhaugh, a fellow of the Geological Society of London, recorded spending the night there in the 1840s. Tax records of the site go back to 1815. Foundations of a two-room cabin with central breezeway, another later cabin, and the old roadbed were excavated. A large proportion of the sherds found at Widow Harris were decorated, with blue transfer-print pearlware being the most common. Other artifacts included both British and French gunflints, many kaolin and clay pipe fragments, a sherd of a glass stemmed goblet, and a pepperbox pistol barrel. Investigation of the site has focused on relating this typical pioneer household to the wider trade networks reflected by the artifacts.

There are a number of known early nineteenth-century towns in the Central Valley. One was even colonized directly from Europe. Greenock, Arkansas, was settled by a group from Greenock, Scotland. Other towns were settled by families from Tennessee and Kentucky. Some excavations have been undertaken at the site of Davidsonville in Randolph County, Arkansas. This town existed only between 1815 and 1830 (Stewart-Abernathy 1980). It was a formally platted town located on the Black River, on the edge of the Ozark Highlands, near the Natchitoches Trace that went from Illinois to Louisiana. The town plan, with a central public square and eight surrounding blocks, was discovered in the county archives (Figure 13.6). The town was once the administrative center of an area composed of the northern half of Arkansas. A brick courthouse was built in the central square. A cotton gin, several mercantile establishments, taverns, and a ferry were also present. Archaeological investigation located the brick footings of the courthouse and a brick chimney belonging to the old post office. Again, the typical early nineteenth-century artifacts such as blue and green shell-edge pearlware, polychrome underglaze pearlware, numerous sherds of thin window glass, and wrought and cut nails were found during test excavations. Davidsonville flourished briefly, and then its residents moved elsewhere, leaving behind a time capsule undisturbed by further building.

Another type of Historic site present in the Central Valley is the boat wreck (Figure 13.7). These appear during times of drought, when river levels are very low. The wreck of the steamboat *South Bend*, sunk in 1860, was found in 1980 and studied by the Tennessee Department of Conservation (personal communication, Steve Rogers). This type of site has the potential of being a true time capsule, preserving merchants' goods and luggage from a tight time period, as did the wreck of the steamboat *Bertrand* in 1865 on the Missouri River (Petsche 1974). Unfortunately, vandalism of these time capsules often destroys forever their potential contribution to history.

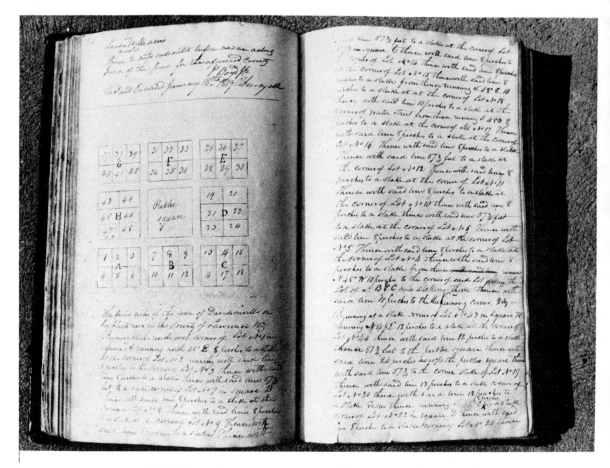

FIGURE 13.6.   Original plat of the town of Davidsonville. [Courtesy of the Arkansas Archeological Survey.]

Nineteenth-century stoneware kiln sites have also been found in the Central Valley area. During a survey of the Strawberry River, Sam Smith found a small local industry that produced utilitarian wares such as crocks and jugs. Again, data on this industry are not present in the local archives, and it was probably pre-Civil War. The large amount of stoneware wasters found in the field caused it to be called an "Indian site" by the local inhabitants.

WHO MADE KING CROWLEY?

After reading Conant's "Footprints of Vanished Races" the writer is convinced that these images were made by the Aztecs and placed on Old Town Ridge and the ridge below Jonesboro, as it is definitely established that the Aztecs once resided in what is now Missouri and Arkansas. Exact replicas of these images were found by Conant in the mounds near New Madrid in 1857. Hence the genuineness of the Rowland Collection is thoroughly established in the mind of the writer [Williams 1930:143].

A series of sandstone statues were "discovered" in the Jonesboro, Arkansas, area and sold to several museums in the 1920s and 1930s. One of these, called King Crowley, was even pictured in an Arkansas history textbook circulated to every school in Arkansas.

The motives apparently were both monetary and the joy of fooling important people. It may have begun as a practical joke; if so, it was successful beyond anyone's anticipation. Respected scientists, politicans, pillars of society, and thousands of Arkansas sixth-graders and their teachers were tricked. People from coast to coast became entangled in a web of chicanery.

At the center was Dentler Rowland (Figure 13.8a), who was born in Alexander, Indiana, in 1856 and moved to Jonesboro, Arkansas, about 1907. Rowland was a "jeweler" and "gunsmith" and lived alone. He was a genuine "character" whose nickname was "Deefie" because of his near deafness.

FIGURE 13.7.   Steamboat wreck in the Central Mississippi Valley. The *South Bend* sunk north of Memphis on December 13, 1860. This wreck measures just over 9 m long. [Courtesy of Steve Rogers, Tennessee Historical Commission.]

a

b

c

d

In 1924 the Smithsonian Institution received the first of many requests (1928, 1932, 1936, 1942, 1966) to examine some extraordinary artifacts (Figure 13.8b–d). All these inquiries prompted the same basic reply: "Our archeologists, after careful examination, report that no one of the 7 pieces exhibits the slightest resemblance to Indian techniques in its carving . . . that all are obviously quite recent in origin [letter with report from Neil Judd, Curator of Archeology to L. C. Castetter, Jonesboro dated Feb 25, 1932]". Nevertheless, we are still being told that the Smithsonian "authenticated" these relics. The web soon entangled a number of individuals who were neighbors of Rowland or who were selling the counterfeits. Some of these latter are included in the Smithsonian correspondence. Everyone knowledgeable in archaeology in the state knew they were counterfeit, and Sam Dickinson even stated so in a 1942 article in the *Arkansas Democrat* (Little Rock).

Dentler Rowland "found" the earliest specimens and most of those offered for sale. He showed the empty hole from which he allegedly excavated the relics to an influential Jonesboro businessman and as a result convinced him of their authenticity. The most famous specimen was King Crowley, whose whereabouts today are as mysterious as Rowland's background. Most of the counterfeits are made of sandstone, artificially aged, with brass harness hardware eyes and other contemporary embellishments, including a valentine style heart. We visited Rowland's house site at 409 North Church Street and in an empty lot roughly where the house once stood found a large sandstone boulder identical in composition to the large counterfeits.

The view that the counterfeits presented a mystery yet to be solved still persisted as late as the August 23, 1971, issue of the *Jonesboro* (Arkansas) *Sun*. During a period of significant advances in archaeological research, nineteenth-century concepts of "Aztec" migration survived among the lay public. They have reinforced an admiration for treasure seeking, and the curio cabinet or private museum remains a focus of most public knowledge of the past.

This general ignoring of professional archaeology's accomplishments is a strange phenomenon. Obviously, archaeologists have not been completely successful in disseminating their results to the very public who support that research. The public is essentially nonscientific and for the most part does not attempt to understand the science of anthropology that is so closely associated with archaeological research. Treasure and Aztec migration are simple and dramatic concepts. History itself is traditionally taught in terms of the individual exploits of leaders rather than in a cultural context. Most people do not think in the way that archaeologists do, and as a result there is a communication gap.

FIGURE 13.8. Artifacts allegedly found by Dentler Rowland near Jonesboro, Arkansas. (a) Rowland posing with artifacts. (b)–(d) Counterfeit artifacts. [Courtesy of the Arkansas Archeological Survey.]

We hope that this book somehow communicates with the general public. In particular, we want to stress the excitement of being an archaeologist. The thrill of discovery is not necessarily that of finding a fine artifact but that of finding an idea translating a hodgepodge of information into a coherent model that predicts what can be found by yet closer examination of sites and artifacts. That is why we became archaeologists and why we wrote this book.

REFERENCES

Baird, David
    1972   *The Osage people.* Phoenix: Indian Tribal Series.
    1975   *The Quapaw people.* Phoenix: Indian Tribal Series.
Bourne, Edward G.
    1904   *Narratives of the career of Hernando De Soto.* New York: A. S. Barnes.
Brain, Jeffrey P.
    1975   Artifacts of the Adelantado. *Conference on Historic Site Archaeology Papers* 8:129–138.
Brain, Jeffrey, Alan Toth, and Antonio Rodriguez–Buckingham
    1974   Ethnohistoric archaeology and the De Soto entrada into the Lower Mississippi Valley. *Conference on Historic Site Archaeology Papers* 7:232–289.
Catlin, George
    1967   *O-Kee-Pa: A religious ceremony and other customs of the Mandans.* New Haven: Yale University Press.
Cleland, Charles
    1971   The Lasanen site: An historic burial locality in Mackinac County, Michigan. *Publications of the Museum, Michigan State University* 1 (1).
Crane, Verner
    1929   *The southern frontier 1670–1732.* Ann Arbor: Mich.: University of Michigan Press.
Ford, James A.
    1961   Menard site: The Quapaw village of Osotouy on the Arkansas River. *Anthropological Papers of the American Museum of Natural History* 48.
Griffin, James B.
    1960   A hypothesis for the prehistory of the Winnebago. In *Culture in history,* edited by Stanley Diamond, pp. 809–865. New York: Columbia University Press.
Hoffman, Michael
    1977   The Kinkead–Mainard site, 3PU2: A late prehistoric Quapaw phase site near Little Rock, Arkansas. *Arkansas Archeologist* 16, 17, 18:1–41.
House, John H.
    1977   Survey data and regional models in historical archeology. In *Research strategies in historical archeology,* edited by Stanley South, pp. 241–260. New York: Academic Press.
Joutel, Henri
    1714   *The last voyage perform'd by de la Sale.* Readex Microprint. London: Bell, Bible, Lintott and Baker.
Klinger, Timothy C.
    1977   Parkin archeology: A report on the 1966 field school text excavations at the Parkin site. *Arkansas Archeologist* 16, 17, 18:45–80.
Lewis, R. Barry
    1974   Mississippian exploitative strategies: A southeast Missouri example. *Missouri Archaeological Society Research Series* 11.

Martin, Patrick
    1977   An inquiry into the locations and characteristics of Jacob Bright's trading house and William Montgomery's tavern. *Arkansas Archeological Survey Research Series* **11.**
Meyer, Roy W.
    1977   *The village Indians of the upper Missouri.* Lincoln, Nebr.: University of Nebraska Press.
Milner, George
    1980   Epidemic disease in the postcontact Southeast: A reappraisal. *Midcontinental Journal of Archaeology* 5:39–56.
Moore, Clarence B.
    1908   Certain mounds of Arkansas and of Mississippi. *Journal of the Academy of Natural Sciences of Philadelphia* **13**: 481–563.
    1911   Some aboriginal sites on Mississippi River. *Journal of the Academy of Natural Sciences of Philadelphia* **14**:367–480.
Morrow, Lynn
    1980   New Madrid and its hinterland. *Missouri Historical Society Bulletin* 36:241–250.
Morse, Dan
    1978   Ancient disease in the Midwest. *Illinois State Museum, Reports of Investigation* **15.**
Morse, Phyllis A.
    1980   The forgotten pioneers. In *Zebree archeological project,* edited by Dan F. Morse and Phyllis A. Morse. Report submitted to U.S. Army Corps of Engineers by Arkansas Archeological Survey.
    1981   Parkin. *Arkansas Archeological Survey Research Series* **13.**
Petsche, Jerome E.
    1974   The steamboat Bertrand. *National Park Service Publications in Archeology* **11.** Washington, D.C.
Phillips, Philip
    1970   Archaeological survey in the Lower Yazoo Basin, Mississippi, 1949–1955. *Papers of the Peabody Museum, Harvard University* 60.
Phillips, Philip, James A. Ford, and James B. Griffin
    1951   Archaeological survey in the Lower Mississippi Alluvial Valley, 1940–1947. *Papers of the Peabody Museum, Harvard University* 25.
Pittman, Philip
    1770   *The present state of the European settlements on the Mississippi.* London: J. Nourse.
Price, Cynthia
    1979   19th century ceramics in the eastern Ozark border region. *Southwest Missouri State University Center for Archaeological Research Monograph* 1.
Royce, Charles
    1899   Indian land cessions in the United States. *Bureau of American Ethnology 18th Annual Report.*
Schoolcraft, Henry
    1821   *Journal of a tour into the Interior of Arkansas and Missouri in 1818 and 1819.* London: Sir Richard Phillips and Co.
Sheldon, Craig T., Jr.
    1974   The Mississippian-historic transition in Central Alabama. Ph.D. Dissertation, Department of Anthropology, University of Oregon. Ann Arbor: University Microfilms.
Smith, Gerald P.
    1969   Ceramic Handle Styles and Cultural Variations in the Northern Sector of the Mississippi Alluvial Valley. *Memphis State University Anthropological Research Center Occasional Papers,* 3.
Smith, Marvin T., and Mary Elizabeth Good
    1982   *Early sixteenth century glass beads in the Spanish colonial trade.* Greenwood, Miss.: Cottonlandia Museum Publications.
Stewart-Abernathy, Leslie
    1980   The seat of justice: 1815–1830. *Arkansas Archeological Survey Research Report* **12.**

Swanton, John
  1939 *Final report of the United States De Soto expedition commission.* U.S. Congress, 76th
        Cong., 1st sess. House Document 71, Washington, D.C.: U.S. Government Printing
        Office.
Thomas, Cyrus
  1894 Report on mound explorations of the Bureau of Ethnology.*Bureau of American Ethnol-
        ogy 12th Annual Report.*
  1899 Introduction. In Indian land cessions in the United States, by Charles Royce, pp.
        527–564. *Bureau of American Ethnology 18th Annual Report.*
Thwaites, Reuben G.
  1900 *Voyages of Marquette in the Jesuit Relations.* Cleveland: Burrows Brothers.
Varner, John, and Jeannette Varner
  1951 *The Florida of the Inca.* Austin, Tex.: University of Texas Press.
Walker, John
  1971 *Excavation of the Arkansas Post branch of the Bank of the State of Arkansas.* Southeast
        Archeological Center, National Park Service, Tallahassee.
Williams, Harry Lee
  1930 *The history of Craighead County Arkansas.* Little Rock: Parke-Harper.

Index

Academic Press, Inc.

Harcourt Brace Jovanovich, Publishers

San Diego   New York   Berkeley   Boston
London   Sydney   Tokyo   Toronto

Academic Press, Inc.
1250 Sixth Avenue, San Diego, California 92101

Academic Press Inc. (London) Ltd.
24/28 Oval Road, London NWI 7DX, England

Academic Press Canada
55 Barber Greene Road, Don Mills, Ontario M3C 2A1, Canada

Academic Press Australia
P.O. Box 300, North Ryde, N.S.W. 2113, Australia

Academic Press Japan, Inc.
Iidabashi Hokoku Bldg., 3-11-13, Iidabashi, Chiyoda-ku, Tokyo 102, Japan

ISBN 0-12-508